DATE DUE

DEMCO 38-296

THE BEST OF

&RESTAURANTS &INSTITUTIONS

WINNING FOOD- SERVICE IDEAS

R&I's keys to success with
the menu, the staff, the customer,
and the kitchen

EDITED BY MICHAEL BARTLETT

John Wiley & Sons, Inc.

New York • Chichester • Brisbane • Toronto • Singapore

Restaurants & Institutions books—co-sponsored by John Wiley & Sons, Inc., and Restaurants & Institutions magazine—are designed to help foodservice professionals build stronger operations.

Publisher: Tom Woll
Senior Editor: Claire Thompson
Managing Editor: Nana D. Prior
Editorial Production: Impressions, A Division of Edwards Brothers, Inc.
Design: Jane Tenenbaum

Restaurants & Institutions is a registered trademark of Reed Properties, Inc., used under license by Cahners Publishing Company.

This text is printed on acid-free paper.

Library of Congress Cataloging-in-Publication Data:

Winning foodservice ideas: the best of *Restaurants & institutions* /
    edited by Michael Bartlett.
        p.   cm.
        Includes index.
        ISBN 0-471-30820-X (alk. paper)
        1. Food service management. 2. Restaurant management.
    I. Bartlett, Michael. II. Restaurants & institutions (Chicago, Ill.)
TX911.3.M27W56   1993
647.95' 068—dc20   93-11409

Printed in the United States of America

10 9 8 7 6 5 4 3 2 1

FOREWORD

Restaurants & Institutions was born in 1937 as a tabloid newspaper called Institutions. It was a year when most eating places deserved the epithet "greasy spoon." Mom and Pop owned most of the nation's eateries, and only the very rich could afford white tablecloth dining out.

Although that year the McDonald brothers opened the store that would eventually revolutionize the way America eats out, we had not yet heard of Ray Kroc and fast food.

Meals for schoolchildren were little more than a radical dream. The food served in most colleges would cause prison riots today. Motels were tourist cabins, retirement homes were poor farms and factory employees ate from lunch buckets. No one observing foodservice in 1937 would have believed that these Depression-weary operations were destined to be fused into the cohesive whole that would become today's $280 billion industry.

But, like the nation itself, foodservice had "a rendezvous with destiny." A national highway system changed tourist cabins into motor inns. Wrenching social change took its toll on the national psyche, but in the process it sent women to work—and families to eat—outside the home.

The search for speed and value spawned giant fast-food empires. But at the same time, awareness of nutrition as a key to quality of life revolutionized the meals served to everyone from schoolchildren to the elderly

We Americans finally rid ourselves of the inferiority complex that had affected our attitude toward our magnificently varied national cuisines. As American chefs became the stars of the culinary world, American diners began to consider quality dining a right rather than a privilege.

During all these years, the editors of Restaurants & Institutions chronicled foodservice as an industry, reporting, teaching and celebrating the ability of operators to solve the problems presented by changing times and to move ahead with confidence.

In the pages that follow, all of us at R&I are proud to share some of the most useful ideas that have appeared recently in the pages of our magazine. Our hope is that these articles will help you bring a sense of excitement to your menu, achievement to your staff and pleasure to your customers.

But most of all, we hope our work will contribute in small measure to your success in this wonderfully challenging industry we all love. ♦

Jane Young Wallace, Vice President/Publisher
for all the editors of Restaurants & Institutions

Running a restaurant is a fast-action business. Whether it's thousands of units in a chain, a multitiered setup in an institution, or a single 100-seat family concern, keeping up is critical. At *Restaurants & Institutions,* our editorial mission is to help each foodservice operator in America not only keep up but grow successfully over the long haul. Our stock in trade is ideas, winning foodservice ideas that you can use *today.*

The *R&I* editors spend a lot of time in restaurants, as customers, observers and, as often as we can, workers. We believe firmly that the business reduces to food + service. Everything that an owner, manager or foodservice director does—buying products, fixing equipment, cleaning, training staff, creating recipes—is a prelude to that moment when the customer is served and fed. If an operator knows the business, each customer eats well, enjoys the experience and plans to return. It's as simple, and complex, as that.

At *R&I,* we isolate four basic aspects of the business—The Menu, The Staff, The Customer and the Kitchen. We call these the Core Four of a restaurant. A foodservice operator who is going through the daily routine of opening a restaurant asks four basic questions: What are we going to serve today? Are there people here to serve it? Is the physical plant in working order? Will the customers come?

In the selections chosen for this collection, we think we provide some solid answers. For example, under The Menu, we help guide your thinking about trends with overviews on where American cooking is in the '90s. We tee up the great nutritional debate and explore the expanding flavor frontier. If you want ideas for dayparts, look under breakfast, lunch and dinner. All of the ethnic cuisines, from the most popular, Italian, to some of the most far out, Chino-Latino, are covered. And when it comes to creating a menu, we give you the best thinking on menu engineering and graphic design.

For help with The Staff and The Customer, we offer personal viewpoints from your employees about their jobs and an insightful, five-part program on how to achieve Exemplary Service. These days, knowing how to treat your employees for maximum benefit and helping them deliver superior service experiences to the customer is a major challenge for all operators. We've included marketing and merchandising techniques that let you reach out to customers and then listen to their feedback. We've even asked restaurant critics what they look for in a dining experience.

When it comes to building and maintaining a restaurant, we start at the beginning—where the money is. Included in the fourth section, The Kitchen, are our award-winning series: The Clean Restaurant, The Accessible Restaurant (dealing with the current need to accommodate disabled customers and employees) and The Secure Restaurant.

Like each issue of *Restaurants & Institutions,* this book is meant to be a compact, all-in-one resource that helps you run a high-quality, profitable restaurant operation. We hope it succeeds, and, if you need more help, feel free to contact us anytime for the best and latest foodservice ideas. ♦

Michael Bartlett
Vice President/Editor-in-Chief

ACKNOWLEDGMENTS

This book is the work of many people.

We want to thank *R&I*'s management, particularly Publishing Director Barry Reese and Publisher Jane Wallace for their guidance in helping produce our editorial product.

Art Director Queenie Burns gives graphic shape to our ideas and Production Chief Laurie Hachmeister makes sure they come off our presses clean and bright.

We want to thank all of our alumni, especially Toni Lydecker, Nancy Backas, Monica Kass, Brian Quinton and Brenda McCarthy.

Most of all, we acknowledge the ongoing efforts of the present *R&I* editorial staff: Lisa Bertagnoli, Jacqueline Rance, Erin Nicholas, Mary Boltz, Nancy Ryan, Karen Straus, Jeff Weinstein, Susie Stephenson, Beth Lorenzini, Rajan Chaudhry, Karen Cheney, Lorry Zirlin, Molly Ingram and Susan Gilleran. ◆

CONTENTS

I

THE MENU
FOOD TRENDS AND TECHNIQUES

In the restaurant industry mix, food is the binding ingredient that brings all kinds of operators together. For example, at an *R&I* Ivy Awards ceremony, internationally known celebrity chef Wolfgang Puck was actually exchanging menu ideas with Marjorie Beasley, Food and Nutrition Services Director of Bloomington (Indiana) Hospital. Though their menus and check averages were poles apart, they could find common ground in a creative pizza recipe.

R&I devotes hundreds of pages each year to food trends, menu ideas, recipes, culinary techniques and merchandising ideas. Virtually every issue features food on the cover. Operators from all over the country provide proven ideas. Specialists and experts in regional cuisines and emerging trends lend authority to each food story. It follows, then, that the first of our Core Four restaurant areas is food.

As the following selections illustrate, there is no end to the public's desire for a variety of taste experiences and the operator's need to satisfy these palatal cravings. In some cases, this may mean well-known comfort foods, such as traditional pastas or a great hamburger. Regional foods satisfy the natives, but often have broader appeal. Since the mid-1980s, flavor frontiers have expanded, as new spice combinations win acceptance. The key here is to master the art of mixing and matching menu items so they keep customers happy and coming back for more. ◆

American Cuisine: Then and Now

by Nancy Ross Ryan

"May you live in interesting times." That's a curse. The ancient Chinese wished their enemies eventful lives, knowing full well that trouble is more interesting than peace and quiet. In our march of progress to the new American cuisine, we have somehow invoked that ancient curse, for we are indeed living in interesting times.

Did we go too fast—from meat and potatoes to caviar and pasta, from salt and pepper to soy sauce and cayenne, from world culinary underdog to top dog—all within 20 years? Did we go too far—from basic sauces to purée of sea urchin, from generous portions that filled the plate to gigantic plates that dwarfed small portions?

Current signposts seem to be pointing us back: to meat and potatoes, to regional and ethnic roots, to smaller heads (but bigger hats) for American chefs, to a more confident, less chauvinistic American cuisine, to good old-fashioned home cooking, in both the restaurant and the home.

Whatever lies ahead, American cuisine has no choice but to continue. As another proverb observes: He who rides a tiger can never descend.

The new American cuisine that began in the '70s with the spontaneous combustion of ideas from many sources lit up our restaurant world like fireworks on the Fourth of July. Or was it the Fourteenth of July, Bastille Day? On closer inspection, however new the new American cuisine seemed, it still turned for inspiration and techniques, if not ingredients, to French cuisine. A white butter sauce by any other name is still a *beurre blanc.*

Americans, since the early 1800s, have had a love-hate relationship with French cuisine, first embracing it, then rejecting it. (In 1840, Martin Van Buren's weakness for French food was successfully exploited by the opposing Whigs in a smear campaign to defeat him in his bid for re-election as president, writes Harvey Levenstein in *Revolution at the Table.*) The new American cuisine was yet another platform from which to pooh-pooh fancy French cooking while praising the American.

Real American, Not Faux French

But Americans also have been ambivalent about their own folk cookery, regarding it by turns as a treasured heritage, or as food of the lower classes. Writes culinary historian William Woys Weaver in *America Eats,* "Hoppin john, a rice-and-bean dish that is now a metaphor for South Carolina cookery, was not at that time in 1859 respectable."

In the '70s, Paul Prudhomme's was not the first voice raised in praise of regional American food. But Prudhomme's Cajun cookery was certainly one of the strongest messages, and it has remained one of the simplest.

Encouraged by the Cajun reception, other chefs came forward. Southwestern chefs—Mark Miller, Stephan Pyles, Robert Del Grande, Dean Fearing—had been busy tracing and pruning the roots of Southwest regional cuisine.

But then a funny thing happened on the way to the restaurant: Down-home, country cooking became citified. Regional fare was refined to fine dining, and the '80s witnessed the phenomenon of low-cost foods—cornbread, beans, rice, brown bread, hash—appearing on menus at high prices and at the table on fine china. Perhaps the ultimate example was Jeremiah Tower's hamburger as described in *New American Classics* (New York: Harper & Row, 1986): It was studded with nearly a half-ounce of fresh black truffles, topped with truffled mayonnaise, and he suggested it be accompanied by a fine Burgundy. Since Tower opened Stars in San Francisco in the early '80s, some stylish burger has always had a place on the menu.

In the '70s and '80s, food became conversation and restaurants entertainment. These decades gave birth to restaurant critics, whose avowed goal was to serve the public.

But which public? Critics could and still can be divided into two camps: The majority of critics serve a public minority, customers with big enough wallets or expense accounts to visit fine-dining shrines. The minority of critics serve the public majority, students, families, senior citizens and singles on limited incomes who eat at fast-food chain restaurants and moderately priced American or ethnic restaurants.

The first camp dismisses fast food as the lowest common denominator, but grudgingly acknowledges that ethnic and American down-home restaurants can deliver tasty cheap eats. (Have these critics ever reviewed a chain restaurant?) The critics who cover cheap eats often subtly reinforce the stereotype of fine dining as pretentious, sometimes unidentifiable and always overpriced food.

Critics still miss the point: Fine-dining ideas trickle down to midscale and fast-food restaurants; simple regional and ethnic fare percolate up to fine dining. McDonald's put Oriental-style chicken salad and crudités on its menu, and Wolfgang Puck at Spago put pizza on his.

In the '90s, as the number of fine-dining restaurants decreases and midscale restaurants increases, critics will be forced to broaden their spectrum and modify their criteria and, we hope, abandon the crutch of the four-star rating system. The '90s are ready for a new restaurant review—kinder, gentler, more informed and informative.

To describe any chef's cooking style in the '80s as "basic" was an insult, and "meat and potatoes" was a term of derision. In the '90s, chefs themselves are talking back-to-basics, finding more fun in regional dishes than in culinary feats of derring-do. Instead of embellishing traditional dishes by adding bells and whistles (Jonnycakes topped with caviar, a $35 appetizer at Jasper's in Boston), they keep it simple. However, they make it lighter, reducing fats, sugar and portion size.

Meat and potatoes are back in style, but with a difference. When meat is the center of the plate, it's a much smaller (3- to 6-ounce) bull's-eye.

Often, meat is a garnish—a little trick we picked up from ethnic dishes such as Vietnamese Rice Sausage studded with bits of chicken thigh meat and dried shrimp (Nicole Routhier's *The Foods of Vietnam,* New York: Stewart, Tabori & Chang, 1989).

If regional American cuisine is one major source of inspiration in the '90s, ethnic cuisines are another. The lure for today's chefs lies (beyond naturally good nutrition) in the thousand-and-one exotic ingredients, contrasting textures, subtle seasonings and surprising presentations offered by the centuries-old cuisines of Asia, Latin America and the Middle East.

Yet before American chefs could yield to the lure of foreign cuisines, they had to drop the culinary chauvinism that burgeoned in the '80s, when we became a world culinary power: Our 1988 U.S. Culinary Team won the world championship in Frankfurt, West Germany; our wines achieved worldwide recognition; our chefs developed and nurtured small food producers, adding superb cottage-industry foodstuffs to the world's biggest larder. Suddenly we developed an attitude: American-only food and wine menus were the hallmark of real American cuisine. Anything imported was culinarily un-American.

But ethnic flavors began to make their way into our hearts by the well-traveled path of our stomachs, and American chefs and restaurateurs took ethnic cuisines in two new directions. The first was traditional, the second, a wholly original culinary hybrid. First they thoroughly researched the ethnic cuisine of their choice, and then created authentic ethnic restaurants in which to serve it. For example, Rick and Deann Bayless ate and cooked their way along 35,000 miles of Mexico, then they wrote a cookbook. Only after their travels did they open their casual Frontera Grill and fine-dining Topolobampo in Chicago.

The second approach to ethnic cuisines has produced and will continue to produce in the '90s some of the most exciting, original food combinations ever put on one plate. Talented, visionary chefs create culinary hybrids by adopting ingredients and elements of one or more ethnic cuisines and adapting them to their style of cooking. For example: Barbara Tropp of China Moon, San Francisco (interpretive Chinese cuisine); Kevin Shikami of Jimmy's Place, Chicago (imaginative Asian-French food); Lydia Shire of Biba, Boston (gutsy, eclectic dishes from anywhere that strikes her fancy).

These three also symbolize a new genre in American cookery: We call it personal cuisine. It works in the hands of a well-trained, talented and skillful chef. From the hands of amateurs, we call that silly cuisine.

The image of American chefs, which went from domestic in 1977 to celebrity in 1980, still is changing as their roles expand. The celebrity chef will not be as prominent in the '90s, not because there are fewer, but because there are more, and their responsibilities have increased. The number of women in a profession previously dominated by men is also on the rise. Only pastry chefs are in short supply.

Whether men or women, chefs are more visible in the media than ever before. However, their appearances are not to promote themselves, their restaurants or their cookbooks, but to end hunger and homelessness, to ease the burden of the mentally and physically ill by working pro bono at endless fund-raisers.

In response to mounting public concern amounting to health-and-fitness mania, chefs are shouldering a responsibility for creating totally new dishes for a menu category that hardly existed 20 years ago: light and healthful. To do so in good faith, chefs today forge new alliances with health professionals. (Emeril Lagasse of Emeril's, New Orleans, while at Commander's Palace, con-sulted nutritional experts at a local hospital to lighten traditionally rich Louisiana fare.)

But many are voicing concern: How Spartan can food get? Will great cheeses fall prey to cholesterol phobia? Will reformed chocoholics hold sway? And will the '90s neo-prohibitionism succeed in ending the time-honored marriage of food and wine?

As if chefs and restaurateurs don't have enough to worry about, along comes the baby-boomlet generation with a new nesting instinct and a return to traditional hearth-and-home values. What's more hearthy and homey than home cooking, formerly a style available mostly in restaurants? Now cooking classes are enjoying a revival, and cookbooks that promise to help readers to produce simple, from-scratch meals fast are on the increase.

Lights are on again in the home kitchens, dear Julia Child, but with a difference. The two-income family is here to stay, and only the most industrious wage-earning adult can bake bread, make soup, frost cakes, in short, make multicourse dinners nightly or throw dinner parties at the drop of a hat. It's most likely they'll fix one or more parts of the meal. Where will the rest come from? And where will they go for that complete experience that they can't have at home? They'll call a restaurant for home delivery, or go to a restaurant for takeout or for a meal. Why? Remember in the '60s, when television threatened the film industry? The film industry pro-mised: "Movies are better than ever." And they really were. Well, in the '90s, restaurants are better than ever. And they really are. ♦

A Regional Album of Great American Food

by Nancy Ross Ryan

In the beginning, ours was a purely regional cuisine. The continent was settled piecemeal, starting with the East Coast. And necessity was the mother of culinary invention as settlers used indigenous American foodstuffs (along with what little they had brought) to recreate the familiar dishes of their homelands. They also adopted Native American customs to create new dishes destined to become American favorites (baked beans is one case in point, turkey another).

What goes around, comes around. Today, we are seeing the renaissance of American regional cookery in professional kitchens from coast to coast. Following, we showcase dishes that use regional foodstuffs (more plentiful than ever) both to revamp traditional recipes and to create new ones.

Because the foods and wines of this country no longer play second fiddle to those of Europe, our culinary confidence allows us to take more pride in the basic, bold, all-American dishes that now are classics, such as the hamburger, the hot dog, barbecue, fried chicken, steak and, of course, apple pie. And we can pinpoint popular new directions that adopted ethnic foods—Italian, Mexican and Asian—have taken in America. So before touring the Northeast, South, Midwest and West Coast to see what's cooking, the portfolio opens with snapshots of perennial American favorites.

When we say something is "as American as apple pie," we've just said a mouthful. Love of pies in general and apple pie in particular came with English settlers, who ate pies for breakfast, lunch and dinner. Although we don't eat apple pie

for breakfast these days, it's as popular as ever for lunch and dinner. According to the *R&I* Menu Census, apple pie appears on 61% of all American foodservice menus (on 50% of commercial menus and on 82% of institutional menus).

Of course, there's apple pie and there's apple pie. In 1758, a Swedish parson in America described apple pie "in country places made of apples neither peeled nor freed from their cores, and its crust is not broken if a wagon wheel goes over it."

Fortunately, today's apple pies are seedless and have fork-tender crusts. The humblest and plainest are good eating, and the great apple pies —topped with ice cream or Cheddar cheese—are slices of heaven.

That same range, from good to great, applies to our other quintessentially American dishes.

Classic American Burgers

Hamburgers are more than popular, they're an American institution. The hamburger is on fine-dining and fast-food menus, in institutional foodservice and on the backyard grill. The *R&I* Menu Census found hamburgers on 77% of American menus and cheeseburgers on 73%.

Burgers come in all shapes and sizes, from the traditional "21" Club 12-ounce burger to the legendary 2-ounce White Castle "slider," and are garnished with everything edible under the sun.

The trend in burgers is to make them leaner: McDonald's McLean and Hardee's Lean Deluxe. The jury is still out on public acceptance, especially because the most current dietary dictums say that although fat intake should be limited to 30% or less and that protein intake be limited to 40%, that formula need not be slavishly followed at every meal.

One truth is self-evident: A hamburger is not a hamburger, nor a hot dog a hot dog, without a bun. (For many, french fries are just as essential.) Although both hamburgers and hot dogs owe their ancestry to Europe, it took Yankee ingenuity to put them between the bread.

Hamburgers came with sailors from Russia's Baltic provinces as minced raw beef (steak tartar), which became popular in Hamburg, Germany. German immigrants brought it to America, where it was broiled and served as Hamburg steak—until we sandwiched it in a bun and made history.

Hot Dog!

Frankfurters, a rendition of a smoked, spiced, pork-and-beef German link sausage, were served and sold in America as early as 1860 in pushcarts in New York City. But the bun and the name came later. Just as with hamburger-bun genealogy, regional debates still rage over who added the bun.

No one, however, disputes who gave the hot dog its name. In 1901, Harry Mozley Stevens (founder of Harry M. Stevens Inc., Cranbury, N.J., a firm now run by third and fourth generations) saw that cold foods at his concession at New York Polo Grounds were not selling. So he sent his vendors out to buy hot "dachshund sausages" with rolls to hold in the heat, and told them to hawk the sausages to baseball fans by yelling, "Get your dachshund sausages while they're red hot!" The then-famous cartoonist "Tad" Dorgan was at the ballgame, and his next day's cartoon featured barking dachshund sausages wrapped in warm buns. But he had trouble spelling "dachshund." So he substituted "Hot Dog" in the caption—and hot dog it has been ever since.

Small independent operators, with stands, small units or pushcarts, still dominate the hot-dog foodservice market, and the nation is divided between two regional hot dog styles: New York (or Coney Island) style, a hot dog garnished only by mustard and sauerkraut, and Chicago (or Midwest red hot) style, a hot dog and "a garden" on a poppyseed bun: mustard, relish, chopped onions, sliced tomatoes, cucumbers, green pepper, shredded lettuce, hot "sport" peppers and, the clincher, a dash of celery salt.

Great American Finger Feast

Fried chicken, an American finger feast that started in the South, has two regional versions: Maryland fried chicken served with cream gravy, and Kentucky fried chicken, without gravy, made famous by "Colonel" Harland Sanders. Kentucky-style fried chicken is also prepared in chains and independent restaurants with a range of regional spicing from mild to Cajun style.

The availability, the affordability and the high quality of fried chicken that Americans take for granted was made possible by a fairly recent revolution in the poultry industry. Before 1934, chicken was an expensive, Sundays-only kind of dish. Then the chicken industry became specialized: One strain of bird was bred for egg laying, another for meat. Scientific formula feeding and mechanized slaughter made possible the factory farming of chicken for the table, and literally put a chicken in every pot and fueled the growth of chicken chains.

Chicken chains today also have introduced leaner, lighter chicken menu options. But only time will tell if customers' stated preference for nonfried foods will affect the popularity of fried chicken.

Bigger Stakes in Smaller Steaks

Leaning toward lean has changed the way beef is bred and raised as well as how that traditional favorite—steak—is served.

As with apple pie, we got our love of beef, along with the science of cattle breeding and the forebears of our modern shorthorn cattle, from

English settlers. But before the 19th century, fresh beef was a luxury in America, and before the refrigerated railroad boxcar in 1882, it was affordable to only a few. But refrigeration, railroads and selective breeding of shorthorns led to mass availability by the turn of the century and consumption that was staggering. In 1894, a double porterhouse steak at Delmonico's in New York City had a trimmed weight of 4.5 pounds; the Gourmet Sirloin weighed 2.5 pounds, and the plain Delmonico Sirloin weighed 1.5 pounds. By 1977, Americans were consuming 97.7 pounds of beef per capita each year.

The beef industry responded to the 15-pound per person beef consumption drop in the 1980s by breeding leaner cattle, and foodservice responded by decreasing the portion size served. Also bolstering beef has been the proliferation of creative dishes such as steak salads and the renewed popularity of regional and ethnic beef dishes such as chicken-fried steak and fajitas.

Despite dietary concerns, not one but two steaks are listed as good sellers by the Menu Census: 57% cite beef fillet as a top good seller, and 51% of operators say sirloin/T-bone steaks are among top good sellers. And steakhouse chains of all types are booming.

Barbecue: The Most Regional of All

Neither fear of fat nor dread of dietary sodium seems to have dimmed America's passion for barbecue. Barbecued items are ubiquitous on menus as appetizers, sandwiches and entrees. And no food is so regionally distinct and so hotly contested. In the South, pork is king of barbecue meats, except for a pocket in Owensboro, Ky., where mutton is the meat of choice. In the West, especially Texas, barbecue means beef. The Midwestern speciality is ribs, and all regions barbecue chicken and sausage.

True barbecue means a cooking process: meat cooked slowly by hot smoking at low temperatures until well done. But to many Americans, barbecue is synonymous with sauce. And the overwhelming favorite, ever since its first commercial bottling in 1948, is tomato-based sauce.

Adopted Ethnics

America's melting-pot character is reflected in its adopted ethnic cuisines, and has resulted in two popular new directions for Italian, Mexican and Asian foods. The first is traditional and authentic: American chefs and restaurateurs study a foreign cuisine, then recreate authentic dishes.

The second direction is to create wholly original culinary hybrids by adapting ingredients and preparation methods from ethnic cuisines to their own culinary styles. Some of these dishes become mainstream, for example, taco and pasta salads.

Pizza, Old and New

Pizza is a perfect case in point. American restaurateurs only recently have begun to prepare an extremely old version of Italian pizza, and its popularity is spreading. Pizza bianca, or white pizza, Roman style, is made without tomato sauce, but with potatoes, garlic, crumbled rosemary or sage, and cheese. (It was a favorite with poor students in Rome because it was cheap and filling.)

At the other end of the spectrum are "designer" pizzas topped with everything from herbs and goat cheese to salmon or grilled vegetables. In the middle are two American regional rivals, New York-style thin-crust pizza and Chicago-style deep-dish pizza.

The Mex-American Taco Salad

Mexican and Asian cuisines have followed similar patterns in their American culinary naturalization. Certainly, the taco salad (one of two top entree salads in the Menu Census) never existed south of the border. Neither did nachos (also one of two top-selling Mexican appetizers) in their familiar American presentation. But regional Mexican dishes making their way into restaurants today do exist. For example, take the *masa*-dough gorditas appetizers stuffed with beans, cheese or seasoned meats, served in authentic Mexican restaurants. And the fast-food refried bean and cheese-stuffed burrito is a version of an authentic regional Mexican burrito.

The Sino-American Stir-Fry

Stir-frying, an Asian cooking technique, has become a source of inspiration for popular dishes on American menus for almost a decade, and the varieties of stir-fry seem endless. Certainly, judging by their ingredients, they are American adaptations, not classical Chinese dishes.

Most recently, Asian wrappers, egg roll and won ton, have captured the imagination of American cooks and restaurateurs, who are using available ingredients and dipping sauces to reinvent the egg roll. And Asian noodles are appearing in salads, soups and spicy side dishes.

As the following regional portfolios show, American cooks are not only searching their own regional roots for inspiration, but turning to ethnic cuisines as well. America's culinary melting pot is still cooking. ♦

Northeast Fare Is as Constant as the Weather

by Susie Stephenson

"When someone comes in the door in January, and the wind is blowing off the water, and it's about 10 degrees outside, what they don't want is three leaves of arugula topped with a single scallop," says Chef Jasper White of Jasper's, Boston.

Indeed, most Northeasterners look askance at frivolous food, and with good reason. Those outside New York City, a region all its own, tend to be practical by nature and tradition. They see food first as nourishment, only later as an art form.

Foods of the Season

It is often said that there is no spring in the Northeast, that the seasons go from winter to mud to summer. But there are treasures that slip up through the moist earth of April. Fiddlehead ferns herald the return of longer and warmer days to those who survive the gloomy days of winter.

In summer, the earth surrounding the cities of the Northeast is plentiful with myriad fruit and vegetables. Northeastern apples—McIntosh, Red and Golden Delicious, Winesap, Northern Spy, Sweet Rhode Island Greening, Baldwin, Rome Beauty, Pippin and Pound Sweet—end up in cobblers, dumplings, pies and sauces that tempt even stalwart dieters. New Yorkers savor dense cheesecakes and nut-filled streusel.

Lobsters, clams, oysters, mussels and scallops come from the salty, tangy water that hits rocky coasts and sneaks up onto Cape Cod and Long Island beaches. The darker-blue, deeper waters are home to haddock, flounder, mackerel, halibut, salmon and cod. Rivers, such as the Hudson, bubble with river herring and shad.

Ethnic Influences

The region's bounty is flavored with the foods and spices of the immigrants who populated the land. Whether they arrived in New Bedford, Mass., Boston, New York or any of the cities between, immigrants brought products from their homeland, and certain tastes for certain foods.

In the 1850s, trying to escape the famine in the country, the Irish came and added potatoes, corned beef and cabbage, kippers, finnan haddie and soda bread to household pantries and restaurant menus. Then came the Italians, Ukrainians, Poles, French, Greeks and Portuguese. They populated the ports, they worked in the factories, they mixed their own traditions with the traditions of this new world.

But in New England, their meals were always tempered by the weather and available foods. New York City dwellers, a more diverse group and further removed from the earth, savored a wider variety of foods from pastrami to blintzes.

The foods of New England were not particularly "sexy," or trendy. And as the residents started to move from working the earth to toiling in factories, many traditional dishes were no longer cooked, or were not cooked as often.

For many years, foods of the Northeast received little attention from either its residents or the chefs of America. Produce varieties disappeared from the farmland, and fields were turned into developments or left fallow. It seems as though New York cuisine was so eclectic it never had an identity and couldn't find one no matter how it tried. New England cuisine, on the other had, knew what it had been, but wasn't sure what it was.

APPETIZERS

- Black-bean and lobster bisque
- Scallops and escargot braised with turnip gnocci and Asiago cheese
- Duck prosciutto on apple kraut with pineapple lingonberry chutney
- Among the pasta selections are large colorful lobster ravioli with scallops in tomato cream, and wild mushroom vermicelli and smoked chicken, pine nuts and goat cheese

Another Revolution

While Northeasterners might not have thrown tea into Boston harbor, a revolution of sorts had taken place. Downscaling began and chefs, particularly those in New England, rediscovered the region's indigenous ingredients.

"These changes didn't happen in a vacuum," says White. "It was going on all over the country. But ten years ago, when the Bostonian Hotel opened, Francophilia ended in this area. That was the first first-class restaurant that didn't try to put on French airs. I know that sounds like a small event, but it was major. The change had to be done on a formal level before it could be successful at all levels.

"Equally important, somebody started to recognize how many beautiful ingredients we do have. The farmers, the dairy and fishing people, they all went up a notch in the quality of their products," White continues. "As a result, the food

purveyors went up a notch, too; thus, the food went up a notch.

"Many of us do different things with the ingredients. For example, Lydia Shire of Biba has a very eclectic menu," he says. But there is a common thread, he notes: "Our food is much heartier than in other parts of the country, especially in the cold months. Our portions are bigger."

But what does this specifically mean when it comes to the foods listed on menus in the Northeast, whether in New York or New England? A look at the dinner menu from the Mills Falls Restaurant in Upper Newton Falls, Mass., gives a pretty good idea of how chefs mesh Northeastern delicacies with the influences of an increasingly diverse population, all the while lightening up dishes without becoming frivolous.

One accompaniment, for example, uses a quintessential Northeast winter vegetable–Honey Ginger Butternut and Spaghetti Squash.

"I tend to cook for where I am," says Walter Zuromski, executive chef at Mills Falls. "As I reach the big four-oh, I've lightened up recipes. Now, there's some resistance to this trend. Many people are steak-and-potato types. But we're tricking them. We're still serving steak and potatoes, but we're changing the sauces, offering chutneys and vinaigrettes, and naturally reduced meat and fish sauces. We're using vegetable purées to thicken sauces and add flavor."

Executive Chef Chris Eiseman from Boston College agrees. "Chefs are using the same prod-

ENTREES

- Native duckling in cider and juniper berries, pecan couscous
- Roasted breast of chicken with cranberry chili
- Rye-crusted scrod, roasted red pepper tartar sauce
- Lobster and sea scallops braised with plantains and white grapes

BOUNTIES OF THE NORTHEAST

Fruit: Apples, cranberries, beach plums, wild grapes and blueberries

Vegetables: Corn, beans, fiddlehead ferns and cabbage; root vegetables such as potatoes, beets, parsnips and turnips

Seafood: Lobsters, clams, oysters, mussels, scallops, haddock, flounder, mackerel, halibut, cod, herring, shad and scrod

Maple syrup

ucts, but they're cooking in a different style. The style is based on customers' needs, which are healthier."

The Taste of Things to Come

But in keeping with the tradition of its heritage, it's unlikely there will be dramatic changes in the future. Says White, "Few of us are doing Northeastern cuisine if you refer to history. Maybe it's in the country inns. But downtown in Boston, it's more international. We're not a bunch of people with brown shoes and blue blazers. Less than half the population is Yankee. There will be a broader view. There are Portuguese here, Italians, Vietnamese, Central Americans. And every group brings something new.

"But there's a sensibility in the Northeast that rubs off onto everybody, Yankee or not," he notes. "And that sensibility is translated into the food. If you look at the restaurants that have succeeded and failed, it wasn't always a matter of talent; it was often a matter of style. It was because the chefs didn't play the right song."

Institutional chefs realize a need to cater to their customers' preferences as well. While the early students at Harvard might have dined on a traditional New England boiled dinner, cus-

---

ON THE ROAD

Maybe it's an arrogance indigenous to the Northeast, but very few native foods travel well; most are too fragile. For instance, although Cape Cod cranberries might grace tables across the nation on Thanksgiving, wild hand-picked New Hampshire blueberries are extremely expensive and just don't taste the same after traveling more than a few hours.

Several native dishes have found their way to menus in other regions: Maine lobster is the specialty at Rooney's Lobster House in Chicago, while baked beans, corn bread and clam chowder are family-dining favorites.

---

tomers at Northeastern colleges and universities today are more likely to opt for salad bars and pizza. "We have selections such as a Yankee Pot Roast and a New England Boiled Dinner on our six-week cycle menu, but the frequency has dropped to once a cycle," says Executive Chef Gino Correlli at Brown University in Providence, R.I. "And I honestly think if we took these items off, no one would be clamoring to have us put them back on." ♦

AMERICAN FOOD PORTFOLIO

Southern Cooking Is Mighty and Fine

by Beth Lorenzini

"What exactly is this I'm eating?" is perhaps the worst insult a guest can hurl at a Southern chef. In the '90s, as the virtues of "comfort foods" are being extolled around the country, Southern cooks will be the first to tell you that they never strayed from simple, good food. And considering the bounties available throughout the region, there is no reason to stray.

Southern waters offer up succulent shrimp, oysters and crabs, and hundreds of species of fresh fish. Southern farmers reap harvests of sweet potatoes, turnips and peanuts, as well as sweet Silver Queen corn and Brussels sprouts. From Southern trees come pecans and tart apples. Classic Southern flavor comes from onions, celery, sweet bell peppers, garlic, parsley and shallots, not imported saffron or truffles. The food of the South is familiar, not only to Southerners, but to all visitors who carry an image of what home cooking is all about.

At Morrison's Cafeterias, based in Mobile, Ala., customers get Southern cooking in its most traditional form. Fresh, boned, roasted turkey with cornbread dressing is a year-round favorite. Broiled cod, mackerel and trout are available with a choice of the day's sides, including black-eyed peas; red, pinto or white beans; and turnip greens. Chicken and beef stews, meatloaf and mashed potatoes in gravy, macaroni and cheese, broiled liver and onions, and fried shrimp are Morrison's menu standards. But Dick Largel, culinary director, admits that customers are more nutrition conscious and that spices, herbs and stocks have replaced ham hocks, salt pork and lard for flavoring.

But the nutrition trend hasn't hit the barbecue capital of the South, Memphis, where sources say there are close to 70 separate barbecue restaurants. "Barbecue is an American ethnic," says Barry Pelts of Corky's. "People will say, 'feel like barbecue' the same way they say 'I feel like Chinese or Italian.'" Slow cooking (rotisserie style for pork shoulder, open pits for ribs) is part of Pelts' secret to good barbecue.

Simple Food Seasoned Well

"The best thing you can do to food is get it at the source and help it taste its best," says Chef Jimmy Sneed of Windows on Urbanna Creek, Urbanna, Va., on the Chesapeake. Sneed is unique in that he doesn't use as many herbs and spices or liqueurs in his cooking as many of his Southern colleagues do. Sea salt, freshly ground black pepper, olive oil and vegetable stocks are more his style. "We have such an incredible abundance of great, fresh seafood and wonderful vegetables down here," says Sneed. "I want to make sure the flavor of those foods comes through."

Chefs around the country are gaining a better understanding of true Louisiana cooking as well, according to Chef John Folse of Lafitte's Landing in Donaldsonville. He says he has ordered a grilled salmon with a side of jambalaya in a Connecticut restaurant and dined on roast lamb with crawfish stuffing while in the Midwest. "All that blackening and heavy use of cayenne pepper is on the wane," says Folse. "That's not what Louisiana cooking is all about." Instead, he says, there will be more smoked seafood, poultry and meats, and more use of andouille sausage, crawfish and tasso (a pecan-wood smoked ham similar to prosciutto) for subtle flavoring.

BOUNTIES OF THE SOUTH

Some foods indigenous to the region are:

- Shrimp, oysters, crabs, scallops, crawfish, turtles and hundreds of varieties of fish.
- Game such as quail, duck, deer and rabbit.
- Root vegetables such as turnips and beets, greens, Brussels sprouts, bell peppers, beans (black, lima, string, etc.), onions, tomatoes, celery, okra, squash, black-eyed peas, sweet potatoes and corn (and cornmeal, hominy and grits), garlic, shallots, eggplant, mushrooms and cabbage.
- Apples, watermelons, pears, peaches, strawberries, blackberries, melons and all varieties of citrus in Florida.
- Rice.
- Pecans, hickory nuts and peanuts.

Simplicity is the key to triumph, says Folse, a truth he picked up from one of his favorite restaurants, The Brass Lantern in nearby LaPlace. "Two sisters, Diana Faucheux and Bonnie Roussel, run it, and I'll tell you, I get cravings for that little garlic roasted chicken on pecan rice they serve. Their place is like a safe harbor—true home cooking at its best."

Nancy Longo of Baltimore's Pierpoint Restaurant says Maryland food combines ingredients and flavorings from several historic influences. In addition to classic Southern foods, such as Longo's Maryland crabcakes smoked over apple and cherry wood, are the inland British influence of sugar, hard cider and vinegar; heavy creams and garlic from Annapolis' French history; and a melting pot of German, Polish and Italian influences from Baltimore. An example of the mix: Longo's Silver Queen corn polenta ravioli served with smoked pecans in brown veal stock sauce.

The emphasis on sauces is minimal at the Trellis Restaurant in Williamsburg, Va. Chef Marcel Desaulniers says vegetables are taking the place of sauces for flavor and moisture. "Steaming or pan-searing meats, poultry and seafood in vegetable stocks and seasonings gives them a better flavor than smothering them in sauces," he says.

Home-Style Presentation

Down South, the portions are big and the presentation simple. "I don't ever want to hear a customer say my dessert is too pretty to eat," says Glenn Powell, director of menu development for the multiconcept, 17-unit Peasant Restaurant Group in Atlanta, who calls one of his dessert sauces "sludge" because it's rich, thick and splatters everywhere when the dessert is being prepared. Sizable slabs of pecan pie, chocolate cream pie that rides high in the plate, big dollops of whipped cream and great gooey cascades of caramel are the order of the day, and patrons are encouraged to share.

Southern chefs in general dislike contrived plate presentations. "If the food looks too arranged, it looks like it's been handled too much. It doesn't look comfortable," says Powell. "People want a presentation that looks like a great value, that says 'dig in.'"

Philip Barden of The Old Post Office Restaurant on Edisto Island, S.C., agrees. For example, he serves 16-ounce portions of grilled rib eye or

ON THE ROAD

Southern trends that have traveled include:

- Big portions that look like a plate you'd get in mom's kitchen.
- Comfort foods with a flavor twist: Mashed potatoes, homemade bread, biscuits, meatloaf, country ham, gravy, vegetables and rice cooked with the right combination of herbs, spices, stocks.
- True Louisiana flavors: "Cajun" flavoring techniques such as blackening and smothering in cayenne will give way to more subtle flavors. Dishes will be lightly flavored with tasso and andouille sausage.
- Lighter sauces: Related to the previous trend, lots of vegetables, stocks and seasonings will provide flavor and moisture.

center-cut pork chops, and all entrees are served with a salad, grits and such sides as crowder peas, butternut squash or sautéed apples on the plate. "It's a glorified meat and three," says Barden.

Florida: Exceptions and Similarities

Even though it's in the South, Florida can't really be called "Southern" in the traditional sense. Many South and Latin American and Caribbean influences have found their way onto Floridian menus. At the business and industry accounts of Total Food Service Direction, a Miami-based contract management foodservice firm, customers will see quesadillas next to lasagna next to cheeseburgers next to Caribbean ropa vieja (shredded pot roast with tomato sauce, onions, peppers, olives and capers).

But some Southern legacies are emerging, according to Gus Gregory, firm president. "We are selling more meatloaf with mashed potatoes and gravy," he says, adding that to the whole generation of people who grew up on frozen foods, such home-style foods have become novelty.

One of the hottest chains to emerge on the Florida restaurant scene is four-unit Pebbles, based in Orlando. "We're giving people what they want: familiar foods with a gourmet twist," says Chef Tony Pace. Pebbles' menu features everything from burgers served on brioche bread buns to honey-roasted spare ribs. Checks average $8 to $12 for lunch, $15 to $20 for dinner everything included. Pace believes Pebbles is creating a new casual gourmet niche: fine foods for midscale prices.

Part of the secret lies in the chain's central commissary, where, for example, Pace prepares homemade soup and gallons of demi-glace for up to 20 kinds of sauces. He also fillets, weighs and portions fresh fish for daily delivery to the units. "Our whole system is designed to allow our chefs to concentrate on what they have to cook that minute, not on what needs to be prepared for tomorrow's menu," he says. Best sellers include chicken Vesuvio ($11.25), a Cajun hamburger with blue cheese ($6.25), and smoked duck and scallops with hot Asian spices on angel hair ($13.50). The food is flavorful, the dinnerware as plain as can be. "And whether customers order milk or a Mouton Rothschild, it's fine by us," says Pace. ◆

The Midwest Offers Country Comfort

by Rajan Chaudhry

The tradition of Midwestern cuisine is as rich as the region's soil. And nowhere are today's mega-trends—comfort, health and freshness—as deeply rooted.

"It seems to me that those of us who have been cooking Midwestern foods for a number of years still lead the way," says Richard Perry, who operates Orchids restaurant, Cincinnati. "The trend now is toward simplicity, freshness and pure flavors, and I think that's what Midwestern cooking has always offered."

The truth is, heartland cuisine has never strayed far from the basics. To this day, it reflects the tastes and values of its first European settlers, and it relies on the fruits of the lands they farmed and hunted.

Down-Home Cookin'

In middle America, as in other regions of the country, economic uncertainty is hastening the flight toward familiar foods. "People around here seem to be moving back toward the homey stuff, comfort-type things, things that they remember their mothers and grandmothers doing when they were little," says Richard Zumwalde, executive chef at the Quality Inn Riverview, Covington, Ky., across the Ohio River from Cincinnati.

Often, however, chefs are giving these old favorites new twists. Zumwalde, for example, has added a meatloaf dish to the menu of the hotel's revolving fine-dining restaurant, The Riverview. Rather than topping it with typical gravy, he uses tomato-onion relish. He serves the meatloaf with pinto beans and cornbread.

Chefs also are rediscovering and updating traditional ethnic dishes that were brought to the region by immigrants from Scandinavia, Germany and Eastern Europe.

At the Minneapolis/St. Paul Airport Hilton, Bloomington, Minn., Executive Chef Byron Korus' specialty is the home-style German-Russian cuisine of the Odessa area of the Ukraine. His most popular items include Kase Knepfla, similar to an oversize ravioli; Fleisch Keukla, a meat mixture in a crisp deep-fried pastry shell; and savory strudel. By altering stuffings and toppings, Korus can create dozens of variations on items guests already feel comfortable with.

Other cultural influences are present in Midwestern cookery as well. Perry, for example, buys free-range chickens from the nearby Amish communities that have existed virtually unchanged for more than 100 years.

Soup and stew, as well as sausage, played an important role in the early days of the Midwest and set the standard for the simple, hearty comfort food of today. "There were very poor people here, so they had to work with the items they had, and use every part of the animal they could," says Korus.

At the Westwood Country Club, St. Louis, Executive Chef John Bogacki offers a simple Farmers Chowder Soup that uses ingredients a local farmer might have had on hand a century ago. The soup combines chicken stock, carrots, celery, onions, cauliflower, pork butt, salt pork, roux, heavy cream, sweet basil, parsley, and salt and pepper.

BOUNTIES OF THE MIDWEST

Produce: Corn; wheat and other grains; potatoes and other root vegetables; peppers; squash; chanterelles; turnip, mustard and collard greens; wild rice; tomatoes; cherries, blueberries, apples and melons.

Meats: Beef, pork, lamb, veal, chicken and turkey.

Game: Bison, deer, quail, pheasant, duck, goose, rabbit and wild turkey.

Fish: Northern pike, walleye, Great Lakes whitefish, farm-raised catfish, trout and salmon.

Beef Is Back

Pork, lamb, veal, chicken and turkey, staples of the farm diet, are hot sellers in the Midwest, but restaurateurs across the region are reporting a resurgent interest in high-quality beef. As with liquor, people might be consuming less, but they are apparently consuming better. At The Grainery, Fargo, N.D.; the Ramkota Inn, Sioux Falls, S.D.; and the Airport Hilton, Bloomington, Minn.; prime rib is still the best-selling entree.

Freshness and Flavor

That is not to say that Midwesterners are ignoring their health. Many operations, such as the Ramkota Inn, offer low-fat cuts of beef, broiled skinless chicken breast, entree salads and seafood items such as steamed halibut. Grilling is growing more popular, and restaurateurs increasingly are showing nutritional breakdowns on their menus.

Even those operators who eschew regionalism agree that freshness and flavor drive business in the Midwest. "In the summertime, I use almost exclusively local produce, but I'm not interested in promoting a Midwestern cuisine or a local cuisine," says Chicago restaurateur Charlie Trotter. "I'm not too much into the indigenous scene. I'm an advocate of obtaining the freshest product possible; I really don't care where it's from."

Korus, on the other hand, cultivates his Midwestern ties. He is even going so far as to reposition his hotel's cafe as a "Minnesota bistro" that will feature cured and smoked pork ribs from Minnesota, trout and king salmon farm-raised in Minnesota, and other local products.

Likewise, Faust's, in the Adam's Mark Hotel, St. Louis, has premiered a new regional menu that spotlights new Midwestern cooking. It includes Ozark Golden Trout with sweet-and-sour eggplant; leek and morel mushroom pie with crawfish and truffles; pumpkin soup with spiced pecans and caramelized apple cream; and skillet-seared mallard duck breast sautéed with Missouri port-wine glaze and Wisconsin sun-dried cherries.

With the possible exception of the West Coast, no region of the country offers the opportunities to use farm-fresh produce that the Midwest does. Corn, grains, tomatoes, root vegetables, squash, pumpkins, melons, berries, peppers and greens of all sorts are only as far away as the local farmers market for much of the year. In some cases, not even that far away: In St. Louis, Bogacki grows his own herbs in a garden right outside his kitchen.

Although the globalization of the food market means produce is available year-round, the culinary rhythms of the Midwest still are tied to the fall harvest. Korus offers a Thanksgiving Day vegetable medley, which includes locally grown rutabagas, parsnips and turnips, which are roasted

ON THE ROAD

Comfort food: Prime steak, stew and soup, meatloaf, berry cobbler and fruit pie, apple butter, cornbread, macaroni and cheese, stuffed pork chops, chicken and turkey, buttermilk biscuits, and baked potatoes.

Food from the "Old Country": Pasta, strudel, sausage and free-range chicken.

Local signatures: Cheese, beer, bratwurst and wine.

Traditional cooking styles: Grilling, smoking and barbecuing.

and then smoked. And Zumwalde features fall desserts, such as an apple dumpling with hot cider sauce and homemade pumpkin caramel ice cream.

Wet and Wild

The interest in healthful fare and the strong tradition of living off the land have converged to reawaken interest in wild game and fish.

Game is familiar and abundant in the Midwest. Pheasant and quail comb the stubble of harvested fields. Deer, rabbit and wild turkey haunt the windbreaks and corn rows. Northern pike and walleye lurk in the cold depths of lakes in Minnesota and Wisconsin. And snapping turtles and crawfish dwell beneath the undercut mud banks of the rivers. The region also is a major flyway for migrating ducks and geese.

In his upstairs restaurant, Korus features a "Pike of the Day," which allows him to spotlight whichever variety of high-quality local pike—primarily Northern or walleye—is available. He also offers wild game. "It's more popular now than it probably ever has been."

To capitalize on the heightened awareness of wild game, Lionel Have, executive chef of the Omaha Country Club, Omaha, Neb., says he concentrates his game specials during hunting season.

These days, because of strict inspection requirements, most game is farm-raised. This increases its appeal for consumers by making the dark, lean meat less gamy.

One of the favorite means of preparing game and other meats is the age-old technique of smoking, which is catching on once again in the Midwest.

As Midwesterns look to their roots to rediscover traditional tastes and cooking techniques, they are reawakening to their unique culinary heritage.

"It wasn't so long ago that this area was the frontier," says Korus. "Now, if there is a frontier here, it is a culinary frontier. People in this area are just becoming aware that they have specific foods and ideas of foods that exist nowhere else in the United States." ◆

AMERICAN FOOD PORTFOLIO

West Coast Cuisine Accents the Possibilities

by Karen Straus

Since the 1960s, the West Coast and its culinary superstars have been innovators, creating culinary styles that influenced a new generation of cooks and helped shape what the rest of the country would cook and eat. The West Coast became one of the geographical centers of the New American Cuisine. Led by Alice Waters, founder of the legendary Chez Panisse in Berkeley, Calif., the area's chefs were the first to forge the farm/kitchen connection.

Tables are being turned now, with the trendy West Coast taking a cue from other parts of the country and emphasizing some culinary basics. No longer the radicchio radicals, West Coast cooks are into comfort in the form of regional, simpler, familiar foods that diners recognize and relate to.

This doesn't mean that West Coast eclecticism is dead. The West Coast still incorporates the major ethnic influences—Italian, Mexican and Asian—into its cuisine, producing hybrid dishes that are uniquely West Coast in style and content. But comfort is more a factor now, and will likely continue to be.

The comfort trend is especially noticeable in the Pacific Northwest, where shifting weather calls for heartier foods, according to Mark Bernetich, sous chef at the Heathman Hotel in Portland, Ore. The Heathman emphasizes regionality and seasonality, rotating its menu every three months. The staff puts up the restaurant's condiments, from jellies and jams to pickles, and cures its own bacon and sausage.

"Portland diners want a good amount of food for their dollar and want it to be fresh and wholesome, like you'd eat at home," says Bernetich.

Popular regional items include game, mushrooms and berries. Some dishes are tinged with Southwestern influences, such as duck leg confit with pumpkin-seed *mole* sauce, served with wild mushroom and goat cheese tamales.

Comfort Condiments

Old-fashioned condiments are making a comeback in the West. "Chowchows, piccalilli and refrigerator pickles—people are nostalgic for these right now," says Thomas Bloom, president and CEO of the California Culinary Academy, San Francisco. The academy operates three full-service, student-run restaurants that are open to the public.

Caprial and John Pence, who opened their own restaurant, The Westmoreland Bistro, in Portland in December, offer grilled tuna in ginger sauce topped with citrus mango chutney. "I'm seeing a lot of compotes, relishes, chutneys or confits, such as an onion confit cooked very slowly," she says.

Economical Meats, Dramatic Garnish

Braising is a preparation technique that is gaining ground, using tougher cuts such as shanks, pot roast and chuck that are both cooked and served in flavorful liquids. "Grilling is not seeing the attention that it did in the 1980s," says Bloom. The use of organ meats is increasing, as is the use of what Bloom calls "ancient grains," such as millet and kasha.

With less expensive cuts of meat being served, chefs are paying even more attention to plate presentation, for example, with condiments and dramatic garnish. One of the most dramatic is potato gaufrette, a lattice of sliced, fried or baked potatoes given height by mounting it on mashed potatoes or chick pea purée.

Nick Fluge, president of the Western Culinary Institute in Portland, Ore., says edible garnishes are growing more popular. "Plate presentation is a result of increasing education of culinary professionals. Even humble restaurants are carefully presenting each course."

BOUNTIES OF THE WEST COAST

Here's a sampling of foods indigenous to the region:
♦ A large variety of seafood, notably salmon, halibut, trout, rockfish, snapper, Pacific ocean perch, shrimp, oysters, scallops, clams and crabs.
♦ Meats such as lamb, veal, game and beef; and game birds and poultry.
♦ Fruit such as oranges, lemons, grapefruit, melons, grapes, kiwifruit, figs, apples and apricots.
♦ The "A" vegetables—artichoke, asparagus and avocado; an astounding variety of lettuces; cultivated and wild mushrooms, including chanterelles and morels; baby vegetables; vegetables with blossoms; organic produce.
♦ Berries such as raspberries, strawberries and huckleberries.
♦ Nuts, notably almonds and walnuts.
♦ Cheeses such as goat cheese, Oregon Cheddar and Monterey Jack.
♦ Fresh herbs of every description.

ON THE ROAD

Fish tacos: Everyone, from white tablecloth to fast food, offers their version of this California craze. The most traditional version, developed by Rubio's, a 10-unit fish taco chain based in San Diego, features a thick, soft corn tortilla wrapped around a deep-fried, beer-battered pollock fillet, shredded cabbage, cilantro-tinged salsa, special white sauce and a squeeze of lime.

Flavored pesto: Pesto isn't just basil anymore. It's anything from combination flavors such as chilies with cilantro to arugula and sun-dried tomato. In Portland, Caprial and John Pence make a tarragon/spinach pesto that they pipe into slits cut into a salmon fillet. They also serve a pesto of roasted red pepper and basil with kalamata olives, Parmesan, garlic and olive oil.

Black beans and chicken: Look around foodservice operations, and you'll see black beans replacing refried beans in Mexican dishes, and chicken taking over for beef and pork in Mexican and Asian dishes. On the University of Southern California campus, Doug Pendleton, assistant director of dining services, says he uses black beans in soup, salad, tostadas, burritos and enchiladas, and as garnish in other dishes because they're more healthful than refried beans prepared with lard.

Broth or flavored-water sauces: These Asian-influenced sauces are replacing fat-based roux sauces and vegetable purées. Pasta, seafood, meat and vegetables are being cooked and served in their own seasoned broth.

Vegetarian nomenclature: There is a trend to move away from the term "vegetarian" in favor of vegetable dishes. "Customers don't always want to be identified as vegetarians," says Thomas Bloom of the California Culinary Academy in San Francisco.

Med to French

In Los Angeles, Michael Roberts of Trumps thinks the Mediterranean trend has crested and will be replaced by a move toward French-inspired cuisine. "Southern California seems to have olive oil coming out of its ears," he says, adding, "I think we'll see a shakeout. Some of these restaurants will start to close, and I think things will go back to something a little more classic: fresh flavors and balance, but without heavy sauces. The French do wonderful things with vegetables that we don't even know about."

The Cobb salad, one of the West Coast's trademark dishes, seems unlikely to diminish in popularity locally or in the rest of the country. Invented by a Los Angeles restaurateur as a late-night snack using only leftovers in the refrigerator, there are as many versions as there are chefs. "There's no such thing as a traditional Cobb salad because everybody and their brother is doing one," says Joseph Rivas, a chef with the Green Hills Country Club in Millbrae, Calif. He uses a variety of lettuces in his version and serves it in a mounded cone shape.

Mining the Southwestern Vein

On the fast-food front, San Diego-based Jack In The Box and Anaheim-based Carl's Jr. both are mining the Southwestern flavor vein, offering jazzed-up versions of familiar foods. Carl's Jr., with 612 units in the West and Southwest, has introduced the Santa Fe Chicken Sandwich and the Southwestern Cheeseburger. Both items are charbroiled and include mild green-chili strips and mayonnaise-based sauce with cayenne pepper.

Jack In The Box, with 1,100 units, offers the Chicken Fajita Pita, combining familiar Tex-Mex and Middle Eastern components. Grilled, boneless, skinless chicken meat is spiced and stuffed in a half pita with lettuce, tomato and American cheese.

Balance and Moderation Are Back

In the West, as in other parts of the country, balance and moderation are reappearing in cuisine. Disappearing, says Bloom, is "cooking through elimination," when dishes were dropped from menus as a result of slavish obedience to dietary dictum. "People are eating more meat, not necessarily a steak, but in a composite dish," he says. "Chefs are also happier to be able to use a little butter and cream to bring out the flavor of foods. We're now serving items we wouldn't have been able to serve two or three years ago."

While the West Coast is returning to basics, its reputation for "far out" food still applies. Innovators are producing "far out" comfort food, such as the salmon hash served by Bradley Ogden at the Lark Creek Inn in Marin County. In nearby Mill Valley, the kitchen crew at the Buckeye Roadhouse jokes about the "Fred Flintstone lamb shanks," so-called because the shanks resemble an oversize drumstick, says Executive Chef Cindy Pawlcyn. The lamb comes with garlicky mashed potatoes, and fennel, orange and mint stew. At Granita, Wolfgang Puck's restaurant in Malibu, whole, small scorpion fish and half lobsters stuffed with couscous are just two ingredients in a hearty Mediterranean fish soup. ◆

Nutrition Debate: Should You Care What Your Customers Eat?

by Brian Quinton

Everybody's going crazy out there, says Victor Gielisse, certified master chef and author of *Cuisine Actuelle*. "The worst thing about this nutritional craze is that 50,000 chefs are now screaming nutrition. What is wrong with a nice roast pork loin with wonderful mashed potatoes and fresh applesauce? What's wrong with that?"

Everything or nothing, depending on where you stand in the Great Diet Debate of the late-20th century. After more than a decade of treating restaurants as temples of pleasure, Americans now seem determined to turn them into gyms, spas and doctors' waiting rooms. On the menu, Sachertortes and hollandaise have been replaced by saturated fats and high-density lipoproteins.

Some of this new clinical approach can be put down to post-'80s puritanism. But much is also due to the growing body of evidence suggesting a real link between diet and disease—much of it produced by the federal government. In July 1988, a ground-breaking report from the Surgeon General's office named overeating America's top dietary problem, replacing nutritional deficiency. Of 2.1 million Americans who died in 1987, nearly 1.5 million died of some ailment that could be associated with diet, the report found.

"What we eat may affect our risk for several of the leading causes of death for Americans, notably coronary heart disease, stroke, atherosclerosis, diabetes and some types of cancer," the report said. "These disorders now account for more than two-thirds of all deaths in the United States." At a press conference introducing the report, then-Surgeon General C. Everett Koop said, "If you are among the two out of three Americans who do not drink or smoke excessively, your choice of diet can influence your long-term health prospects more than any other action you might take."

More recent research by the American Cancer Society suggests that diet alone might be a factor in as many as 35% of all cancers, and recommends that Americans reduce their fat consumption, eat more foods rich in vitamins A and C and high in fiber, and consume greater amounts of what are known as the cruciferous vegetables: broccoli, cauliflower, Brussels sprouts and cabbage.

Studies such as these culminated in a new set of dietary guidelines from the Departments of Agriculture and Health and Human Services. The new document targets specific reductions in dietary fat (from an average of 37% of total calorie consumption now down to 30%) and in the average proportion of daily calories from saturated fat (from 17% now down to 10%). It also sets a recommended number of daily servings of fruits, vegetables, and grains—all this in a positive tone that stresses dietary dos rather than don'ts.

Restaurants' Responsibility

But what sounds positive in the halls of government can seem awfully confining on the cooking line. The new emphasis on the diet-disease link has rebounded onto restaurants. This is understandable, since about 43% of total food spending goes for meals eaten away from home. The National Academy of Sciences' Institute of Health recommended that full-service restaurants be required to give patrons a complete nutritional breakdown of their standardized menu offerings.

The National Restaurant Association's response was instantaneous. Such requirements, a spokesperson said, would be creatively restrictive to independent chefs, unfeasible for chains and a financial burden to all.

Some operators—already under pressure to turn a profit and keep up with the public's mercurial tastes—have balked at the notion of becoming nutritional cops, charged with making sure customers eat their broccoli. Many espouse a kind of nutritional laissez faire, relying on the wisdom of the patron to know what he or she needs. "I don't feel it's my responsibility to serve healthy food," says Richard Melman, founder of Chicago-based Lettuce Entertain You Enterprises. "A number of years ago, I did feel it was a real responsibility, and I tried twice and failed both times. I'm in business to give people what they want. The smart operator knows that 10% of the people want healthy choices, and he provides them. But I'm not a doctor."

"It's just not my concern what shape my customers' diets are in," says one Midwestern hot-dog stand operator. "This whole business is built on *choice*. Customers want a whole range of things, depending on their tastes, their moods and their wallets. You do your best to provide as much of that range as you can, then you stand back and let them choose. If people want burgers and shakes, I've got them. If they want grilled fish or a low-cal salad, I'll sell that to them. If they want sprouts, they have to go somewhere else."

But especially at the upscale end of the dining spectrum, more and more operators are acknowledging some need to formulate menu items with an eye to their nutritional value. They're still not pushing Brussels sprouts, but many are seeking substitutes for ingredients that a great number of diners probably should cut back on. At Nosmo King in New York, Scott Posner uses no dairy products in his entrees except the occasional special cheeses. Desserts contain some dairy, but many are sweetened with rice or maple syrup instead of white sugar. And there's no red meat at all on the menu.

"Obviously, we are not monitoring our customers' diets," says Posner. "It's not the restaurateur's responsibility to know what they're consuming on a one-to-one basis. But we restaurateurs are 100% responsible for providing a completely nutritious, healthy meal."

For a joint project with the American Cancer Society, Gielisse modified his restaurant's signature pecan-breaded catfish by replacing some of the high-fat nuts with a portion of bran flakes and substituting apple cider for apple jack in the sauce. Notwithstanding his high opinion of roast pork and mashed potatoes, Gielisse is willing to go looking for healthful replacements for fats and oils. "When modifying the menu, we are conscious of how many sauces we do with cream as opposed to vegetable purée or sauces with citrus and fruit vinegars."

"The public now really put themselves in the hands of the chef," Gielisse says. "There's a big trust level there. I get a lot of people in here who are conscious of their cholesterol levels and just want a piece of plain fish. They ask me if I can do it for them. If they call and say they don't want any olive oil or butter, I'll eliminate that for however many people are at that table. We're an 80-seat restaurant and we've established a regular clientele, so I'll go out of my way to accommodate their needs."

Free Will and French Fries

Such customization is at least possible in a white-tablecloth setting, where high-income, nutritionally informed diners can control their intake with a simple talk to the chef. But advocacy groups such as the Center for Science in the Public Interest complain that those same basic tools—understanding, information and choice—are often withheld from the much larger audience that patronizes only midscale and fast-food restaurants. Too few of these customers, they say, are empowered with a working knowledge of what good nutrition is and how it translates into the menu down at their local pizza place or coffee shop.

And while healthful food is finding its way onto chain menus around the nation, it is by no means everywhere. "I was traveling across Colorado looking for a place to eat late at night," says former American Dietetic Association (ADA) President Mary Abbott Hess. "I went into a Denny's with a 24-hour menu and almost everything on it was fried. You could get soup or salad, but in this day and age to have french fries as the only starch is ridiculous."

The most moderate of these groups stop short

of demanding mandatory nutritional labeling. The ADA, for example, has called on restaurants to volunteer information on calories, protein, carbohydrates, fats (including saturated fats), cholesterol, sodium and fiber—but only for those items promoted as healthful options. Privately, Hess says she sees no reason why chains, with their highly standardized, highly stable menus, should not be able to make all such information easily available.

Advertising further complicates the question of choice; free will becomes a problematic concept when billions of dollars are deployed behind prime-time TV campaigns to sway the purchase decision. In the first six months of 1990, the top ten restaurant chains spent $638 million on advertising—much of it targeted to specific splinter markets predisposed to buying fast food, such as children, teens and minorities.

Minorities pose a special dilemma because their particular health problems seem to be closely linked to diet. National Institutes of Health statistics show that almost half of African-American women and one-third of African-American men exceed their normal body weight by 20% or more, compared with about one-fourth of white men and women. Hispanic men are 2.5 times more likely to develop diabetes than non-Hispanic men, and blacks are 40% more likely to suffer high blood pressure than whites.

"I keep reading where fast-food executives say their menus are healthy when part of a balanced diet," says Ellen Charters Tower, a registered dietitian in Newark, N.J. "But in many low-income neighborhoods the fast-food restaurants are the diet of choice for people who can afford it. Fast food *is* what they think of as good food. And for lack of better nutritional knowledge, it's what they think of as *healthy* food, too. Fast-food chains need to provide healthful selections within their menus, not just tell people to go elsewhere for the good stuff."

Is Peace at Hand?

Of course, chains of all kinds are providing nutritious options and information in greater and greater quantities. Fast-food chains in particular have caught the scent of incremental sales from items with the healthful-food halo, and they are likely to roll as many of these as their menu boards can hold. Oak Brook, Ill.-based McDonald's delivered a one-two punch by building up its healthful menu with items from low-fat shakes to the Lean Deluxe hamburger and with an expanded program of informational booklets, posters and tray liners giving nutritional analyses of its menu. The wide expectation is that if McDonald's does these things, other chains will find it worth their while to catch up.

Not that everyone in the nutrition camp is ready to make peace with the quick-service chains. The ADA's Hess points to deception in much nutritional data. "A single-serving package of chicken salad with dressing holds 2 ounces, but they do an analysis based on a half-ounce," she says. "Who are the other three people sharing my chicken salad? I don't like it when people play games with customers. That's dirty, unfair and insulting."

Nutritional marketing is having a spillover effect outside the fast-food arena in midscale dining, as chains such as Minneapolis-based Country Kitchen redesign menus to highlight dishes low in calories, sodium or cholesterol. Even Howard Johnson is testing flavors of ice milk to add to its original list of 28 ice cream flavors. And buffet concepts such as Fresh Choice and Restaurants Unlimited's Zoopa! are tapping a strong niche market for fresh, healthful dining at a low price. "Good nutrition and value are closely linked," says Martin Culver, president of Santa Clara, Calif.-based Fresh Choice. "Value isn't just a quantity of food in front of you for a reasonable price, but also its quality and nutritional value. We are banking on the fact that people will demand higher quality at a reasonable price."

Beyond Fear of Food

Perhaps the most hopeful development on the diet front was symbolized when the American Institute of Wine and Food (AIWF) brought 50 chefs, nutritionists, anthropologists, food editors and cookbook writers together for a three-day symposium on food and nutrition. Attendees included fine-dining notables such as Bradley Ogden of Lark Creek Inn in San Francisco and Julia Child; the science contingent included Dr. Wayne Calloway, an endocrinologist at George Washington University, Washington, D.C.; and Johanna Dwyer, director of the Frances Stern Nutrition Center at the New England Medical Center, Boston.

The end result was a report outlining a new way for cooks, dietitians and consumers to look at food: with common sense. Stipulating that there are no "good" or "bad" foods, the group recommends that diners track their food intake over a period of several days rather than by individual dishes or meals.

For nutritionists, this means recognizing that everything, pork and mashed potatoes included, can be part of an intelligent diet, if eaten in moderation and balanced with low-fat, low-cholesterol foods at an ensuing meal. Food's social and psychological value is given equal weight as its power to fuel the body. "This wasn't a concession on the nutritionists' part," says Jan Weimer, a Los Angeles-based food writer and one of the meeting's coordinators. "Nutritionists have a scientific bent, but they eat, too. The importance of taste and pleasure in food was already there for them."

Chefs and restaurant owners, on the other hand, should recognize their role in combating the epidemic of poor eating in America, the report says. They should use a diversity of high-quality raw materials of optimal nutritional value, putting taste above appearance and reserving fats for dishes where their use makes a big difference in flavor and texture. They should also try to comply with the aforementioned USDA guidelines on reducing fats, saturated fats and cholesterol, and should make these basic contents known about the dishes they serve.

What's really new about this more forgiving approach to the nutrition argument is the revelation that all parties to the debate have valid points to make about food. No one is made a scapegoat for the nation's poor diet, and all sides are given partial responsibility for correcting it, educating consumers into a new, more benevolent view of what food can do to, and *for*, their lives.

The Need to Know

Since the early 1980s, consumer advocate groups such as Public Voice and the Center for Science in the Public Interest (CSPI) have asked Congress to require foodservice operations to list the ingredient and nutritional content of menu items. While the industry opposes such legislation and new labeling laws continue to exclude foodservice, an ever-growing number of operators are voluntarily complying to meet growing consumer interest in health and nutrition information.

As of 1991, 78% of chain operators have nutrition information available for customers, according to a National Restaurant Association survey. About three-quarters offer data relating to menu ingredients. Approximately 80% of the survey respondents have these details available through corporate headquarters. Two-thirds have printed material about nutrition in units; 35% have ingredient listings at unit sites. Another 25% of chain operators report having either a toll-free telephone number or wall posters listing nutrition and ingredient data. The survey also finds that nutrition facts can be found on 19% of chain tray liners and 10% of packages.

But the controversy continues. Spokespeople from the leading chains say that requests for such information continue to be limited. And CSPI complained after a March 1990 survey that voluntary compliance varied widely among five major chains. In that case, its test of 60 stores in nine states revealed that one chain had nutritional information available in 83% of its outlets: another, in none of its stores.

Food for Thought

How much do consumers know about what constitutes a good, healthy diet? *R&I* recently administered a moderately difficult American Dietetic Association quiz to 50 people. The quiz asked simple questions such as whether an ounce of Cheddar cheese has more saturated fat than two tablespoons of peanut butter (the cheese does) or whether running a mile burns more calories than walking a mile (they're the same).

The response to this admittedly unscientific survey—the average score was 65%, or barely passing—supports what experts have concluded about the nation's nutritional savvy: namely, that the typical American diner is no longer completely nutritionally illiterate—only somewhat ignorant. A 1990 Food and Drug Administration survey concluded that 80% of all retail food shoppers have a "functional understanding" of terms such as cholesterol, calcium, preservatives and sodium. About 70% understand terms such as protein, calories and fiber. One in eight is familiar with polyunsaturated fat and hydrogenation, and only a handful are acquainted with riboflavin, niacin or potassium.

But familiarity with terms doesn't mean grasping concepts. A 1990 Gallup survey for the American Dietetic Association shows that 40% of consumers don't know that the marbling in red meat is fat. And almost 68% don't know that cholesterol is found only in animal products.

Branded Foods in School

One of the biggest problems at school foodservice operations is getting students to believe that the food served is of decent quality. To gain students' trust and keep them on campus at lunchtime, directors are bringing in branded items. At the Minneapolis School District, Foodservice Director Jo Ellen Miner is testing both Pizza Hut and Subway products, delivered daily by local operators. She says student recognition of branded products improves the credibility of her program.

"Nutrition is a concern, but it is very difficult to get students to eat food that is good for them," says Miner. "Maybe the Pizza Hut product is a little higher in fat, but there has to be a balance. If we are feeding students one meal a day for 170 days a year, that is about 15% of the food they eat during a year. So you must look at the branding program with perspective. It has been good for school's public relations and keeps more students on campus."

As for teaching children to develop healthy eating habits, Miner says her program is in no financial position to provide the necessary educational components. "For too many years, school foodservice has been seen as a stepchild of the district and not an integral part of the education program," says Miner. "Statistics show how diet affects children's ability to learn but educators never perceive nutrition as a necessary part of the educational program."

Miner says school districts must integrate nutrition education into curriculum so students understand what foods are good for them. She adds that programs also must be creative so students respond to the education. ♦

Flavor: The American Palate Awakens

by Nancy Ross Ryan

Remember the story of Dr. Frankenstein? Using his native ingenuity, a lot of energy and materials at hand, he created what he believed would be the perfect human. However, because of a slight miscalculation, his creature became forever famous as "Dr. Frankenstein's monster." American chefs and restaurateurs may have unwittingly unleashed their own monster: The New American Cuisine has given birth to the New American Palate—and at this very moment it is on the prowl in search of flavor.

What it craves is not any one flavor, but flavor itself—a complex phenomenon depending not on taste but on smell for 80% to 90% of its impact. This new American appetite is neither easy to gratify nor as simple as the recent taste for hot and spicy food. Cajun fever may have electrified American taste buds and paved the way for the sudden popularity of Southwestern and other regional and ethnic cuisines to follow. But the four-alarm fire that Paul Prudhomme ignited has spread.

Items such as elephant garlic, ancho peppers, sea urchin, fermented fish sauce and garlic chives are all finding their way into American restaurant kitchens. In the last ten years, Americans consumed 170 million pounds of spice *more* each year than during a comparable period a decade before.

"Ten years ago, we held wine-tasting parties. Now we hold food-tasting parties," comments Jenifer Harvey Lang, chef, writer and author of *Tastings: The Best from Ketchup to Caviar.* Lang was among the experts *R&I* called on to help unravel the mysteries of flavor: What it is—and isn't; what it was that made our Main-Street American palate suddenly veer into the fast lane; what are today's favorite flavors—and some of tomorrow's; a catalog of suggested flavors for listless menus; and some spicy tidbits.

Pleasing the customer's palate is not an easy matter. Flavor depends on much more than the taste buds in our mouths, which respond only to four basics: sweet, sour, salty and bitter. Flavor, a complex perception, depends on the sensations of taste, smell, feeling and sight when food is being eaten, according to Nancy Smith, manager, Food and Sensory Sciences Unit of Arthur D. Little Inc., Cambridge, Mass., a firm that she says developed the first "descriptive sensory technique" in the United States. "Smell is especially critical to flavor," says Smith, "And smell is what tells you the difference between basil and dill. It is not taste that differentiates the flavors, but the aromatic quality of the herbs. For the same reason, people with colds often complain that food has no flavor."

"The whole world of sensory measurement has gone from art to science in the last 10 to 15 years and is now well-respected and relied on as a tool in product development by food and beverage companies," says Smith. The science of flavor reveals other components involved (in addition to the taste buds' basic four and the important role played by smell): One is feel (the mouth perceives both textures—the crunch of potato chips—and chemical stimuli—the heat from red peppers); another is sight (we expect strawberry sauce to be red, champagne to be effervescent and beer to have foam); and a third is sound (crisp vegetables should make a crunch).

However complex flavor may be, the majority of Americans liked theirs simple until about five years ago. "We all have childhood memories of the kitchen spice shelf," says Lang. "It held salt, preground pepper, cinnamon, maybe paprika for color and perhaps oregano for spaghetti sauce. Parsley is what you got in restaurants on a plate—and didn't eat."

Lang points out that 75% of Americans originally came from Northern European countries with conservative tastes. Of that 75%, half came from Germany, half from England, Scotland and

Ireland. "Since the majority reflected these origins, the minorities wanted to conform and so dampened their own tastes," she says, adding "Cold countries had fatty diets, and fat carries flavor."

So does salt. "Salt does more than give food a salty taste," says Smith. "It blends flavors and gives fullness." "Sugar blends, too," comments B. J. Doerfling, home economist and test kitchen manager, who was recipe coordinator and food stylist for *Cooking with Sunshine,* a citrus cookbook. "In developing recipes, I've found you can omit salt, fat and sugar completely and still retain flavor." But Americans' current preoccupation with health and fitness has caused them to question, in varying degrees, all three. Chefs and restaurateurs have responded by developing and serving increasingly flavorful healthful foods, (two prime examples being New York's the Four Seasons Spa cuisine and the marvelous meatless meals at San Francisco's Greens Restaurant). "Where do most people try something new?" asks Doerfling. "At a restaurant."

The American palate also owes its awakening to travel, at home and abroad. Travelers abroad collected a palette of exotic flavors, and travelers at home came in contact with intensely regional cuisines such as Cajun and Southwestern.

Many of these cuisines use herbs and spices previously unfamiliar to mainstream America. Not surprisingly, fresh herbs are one of the main flavor catalysts of today. Emelie Tolley, author of *Herbs: Gardens, Decorations and Recipes,* offers some sage advice: "You *can* use herbs for flavor in place of most or all the salt in a recipe; roasted nuts can add flavor without salt. Herb vinegars intensify flavor in salad dressings. Chefs no longer think chicken means tarragon, salmon means dill. They are rethinking how they use herbs and coming up with some entertaining and innovative dishes."

Tolley decries, however, "herbs as a buzzword to sell things (shampoos and soaps)," and the all too frequent tendency to condemn dried herbs (and spices), much the way that Americans' love affair with fresh pasta has resulted in labeling dried pasta as inferior. (Italian chefs repeatedly stress the two are different products, equally good.)

"If you can't have fresh herbs all year round, then use those dried herbs that hold their flavor, for example, thyme, rosemary and bay. And don't overlook herbs preserved in oil—such as basil, or frozen and freeze-dried herbs such as chives. Above all, experiment."

Someone whose experiment with herbs turned into "a real asset to the restaurant," is Janet (Mrs. Howard) Melvin, co-owner of The Heritage Restaurant in Cincinnati. "I grew herbs for years at home and used to take them to the chef. The Heritage sits on four acres, so I started a four- by six-foot herb garden in back. Customers became more interested when servers would describe the herbs from the garden that flavored their meals, so we started letting them back to see the garden. Howard finally said, 'If you're going to keep bringing people back here, we'd better spiff it up a bit.' That was five years ago. Today we have a huge garden with 500 varieties of herbs and flowers and do garden tours and herb luncheons."

PALATE PLEASERS

To produce the assertive flavors that please the palate, chefs use a variety of preparation and cooking techniques:

- Varying how ingredients are cut to affect flavor.
- Marinating ingredients before cooking in liquid and dry paste marinades.
- Using sauces to contrast or complement the flavors of the central dish.
- Seasoning prepared dishes directly with fresh herbs and with signature dried herb-spice mixtures.
- Slow cooking (braising, stewing); combining different cooking methods in the same dish.
- Layering flavors, contrasting or complementary, within the same dish.
- Using ingredients with high-flavor profiles and familiar ingredients in unexpected ways.

The American palate has awakened and is calling for its favorite flavors, herbs and hot red peppers among them. Keeping in mind that all these flavors must be distinct (nothing namby-pamby will satisfy), we asked our experts what flavors were popular today. Smith says: "Chocolate is still extremely popular, so are raspberry and strawberry. But tropical fruits are gaining ground—guava, passion fruit, mango, kiwifruit, papaya; so are cranberry and blueberry flavors showing up in products where they were never used before." Lang says, "in addition to exotic fruits and vegetables, the Indo-Chinese influence is quite extraordinary—coriander, lemon grass, fish sauce, and the Chiu-Chow cooking of Canton, China."

We also asked them what lies ahead. Tolley predicts the interest in herbs and her gardens, "which has really been building for ten years," will accelerate as will their use in foodservice, including fast food.

Lang predicts the next revolution will be in the art of tasting itself. "Smarter people are going into foodservice; they are beginning to question why we do what we do and to investigate. We will pay more attention to so-called healthy foods, but I don't think we know as much as we think."

Says Smith: "The desire for new kinds of flavor sensations will continue. Whatever else, we will *not* (as some have predicted) eat pills as our source of nutrition. Eating is pleasurable and social. Americans enjoy eating and will continue to look at, taste, smell and experience food." ◆

America's Cheeses Come of Age

by Nancy Ross Ryan

"Cheese is milk's leap toward immortality," said American lexicographer Clifton Fadiman in the '60s, eloquently defining the food most often compared with wine. By the '80s, Americans had not only transformed grape juice into wines that command worldwide respect, but also had immortalized milk into cheeses that equal Europe's finest. Today, from the bounty of factory cheeses to hundreds of specialty farmhouse cheeses, domestic cheese in all its variety is taking its rightful place in restaurants: not only as the cheese course, or a natural companion to wine, but as a round-the-clock food, for breakfast, lunch and dinner, and above all, as a cooking ingredient with a Midas touch.

Even though all cheese begins with milk—from cows, goats, sheep, water buffalo—and is made by separating curds from whey and pressing the curds to form a solid, the end products can differ so much that it seems as though some varieties of cheese belong to a different food group altogether. Consider, on one hand, 8-ounce blocks of soft, white, mild, smooth cream cheese ready to eat a few hours after being made and, on the other, 80-pound wheels of firm, orange, sharp, crumbly Cheddar, aged for up to three years. (See profiles on natural, process and substitute cheeses at the end of this article.)

We owe today's wide variety of domestic cheeses both to giant factories that mass-produce high-quality popular cheeses and to hundreds of smaller co-ops and farmhouse cheese makers. These pursue traditional cheese-making methods to produce cheeses patterned after their European namesakes, but with distinctly American flavors. An authoritative sourcebook that includes recipes is *American Country Cheese: Cooking with America's Specialty and Farmstead Cheeses*, by Laura Chenel and Linda Siegfried (New York: Addison-Wesley, 1989).

Cheese for Breakfast?

Most Americans consider cheese in breakfast omelets fairly standard. But cheese for breakfast? A selection of cheeses is offered daily on the breakfast buffet at the Cafe Suisse, Swiss Grand Hotel, Chicago. At $13.50, the buffet is the single most popular breakfast. In addition to American breakfast foods, the buffet has a traditional European side. There, guests will find Buendnerfleisch (cured, air-dried beef thinly sliced), the traditional muesli (uncooked oats mixed with milk, chopped fruits and nuts) and, the stars of the buffet—a selection of traditional Swiss breads and fine Swiss cheeses. Cheese eaten as it is, a European tradition, lends itself to breakfast as a protein source, especially when paired with whole-grain, rye and egg breads, freshly baked on the premises.

Dozens of other breakfast and brunch menu items derive their flavor, texture and character from cheese. The following breakfast menu items (from *American Country Cheese*) illustrate creative uses for four different domestic cheeses: Poached eggs on a bed of chopped tomatoes and grated smoked mozzarella in crisp potato baskets; Ricotta Pancakes (using 2 cups of ricotta in a 6-egg batter); a savory Brie Pancake; and popovers baked with Muenster or brick cheese in the batter. What's good for pancakes and popovers applies as well to waffles and breakfast breads.

Cheese at Lunch

Soup and sandwiches are two menu item categories synonymous with lunch. And tried-and-traditional cheese dishes are enjoying a renaissance: Cheddar cheese soup, cheese and broccoli soup, corn and cheese chowder, gratineed onion soup, croque monsieur, the Reuben, Philadelphia cheese steak and the grilled cheese sandwich.

But beyond the standards lie a new generation of luncheon soups and sandwiches. Examples: Black Bean Soup with Pumpkin and Chevre Purée (from *American Country Cheese*); a New England seafood chowder with Gouda cheese; a Reuben chowder made with cream of celery soup, sauerkraut, sausages, Swiss cheese and caraway seed; Poblano and Cheese Soup with Yellow Pepper Sour Cream, a specialty of chef/partner Stephan Pyles, Routh Street Cafe, Dallas.

Cheese sandwiches can be grilled in new ways. For example, a grilled sourdough bread can be filled with roast beef, turkey breast, Cheddar and Swiss cheeses, lettuce, tomato and fried onions. It's listed on the menu of Dayton Hudson, Minneapolis, as a Frisco Sandwich, and served, not with french fries, but with fresh fruit. The Greenery Restaurant in Barrington, Ill., features only American food products and American beers and wine. Two of chef/owner David Koelling's signature sandwiches are: Eggplant, Tomato and Cheese Sandwich on Rye, which features mozzarella, smoked Cheddar, both sliced and grated Asiago; and Breast of Chicken topped with Goat Jack and Sautéed Onions.

Old Dishes Learn New Tricks

Updates of traditional cheese favorites include the soufflé and the quiche. The old-fashioned cheese soufflé is finding new-fashioned favor when made with today's cheeses; for example, a hearty combination of bread, mustard and Colby cheese baked with an egg custard rises to new heights. In *Cheese* (San Francisco: Chronicle Books, 1986), James McNair transforms Southern cheese grits into a light soufflé using eggs and a combination of Monterey Jack and Parmesan cheeses. McNair, author of 19 single-subject cookbooks, has a knack for injecting new life into old favorites: Pasta with Four American Cheeses (goat's milk, blue, brick and Monterey Jack), and Blue Cheese Blintzes. His update of quiche is a sizzling Chili and Chorizo Quiche, combining Cheddar and Monterey Jack, spicy sausage, fresh hot chilies, garlic and a pinch of cayenne for good luck.

A contemporary version of quiche is often deep-dish. One is featured on the menu at Dayton Hudson, Minneapolis, and another is offered seasonally on the luncheon menu of Le Crocodile, Edd Wheeler's new restaurant in Atlanta. Le Crocodile's Deep-Dish Quiche of the Day (two inches deep) is baked in a puff pastry shell, and the egg-cream-Swiss cheese custard includes untraditional combinations such as smoked turkey and wild mushrooms.

Another old-fashioned favorite, macaroni and cheese, is being given a new look by today's chefs. The macaroni used is seldom elbow; chefs choose from wagon wheels to shells and corkscrews. One current version of macaroni and cheese calls for spinach pasta, tomatoes, Swiss chard, onions and a combination of blue and Monterey Jack cheeses.

Other popular luncheon items that offer opportunities to feature cheese include, at Dayton Hudson, Spinach Terrine with Roquefort, Pasta with Goat Cheese, and Smoked Cheddar Steak Burger; a ratatouille au gratin (baked with Swiss cheese), a pizza soup so hearty it is almost a stew (pizza ingredients simmered in a rich tomato base and topped with mozzarella), the stuffed potato in its endless variety and cheese fries (french fries smothered in cheese sauce). And popular fried cheese has moved from its niche as an hors d'oeuvre and appetizer to topping all manner of salad greens.

Cheese Stars at Dinner

Dinner is the meal when cheese can star from first course, through entree, the cheese course, to dessert.

Interesting cheese appetizer courses range from the simple, skewered fruit-and-cheese kabobs, flavored cheese dips, fried cheese, nachos and bite-size pizza squares—to the complex, miniature cheese pastry puffs, crisp cheese straws and biscuits, tiny chevre-stuffed phyllo triangles, nut-crusted cheese truffles, and savory cheesecakes such as the Greenery's Salmon Cheesecake with Red and Green Onions; Chef Jean Joho's sliver of Alsatian Leek and Cheese Tart at the Everest Room, Chicago; or Chef Jasper White's New England Cheddar Cheese Pie with Green Onions and Walnuts, made with aged Cheddar cheese and served in small wedges as a combination cheese-and-salad course at Jasper's in Boston.

There are menu signs that interest is reviving in a hearty, old-fashioned first course: cheese fondue made with nontraditional cheeses such as Cheddar and incorporating nontraditional ingredients such as a combination of crabmeat and caraway seed.

Another dish from Switzerland is reappearing on cold-weather dinner menus as an entree: raclette (from the French verb to scrape, *racler*). This traditional Swiss meal consists of herb-roasted potatoes, smoked ham, salami or sausage, sliced apples and sliced French bread with a garnish of cornichons and pearl onions; and at its heart are servings of melted cheese that has been scraped from a wheel or wedge of any firm or semisoft cheese. And in *American Country Cheese*, a recipe for New World Raclette includes yams and white potatoes, red onions, medium hot chilies (Anaheim or Poblano) and duck sausages.

Ethnic Dishes Redesigned

American chefs are redesigning ethnic classics with cheese. For example, lasagna no longer necessarily means ricotta, mozzarella and Parmesan, but can be made of cheese combinations of Cheddar, Monterey Jack, provolone and Swiss, matching flavors to complement sauce and other ingredients. (Swiss and spinach are flavormates, and so are Cheddar and Monterey Jack with tomatoes.) Mexican classics are getting new attention: Chilies Rellenos at Santacafe, Santa Fe, are stuffed with mild chevre, cream cheese and sun-dried tomatoes; quesadillas can be filled with Gouda and accompanied by pineapple salsa; and the queen of comfort dishes, kugel, is no longer relegated to traditional Jewish home kitchens thanks to American chefs who are creating unsweetened versions of this noodle pudding as a savory side dish that uses cottage cheese and Parmesan with sour cream.

In addition to revamping hearty ethnic comfort foods with cheese, chefs today are creating new entrees: grilled chicken breast topped with prosciutto and melted Camembert; boiled beef with Swiss cheese dressed in a flavorful parsley vinaigrette; for vegetarians, a wild mushroom and wild rice strudel layered with Swiss, Parmesan and goat cheeses; and Double-Cheese Polenta with mozzarella and Parmesan served with grilled tomatoes and sautéed spinach from Chef Denis Bold, The Station House Cafe, Point Reyes, Calif.

The Cheese Course

After the main course and before dessert, it has been a European tradition to serve the cheese course, says Jean Pierre Legand, food and beverage director of Hotel Sofitel in Rosemont, Ill. The Sofitel offers a cheese course in its fine-dining operation, Cafe De Paris. Legand says that the Sofitel offers fruit with the cheese course "for presentation and flavor, but in the very old school, fruit was never served." Criteria for a cheese course, according to Legand, include a selection of three or four different cheeses with contrasting flavors and textures (soft, semisoft, hard; mild, ripened, aged). He recommends that, with the exception of baked cheeses for cold weather, cheeses be served at room temperature for the best flavor.

As Americans become more familiar with fine domestic cheeses, they will be more interested in finding the cheese course on American restaurant menus. A pioneer on behalf of made-in-America cheeses is Richard Perry, who, a decade ago, began offering customers at Richard Perry Restaurant in St. Louis a sampling of five or six domestic cheeses.

Cheese Desserts

Although some customers might opt for the cheese course in lieu of dessert, they might easily be swayed by any of the following: cheesecake in all flavors; Coeur a la Crème, molded in heart shapes, made with cream cheese, cottage or farmer cheese and cream, served with strawberries and chocolate or raspberry sauce; for chocoholics, this dessert can be made with chocolate.

Wine-poached pears can be filled with a blue-cheese mixture or with sweetened American-made Mascarpone, which can be used to fill dessert crepes and is also central to the traditional Italian Tiramisu. Pears also can star in a sweet pastry dough tart with slivered almonds and blue cheese, a creation of Chef Seppi Renggli. Cream cheese can be combined with gelatin, cream and flavorings such as lemon juice, vanilla, maple syrup or liqueurs, molded, chilled and served with a berry sauce or apricot purée. And the addition of cream or farmer cheese can enrich any version of bread pudding, as can Monterey Jack or a combination of tart apples and Cheddar cheese. And what is more appealingly American than a wedge of warm apple pie topped with sharp Cheddar?

Choice in Cheese: Natural

The 2 billion pounds of cheese produced in the United States last year can be divided between Natural Cheese and Pasteurized Process Cheese. Although there are about 800 different names for natural cheeses, there are only 18 different types; their distinguishing characteristics come from the method by which they are made. Examples of these 18 types are: brick, Camembert, Cheddar, cottage, cream, Edam, Gouda, Limburger, Neufchatel, Parmesan, provolone, Romano, Roquefort, sapsago, Swiss, Trappiste, and whey cheeses such as ricotta.

Natural cheeses also can be classified in four categories:

1. Hard, ripened by bacteria: Grating cheeses such as Parmesan, Romano, old Asiago.
2. Firm, ripened by bacteria, without eyes: Cheddar, Edam, Gouda, provolone. With eyes: Swiss, Emmenthaler.
3. Semisoft, ripened by bacteria: Brick and Muenster. Ripened by bacteria and surface micro-organisms: Limburger, Port-Salut. Ripened by blue mold in the interior: Roquefort, Gorgonzola, blue, Stilton.
4. Soft, ripened: Brie, Camembert, double- and triple-cremes. Unripened: Cottage, pot, cream.

Choice in Cheese: Process

Standards of identity for pasteurized process cheese are set by the U.S. Food and Drug Administration as follows:

1. Pasteurized Process Cheese: A blend of natural cheeses, mixed with an emulsifier and heated to prevent further ripening. Moisture content may equal 40%; fat content must be 30%; implied cheese minimum is 81.5%.
2. Pasteurized Process Cheese Food: Made like process cheese but slightly higher in moisture (up to 44%) and lower in milkfat (23%). Cheese must be at least 51%. Additional flavoring ingredients (vegetables, meats, seasonings) may be added, along with optional dairy ingredients such as cream, milk, skim milk, buttermilk, nonfat dry milk solids or whey.
3. Pasteurized Process Cheese Spread: Made like process cheese food with addition of an edible stabilizer. Slightly higher in moisture and lower in milkfat.
4. Pasteurized Process Cheese Product: Made like process cheese spread but higher in moisture (up to 80%) and lower in fat (less than 20%). Cheese ingredients must be 51%.

Choice in Cheese: Alternates

Sometimes called cheese analogs or alternates, the products that are officially classified by the FDA as Substitute Cheese and Imitation Cheese are made primarily from casein or caseinate (a milk protein) and vegetable oils (partially hydrogenated), whey, water, natural and/or artificial flavor and color, and vitamins. Producers cite their products' lower food cost, convenience and long refrigerated shelf life. The most commonly produced cheese substitutes are American, Cheddar, mozzarella, Swiss and Monterey Jack cheese substitutes. According to Simmons Market Research Bureau, New York, Substitute Cheese and/or Imitation Cheese is used by 17% to 18% of foodservice operators. According to FDA standards, Substitute Cheese must be nutritionally equivalent to its counterpart, process cheese. Imitation Cheese need not be nutritionally equivalent to its counterpart, process cheese. ♦

Smoke Catches Fire:
The Flavor and Texture of Smoked Food Is Catching On Like Wildfire

by Nancy Ross Ryan

Until very recently, the only places Americans could satisfy their hankering for the unique flavor of smoked foods were a regional BBQ joint (or a pig-pickin'), a "new Southwestern" restaurant, a trendy California bistro—or in their own backyards over the home grill. Suddenly, smoked foods started catching on like wildfire on menus from coast to coast. But many operators are discovering that where there's smoke—there's confusion: to grill, to hot smoke, to brine, to dry cure (aye, there's the rub!), to cold smoke, to smoke roast, or to purchase presmoked products? Those are the questions.

To clear the clouds of confusion, *R&I* offers a mini-lesson (everything you ever wanted to know about smoking foods), how-to tips (on how to do it simply in the restaurant kitchen), and ideas for menu items.

To learn about the basics of smoking, we interviewed David Kellaway, CMC, chef-instructor, The Culinary Institute of America, Hyde Park, N.Y. Kellaway not only teaches the subject as part of the curriculum, but he grew up with it. Raised in Texas, he was weaned on regional barbecue at the "Salt Lick, in Driftwood, right outside of Austin. It's great! And every time I go home, to this day, I go back there." Then he adds, "For some beef brisket, that is. Uncured. Hot smoked," thus beginning our lesson on smoking. "If there is any confusion between grilling and smoking," says Kellaway, "it stems from the fact that as items are cooked (on a grill or rack) above a bed of fire or coals, flames are combusted, creating smoke, and the food acquires nuances of flavor from the smoke. But in the true smoking process, the food

obtains the majority of the flavor from the smoke itself."

Cold and Hot Smoking

The two basic smoking processes are cold and hot. In cold smoking, food is placed in a cold-smoke environment where the air temperature is lower than 100F; no cooking takes place. Cold-smoked foods are cured before smoking.

Hot smoking takes place typically in a closed hot-smoke environment where temperatures are maintained between 150 and 250F; cooking takes place. Hot-smoked foods typically are not cured before smoking. "Temperatures higher than 250F signal the realm of smoke roasting, where the food cooks faster, allowing for less smoke penetration."

Basic steps to prepare food for cold and hot smoking are:

♦ **Fabricate item:** Rid it of excess fat, bone or sinew; break it down into uniform sizes to allow for consistent curing and smoking.

♦ **Cure:** (Cold Smoking) Apply brine, a mixture of salt, curing salt (4% sodium nitrite and 96% salt), sugar and seasonings (spices and herbs); or dry cure (not a liquid but a rub). The cure draws out water, changes the texture, making it slightly more dense; inhibits bacterial growth; gives product salty flavor; sets color; extends shelf life.

♦ **Rinse:** (Cold Smoking) Rinse product under clean running water to stop cure, remove excess salt.

♦ **Dry:** (Cold Smoking) Blot dry small items or air-dry, refrigerated, large items. Drying time for some items is drastically extended (pro-sciutto-crudo, salami); drying times for small items range from four hours (smoked salmon) to two to three days (cured sausages). Air dry-ing on skinless items forms a pellicle, a layer of dehydrated protein, creating a skin-like covering that gives the cooked item even color and shine.

♦ **Smoke:** To cold smoke, place item in smoke environment maintained below 100F. Source of smoke is usually indirect; fuel is typically hardwood, presoaked in water, chips, shavings or sawdust (hardwood is low in resin) from fruitwoods or mesquite.

To hot smoke, place item in, typically, a closed environment; introduce smoke at the same time heat is maintained above 150F up to 250F. Many variations and interpretations of hot smoking include Texas-style barbecue where uncured brisket is suspended over low-burning hardwood coals in an open environ-ment to slow smoke roast. (Commercial smoke houses have additional technologies to expand the range of effects from their closed environments, such as varying levels of humidity, fan-forced air, and automatic cold showering of products.)

Simplified Hot Smoking

To cold smoke foods requires more elaborate equipment and sophisticated techniques than the average restaurant kitchen can supply, although there are chefs who are at ease with both cold- and hot-smoking techniques, for example, Michael Russell, CMC, *chef de cuisine,* Travis Pointe Country Club, Ann Arbor, Mich. Russell, who hot smokes everything from chicken and salmon to wild boar sausage and venison jerky, in everything from cast-iron skillets to buffet pans to converted food warmers, does not recommend cold smoking or elaborate equipment "until you are familiar with the process." But he does recommend hot smoking on top of the range, using either a cast-iron skillet or a makeshift smoker from hotel pans.

For skillet smoking, place cast iron skillet on heat, put fuel (presoaked wood chips) in bottom,

place item to be smoked on rack above fuel, and cover with foil, lifting or venting to prevent too heavy a smoke flavor.

For a makeshift smoker, put presoaked chips in full-size hotel pan, cover with foil, cut slits in foil to allow smoke to vent. Put fuel-filled pan on heat, place perforated hotel pan above it. Place food to be smoked in perforated pan; cover with foil, lifting occasionally to prevent too heavy a smoke flavor. Cooking times vary according to size and thickness of item.

Russell's tips for chefs unfamiliar with smok-ing foods include:

♦ Get a good book on smoking. For years he has relied on *The Easy Art of Smoking Food,* by Chris Dobbs and Dave Heberle (Winchester Press, 1977, New Century Publishers Inc., 220 Old New Brunswick Rd., Piscataway, N.J. 08854).

♦ Learn the basics: brining, drying, fuels, heat and timing.

♦ Do one item until mastered, then move on to the next. He started with salmon, progressed to other fish, then moved on to poultry. "The most forgiving," he says, "because by remov-ing the skin you can diminish the smoke fla-vor if you have overdone it."

♦ Smoking meat, poultry and fish bone-in imparts more flavor.

"Smoking foods adds a dimension to a chef's repertoire that is very popular right now, and will be, I think, for a long time. And hot-smoked foods that are not cured are an attrac-tive flavor alternative to customers on low-sodium diets." Russell, who is willing to share what he has learned, urges chefs unfamiliar with the process to talk to him and to other chefs who are already doing it successfully.

Contemporary Menu Ideas

Jeffrey Gabriel, CMC, chef-instructor at School-craft College, Livonia, Mich., who owns Califor-nia Pasta Shops Inc. (a retail takeout and whole-sale operation), agrees that smoked foods have hit an all-time high on restaurant menus, but ascribes their popularity to several causes: "First, smoking imparts more flavor, more depth to food; you can taste the cooking method. People like that outdoorsy aroma; it reminds them, I think, of backyard barbecues. But smoked foods in the ambiance of a restaurant dining room adds a new dimension."

"Smoking foods can enhance the perceived value," says Russell. "A smoked chicken salad has more perceived value than a roast chicken salad." "And," adds Kellaway, "smoked meats can be used in a matrix of pasta, greens or rice."

Some of Gabriel's smoked menu items include: Cornish game hen—deboned, used hot or cold with a natural reduction of fresh poultry bones, or in a spinach salad with dried cherries, mushrooms and an orange vinaigrette; pork loin and pear salad; house-made chicken sausage; a variety of smoked fish, served cold.

Russell's popular smoked menu items include: hot-smoked salmon served with a coarse-chopped egg, fresh herb, cream and white wine sauce, or a fresh tomato concasse with garlic and tarragon; a natural fish reduction; or with lentils, spinach and stewed mushrooms. His smoked oysters star in a red-skin potato salad with fresh chopped lemon thyme, tarragon and cilantro or flat-leaf parsley. Russell smokes shrimp with the shells on, removing them while warm, and favors the ducks bred for leanness for smoking for salads, pastas, entrees. Russell's smoked repertory includes duck and wild boar sausage, beef and venison jerky, frog legs and cheese (Swiss and Gouda).

But two of the chefs interviewed, Kellaway and Gabriel, mention a smoked item that may take some time before setting menu trends: rattlesnake. Kellaway remembers eating it "years ago in Texas at a rattlesnake roundup—they still hold them. It was really quite good. The flavor was delicate, and the oil content of the meat made the texture melt in your mouth." ◆

WHERE THERE'S SMOKE THERE'S:

Seafood: Mussels; clams; oysters; snails (California grey snails); shrimp; squid; eel; and fatty fishes such as salmon, fresh water whitefish, lake trout, bluefish and mackerel. Usually fish are cured, cold-smoked and served cold, but today's chefs also hot pan-smoke fish and serve with a variety of sauces.

Poultry: Chicken, duck, Rock Cornish game hen, turkey and goose.

Game and game birds: Venison, elk, rabbit, partridge, grouse, chukar, pheasant and quail.

Cheese: Swiss, Gouda and white Cheddar.

Vegetables: Garlic, elephant garlic, onions, potatoes, chestnuts, chilies, sweet peppers, eggplant, corn, acorn squash and mushrooms.

Meat: Beef, lamb, and pork.

Herbs: Juniper, thyme, bay, marjoram, tarragon, dill, sage, mint and basil; added to fuel for heightened aroma.

Sausages: Meat, seafood, poultry and game.

Convenience: A long inventory of quality commercially produced smoked foods can expand menu offerings. And using liquid hickory smoke-flavored extract has a long precedent: Before its commercial beginnings in 1895, Confederate General Thomas "Stonewall" Jackson had his men pour water over burned wood, then add to pork being barbecued because he liked its smoky flavor.

Food on the Move

by Lisa Bertagnoli and Beth Lorenzini

By 1993, the market for takeout food accounted for about $100 billion of total foodservice sales. More than a few operators were part of that sum: The National Restaurant Association estimates that 38% of all upscale and 56% of all midscale restaurants offer takeout meals. But food to go requires more than packing the daily special into a plastic carton. As this article shows, operators who succeed with takeout and delivery carefully tailor their plans to their own businesses.

Upscale restaurants, for instance, treat food to go as an adjunct to normal operations. Takeout orders and delivery schedules do not interfere with the dining experiences of on-premise customers, nor do they overtax the kitchen. In the words of Barry Wine, chef/proprietor of the Quilted Giraffe (which Wine shuttered in 1992): "We want to maintain our reputation as a special restaurant."

Foodservice operations without extensive sit-down facilities find success in offering unusual fare. A waitress at a Spanish restaurant in Austin, Texas, for instance, continues to make and deliver orders, even though the restaurant closed a year ago. Universities and hospitals have launched successful takeout and delivery operations in previously underused kitchen and dining facilities.

The following examples show that a creative approach is best for operators considering food to go. After all, a $100 billion market is too big to ignore.

♦ A customer at Le Petit Cafe, Chicago, was responsible for hooking up the restaurant with Room Service, a company that delivers food from 11 restaurants in the city. Before the matchup, Le Petit Cafe provided limited delivery service and was not pleased with it at all. Customers would call in lunch orders at the last minute and expect instant delivery, says Le Petit owner Dalia Azevedo. Furthermore, the small amount of business did not warrant hiring a delivery person;

instead, waiters or kitchen help would deliver the order, thereby leaving the restaurant short-handed during peak periods. "We weren't too crazy about delivery," says Azevedo.

One of Le Petit's regular customers, however, is married to one of the owners of Room Service. Room Service, then only a month old, needed a restaurant specializing in lunch to balance its heavy load of rib and pizza restaurants. The delivery company experimented with Le Petit's menu for a month to find out which items were most conducive to delivery. The two companies then signed a year-long contract.

Orders are transmitted via fax machine from Room Service's order-taking office to Le Petit's kitchen. Le Petit is required only to cook and package the food. Room Service delivers it, tacking a 20% service charge and $3 delivery charge on to the menu price.

♦ The Quilted Giraffe's Wine prevented delivery from taking over his kitchen by offering a limited menu to a limited number of customers.

When Wine started thinking about a delivery business, however, he planned to make it a business that could grow on its own. Once he started delivering, problems such as Manhattan traffic and maintaining food quality forced Wine to reconsider.

The Quilted Giraffe offered delivery of two menus, priced at $25 per person, to regular customers. The Spa lunch consisted of a goat cheese and vegetable salad, jalapeno shrimp, grilled Norwegian salmon and fresh fruit. The Executive menu offered cabbage slaw, smoked salmon, duck confit and assorted cakes. A waiter attired in a black satin Quilted Giraffe jacket delivered the food in black lacquer Bento boxes, which are picked up after lunch. The kitchen required advance notice of two to three days for lunch delivery, especially for large parties or corporate lunches.

◆ Brigitte de Roch delivers paella, salad and dessert to residents of Austin, Texas. She started the business, Paella Plus, after the Spanish restaurant she worked in closed. "There are a lot of educated people in Austin who like fine food," de Roch explains. She and her partner, Michael Niland, deliver about 25 orders each week.

The standard order consists of paella for two, salad and small fruit tartes, and sells for $32. (Paella for four costs $48, and in reality serves six, de Roch says.) She does all the cooking herself, even during peak holiday seasons. She and Niland have no plans to take the business outside Austin or expand the menu.

◆ For $31.50 plus $5 for delivery, Original American Scone, Chicago, delivers a dozen warm scones and two jars of jam packaged in a cardboard "briefcase" to downtown businesses. The restaurant delivers about 25 cases a week, according to owner Jeff Hopmeyer. Hopmeyer says the briefcases, which are white, green or hot pink, were popular corporate Christmas gifts. "A lot of the buyers are customers who come in to the restaurant for their morning coffee breaks," he says.

◆ Takeout helped Nick Spinelli, foodservice officer of First Wisconsin National Bank, get the bank's foodservice department back in the black. "We had already been doing some carryout business," says Spinelli, "so it was just a matter of refining the process. We had to market it properly so that it would generate revenues that would let us operate without subsidies."

Refining the process included adding takeout items not featured on the regular menu for breakfast and lunch, as well as adding a line of dinner entrees that are ready for the microwave. Bulk snacks, such as nut mixes and candies, and yogurt, all sold by the ounce, add to takeout revenues, which account for 12% of total sales.

Most takeout transactions are made at lunch. Soups, salads and sandwiches, sold separately or in combination, generate check averages of about $2.40. Lunch items are presented in the salad-bar area of the cafeteria. "At the salad bar, customers expect a potpourri of sorts, so the various items move fastest when presented in that format," says Spinelli.

The most innovative addition to the takeout program is the dinner entree service that Spinelli created to compete with the frozen and prepared foods sections of local markets. Beef stroganoff, lasagna, pork and chicken dishes and stews, among other entrees, sell for an average of $2.20.

The cost of the extra labor incurred for takeout is minimal, says Spinelli. The staff has simply become more productive, and preparing extra quantities of items has been scheduled into the normal routine. One employee stays an extra hour each day to sell the dinner entrees to outgoing employees.

◆ Blue Plate, a Chicago catering company turned food shop/restaurant, offers home-style food and hot soups to customers who are tired of cold marinated salads and deli sandwiches. The restaurant offers two hot daily specials from a master menu of 40 items, which includes everything from pot roast with potatoes, onions and carrots to hefty portions of lasagna. Prices range from $4 to $6.50 a serving. Customers can supplement their meals with baked goods and wine from the store.

While catering for parties and film crews accounts for 75% of Blue Plate's business, the owners want to expand the business and eventually add delivery. According to Bob McDonald, Blue Plate founder and vice president of marketing, the company will soon package the food to go in microwavable containers. The company is also developing custom-printed packaging; currently it uses white paper bags and stickers imprinted with the Blue Plate logo.

◆ San'wiches restaurant in San Diego uses a fax machine to take orders. When owners Jordan Lansky, a former partner with Kaufman, Lansky, Baker advertising in San Diego, and Jay Chiat, chairman and chief executive of Chiat/Day in New York, opened the 35-seat restaurant, the fax machine was part of the plan.

Any one of the 22 sandwich selections, ranging from peanut butter and jelly to traditional deli sandwiches, can be ordered by fax and delivered within 30 minutes to corporate offices in the area. Faxing saves time over ordering by phone and ensures accuracy, a blessing to hungry workers with limited lunch hours.

♦ San'wiches is not alone in its use of the fax machine. Restaurant Associates in New York has installed machines in its Brasserie and Trattoria restaurants. Fax menu sheets in 25-count pads can be picked up or sent to offices by mail. Orders must be received three hours in advance. In an effort to increase large orders, Brasserie and Trattoria offer free delivery for orders of ten lunches or more.

♦ Even quick service has jumped aboard the fax bandwagon. A Burger King restaurant in Danbury, Conn., uses a fax machine to take orders from workers at the nearby Fujitsu Imaging Systems of America factory. Employees can pick up their orders in about two minutes, avoiding lunch-hour lines, once they get to the restaurant. About $100 worth of orders are taken by fax each week.

♦ Cap'n Taco, a small chain of full-service Mexican restaurants based in Cleveland, uses a SWAT-team approach to deliver lunch orders to downtown Cleveland office buildings. First, customers must phone in lunch orders by 10:30 A.M. They order from menus distributed in the office building, and often order for an entire floor, says Cap'n Taco President Ray Brown. The cooked orders are packed in big blue coolers, which are loaded into a van, along with five uniformed delivery people. Delivery people and food are deposited on various city blocks; the food is delivered while the van circles the blocks (necessary to avoid parking tickets).

Brown says the chain aggressively advertises delivery and took pains to obtain a special phone number. Delivery accounts for 80% of business at the chain's Cleveland restaurant; delivery checks average $25 to $30. At the Cap'n Taco in Brook Park, Ohio, orders delivered to area schools and factories account for 28% of sales. Popular delivery items include taco salad ($3.25) and crab salad ($3.59).

♦ Nutritional takeout meal programs are showing up in hospitals across the country. For United Hospital in St. Paul, Minn., the Nutritional Cuisine program developed six years ago is a way of offering meals that are low in sodium, salt and sugar to patients (especially elderly ones) recuperating at home. "Meals on Wheels doesn't deliver on weekends," says Kaleen Kregel, administrative dietitian for the hospital, "and we're concerned that patients are not eating as well as they should."

The hospital developed 24 varieties, ranging from casseroles and lasagna to Cod Amandine, to be produced and distributed by a manufacturer. Each entree also includes soup, a vegetable, a starch and dessert. Large, easy-to-read labeling on each package lists all ingredients. Cases containing six entrees for $20, as well as individual selections, are sold from a refrigerated display in the hospital's cafeteria. So far, hospitals in 20 states have picked up the program.

♦ California State University at Fresno used its holiday basketball tournament to launch a Thanksgiving-to-go program. Every year, the school hosts four teams for the tournament, and keeps a kitchen open to cook Thanksgiving dinner for the players. "We've always enjoyed doing the banquet," says Rick Finlay, administrator of campus foodservice, "but keeping the staff on and keeping the kitchen open to feed 100 students was expensive."

The foodservice department decided to market a Thanksgiving-to-go program to students and faculty who planned to stay on campus during the holiday. In early October, the university advertised a feast of roast turkey, rolls, butter, gravy, stuffing, a vegetable and pumpkin pie for $44.50. Orders for the 58 dinners available to the campus sold out in one week. The success of the Thanksgiving-to-go promotion ensures that it will be offered again next year.

♦ At the University of Southern California's Vieni Vieni bake shop, the line forms to the right, daily. What makes the shop so appealing, in addition to a tempting array of muffins, pastries, juices and fresh coffee, is the fact that university meal cards are accepted as payment.

The bake shop is just one of many ventures into the takeout market on the Los Angeles campus. Homemade pizzas can be ordered for delivery and USC meal cards are accepted. The option to pay by meal card draws orders from students who may be short on cash and makes ordering a university-made pizza over one from a local shop that much more appealing.

♦ Dallas-based Embassy Suites has begun to package its complimentary breakfasts to go. Such amenities help keep occupancy rates at the chain at 80%, 15% above the national average, says Doren Chisholm, corporate director of food and beverage.

The breakfast menu was changed a bit to accommodate the takeout program, Chisholm says. Bananas, apples, oranges and other fruit are served whole instead of sliced. Yogurt is offered in the cup, and muffins, doughnuts and sweet rolls are wrapped and ready for patrons to pick up on their way out.

♦ Dairy Queen tried Telechef. General Mills has experimented with Order Inn. Jean Sippy has started Home Cooking, and delivers about 150 dinners a week to office workers in Santa Ana, Newport Beach, and Irvine, Calif.

Sippy, a banker before she founded Home Cooking, works out of a rented kitchen in Santa Ana. She distributes menus to office buildings, and relies on word of mouth for advertising. Orders must be placed four hours before the customer wants it delivered. Home Cooking's menu offers six different entrees a day; popular items include Chinese chicken salad ($6 per serving) and pot roast ($6.50 per serving). About half the deliveries are made to work places; half are made to residences. Checks average $15.

♦ Canteen Co. tapped into the takeout market by introducing its signature Pazzelli's Pizza. The pizza is available in 7-inch individual or 14-inch, eight-slice pies. Canteen clients order ready-to-bake crusts and prechopped toppings, such as Italian sausage, pesto sauce, a five-cheese mix and pine nuts, from distributors, and assemble the pizzas by hand on site. Twice a year, Canteen introduces new topping packages, like seafood or Mexican, for special promotions.

Business and industry clients are the biggest fans of Pazzelli's, says Jean Robinson, director of dietetics for Canteen. In addition to taking individual pizzas back to the desk, many offices order large pizzas for lunch. An average of 400,000 portions are sold each month.

♦ Executive Box Lunch, an offshoot of ARA's Classic Cuisine catering service, succeeds due to a combination of good food and sharp packaging, according to Paul Quintavalla, director of marketing services for ARA's business, convention and personal dining division. The program generates a 20% to 25% profit margin because the lunches are made in off-peak periods without additional overhead costs.

The individual boxes are made of gray laminated cardboard with lids held on by a silver elastic band. Glossy black plates rest on cardboard platforms inside the lunch box, which keep the lunches from crushing each other. The boxed lunches are carried to the site in ARA's custom-carry box, which is waterproof, washable, insulated and can hold up to 65 pounds.

The box-lunch menus include upscale sandwiches: for example, roast sirloin of beef on a kaiser, turkey with ham and Swiss and the overstuffed Dagwood Deli. Side salads of cheese tortellini in basil vinaigrette or German potato salad and desserts also are included. The lunches cost between $6 and $7. ♦

Build a Better Breakfast

by Nancy Ross Ryan, Karen Straus and Brenda McCarthy

The morning news: 20% of adults eat breakfast out at least once a week. Breakfast traffic grew 2% from 1990 to 1991, outpacing other dayparts. And in the past decade, breakfast traffic has advanced 19%. To help you build your breakfast business, the editors of *R&I* serve you the best breakfast information and ideas on the market today.

For example: Members of higher-income households are more likely to eat breakfast away from home, as are households where the female head of the household is employed. For seniors, breakfast represents a greater share of restaurant visits. However, across the board, breakfast is the most-skipped meal.

Most important, we offer a buffet of hot-selling breakfast foods. Today's breakfast flavors are livelier. Garlic is big and bold in potatoes and sausage. Hot peppers heat up egg dishes and hash. Traditional breakfast meats benefit from the back-to-basics trend, while lighter versions and nontraditional breakfast meats (veal bacon, poultry sausage, gravlax) are carving their own menu niche.

Fruit—fresh, grilled and marinated—plays new roles at breakfast and brunch. Breakfast breads, more popular than ever, branch out as signature breakfast sandwiches and pastries. Hot and cold cereal is bigger than ever in portion size and variety.

And breakfast beverages can no longer be taken for granted. Witness the surge of exciting specialty coffees, premium and herbal teas, and house-mixed fruit drinks.

Eggs

Nothing says breakfast quite like eggs. And no other single ingredient is as versatile as the following menu ideas show. The best nutritional news bulletin is that the cholesterol content of a large egg—once calculated at 274 mg—has been revised down 22%, to 213 mg. In addition, for customers on restricted diets, the marketplace offers operators a choice of good-tasting no- or low-cholesterol egg products for scrambling and omelets.

Many operations highlight these egg products with special promotions. For example, at the Chicago Downtown Marriott, banquet chef Hector Arroyo prepared filled omelets made with a reduced-cholesterol egg product at an omelet station—a perennially popular form of exhibition cooking. Meanwhile, the breakfast buffet featured burritos and scrambled eggs also made with egg product.

Hyatt Hotels and Resorts is having great success with its all-natural light menu, called Cuisine Naturelle. Eddie Sipple, corporate F&B director for the Chicago-based company, cites two breakfast items. The first is the no-cholesterol egg-white omelet made with chopped chives, white wine, blueberries and strawberries, and served with a fresh strawberry sauce (116 total calories). The second is egg-product huevos rancheros served with black bean salsa. The reason for the systemwide success of the menu is, he says, very simple: "The flavor is there."

When it comes to flavor, fresh eggs need no enhancement. Unadorned eggs—sunnyside up, over easy, poached, soft boiled and scrambled—are the cornerstones of the breakfast menu. They also are building blocks for traditional regional and ethnic egg dishes making menu news today. The Dining Room at Ford's Colony Country Club, Williamsburg, Va., features poached eggs on toasted Sally Lunn with shaved Virginia ham, spinach and hollandaise.

"Eggs lend themselves to sauces," writes Terence Janericco, Boston caterer and author of *The Book of Great Breakfasts and Brunches*. His book features 24 recipes for poached eggs with sauces, ranging from the well-known eggs Benedict to Tschimbur (poached eggs with garlic yogurt sauce) and Oeufs Poches a la Haut Brion (poached eggs with potato cakes, ham and a red wine sauce).

Fried eggs are familiar as huevos rancheros. Margaret Fox, chef-proprietor of Cafe Beaujolais, Mendocino, Calif., serves two eggs on two corn tortillas with Monterey Jack or Cheddar cheese, black bean chili, shredded lettuce, chopped black olives and sour cream. The secret: The eggs are cooked in salsa. For breakfast burritos, she scrambles eggs with hot pepper sauce.

Another egg dish, souffle, is enjoying a morning revival, especially at brunch. Oeuf Souffle a la Moutarde was developed by Chef Krista Wibskov as a special-occasion dish. The dish has a low food cost, but is labor intensive. However, it can command an $8.95 menu price. Wibskov says only an operation's oven capacity limits how many souffles can be made.

Breggfast Eggsperiments

Operators are no longer leery of innovative eggs on the breakfast menu. Following are R&I's suggestions for far-out breakfast eggs that might be in someday soon:

Egg foo yung: What is egg foo yung if not an Oriental vegetable frittata with gravy? Make breakfast egg foo yung with a lemon-soy-ginger sauce, peanut sauce, or cilantro-green-onion-tomato salsa with a dash of soy or a drop of sesame oil.

Egg rolls and spring rolls: The perennially popular deep-fried egg roll and fresh spring roll both lend themselves to egg (scrambled or hard cooked and chopped) as one stuffing ingredient in combination with chopped vegetables, seafood, meat and/or poultry. Breakfast egg rolls should omit hot mustard sauce and instead be served with light sweet-and-sour fruit sauce.

Scotch egg: Traditionally an appetizer or pub food, the hard-cooked egg coated with sausage, dipped in beaten egg and breadcrumbs, then deep-fried would make a stunning hearty-breakfast item served hot, halved lengthwise, accompanied by small buckwheat pancakes or authentic Scottish scones made with oats and griddle baked.

Flan: Who are we kidding—flan or creme caramel is too sweet for breakfast? Sweeter than French toast, waffles or hot cakes drenched in syrup? Flan provides its own syrup, and makes dramatic presentation unmolded from individual ramekins and served warm with a compote of fresh seasonal fruits and a croissant.

Rise and Shine with Breakfast Meats

In California, not far from the vineyards of Napa Valley, an Israeli-born chef serves home-cured pork loin, gravlax, veal bacon and chicken sausage to breakfast guests staying at a century-old hotel.

In Burlington, N.C., Biscuitville, an upscale chain of breakfast restaurants noted for traditional Southern favorites such as sausage, country ham and made-from-scratch biscuits, recently introduced a low-fat, Southern-style pork sausage.

And in Westport, Conn., Winslow's Restaurant offers customers a Country Breakfast Buffet featuring hash made with smoked pastrami, skin-on potatoes, onions and green pepper, topped with a poached egg and chipotle hollandaise.

Breakfast menus are offering meat in more forms than ever, from traditional bacon, sausage, ham and corned beef hash, to new, leaner variations of the classics, to nontraditional meats, fish and poultry.

Hash is a breakfast menu standard. Despite the simplicity of the ingredients—finely chopped meat, cooked potatoes and seasonings—hash can easily be up- or downscaled, depending on the operator's needs. At Chicago's Drake Hotel, the corned beef hash is definitely upscale. Made from scratch, it is topped with a poached egg and served with a hot baked apple, English muffin and beverage for $12.25.

John Carlino, chef-partner at Winslow's, makes his hash with smoked pastrami instead of corned beef. Says Carlino, "Corned beef shrinks a lot during cooking. With pastrami, which is already cooked, there is less waste. It is also leaner and has a nice smoked flavor."

At the 100-year-old Union Hotel in Benecia, Calif., filmmaker-turned-chef Lev Dagan offers a pork loin he cures himself. He ran across the dish in Germany and now serves it regularly. To prepare the dish, Dagan cleans and trims a 4-pound boneless pork loin, then cures it for two days in a brine solution. After hanging in the walk-in for 10 to 14 days, the meat is sliced paper thin, like prosciutto. During curing, seasonings such as fennel, peppercorns, or soy sauce and star anise flavor the meat.

Dagan also cures his own gravlax. "I love curing meats and fish," he says. "We make all our own sausages in-house, and we serve veal bacon, which we get from a local purveyor. It's much leaner." His house-made sausages include chicken, lemon and basil; chicken, garlic and chive; Italian and Portuguese; and a Moroccan offering seasoned with jalapeno peppers, turmeric and garlic.

Of the approximately 17 billion pounds of processed meat (cold cuts, sausage, ham and bacon) produced annually in the United States, more than 5 billion pounds is sausage. Sausage comes in many forms: fresh, uncooked and smoked, cooked and smoked, dry and/or semi-dry, and loaves and other specialty forms.

New sausage products on the market contain 10% to 20% fat by weight and, at 114 calories per serving, have about half the calories and fat of traditional whole-hog sausage. Fat reduction is accomplished by using lean meat or poultry; by adding water and fruit juice; using extenders such as hydrolyzed vegetable protein, oat bran or potato; or by adding moisture retainers such as carrageenan.

Biscuitville, with 34 units in North Carolina and Virginia, recognized the importance of offering traditional Southern fare such as country ham, whole-hog sausage and breaded, fried pork tenderloin, yet also saw the need to offer more healthful fare. The chain introduced a low-fat pork sausage with 10% fat. After a month on menu, the Biscuitville Pork Sausage Lite accounted for 20% of the chain's overall sausage sales.

The mix of traditional meats and new, healthier products will continue to expand on the Biscuitville menu. While the best-sellers remain the biscuit with regular sausage and salt-cured country ham on a biscuit, new breakfast items will include grilled, nonbreaded boneless pork tenderloin and grilled, marinated chicken biscuits.

Breakfast Breads and Grains

Breads and their carbo-loaded colleagues—cereals and hot cakes—command more attention at breakfast than at any other meal period. All the more reason to give them the attention they deserve.

Some things never change—the popularity of biscuits, for example. According to the *R&I* Menu Census, biscuits with sausage and biscuits with gravy still top the list of breakfast breads operators call good sellers (52% and 50%, respectively). The Menu Census lists the following breads as good sellers: bagels (47.6%), doughnuts (44.3%), cinnamon rolls (42.7%), Danish/sweet rolls (39.6%), muffins/quick breads (38.9%), toast (38.2%), coffee cake (32.7%), English muffins (31.4%) and plain croissants (27%).

But some things do change: Witness the growing popularity of unusual breads and breakfast sandwiches. John Storm, manager of Samplings Bar, Holiday Inn Crowne Plaza, New York, says the following breads on the *prix-fixe* $17.95 buffet brunch are extremely popular: Irish soda bread, pumpernickel-raisin rolls, sourdough bread and, a New York favorite, salt sticks (caraway-seed bread sticks coated with coarse salt).

The breakfast menu at Doug Arango's restaurant in Palm Desert, Calif., includes a la carte listings for toasted currant Irish soda bread ($1.50), and toasted Russian health bread ($1.25). In Chicago, Country Bruschetta ($2.95) is featured on the brunch menu of Christopher's on Halsted, and fresh-baked scones ($1.50) are popular for brunch at Noble Griffin.

The Apple Oat Squares from A La Carte, Wilmette, Ill., started out as a signature breakfast bar created by owner Lisa Kuk, with a flavor cross between apple pie and oatmeal cookies. Good taste travels fast. Word-of-mouth spread to several Chicago-area coffeehouses, where her oat bars are now regularly delivered and served.

Signature Breakfast Sandwiches

To McDonald's goes the credit for creating the breakfast sandwich that launched fast-food breakfast. However, signature breakfast sandwiches didn't start or stop with the Egg McMuffin. Our menu search uncovered more signature sandwiches: Lupo's S&S Charpit in Binghamton, N.Y., and Lupo's Quality Deli in Vestal, N.Y., have two signature sandwiches on the menus: the Deluxe Sandwich of eggs with sausage or bacon and

cheese and the breakfast BLT Sandwich, both on choice of roll, bread, bagel or muffin, and both at $1.69. Sam Lupo, president, says that sandwiches are cooked to order and customers can have the eggs cooked any style, or request low-cholesterol egg product and margarine instead of butter.

Other noteworthy breakfast sandwiches include the warm croissants stuffed with applewood-smoked turkey breast and mozzarella on the new weekend brunch menu of Le Mikado, Chicago, and a reminder of what probably was the original breakfast sandwich, lox and bagel on the Hala Terrace menu, The Kahala Hilton, Honolulu.

ALL ABOUT EGGS

Nutritious, versatile, and with low food -and labor-costs, the egg performs perfectly if all these tips are followed:

PURCHASING: Specify grade and size required: AA and A (ideal for poaching, frying, cooking in shell); B (good for scrambling, baking and as an ingredient); jumbo (30 oz./doz.); extra large (27 oz./doz.); large (24 oz./doz.); medium (21 oz./doz.); small (18 oz./doz.); and peewee (15 oz./doz.). Accept only clean, sound, odor-free eggs, snugly packed in fiberboard boxes, under refrigeration or cooled to below 55F.

Purchase only pasteurized, USDA-inspected products by type (fresh, frozen, dried, whole mixed, yolks, whites, blends, prepeeled hard cooked). Do not accept frozen product with signs of thawing.

STORAGE AND HANDLING: Rotate first in, first out. Store shell eggs in their case, away from strong-smelling foods, at 45F or below; do not freeze. Eggs at room temperature lose more quality in one day than in one week refrigerated.

Use only clean, uncracked eggs. Use sanitized utensils and equipment. Never mix shell with internal egg contents. Never reuse containers that have held raw egg mixture without sanitizing.

Store frozen products at 0F or below. Defrost in refrigerator or under cold running water, not at room temperature. Use defrosted product promptly and unused portion within three days.

Store refrigerated egg products at 40F with seal intact for up to six days unopened. Once opened, use immediately.

Store dried egg products tightly sealed in cool dark place. Refrigeration is recommended. Reconstitute only the amount to be used.

PREPARATION: Pasteurization occurs when a whole egg reaches 140F for 3.5 minutes. Cook until white is completely set and yolk begins to thicken. Scrambled: 250F for 1 minute until firm throughout. Poached: 5 minutes in boiling water. Sunny side: 7 minutes at 250F one side; turn and fry another 2 minutes. Soft cooked: 7 minutes in boiling water.

Cereals

It's no secret that cereal consumption is rising, and along with it, some interesting cereals. Individual portion packs of cold cereal now come in a larger size, closer to USDA's data on the amount of cereal Americans normally eat in a serving.

Two hearty cold cereals that made a strong showing in the '70s—bierchermuesli and granola—are making a comeback in the '90s. Granola is offered at Doug Arango's; the Fiddlehead Restaurant and Bakery, Juneau, Alaska; and at Noble Griffin. Hyatt Hotels and Resorts lists whole-grain cereal with fresh berries as one item on its Cuisine Naturelle menu, and house-made bierchermuesli is a popular breakfast item at the historic Westin St. Francis hotel, San Francisco.

Among hot cereals, old-fashioned oatmeal is a new-fashioned favorite that comes in new-fangled flavors: Mexican Oatmeal at Cafe Las Bellas Artes, Elmhurst, Ill.; Irish oatmeal at Daily Grill, Encino, Calif.; and apple-cinnamon oatmeal, a Hyatt Cuisine Naturelle item.

Pancakes, French Toast, Waffles

Innovative operators are sparking new interest in popular pancakes, French toast and waffles by giving them creative twists. At Mirador, Chicago, for example, the new brunch menu features thick-cut brioche French toast. Margaret Fox, Cafe Beaujolais, Mendocino, Calif., makes both a sweet (ricotta) and a savory (goat cheese) stuffed French toast, and Hyatt offers whole-grain French toast, whole-wheat pancakes and cornmeal pancakes. For children's menus, silver-dollar pancakes, miniature waffles and Lilliputian French toast triangles are a big hit.

Doug Arango's menu lists Russian pancakes made with shredded apples, and Primavera Restaurant, Fairmont Hotel, Chicago, features Pancakes Oscar with brown sugar, marshmallow meringue and hot strawberry sauce. Pecan waffles with smoked bacon and maple syrup ($6) is a popular breakfast item at the Dining Room, Ford's Colony Country Club, Williamsburg, Va. Whole-wheat and wild-rice waffles and tropical waffles with macadamia nuts and toasted coconut

ABOUT BACON

Bacon is produced from smoked pork bellies. The belly is the boneless side or underside of the pork carcass.

Pork bellies are smoked and processed to an internal temperature of about 130F.

Canadian-style bacon is made from the top loin muscle of pork, usually from heavier hogs.

Bacon is available in slab and sliced form. Depending on usage, bacon is sold in slices per pound for operator portion control. Bacon packs include tray pack, layer bacon (shingled) and bulk sliced.

Layer bacon is packed in 1-pound lots per layer, generally in 18 to 22 and 20 to 24 slice counts. Other counts are available for specific operator needs. Layer-packed bacon is often used in high-volume operations where portion control and fast preparation are essential.

Bulk-sliced bacon is best used by cost-conscious operators who do not require specific portion-control product.

Source: National Live Stock and Meat Board

are only two of the wonderfully wacky waffles at Cafe Beaujolais.

Jam Session

Hot, hearty, breakfast fare is more creative than ever. Pancakes are fortified with fruit, nuts and cheese; French toast is sliced thick from specialty breads such as brioche, whole-wheat, multigrain or cinnamon raisin; and ham, eggs and sausage are stuffed into brioche and croissant dough and baked.

And topping today's bountiful breakfasts are creative condiments—syrup blends with fruit and spices; preserves such as spiced pear butter or ginger-lime marmalade; cream cheese blended with garden vegetables; and butter flavored with candied nuts and spices.

HOT TRICKS WITH FROZEN DOUGH

Jerry Flinn, bakery manager, SUNY Brockport, offers tips for transforming frozen bread dough into signature items:

- Before baking, spray thawed, proofed Italian dough with water and top with sesame, poppy, caraway or dill seeds; cornmeal; oat flakes; or Parmesan. Or spray with garlic mist and sprinkle with dried onion.

- Combine one each light and dark rye doughs, kneading to marbleize; bake in football shape. Hollow out center for dips; cut croutons from center.

- Roll out thawed, frozen breadsticks; proof; shape into names or messages and bake.

- Roll out thawed, frozen Italian dough; shape into peace dove for Christmas, turkey for Thanksgiving. Color dough for turkey wattles with red food color before baking.

- Use small balls of dark and light rye doughs to form grape cluster. Cut leaves for top; color dough with green food color. Proof and bake.

- Make bread dough bowls for chili: Roll dough in circles, ease into 8- to 12-inch soup bowls, proof, bake.

Condiments are an easy way for operators to bridge the gap between ordinary and outstanding morning fare. A signature condiment, even something as simple as a flavored butter, dresses up a dish, enhancing the diners' experience and adding value to the meal.

Chicago's Pump Room offers a number of signature condiments at breakfast. Executive Chef Andrew Selvaggio tops crisp, golden pecan waffles with pecan butter, a blend of chopped pecans, sugar and cinnamon whipped with unsalted butter. Oatmeal comes with apple cream, a mixture of caramelized apples, golden raisins and sugared walnuts simmered in heavy cream, puréed and strained.

The pecan waffle sells for $6. The 1 1/2-ounce pecan butter serving, piped from a pastry bag with a star tip, costs about 15 cents per portion. "The waffle is a very profitable item for us," says Selvaggio. In addition to pecan butter, the waffle is served with warm maple syrup. At about $27 a gallon, it is the highest-cost ingredient of the dish.

Show-Stopping Topics

When guests go through the breakfast buffet at the Wigwam Resort in Litchfield Park, Ariz., they can choose whole-wheat-raisin, blue-corn, buttermilk or buckwheat pancakes. In crocks next to the pancakes are show-stopping toppings, including macadamia nut butter and prickly pear butter.

Breakfast buffets at the Wigwam are priced between $13 and $20. "The actual cost of the condiments per person is minimal," says Executive Chef Michael Garvin. For plated breakfasts, the chef portions flavored butters into rosettes.

Garvin also prepares fresh fruit sauces as alternatives to syrup. He serves marmalade made from Seville oranges grown on the property. A fig tree on the property produces fruit for a compote that tops waffles and pancakes.

Fruitful Condiments

Fruit condiments in many forms are on the breakfast and brunch menu at Betise, a bistro in Wilmette, Ill. Executive Chef Kent Buell makes fruit into spreads, compotes and fruit-and-nut butters. He also flavors plain, nonfat yogurt with honeyed apples or fresh strawberries as a topping for house-made granola.

To serve fresh fruit as a condiment, the chef warms the sliced fruit in a sauté pan with just a little unsalted butter to bring out the natural sugar flavors of the fruit. To top French toast, he sautés bananas until they begin to caramelize. He also stuffs French toast with berries mixed with cream cheese and vanilla.

The bistro uses unsalted butter for cooking

and serving. Croissants and brioche come with the classic accompaniments, sweet butter and strawberry or raspberry preserves. The chef recommends bringing the butter to room temperature before serving. At Betise, butter portions, made with a Parisienne scoop, are served in individual ramekins.

Portions are refrigerated until use, with enough time built in to temper.

"Light" Condiments

Low-sugar fruit preserves, "light" cream-cheese spreads and cholesterol-free margarine are breakfast staples at the Brown Bag, Rockland, Maine. Anne Maher, one of four sisters who own and operate the cafe, says she has seen the use of low-sugar fruit preserves increase significantly. "If we run out of low-sugar jam, I hear about it right away. Five years ago, people didn't care."

Increasing numbers of Brown Bag customers are ordering dry toast, forgoing butter in favor of low-sugar jam, Maher adds. The cafe also serves low-sugar fruit jam mixed with reduced-fat or regular cream cheese as a spread, and offers 1-ounce portions of no-cholesterol margarine.

Cream Cheese, Please

"You name it, if it's something we can spread on a bagel, we've made it," says Andy Allen, a dining services production manager at Brandeis University, Waltham, Mass. At the campus dining facility, a luncheon salad bar becomes a condiment bar that displays cream-cheese spreads, jellies, jams, butter, margarine, syrups and peanut butter. Students go through the cafeteria line, pick up a bagel or breakfast bread, then toast it and top it at the condiment bar.

Cream-cheese spreads are the most popular topping. Cream-cheese blends include lox, olives, vegetables, nuts and herbs. Some spreads are whipped smooth; others, such as lox, are left chunky. To make a smooth spread, Allen recommends whipping cream cheese thinned with milk, half-and-half or cream. After whipping, fold in puréed ingredients. Thinning keeps the mixture

spreadable after refrigeration. Reduced-fat cream cheese doesn't need to be thinned during whipping.

Potatoes Color Breakfast Red, White and New

Potatoes are breakfast's comfort food. Minimally seasoned dishes such as hash browns and home fries are morning favorites, adding taste and substance to any menu. And because their tastes and textures hold their own, red, white and new potatoes all stand up well to additional seasonings.

ABOUT SPREADS

Researchers are developing new butter products, including cholesterol-free butter and "light" butter. Specific parts of butterfat are isolated, based on their individual melting points. "Light" butter would contain 52% butterfat.

By law, regular butter must be at least 80% butterfat. The remaining 20% consists of water and milk solids. It may be salted or unsalted. Unsalted butter is sometimes called sweet butter. Whipped butter has air or other gases whipped into it for greater volume and improved spreadability at colder temperatures.

Margarine, made with vegetable oils, was developed in the 1800s as a butter substitute. Margarines lowest in cholesterol are made with polyunsaturated safflower or corn oil. By law, margarines must be at least 80% fat. The remaining 20% consists of liquid, coloring, flavoring and additives.

Butter-margarine blends are usually proportioned at 40% butter and 60% margarine. Soft margarine is made with all vegetable oils. Whipped margarine has air beaten into it. Liquid margarine is soft enough to be poured when cold. Diet spreads contain only 40% fat and approximately half the calories of butter or margarine.

"Unbreakfast-like" seasonings, even. A dash of hot sauce, a dose of garlic or a sliver of bell pepper added to a breakfast potato dish can jump-start the morning.

At the Fiddlehead Restaurant and Bakery in Juneau, Alaska, Chef John DeCherney offers Halibut Hash every weekend as a breakfast special. Combining the flavors and textures of potatoes, halibut, hot sauce and bell peppers, DeCherney's breakfast special is decidedly un-breakfast-like.

Owner Deborah Marshall names Halibut Hash as one of her favorite meals and recommends experimenting with different-texture potatoes. "It's good with new potatoes, and with russets, it's delicious," says Marshall. "We leave the skins on to add to the texture. It makes a big difference, and that's where all the vitamins and minerals are."

Because fish and seafood are so readily available in Juneau, Marshall emphasizes the dish's cost-effectiveness for that region. It sells for $9.95 and comes with scrambled eggs and a side of either salsa or ketchup.

Garlicky Potatoes hail from Ina's Kitchen in Chicago, and are an addicting breakfast treat for Ina's customers. Owner Ina Pinkney says she fol-lows no written recipe to make the dish. The cooks simply dice potatoes, boil them until they are cooked and put them in a single layer in a half hotel pan. The potatoes are seasoned with salt, pepper and crushed garlic, then moistened with whipping cream. They bake for 40 minutes at 400°F, until they are very brown on top. The potatoes are stirred before serving to distribute the brown topping.

Pinkney says that of the thousands of servings of Garlicky Potatoes that have sold at breakfast, the restaurant has received only four comments that the potatoes have too much garlic.

"First the customers are surprised and then they're addicted. Now they even order them as a side for pancakes," says Pinkney. As a side, the potatoes sell for $1. They are served with egg and omelet orders, as well.

Popular Pancakes

At Melville, N.Y.-based Pancake Cottage, customers have been ordering potato pancakes since the chain opened in 1964. Back then, the potato pancake was made from scratch.

"Today, we're experimenting with flash frozen and *sous-vide* products that have the consistency

---

ABOUT BREAKFAST POTATOES

Russets: Have low moisture and high starch content; make great hash browns and mashed-potato pancakes.

Round Reds, Round Whites: Because of their low starch content and waxy texture, these stand up well to slicing and boiling, making them ideal for home-fries recipes.

Long Whites: These bake, boil and roast equally well; can be used for any breakfast potato dish.

New Potatoes: Young versions of any potato type. They share qualities with round reds and whites and make excellent home fries. Since their skin is so feathery, they are delicious cooked skin-on.

Potato Stretchers: Follow these tips to improve potatoes' cost-effectiveness.
♦ Cut leftover baked potatoes into hash browns for breakfast.
♦ Create mashed-potato pancakes from leftover mashed potatoes.
♦ Slice leftover boiled potatoes into pan-fried breakfast potatoes.

and quality that we require," says Christopher Levano, vice president of Captain's Cottage Franchise, owner of Pancake Cottage.

Today's product is the same basic blend of potatoes, onions, eggs and seasonings as the original pancake, only now, says Levano, it is consistent from unit to unit. In 1988, it came off the menu and became a 3.5-ounce side order, and in 1992, it resumed its position on the pancake menu with an increased serving size. For $4.50, the customer now gets three 2-ounce pancakes served with sour cream or apple sauce.

At the Rose restaurant in Baltimore, only one breakfast potato dish is served: home fries. But it's a customer favorite, and is served with most of the breakfast entrees. It also sells as a side dish for 95 cents. The dish is made with the simplest ingredients—baking potatoes, onions, salt and pepper—but it's on the menu to stay.

At the Fiddlehead, the home-fried potatoes have a little zing. Unpeeled red potatoes are boiled, cubed and fried in oil and butter. Then they are sprinkled with a seasoning mix made of garlic powder, salt and Fiddlehead's "secret" ingredient, brewer's yeast. The potatoes sell for $2.50 as a side dish.

Side Dishes Take Center Stage

Just as eggs, breads and meats are getting special treatment at breakfast, so are side dishes. Grits, fruit dishes and other sides are benefiting from innovative ingredients, bold flavors and healthful preparations.

Side dishes get star treatment at Chicago's "Heaven on Seven." The restaurant, specializing in Cajun-Creole dishes, also features sides that include cheese grits. Chef-owner Jimmy Bannos dresses up grits with white and yellow Cheddar cheese, Asiago cheese (a semifirm Italian cheese noted for its nutty flavor), cream and butter. Other grits dishes are flavored with shrimp marinated in hot sauce, and tasso, a Cajun specialty of highly spiced, cured pork. Cheese grits as a side sell for $2.50; shrimp and tasso grits are $6.50.

At the hands of Executive Chef Rick Federholt of the Scottsdale Plaza Resort in Scottsdale,

Ariz., grapefruit gets center-of-the-plate handling. Federholt grills honey-basted grapefruit slices over a mesquite wood fire. The fruit is served hot with Mexican-seasoned frittatas, omelets and scrambled eggs.

Fruit offerings at Eggs 'n Things, Honolulu, include the Hawaiian Delight, half a fresh papaya filled with blueberries and strawberries, topped with whipped cream, for $3.75. Other breakfast side dishes popular in Hawaii include rice, fresh fish, Portuguese sausage and Spam, otherwise known as "Hawaiian steak," adds chef-owner Jerry Fukunaga.

Looking at Old Town Bakery's menu, the sides look pretty standard—home-fried potatoes, sausage, bacon, biscuits and gravy. But talk to chef-owner Amy Pressman, and you learn that her sides are different. Sausage patties are made with chicken, the country bacon is meaty and preservative-free, and gravy for the biscuits is made from chicken gravy thickened with potato in order to cut down on fat.

A house-made chicken sausage patty at the 75-seat Pasadena, Calif., restaurant sells for $1.95; country bacon, cured with brown sugar, is $1.95; and a large cream biscuit with gravy is $1.25.

All-Purpose Quiche

In Youngstown, Ohio, people drive from miles around to pick up a quiche from Mister P's, a deli-restaurant operation with 164 seats. The breakfast menu features quiche with hash browns and seasonal fresh fruits for $4.95. Quiche as a breakfast side sells for $3.25.

Patrons who call ahead can order quiche made with skim or 2% milk and a reduced number of egg yolks. Chef-owner Mark Pearce runs contests among the kitchen staff to come up with new ideas for quiche. The staff makes the quiche, tastes it, and writes up the recipe.

Simple Garnishes Garner Praise

When Executive Chef Michael Fekr garnishes brunch dishes, he keeps three simple rules in mind: The garnish must be edible, must complement the flavors of the dish it is served with, and should not be on the plate just for beauty.

Fekr, who jokes that he is the only Iranian-Italian chef in Los Angeles, is co-owner of Il Mito, a 60-seat restaurant in an Art Deco building. The brunch menu is Italian and Middle Eastern, with dishes such as poached eggs with olive oil, Persian basil and fresh tomatoes; eggs with eggplant and spicy tomato sauce; scrambled eggs with Parmesan cheese, Italian parsley and roasted garlic; and Italian sausage with lentils.

Fekr garnishes dishes with the same fresh herbs used in cooking the dish, providing different flavors and textures, but at the same time echoing and enhancing the cooked herbs. To garnish an omelet, he uses uncooked, julienne garden vegetables that have been lightly tossed with olive oil, salt and pepper. The omelet is filled with the same mixture of cooked julienne garden vegetables.

One of Fekr's most unusual garnishes is whole strawberries marinated in balsamic vinegar, powdered sugar and vanilla extract. "In the morning, after waking up, your palate needs to be cleared. The acidity in the vinegar does this." In winter, when strawberries are not available, the chef substitutes marinated grapefruit segments for garnish.

A.M. Percolators

Whether it's the jolt of java or the refreshing splash of juice, breakfast beverages are the ritual that get the day going. The major players, coffee and orange juice, still are the beverages of choice for many breakfast customers, but those with more adventuresome taste buds are finding new ways to get their A.M. wake-up call. Today, specialty coffees, herbal teas and fruit-juice-based drinks are gaining popularity at breakfast and converting more than a few beverage customers.

Coffee still is an overwhelmingly popular breakfast drink. According to the Winter 1991 Coffee Drinking Study conducted by the National Coffee Association, 53% of all coffee consumed is consumed at breakfast. The study also notes that 44% of the American population drinks coffee at breakfast.

The same study tracked espresso and cappuccino consumption for the first time in 1991 and found that 1% of the population drank these, although no time of day was specified. Operators who offer specialty coffees, however, are seeing bigger jumps in specialty coffee consumption at breakfast.

At the Willard Inter-Continental Hotel's Cafe Espresso Bar, Washington, customers still drink a lot of regular coffee, says Manager Jennifer Newby, but she estimates a 40% to 50% increase in espresso, cappuccino and flavored coffee orders at breakfast during the last two years. Newby attributes specialty coffee's surging popularity at the operation to a general increase in customer awareness about the coffees.

Price does not seem to hamper specialty coffee orders at Cafe Espresso. Regular and decaffeinated coffees sell for $1.75, and specialty coffees range from $2.50 for an espresso to $4.50 for Cafe Chocolate: a mixture of espresso, hot chocolate, whipped cream and cinnamon.

Newby also notes regional preferences, with customers from Washington state and California nearly always opting for espresso, cappuccino or caffè latte at breakfast. East Coast customers are just as likely to order a specialty coffee as a regular coffee, she says, and Southerners opt for soft drinks.

Barnie's Coffee and Tea Company of Orlando, Fla., is a combination cafe and retail vendor. Its coffee menu now includes nearly 50 varieties. According to Jay Downer, spokesman for the 80-unit chain, the further the coffee menu expands, the more exotic coffee orders the chain sees. "Specialty coffee is the growth area in coffee," says Downer.

For summer, Downer suggests a breakfast coffee that surprises and pleases—with a cool temperature and frothy texture. The Iced Coffee Shake blends strong roast coffee with the customer's choice of flavored coffee, sugar, cream and chipped ice.

Tea offerings are increasing in variety and popularity as well. Newby of Cafe Espresso notes an increase in herbal tea orders along with the increase in specialty coffee orders at breakfast.

Barnie's features 98 varieties of teas, including flavored, spiced, blended, herbal and decaffeinated. Its Orange and Spiced Iced Tea, for example, blends flavored tea with orange zest, orange juice, candied ginger and sugar.

At Southern Methodist University in Dallas, fruit juices are the most popular breakfast beverage in the cafeterias, with orange juice leading the pack. According to Merle Parker, director of dining services, dairy products are No. 2, followed by soft drinks and coffee. Parker adds that breakfast is the time of day when most beverages are consumed.

"It's not unlikely to see three or four beverages on one tray," says Parker, noting that that includes multiple orders of the same beverage, such as two milks and two orange juices.

Throwing consumption trends to the wind are customers at Sarabeth's in New York, whose favorite breakfast drink, Four Flowers, is an exotic mixture of fruit juices and purees. The drink is sold in 8-ounce servings for $3.50 each. ◆

Fast Takes for Lunch

by Nancy Ross Ryan and Karen Straus

Essentially speaking, lunch is about good food fast. Following are what *R&I* believes are perfect lunch foods: They're popular; quick and easy to prepare, serve and eat; and best of all, these double-duty foods can be served on premises or packed for takeout.

The perfect lunch foods have always been fast and easy—to prepare, to serve, to eat and to transform into signature specialties. But now a new dimension has been added: portability. With the increase in carryout trade, today's perfect lunch foods do double duty on and off the premises. Sandwiches remain the perfect example: Witness the phenomenal growth of the sub—a.k.a. hoagie, grinder, hero, po' boy. Sandwiches are on the menu of 91% of all foodservice operations surveyed in *R&I*'s Menu Census. And their popularity is growing: They ranked No. 4 in the top 10 items operators said they had added to their menu in the past year.

Signature sandwiches, long the staple of fast food, delis, midscale restaurants and institutions, have made a bold move to fine dining. Delmonico's in New York recently launched a new "Light Entree" luncheon menu, offering a free bottle of sparkling mineral water with any Light Entree order. One of the most popular menu items, proving that light is not synonymous with salad, is the Delmonico Steak Sandwich. Piperade restaurant in Cleveland offers a Tuna Club sandwich (yellowfin tuna, arugula, slab bacon, roasted red peppers and lemon-garlic mayonnaise, $7.50) and Grilled Portobello Mushrooms and Onions on Toasted Peasant Bread ($5.50). And the Manor, West Orange, N.J., features a Smoked Salmon Club Sandwich ($8.25) as one of the menu items designated as light fare.

Chili closely follows sandwiches in versatility and portability. Sidestepping the fierce regional debate about true chili (meat without beans), chili in its most popular form is an ideal eat-in or carryout lunch food. More than a soup, it's a meal in itself, complete with garnishes that range from traditional (chopped onions, shredded cheese, sour cream and crackers) to innovative (diced cucumber or tomato, corn kernels, crème fraîche, and blue- or red-corn tortilla chips).

Like the sandwich, chili goes from fine-dining to midscale to economy operation with ease. In addition to black-bean chili, white-bean chili, black-eyed-pea chili and mixed-bean chili, some current chili signatures include: venison chili; turkey chili; Vegetarian Red Bean Stew with carrots, celery, turnips, parsnips, squash and potatoes, from Susan Feniger and Mary Sue Milliken, Border Grill, Santa Monica, Calif.; Muscovy Duck Chili, a creation of Chef Jody Denton for Wolfgang Puck; and Bowl of Green with Chilied Melon, puréed green-chili-potato soup with hot-spicy melon salsa served cold from Chef John Sedlar.

Last year, pizza enjoyed renewed popularity in the form of individual-size appetizer pizzas. In the Menu Census, appetizer pizza was called a good seller by 57% of all operators surveyed. And it ranked No. 2 in the category of appetizers added in the last year. Just as sandwiches are making a move to fine dining, personal pizzas are finding a new niche at lunch.

They're an obvious choice for Italian restaurants that already are equipped with deck or wood-burning ovens. But lack of space or ovens shouldn't stand in the way of putting this popular, profitable item on the menu, says Chef Greg Christian, director of At the Tracks catering, Chicago. Christian has a local Italian bakery deliver half-baked sheet pans of focaccia to his door. Depending on toppings, "You can really load them with top-quality roasted vegetables, sauteed Italian sausage, mozzarella and Parmesan cheese," he says. The menu price can be up to

$3.95 for a 4-in.-×-6-in. portion. Christian tops the focaccia and bakes each in a convection oven at 400F for 5 to 10 minutes.

Operators already have all the product needed in the kitchen for an endless variety of signature pizzas, says Christian. For example, he spreads the dough with either pesto, tapenade or dried tomatoes, and tops with a variety of ingredients for pizzas du jour. He also cuts the sheet pans into 100 portions and serves them at catered functions as hors d'oeuvres.

Sam's in New York has another word to add to the portable pizza. It's called bombalone bread, a Sam's signature. Bombalone dough (like pizza or focaccia dough) is rolled out flat into small rectangles. The dough is topped with ingredients that range from asparagus and provolone to dried tomatoes, sweet Italian sausage, roasted peppers, onions, mozzarella and ricotta. Then it's rolled, jellyroll fashion, sealed and bent into a horseshoe shape. The bread is brushed with egg wash and coated with sesame and poppy seeds before baking.

As a lunch entree, bombalone breads sell for $7. They also are a popular offering at the bar. This horseshoe shape, says Executive Chef Michael Ammirati, makes bombalone breads ideal to slice into appetizer portions for lunch or dinner.

There's nothing but good news when it comes to salads: They're everywhere, in fast food, fine dining, colleges and catering. They're timely, perceived both as light and healthful and, with the advent of entree salads, as hearty complete meals. They're innovative; a signature salad is born every day. And they're terrific for takeout.

According to the *R&I* Menu Census, salads and entree salads are on the menus of 95% of all foodservice operations surveyed. The Menu Census lists the top 10 best-selling salads (in descending order): tossed green salad, taco salad, chef's salad, signature house salad, Caesar salad, chicken/turkey salad, tuna salad, coleslaw, pasta salad and potato salad. And, salads/entree salads were the No. 2 item most often added to menus in the past year, according to the survey.

Salads can be trendsetters, too. Three timely salad trends are light, low-fat salads, salad sampler plates and salads composed of grains and legumes.

Even the salad bar is going light and healthful. At Michael's Restaurant in the Holiday Inn, Harvey, Ill., the hotel's food and beverage department has responded to guests' requests for lighter items by designating 40% of its luncheon buffet as low-cholesterol and low-fat. On Thursdays, a complete low-cholesterol, low-fat buffet is offered. On other days, in addition to fresh vegetables on the salad bar, the hotel serves a number "heart-healthy" salads including three-bean salad in oil-free vinaigrette, bean sprout salad, and pasta, basil and tomato salad. The cost of the total salad bar and buffet is $7.25.

At Home restaurant, described by owner Joan Kurlan as an unpretentious storefront in Chicago's gallery district, the assorted salad plate has become a best-seller. On Home's menu, Chef Saul Wax offers a choice of three of the following salads for $7.95: curried chicken salad with garden vegetables and mango chutney; fresh asparagus in season in balsamic vinaigrette; orange dill potato salad; red rice salad with corn, tahini, tarragon and tomatoes; black bean salad with fresh corn in cilantro-lime dressing; lentil feta salad with lemon olive oil dressing; and caponata. The salad selections change weekly—at least 15%—and more from season to season.

R&I's annual food trends forecast predicted there would be a hill of beans, legumes and grains. Not only have these humble ingredients found a home in fine dining, but they have fit nicely into menu categories of appetizers, soups, salads, sides and entrees. At Convito Italiano, which has two Chicago locations, Executive Chef Rich Ladd is taking couscous, barley, cannellini beans, white beans and lentils to new levels. For example, his trio salad plate consists of barley with toasted almonds and golden raisins, curry chicken salad, and fresh fruit salad.

Los Angeles Chef Michael Roberts says he's incorporated more grains and legumes into his dishes, such as grain polenta made with barley, bulgur, quinoa and cornmeal. His luncheon chopped salad of stir-cooked vegetables now has split peas and lentils.

Signature salads sell in direct proportion to their popular appeal and creativity. For example, at the Blue Ribbon Cafe in Michigan City, Ind., one of the best-selling items is the salad du jour. The luncheon menu advises customers to ask about details of the Day's Special, a specially prepared salad plate for $4.95.

At the American Cafe, Newport, R.I. (the latest venture of Ivy-Award winning Chef George Karousos of Sea Fare Inn), signature luncheon salads include Chilled Lobster Salad (on fresh greens, cucumbers and tomatoes with tarragon vinaigrette, $9.95), and Grilled Salmon Salad (on endive and mixed greens with balsamic vinaigrette, $9.25).

Signature salads stand out on the Executive Order *prix-fixe* luncheon menu introduced this spring at the Willard Inter Continental in Washington. The $16.95 menu consists of six two- or three-course menus with coffee. Salads accom-

pany five of the six menus. Notable signatures include Sliced Plum Tomatoes with Arugula, and Chesapeake Crab Cake Salad.

Pasta is one of the perfect lunch foods: for table service, self-serve lunch buffets and bars, pasta carts in institutional foodservice, and takeout, too. Lunch pasta specials at Michael Roberts' Trumps include Angel Hair, Spaghetti Squash and Duck Confit ($12); Green Noodles and Garlic Rock Shrimp ($14); and Riso Pasta Primavera ($12).

At Buckhead Diner in Atlanta, the most popular lunch item is mostaccioli with smoked chicken, roasted peppers, basil and Asiago cheese ($8.25). Pricci, another of Atlanta's Buckhead Life Restaurant Group concepts, promotes lunchtime pasta made fresh daily and combined with a variety of ingredients that include baby artichokes, spinach, pesto, sage, ricotta, Italian sausage, veal, shellfish and plum tomatoes. And the marketing is just as creative as the pasta: Billed as a "light-hearted lunch," Pricci's lunch hour stretches luxuriously from 11 A.M. to 5 P.M. ♦

Lunch to Go

by Brenda McCarthy

Who are lunch-to-go customers? They are the people you see every day, like the man running errands at noon, sandwich in hand. Or the woman relaxing on a park bench, enjoying her salad and the change of scenery.

They also are the people you don't see: the ones in an all-day meeting waiting for the much-needed break the catered lunch will provide. Or the ones holed at their desks, waiting for the return of a co-worker who volunteered to pick up lunch.

Which is why you should view serving lunch to go as an opportunity to win customers. You want to be the operation they think of when they want lunch on the run.

Lunch-to-go customers' expectations are high: They want a good meal that travels well. They don't want to go into debt paying for it. They want it fast.

Four operators that are surpassing those expectations are Corky's, Memphis, Tenn.; Convito Italiano, Chicago; The Market at Larimer Square, Denver; and Bon Appetit corporate food-service division, Minneapolis. All have targeted lunch-to-go business and turn a profit doing so.

Thanks to a quartet of off-premises programs, people all over Memphis lunch on Corky's barbecue ribs and pork shoulder. Off-premises catering, bulk orders, a takeout window and a program with Memphis Hospital account for about 50% of the restaurant's yearly sales, says owner Don Pelts.

Office workers located close to Corky's account for most of the restaurant's individual takeout orders. Pelts says he occasionally distributes a flier to the buildings, but finds it's not necessary.

"Our biggest worry is not getting more business, but taking care of the business we've got," he says. He also has nixed the idea of orders by fax: "It's too confusing . . . people might not have a menu to look at, and the orders could get mixed up." Instead, workers at six phone lines handle

orders for barbecue ribs, pork shoulder, sandwiches and barbecue chicken from opening time, 8:30 A.M., until the lunch crunch is over. Pelts declines to guess the number of orders Corky's gets on a busy day.

And thanks to a program started last year, Corky's fans who happen to be patients at Memphis Hospital can choose Corky's for lunch on Saturdays. The food is delivered cooked to the hospital, kept warm, and then served. Pelts says about 200 patients each week choose the Corky's special, which is listed on the menu along with the restaurant's logo. In addition, once a year the restaurant participates in the hospital's Visiting Chefs program, and serves barbecue to employees and visitors.

Likewise, Corky's barbecue is on the lunch menu at one of the Marriott hotels in Memphis, and is offered through several hotels' catering departments as well. Pelts adds that the hotels' wait staffs trained at Corky's before they started serving the restaurants' food at catered affairs.

The secret to the successful program is the packaging, Pelts says. Bulk orders are packed in disposable serving containers—patrons set up the aluminum pans buffet-style, peel back the foil and let their guests dig in. Single orders are packed in sturdy foam containers. "The packaging costs us a lot more, but it's real easy for people to handle," he says.

Pelts says check averages, $9.50 in the dining room, are hard to gauge for takeout, although bulk orders average about $3.60 a person. "Why, just today we had an order for $900 from a bunch of doctors," Pelts says. "Why they don't want to spend the extra $200 to get served, I don't know."

Convito Italiano is a combination full-service restaurant/cafe, food shop, deli, bakery and wine shop offering carryout and catering services. The store designed one whole section, Pronto, for quick lunches. The Pronto case always contains at least four different sandwiches, two pasta salads, two vegetable or grain salads, and one fruit salad. The takeout menu is more limited than Convito's conventional menu, but it changes every day, offering repeat customers variety. And though the Merchandise Mart store has only been open for one month, repeat customers are already in evidence as the number of lunch customers Pronto handles steadily increases.

"We think it will be 50% of lunch business soon," says Barocci. The average price of a Pronto lunch is between $5 and $7. Barocci says sandwiches are a popular lunch-to-go item, but notes rising salad orders, too. "Our grain salads, like the ones made with barley, lentils and couscous, have become much more popular," she says. Barocci also is developing a reusable lunch bag that repeat to-go customers can buy. The nylon bag will bear the store logo and have a Velcro® closing, and will be purchased by the customer for multiple uses.

The Market at Larimer Square takes takeout one step further and offers Denver customers every menu item to go.

"We have a seating area of 200," says owner Mark Greenberg. "But everything we make is served on paper and in recyclable takeout containers." The Market serves 800 meals a day, a majority of which are at lunch. About 40% of that lunch business is takeout.

Greenberg is quick to point out his operations's strong suits. "What's different about us is that this is a fast-food operation, but the food is all made in the building," he says. "I go all over the country looking for new ideas," he adds. "I'm doing the most creative things I can find out there."

One creative and popular dish is Russian Runzas, pie dough wrapped around ground beef, cabbage, onion and Oriental seasonings baked and served warm in a microwavable container ($2.75). Another is the boneless breast of chicken with herb cream cheese served on a bed of rice. It comes with the customer's choice of salad for $4.75.

Like Convito Italiano, The Market offers a broad spectrum of services and products to customers. Its ten-year-old espresso bar serves 1,600 to 1,700 cups of coffee daily, 500 of which are espresso drinks.

The 5,700-square-foot restaurant also holds a deli island in the center of the floor. One side serves sandwiches; another is a self-service salad bar. Pastries fill the third side, and a combination hot-food service area/antique deli case completes the square. Different salads are displayed in artsy bowls

TAKEOUT TIPS

Follow these packaging tips to ensure that your customer's lunch can hit the road without spilling, leaking or toppling over.
- When filling a takeout bag, think grocery bagging: Always put flat-bottom items in first.
- Stack heavier items on the bottom, and lighter items on top.
- Crushable items like cookies should go into a covered tray and be packed on top.
- Package hot items together in one bag and cold in another to keep optimum temperatures for both.
- To keep sandwiches fresh and salads from wilting, pack mayonnaise spreads and salad dressings in separate condiment containers for customers to add themselves.
- Prewrap takeout utensils in napkins and secure with ties or ribbons in large quantities. When you get the takeout call for 50 lunches to be picked up in an hour, the utensils will be ready.
- When putting liquid in a container, wrap the container—lid and all—in plastic. It could end up on your customer's clothes or car seat, and you could end up paying for it.
- Always package hot items in a microwavable container. When it arrives at its destination, it might need more heating.

within the antique display case and are sold by the pound for sit-down lunch, or for lunch to go.

The average lunch check at the Market is $6 and includes either a sandwich, salad or hot meal, along with a pastry and beverage.

Speed is a key element in the operation as well.

"We consider our competition to be McDonald's and any other fast-food restaurant, because we want the customer who wants to come in and be served quickly and courteously," says Greenberg.

But in no other operation is time more important than in catering. The customer waiting for a catered meal to arrive watches the clock because timing is part of the contract.

In Minneapolis, Bon Appetit's corporate foodservice division keeps winning those contracts. By offering a summer catering discount of 10% to one of its clients, Bon Appetit saw a 7% increase in catering orders.

Bon Appetit personalizes its catering service for each one of its clients by offering them custom menus and catering packages. Employees at one client, Cray Research Park, can choose among VIP Sack Lunches, regular Sack Lunches, Cold Luncheon selection, Luncheon Buffets and the regular Lunch Menu.

One VIP Sack Lunch offers grilled marinated breast of chicken served on a kaiser roll with tomato, lettuce and Swiss cheese. A side of pasta salad, fresh fruit and a home-baked cookie are included in the $6.95 price.

Selections from the regular Lunch Menu come with soup, a salad or appetizer, rolls, butter and dessert. Main courses include Pork Loin Dijonnaise served with potato and vegetable for $9.95, and Fresh Filet of Cod with Mushrooms, served with asparagus and rice ($10.95).

Like Corky's, Convito Italiano and the Market, Bon Appetit uses lunch to go as an opportunity to win and wow customers. All four realize that (barring 5 P.M.) lunch is the most anticipated time of the work day for many customers. And their quick, portable menus are turning their lunch-to-go customers into people they see every day. ♦

Fixe-ing Dinner

by Karen Straus

When New York restaurants were downscaling to cope with the recession of the early '90s, an American/French restaurant opened in Manhattan's picturesque Flatiron district. The restaurant, Prix Fixe, designed its menu—moderate, fixed-price lunches and dinners—for survival in a tough market and a tougher economy.

But Prix Fixe has done more than just survive. It has garnered praise from hard-to-please New York critics and developed a strong customer following with its fixed-price meals.

For many operators, charging a fixed price for a meal has become a menu fixture. The practice has its roots in the hotel industry, when towns were small, competition scarce and supplies hard to come by. Lodgings were often the only place to get a meal, and you ate what the host put on the table. This came to be called table d'hote or "the host's meal." This was an entire meal offered at a fixed price and often at a set time.

As towns grew and competition increased, customer demand for more choice increased. Commercial restaurant menus evolved into two basic pricing structures, table d'hote or a la carte. A la carte literally translates to "according to the menu." *Prix fixe* is French for "fixed price" and is the same as table d'hote. (Another menu form, degustation, is a fixed-price meal designed for sampling a wide variety of food and wine. It is from the Latin, *degustare,* "to savor or relish as a connoisseur.")

When a la carte pricing first developed, it was partly in response to the economy. Diners wanted to pay only for what they were going to eat, not for anything extra. In today's economy, fixed-price offerings are perceived as a bargain, because customers who order *prix fixe* generally get one course free compared with ordering the same meal a la carte.

Most operators, from chains to institutions to independents, offer both a la carte and fixed-price options. Quick-service menu boards price items individually, but also offer meal deals for a fixed priced. In addition to its a la carte menu, Elias Bros. Big Boy Restaurants, based in Warren, Mich., has offered an all-you-can-eat Shrimp, Seafood & Crab Bar that includes soup, salad and fruit bar for $9.95. Marriott Management Services offers its B&I contractors monthly themed promotions featuring a combo meal, for example, a soft drink, fruit cup and turkey croissant sandwich.

At Prix Fixe, all meals, lunch and dinner, are fixed price, with several price levels. For the $24 *prix-fixe* dinner, Executive Chef Terrance Brennan offers two menus of three courses each: appetizer, entree and dessert. The $36 *prix-fixe* dinner, also three courses, features more expensive ingredients such as foie gras and lobster. Some evenings, a $30 menu is offered as well. At lunch, two-course meals of appetizer and entree are $13.50 and $18.50.

"The whole *prix-fixe* concept has worked very well for us," says Brennan. "Customers get a fine-dining experience for very reasonable prices. The $24 menu, for instance, has dishes that are a very good value, such as salmon, cod, and salmon tartare."

To make a profit, Brennan balances high- and low-cost ingredients. "Salmon is one of our higher food costs, so I balance it with chicken choices. On the $24 menu I can't afford to use sea scallops. Instead, I use vegetable appetizers, or because we go through a lot of salmon, I can make tartare from salmon medallion trimmings."

Brennan says fixed-price menus cut down on waste and streamline purchasing. "We have 180 seats and can do up to 400 covers a night. Because on any given night we'll have only two kinds of fish on the menu, I can control costs. I can almost guess to the fish what I'll sell because there's a definite pattern. Let's say I had four different fish on the menu, and halibut and salmon sell, but cod and trout don't. I'd have to throw cod and trout out and get fresh in.

"Because we order in quantity and have very high turnover on product, we have considerably less waste overall; nothing sits in the box. We shoot for a 22% labor cost and a 28% food cost. We work from menu price down. If the payroll goes up or the cost of ingredients, we have to look how to squeeze a little more. We make the food fit the price, rather than raising the price." With a computerized inventory system, Brennan says he knows the cost of every plate that goes out. He calculates food costs weekly and sets up target food costs for the season.

To meet the bottom line on her nonsubsidized food budget, Linda Wenman, executive chef at St. Joseph Medical Center, Wichita, Kan., balances a high-cost entree with a low-cost entree on the four fixed-price meals she serves daily (two at lunch and two at dinner). House-made vegetable lasagna (food and labor cost, $3.90 a pound) is a high-cost item because it is labor-intensive and contains a lot of cheese. It is paired with Salisbury steak (food cost, $2.40 a pound), which arrives frozen and only has to be heated.

Fixed-price meals at St. Joseph include soup, entree, vegetable du jour, fresh-baked bread, dessert and beverage for $2.75. (Employees get a 30% discount.) Soup and desserts are house made because it is more economical, says Wenman.

Once a month, Goose Island Brewing Co., an independent brewery-restaurant in Chicago, offers a five-course *prix-fixe* dinner. "A lot of our regulars come to these and bring their friends. They have brought in a lot of new people," says Manager Tim Ryan.

Goose Island's *prix-fixe* dinners pair hearty German food—sausages, veal shanks, potato pancakes, oxtail soup—with exotic microbrewery and imported beers. "The price, $35, is

attractive to customers," says Ryan. "They get five courses, plus more than ample beer with each course. Even though the *prix fixe* is roughly double the price of a normal meal, with menu prices ranging from $5.95 to $14.95, it's still perceived as a value because of the number of courses and the beer."

Like other operators, Goose Island managers started with a price they thought the market would find attractive, then worked back from there to make the food fit. Goose Island also builds in entertainment, offering live jazz or polka music on *prix-fixe* nights.

The chef and general manager work together to come up with a theme, menu ideas and beer selections. The chef comes up with food costs. If it's under or over, adjustments are made in the menu. Food costs are kept at 20% to 25%, "although it gets a little sticky here," Ryan says. "Some things we serve on *prix-fixe* nights aren't always in house; there's a lot of special ordering. This is where we have to compromise between the entertainment, labor, food cost, house beer and outside beer."

At Fullers, in the Sheraton Seattle Hotel & Towers, the *prix-fixe* menu offers patrons samplings of the restaurant's most popular a la carte dishes. For $38.50, customers can try pheasant pate, tomato-carrot bisque with warm scallop chutney, sweet and bitter greens with roast beet and shallot vinaigrette, grilled halibut with warm tomato-herb vinaigrette, grilled beef medallions with spicy ragout of white beans, and a dessert. At the Maile restaurant, the fine-dining venue at the Kahala Hilton, Honolulu, patrons can create a customized fixed-price dinner from the regular menu. For $62 per person, diners choose any appetizer, soup or salad, entree (except Maine lobster, for which there is an additional charge), dessert, and coffee or tea. By ordering the fixed-price dinner package, customers save an average of 30%, says Greg Mendoza, executive assistant F&B manager. ◆

Italian Renaissance

by Nancy Ross Ryan and Karen Straus

Is this a renaissance or a carnevale? Another day, another Italian restaurant opens. Old or new, most fit into three categories: the old-fashioned family-owned and -operated restaurants; the fashionable trattoria and fine-dining Italian restaurants; and last, the fantasy restaurants that base their menus and decor on imagination and showmanship.

Hindsight offers insight into today's Italian restaurant scene. And for a fix on the future, we talked with some of the acknowledged maestros of the Italian restaurant world. So *benevenuto* to our tour of Italian restaurants, *alla famiglia, alla moda* and *alla fantasia.* Today's Italian restaurant scenario owes its curtain raiser to an unsung hero: Gennaro Lombardi, who opened America's first pizzeria in New York City in 1905. It has served as the model for New York-style, as opposed to Chicago-style, pizzerias throughout the country.

In the 1930s, Lombardi added tables to the restaurant and spaghetti to the menu, thereby evolving into a second style of Italian restaurants just then beginning to proliferate: the family-owned and -operated Italian restaurant.

The ties that bind family-owned and -operated Italian restaurants, past, present and future, are heartstrings. "I've always felt that the restaurant is something sacred aside from the business. There has to be a warm, family-type setting in order to give your patrons something from the heart," says Alfredo Capitanini. Capitanini, his brother Frank and sister Gina are the third generation of Capitaninis to operate the Italian Village in Chicago. The Village is a microcosm of Italian restaurants in America, housing three restaurants in one. On the lower level is La Cantina, specializing in classic Italian seafood dishes in an informal setting; on the first floor is the fine-dining Vivere, with an award-winning design and wine list.

And on the top floor, a reminder that the '90s didn't invent concept creation, is founder Alfredo Capitanini's Village, which he opened in 1927 as a recreation of an Italian village of the last century. Lights in the ceiling simulate stars in the sky over the main dining area resembling the town square. Around it are tiny private rooms bearing names such as Casa Reale (king's palace), La Banca (the bank), etc. The menu is traditional Northern Italian, and the kitchen tries hard to keep one secret: that from the old brick oven with limited production capacity comes some of Chicago's best thin-crust pizza.

Many of the Italian restaurants and chains that opened in the '80s and '90s feature elements of make-believe: imitation bricks to simulate old-style pizza ovens, walls adorned with fictitious family portraits, wait staff with vocal chords who deliver a burst of song as well as a plate of pasta.

Coexisting are their prototypes, original first- and second-generation family-style restaurants, many of which predate them by decades.

When Emilio Baglioni was a little boy in Italy, he learned to play the concertina. He immigrated to the United States, where he opened a restaurant and raised a family. His children had never heard him play. One day his children bought him a concertina, and now he plays tarantellas and waltzes in the aisles of Emilio's, the family restaurant in Los Angeles—when he's not entering concertina competitions in Italy.

Milo Baglioni is one of Emilio's six children who work at Emilio's and Il Piccolino, a casual pizza place next door to Emilio's.

"Emilio's is an extended family for a lot of people," says Milo. "Sixty-five percent of our patrons are people I've grown up with for the past 20 years. We know them on a first-name basis, and we've held their wedding receptions and graduations."

A regular Sunday feature is a buffet with roast suckling pig. Patrons can order dishes that they have enjoyed for 20 years, but also can try something new. Every six months, chefs from Italy visit Emilio's kitchen to update regional specialties.

At Marliave Restaurant in Boston, Roy Rossetti is the second generation of his family to run the operation. His father opened the restaurant in 1934, and now Roy's daughter, Karla, runs Marliave with him.

Roy's father, the late Anthony Rossetti, came from Italy at the age of 18 and worked first as dishwasher and then waiter, before becoming an ice cream chef. In those days, Roy explains, ice cream and ice cream desserts were handmade specialties, often molded into multilayered bombes using special forms. Roy recalls his father making spumoni and other ice creams by hand from whipping the milk mixture to skinning and toasting almonds.

Food prepared from scratch is still a hallmark at Marliave. The restaurant prides itself on its minestrone, which hasn't changed since Anthony first served it. Beef stock is made fresh daily and all the vegetables used are fresh. "It's soup made with time and attention. We take pride in what we're doing and it shows," says Rossetti.

Other family operations taking pride in their work are Mosca's in Jefferson, La., Marsi's in Chicago, and Regina's in Arlington Heights, Ill.

John Mosca's wife and 6-year-old daughter help out in the restaurant (the daughter peels garlic). "Our customers return because we are consistent. They always know they can get the same things," says Mosca. One of the restaurant's most popular dishes is Chicken a la Grande, a whole chicken cooked in olive oil, garlic and white wine for $16.50. Customers order it with fresh crabmeat salad and a side of spaghetti.

At Marsi's in Chicago, owner Gabriel Sorci's wife and five children work in the restaurant with him. "Customers come back because they love the food," says Sorci, who came over from Italy 14 years ago. Sorci, who was raised in a restaurant family, takes special pride in presentation, taste and creativity: veal with artichoke hearts, black olives, onions and mushrooms in Marsala sauce for $12.95; orange roughy in parchment with a light sauce of plum tomatoes and oregano for $11.95.

"When I came to this country from Sicily, my first job was working in a pizza place in Chicago. Being Italian, I enjoy cooking and eating," says Phil Campanella. Soon Campanella and his wife, Regina, opened their own pizza parlor in Chicago. By the time they moved Regina's to its present location in Arlington Heights, a free-standing facility with two dining rooms, it became clear that "People had finally figured out that pasta's not fattening and pizza's not junk food."

Campanella shows his marketing skills with platters for two with enormous portions: The Godfather platter (lasagna, veal Parmigiana, deep-fried zucchini, meatball and sausage, $26.95) and the Festa di Pasta platter (house-made gnocchi, spinach tortellini, cheese ravioli and cappelletti, each with its own sauce, $22.95). The most encouraging note, he says, is that the daily specials represent the highest percentage of sales. "Our pizza is great, still made from scratch, and so are our sauces. But for me—I live for the specials."

"You want to talk to the manager?" a voice said when R&I called Vinnie's Pizza on New York's West Side. "Well, I'm the manager, I'm the owner, I'm everything else."

It was Vinnie himself, who goes by his first name only, and interrupts himself every few seconds to fire rapid instructions in Italian to people on his end of the line. Vinnie is one of two owners and both, of course, are from Italy. "If you come from Italy, you have the kitchen in the blood," he explains. The success of Vinnie's no-frills operation, he says, is "good ingredients and no machines. Everything by hand. If you want machines you can go to . . . well, you can go somewhere else."

After family-style operations such as these, and often out of these, came the stylish trattorias and fabulous fine-dining Italian restaurants that add luster and pizazz to America's major cities.

Piero Selvaggio's famous Valentino in Los Angeles opened 20 years ago as a storefront trattoria before the word had much of a meaning in America. "I wanted to bridge the gap between formal dining and the mamma-and-poppa tradition of our childhood," he explains. Valentino had informality with style, a tablecloth restaurant with quality food and professionalism, where the owner wrote the menu afresh every day and came out to greet guests. It was a phenomenal success. "Valentino evolved, grew in the right direction of improving the image of Italian cuisine that was my heritage."

After Valentino in the '70s, Selvaggio opened Primi in the '80s. The menu, which lists all small courses, anticipated the change in American eating habits from three squares a day to unstructured meals.

In 1991, Selvaggio opened his third restaurant, Posto, to emphasize what he considers will be a strong direction in Italian food and restaurants: a rediscovery of the south of Italy.

"You don't have to be Italian to cook Italian food—you do have to understand what it is," Selvaggio says. His current concern is the number of what he terms "ersatz Italian restaurants" and their potential to set back the progress of Italian food in America. "Nothing is more offensive to me than to see misspelled menus, sloppy dishes and complete confusion about the delivery of certain dishes. Fantasia? Yes, there's a lot of space for fantasia. But it doesn't have a solid base. This much we know: The fantasia of the early '90s won't be the fantasia of the late '90s."

Sharing his optimism and his concern about the future of Italian food in America are other maestros of Italian food and wine, Giuliano Bugialli, Marcella Hazan and Pino Luongo.

"There are really two Italian foods, real Italian and production Italian," says Bugialli, who teaches classic Italian cooking in his own school and whose newest book is *Giuliano Bugialli's Foods of Tuscany* (Stewart, Tabori & Chang). "So you have to judge restaurants: if they are real or an adaptation." Still, he thinks that in the United States there have been dramatic changes in Italian food in the past five years. "We have moved from the straw wine flask to refined wines, and there has been an incredible upgrading in the level of dining Italian-style. I have to say, I'm really surprised. I never thought we could reach this level outside of Italy."

Bugialli sees the future of Italian food as end-

less because of the research into regional foods. His predictions: Tuscany will continue to be a popular region. The south of Italy will be the next strong region, especially Sardinia. And, finally, Piedmont if it can emerge from the culinary shadow of Provence.

Marcella Hazan, like Bugialli, owns and operates her own cooking school. Her latest book is *Essentials of Classic Italian Cooking* (New York: Alfred A. Knopf). She emphasizes the simplicity and the difficulty of Italian cooking. "It is simple cooking, but it is very difficult to do because there are no disguises available, no reductions, concentrates, cover-ups, no surprising combinations of exotic ingredients. When honestly and competently executed, it is, along with real Chinese cooking, the one cuisine that you can turn to every day of your life, that will nourish without ever fatiguing."

Hazan makes a sharp distinction between improvisation and self-indulgent novelty in Italian cooking: "There is unlimited space for improvisation. But there is no room for self-indulgent novelty. To appeal to taste through novelty is self-defeating . . . truffle-flavored olive oil, runny polenta, goat-cheese pizzas, incongruous stuffing for oversize ravioli, pesto slapped on everywhere—these cliches of novelty Italian operations have no connection with everyday Italian cooking and its timeless pleasure-giving principles."

Pino Luongo, chef-owner of restaurants in New York, Chicago, Dallas and Houston, says that although the process of improving Italian dining in America is a slow one, it's happening. "Basically, we're getting much closer to how people eat in Italy," he says, attributing this in part to efforts of chefs like himself and in part to improved ingredients—some still imported but many produced here. However, he warns of the misconcept dinosaur: "There are still plenty of entrepreneurs opening restaurants who don't know what it's all about, and who knows where their chef came from? They're still out there creating misconcepts."

Are today's Italian fantasy concepts good fun or gaudy fakes? Will they last, or will they pass?

While the jury is still out, we'll venture the following:

Everything changes. As Selvaggio points out, the fantasia of the early '90s will not be the fantasia of the late '90s. And success breeds success: The better operators become, the better their restaurants become.

And there are two other factors to consider: first, Americans' unquenchable appetite for experience. They're hungry for more, and they're constantly trading up. Second, the seductive nature of Italian food. The more operators experience, the deeper they delve into the cuisine of Italy.

And while some might dismiss and others might rail against the new breed of Italian restaurants alla fantasia, most are giving Americans their first but not their last taste of and for Italian food in friendly, imaginative surroundings for a very good price.

For example, the consummate concept creator, Chicago's Rich Melman, has spawned four Italian fantasy restaurants. The first was Scoozi, where the giant tomato still hangs over the crowd outside, and inside, the make-believe Italian artist's "warehouse" sports carefully exposed brick, elaborate restrooms, and a grazing menu of Italian "tapas." Next came Tucci Benucch, described by *Zagat Guide* as New Age Italian fantasy: an Italian country villa incongruously located in a postmodern mall with Bloomingdale's. After Tucci Benucch came Tucci Milan with hip crowds and a more sophisticated menu. And latest is Maggiano's Little Italy. On one side of the restaurant under family portraits of somebody else's family, Chicagoans dine on red-sauced pasta. On the other side, they take home amazingly good country breads from a full-scale bakery.

Also in Chicago is Vinny's, created by Joe Carlucci, who already opened two highly successful namesake fine-dining restaurants. And Carlucci is Italian.

Vinny's he describes as a "recreation of the family restaurants I used to go to as a kid."

Vinny's menu is a recreation of the home cooking of two very real relatives—Carlucci's Uncle Babe and Aunt Tessie. When the menu was being created, he invited Babe and Tessie to come and cook for his chefs, resulting in some of Vinny's most popular menu items, for example, Babe's Bonzetti (a giant portion of stuffed veal breast for $9.95). "Bonzetti means fat kid," explains Carlucci.

Fantasia lends itself to Italian chains, large and small. According to *R&I*'s 1993 400 survey, the big Italian chains are the third-largest foodservice segment in sales and rang up $12.8 billion last year. Although the three top chains were pizza concepts, the fourth chain, the 420-unit Olive Garden, with headquarters in Orlando, Fla., specializes in family-style Italian dining. Smaller chains, located coast to coast: New York-based, 14-unit Sfuzzi; the 6-unit La Prima with headquarters in Washington; the 5-unit Garibaldi's with headquarters in Hoffman Estates, Ill.; and the 4-unit Beau Jo's, with headquarters in Idaho Springs, Colo.

Far from being carbon copies of one another, each and every chain has its own identity. At the Olive Garden, it's "hospitaliano," complimentary and unlimited garlic sticks and salad and lunch for as little as $3.95, dinner as low as $7. At Sfuzzi, it's Sfuzzi Sfamily Sfeast—family-style dining on Sundays. At La Prima, it's an Italian market atmosphere. At Garibaldi's, it's rock-and-roll Italian with neon art and flying fish. And at Beau Jo's, it's the robust ingredient-packed Colorado-style pizza dubbed Mountain Pies, a napkin art gallery and salads served in (miniature) ceramic claw-foot bathtubs. Also, there's the small matter of that ongoing promo: "The Challenge Pie." Any two people capable of eating this 14-pound grand Sicilian pizza, crust and all, in one hour, one sitting, wins the pie free of charge, a $100 cash prize and two Beau Jo's T-shirts. Hopefully, extra large. ◆

Beyond the Combo Platter

by Karen Straus

Mexican cuisine, firmly established with Italian and Oriental in the triad of ethnic favorites, is more popular than ever as the American public takes to its assertive flavors and good value. And, thanks to low-fat, vegetable-based salsas and new dishes using more vegetables and less fat, diners also are beginning to look at Mexican food as healthful.

Operators are offering boiled, spiced black or pinto beans, for example, as an alternative to refried beans, and lentils are appearing as an alternative to meat fillings and entrees.

Traditional combo platters also are moving over for *platos pequenos,* or small plates of appetizers, that diners can sample and share. Nontraditional combinations of Mexican and other ingredients are gaining ground as well. Two Cincinnati chains, Empress and Skyline, have put that city on the culinary map with their versions of chili-topped pasta, while in Miami, Yuca, a Cuban restaurant, offers rice primavera with asparagus, peas, chayote, corn, peppers and grilled eggplant, and paella with saffron linguine.

Chimichanga Changes

The chimichanga, a specialty burrito from the Sonora region of Mexico, is an example of a traditional dish that midscale operators are lightening up. Chimichangas are flour tortillas filled with shredded beef, pork or chicken, grated cheese, rice and beans, folded with the ends tucked in and fried or deep-fried. With sour cream and guacamole, the calorie count is 500.

Dominga Garcia, chef-owner and namesake of Minga's in Glendale, Ariz., who shed 36 pounds after joining a Weight Watchers® group, knew there had to be a better way. Incorporating

diet tips learned at Weight Watchers®, she developed a tortilla made with canola shortening instead of lard. The tortilla is stuffed with artfully seasoned zucchini, celery, cucumbers, carrots and green chilies, then oven-baked. Skipping guacamole and sour cream, the chimichanga weighs in at 150 calories.

Garcia calls her cuisine Ultra-Lite Mexican and has trademarked it. She uses canola oil for frying, soaked, cooked and mashed beans, and seasonings to replace traditional lard.

At Rooh's Cafe Salsa, an eight-unit chain in northern California, lentils and pinto beans are cooked without the addition of oils or lard. Beef and poultry also are steamed-cooked without added fats or oils. Rooh's offers two kinds of tortilla chips: its own trademarked Toastillas, corn tortillas that are toasted, not fried, and corn tortilla chips that are toasted, then lightly fried in canola oil. All other Cafe Salsa dishes are grilled or oven baked.

Fajitas Test

Louisville, Ky.-based Chi-Chi's, a chain of more than 200 units with most locations east of the Mississippi, is testing vegetable Chajitas in the Louisville market. (Chajitas combines the Chi-Chi's name with the word *fajitas.*) The product was developed as a result of increased customer interest in vegetable items, says Ann Olmsted, Chi-Chi's marketing manager.

The test Chajitas consist of broccoli, carrots, green peppers, onions, zucchini, mushrooms, tomato and a banana pepper sautéed with Mexican seasonings and served on a sizzling skillet. The Chajitas come with flour tortillas and shredded Monterey Jack and Cheddar cheese, *pico de gallo,* sour cream, guacamole and lettuce. One side dish of Spanish rice, refried beans, black beans, french fries, fiesta corn or a jalapeño stuffed potato is included.

Small Plates, Large Plates

Chicago restaurateurs John and Linda Terczak call their unique brand of cuisine "Gringo-Mexican," or "Mexican joints for American taste buds." Chameleon offers a variety of platos pequenos such as goat cheese and mushroom quesadillas and pumpkin tamales. Platos grandes offerings include grilled fish chayote with guajillo chili sauce, black beans and roasted corn; and torta de pollo, chicken layered with whole-wheat tortillas, salsa, cheese, garnishes and roasted tomatillo cream sauce.

Tamales, the Terczak's other Mexican-inspired restaurant, offers a similar menu. Appetizer prices at both establishments range from $1.50 to $6.75, with entree portions priced from $5.50 to $11. As at Spanish tapas bars, customers are encouraged to order several platos pequenos and share them. Large plate orders can be halved. ♦

Mexican for the Masses

by Rajan Chaudhry

When foodservice operators say Mexican dishes are among the hottest items they offer, they're not just talking jalapeño peppers.

Indeed, the growth of the Mexican segment, the fastest among all quick-service segments, suggests that America's appetite for low-priced Mexican fare is far from satisfied.

From 1986 to 1990, traffic at quick-service Mexican restaurants advanced 42%. By comparison, total quick-service traffic increased less than 6% during the same period, according to NPD CREST, a survey conducted by the NPD Group, Park Ridge, Ill. During the same time period, the number of Mexican entrees on menus swelled 180%, according to the National Restaurant Association's menu census.

But even those figures belie the far-reaching impact of Mexican foods and flavors on American menus.

Oak Brook, Ill.-based McDonald's, with some 12,000 restaurants worldwide, is among those banking on Mexican foods for new business. McDonald's has added breakfast burritos and chicken fajitas to its menu. The chain has also launched tests of hard-shell tacos (59 cents each) and beef burritos (79 cents each).

Wendy's, Dublin, Ohio, also is exploring extensions to its Mexican line. Like McDonald's, the chain is searching for products that will attract more families and lift traffic during evenings and weekends.

Since 1988, Wendy's has offered a make-it-yourself taco station as a permanent part of its SuperBar, an all-you-can-eat hot and cold buffet. For about $3.50 to $4, the bar includes fixings for tacos and burritos as well as side items like Spanish-style rice.

New products, such as chicken burritos and chicken fajitas, are in "very small-scale testing," says Denny Lynch, vice president of communications. "Right now, we have a lot of flexibility. You can make nachos if you want, or tacos or burritos, or any variety of combinations. But we are looking at new food items that could offer the same flexibility and provide another reason for a customer to come to Wendy's."

Lynch credits Taco Bell and other fast-food specialists for increasing awareness of Mexican-style foods. "They've created a market, and everyone will get to benefit from it," he says.

Despite undeniable interest in fast-food Mexican products, the discount-pricing strategy of 3,500-unit Taco Bell, the Irvine, Calif.-based leader among Mexican quick-service chains, has undercut many traditional taco and burrito programs.

Most operations simply don't have the size, with its attendant economies, to match Taco Bell's prices, typically 59 cents for a basic taco. To compete, many operators have begun diversifying their offerings to include more upscale and healthful alternatives.

Taco John's, Cheyenne, Wyo., is a case in point. The 440-unit chain recently launched a new mall concept, Taco John's Mexican Fiesta, in Jacksonville, Fla.

Besides Taco John's standard fast-food fare—tacos, chimichangas and burritos—the new concept will carry new chicken fajitas and beef fajitas ($1.99), entree-size chicken and beef fajita salads ($2.99), Mexican-style hot chicken wings ($1.99 to $3.99), Sierra nachos ($1.99), a Sierra chicken fillet sandwich ($2.49 to $2.69), and baked potatoes with Mexican toppings ($1.99).

Taco John's Mexican Fiesta also departs from the chain's traditional counter-service layout, showcasing the new menu items along a cafeteria-style trayline.

In part, the changes are recognition that mall customers might be more open to display merchandising than customers on the street. "Mall patrons carry along the same shopping mentality when it comes to a food-court occasion as they would if they were in a department store. We decided to take more advantage of that and put our food up front so that the consumer could do a little window shopping," says Gary Wofford, vice president of operations and franchise services.

The company's new chicken sandwich consists of a chicken breast fillet on a pita-style Mexican bread formed in the shape of a taco shell. It is topped with dressing, salsa and cheese. ARA Services, the Philadelphia-based contract-feeding company, is another operation that has felt the impact of Taco Bell's price cutting. The company has shifted its attention to more upscale items. ARA has developed a concept that will bring the spices of Mexican foods to new dishes, including grilled items and seafood, often prepared in exhibition fashion. It is also exploring more center-of-the-plate combinations and trying to de-emphasize burritos, tacos and nachos.

As the changes at ARA and Taco John's suggest, marketing healthfulness is one means operators are using both to appeal to new customers and to distance themselves from the commodity taco business. For instance, Eugene, Ore.-based Taco Time now offers a vegetarian burrito, priced at $1.69. It features a whole-wheat tortilla, lard-free refried pinto beans, brown rice, Cheddar cheese, sunflower seeds, sour cream and salsa. And already, the new cafeteria at the Florida Hospital Medical Center, Orlando, says it is experiencing a "never-ending want" for meatless Mexican foods. The vegetarian cafeteria devotes half of its salad bar to Mexican items at all times.

The inclusion of traditionally Mexican ingredients in non-Mexican items is testament to the cuisine's growing importance. Denny's added an all-American roast beef and ham sandwich with a decidedly Mexican twist. The product, the Megamelt Slam, is topped with Monterey Jack cheese and mild green chilies. Likewise, Denny's features guacamole with some of its hamburgers. Its newest Southwestern product, Santa Fe Steak, is a hamburger topped with salsa, sour cream, Cheddar cheese and green onions. The burger is served with refried beans, tortilla chips and more salsa on the side. Price: $4.99.

Similarly, Austin, Texas-based Schlotzsky's new menu includes jalapeño cheese bread as an option for all its sandwiches. And Jack in The Box, a San Diego-based hamburger chain, offers items like the "fajita pita," which combines Mexican and Mediterranean elements. The chain's latest Mexican item is a finger-size minichimichanga.

Despite the new opportunities for spicing up non-Mexican items, most downscale efforts are aimed at supplementing, not replacing, popular traditional items like taco salads and burritos.

To meet demand for the downscale Tex-Mex food without sacrificing their own margins, a growing number of operators are turning to partnerships with the very force that pushed them away from the cut-rate fare: Taco Bell.

Marriott Host International is pairing its Arriba Margarita bars with Taco Bell Express units in airports, and Clemson University, Clemson, S.C., added a Taco Bell Express kiosk to its campus. Even ARA has begun testing Taco Bell carts in some accounts. ◆

Inside Mexican Fillings

by Nancy Backas

Tortillas are the foundation of many different Mexican items. Each variation has a name based on the filling, how the tortilla is stuffed or folded around the filling, and the sauce, if any. The tamale, a close relation of the tortilla, consists of a nonedible covering, usually a corn husk, around cooked *masa* (specially treated cornmeal) and its filling. Tortilla-based items and, to a lesser extent, tamales can be found in every corner of Mexico, from sidewalk fast-food stands to fancy restaurants, and in every home, rich or poor. Although Americans are very familiar with corn and flour tortillas, they might be confused about the various dishes for which tortillas are used.

A tortilla is a thin, round, unleavened pancake made with *masa* or, more often in the United States, with *masa* flour, called *masa harina*. It can also be made with wheat flour.

The time-honored way of making the *masa* itself is still practiced. Dried corn kernels are covered with, or cooked briefly in, an unslaked lime and water solution to soften the hulls and left to steep until partially cooked. Then the kernels are washed and, while still moist, the hulled corn is ground between lava stones.

Restaurants in the United States wishing to make their own torillas (a labor-intensive procedure) can either buy fresh *masa* (available in cities with a large Mexican population) or use *masa harina*. A tortilla press is useful in pressing the tortillas to the proper thickness before briefly heating on a griddle or hot pan until small brown spots appear. But the dough can also be pressed between two layers of waxed paper and rolled. Quality packaged tortillas are readily available throughout the United States.

The list of fillings for tortillas can fill a thick cookbook, but there are categories of dishes, all using tortillas.

Enchiladas are tortillas that are either fried very briefly in deep fat, dipped into a heated sauce, filled and rolled; or dipped into a sauce, fried, filled and rolled. A heated sauce usually is poured over them, and they are garnished with shredded cheese and run under the broiler or served with fresh ingredients such as shredded lettuce and avocado slices.

Tacos, as we know them in the United States, are tortillas that have been folded over, fried crisp, and filled with ground or shredded meat, shredded lettuce, cheese, green chilies, tomato and sauce. In Mexico, tacos most commonly are served in soft, filled and rolled tortillas, doused in sauce and eaten like a snack.

Tostadas are tortillas fried flat and used as bases or plates for any number of fillings. Many U.S. restaurants serve salads in large fried tortillas that have been formed into hat-like bowls.

Burritos are made with flour tortillas and usually are folded envelope fashion to make a package. Any of the fillings for enchiladas can be used for these. Chimichangas are burritos that, after the filling is added, are fried in an inch of oil until brown on each side. Often, these are served on a bed of lettuce and topped with guacamole and sour cream.

Flautas are so-named because of their flute-like shape. They are made either with one large soft tortilla or two overlapping soft tortillas. They are filled wtih chicken or meat, rolled snugly, fried until crisp, and served without a sauce.

Quesadillas are made with medium to small uncooked tortillas, either corn or flour varieties. The filling used to be cheese with strips of green chilies, but today turkey or chicken, meats or shrimp often are added. The filling is put on half of the tortilla, which is folded over like a turnover and secured with a wooden pick.

Panuchos hail from the southern-most part of Mexico, the Yucatan. They are made from very fresh tortillas that are placed on the grill until they puff into pillows and then are filled, usually with bean paste and hard-cooked egg, garnished lavishly and topped with a piquant sauce.

Tamales are a category all their own. While the nonedible covering varies (it can be dried corn husks, palm leaves or banana leaves), the one thing all tamales have in common is the *masa* filling, which can be sweet or savory. All tamales are tied into packages and steamed.

Mexican cookery also has its own version of turnovers, called empanadas, pastry dough filled with savory or sweet combinations that are then baked or fried.

For authentic Mexican recipes, consult: *Authentic Mexican*, by Rick Bayless with Deann Groen Bayless (New York: William Morrow & Co., 1987), or *The Art of Mexican Cooking*, Diana Kennedy (New York: Bantam Books, 1989). ◆

MEXICAN EXPANSION

Southwestern Cooking Heats Up

by Jeff Weinstein

No matter how complex the recipe, simple ingredients—corn, chilies and beans—form the base of most menu items found at traditional Mexican restaurants as well as trendy Southwestern cafes.

Mainstream consumers, however, are just starting to understand what Southwestern and Mexican cuisine is really all about. It hasn't swept the country the way Cajun cooking did because it has no charismatic promoters such as Paul Prudhomme.

"Southwestern cuisine is still in its infancy," says Mark Miller, chef-owner of the Coyote Cafe in Santa Fe, N.M., and Red Sage in Washington. "As more Southwestern restaurants open across the country, people are starting to understand the food's complexity. They are asking more questions and doing more comparing. It is no longer a novel dining experience."

Blame for the misunderstanding about Southwestern food might fall to chefs who don't know how to handle the wide variety of chilies and spices. "There is an old Mexican wives' tale," says Nancy Beckham, chef-owner of Brazos in Dallas. "If you are mad at your husband, put two peppers that don't belong together and you can kill him."

For Beckham, doing Southwestern cuisine right means using an ancho chili with chocolate for a mole sauce because the ancho has a sweet raisin-like flavor that complements the chocolate's richness.

Lenard Rubin, chef at Windows on the Green at the Phoenician Resort in Scottsdale, Ariz., concentrates on textures as well as flavors. To give a dish crispness and taste, he pan-fries sea scallops and serves them with orange grit cakes. "What I do is what Southwestern cuisine is evolving into—more refined and not as spicy," says Rubin.

In the early 1980s, Southwestern chefs tried to stick to certain guidelines for traditional regional cooking. But today, they are looking for influence in a variety of ethnic traditions: Asian, Italian and French.

Whatever the cuisine, fusion cooking is catching on in the region. "Anything goes with indigenous ingredients today," says Dallas chef Stephan Pyles. For example, Pyles makes a tamale tart with roast garlic custard. He tops it with Mediterranean products such as kalamata olives and artichokes. He also is using more olive oil, basil and Italian cheeses, noting similarities between Italian and Southwestern cooking. "A big part of the Southwest repertoire is beans," says Pyles. "It is the same in Tuscany, Italy. Both styles are rustic and hearty."

At the Coyote Cafe, Miller serves contemporary Southwestern cuisine. He says beans, corn and low-fat game such as Texas venison, Mexican rabbit and quail are his hottest commodities. In addition, he notices more requests for vegetarian entrees.

And Beckham is among the Southwestern chefs singing the praises of an herb called *hoja santa*. The large heart-shaped leaf, available May through November, has a smoky, anise flavor. Hoja santa is used in sauces and as a wrap for steaming and baking entrees.

Consumers looking for value in Southwestern cuisine won't necessarily find it in bigger portions, which prevail in other regions. Instead, presentation has come forward as a differentiating factor.

For instance, Rubin at the Phoenician has switched to heartier side dishes. An 8-ounce steak (as opposed to a 10-ounce steak) is accompanied by rattlesnake polenta, chayote squash or white bean purée.

Miller says better-quality ingredients enhance value even more. He has his own organic farm and can offer 52 varieties of tomato, and something as exotic as corn fungus stuffing for beef.

Pyles' philosophy is different. He favors portion sizes that are bigger than ever. He used to present a seafood medley with a sauce and vegetable. Today, it comes in a big bowl with black bean and smoked-tomato ragu, smoked scallions and fried leeks.

Southwestern cuisine finally is gaining an identity. More people know what red chili sauce is and why tomatoes are roasted. And more chefs are showing interest because the flavors of the Southwest are exciting and the food has numerous applications.

In addition, ability to cook Southwestern style will grow because the abundance of Latin American communities in the United States makes more fresh product available. In cities like St. Paul, Minn., the presence of a large Hispanic community now makes it easier to get fresh tortillas, tamales and chilies. In fact, Pyles offers such fare at Tejas, his restaurant in Minneapolis. ♦

ASIAN ENLIGHTENMENT

The Asian Influence

by Karen Straus

The Asian influence on American cuisine has its roots in the 1960s, when Americans began to reevaluate their meat- and fat-heavy diet. In the 1970s, nouvelle cuisine experimented with Asian seasonings, and by the 1980s, Asian dishes had mushroomed on menus faster than you could say "shiitake."

In the '90s, the Asian population continues to grow, as does the popularity of Asian cuisine. According to the *R&I* Menu Census, Asian food ranks among the top three ethnic menu segments, along with Italian and Mexican. And by 2000, the Asian-American community is expected to top 8 million, says Hugh Carpenter in his new book, *Chopstix, Quick Cooking with Pacific Flavors* (New York: Stewart, Tabari & Chang, 1988). Carpenter is the founder of Chopstix Dim Sum Cafes in Los Angeles, which offer fresh, American ingredients paired with Chinese, Thai and Mexican seasonings, a cuisine he calls "Pacific flavors."

But Asian influence has penetrated regions beyond the West Coast. In Rehobeth Beach, Del., at a restaurant called La La Land, diners enjoy poached shrimp that has been marinated in soy, peanut oil and Chinese chili sauce, then plated in a pool of chili-spiced red pepper coulis.

For appetizers, visitors to LP'S Spruce Pond Inn in Stowe, Vt., can order vegetable nori rolls (toasted seaweed wrappers stuffed with vegetables and vinegar rice, similar to sushi) with wasabi, pickled ginger and tamari-sake sauce. Another dish is green onion pancakes with sliced, fanned Chinese barbecued pork.

And at Hat Dance, an upscale Mexican restaurant in downtown Chicago, one of the most popular appetizers is avocado sashimi, served with soy and sake vinaigrette and garnished with red pepper and tomatoes.

A Difficult Cuisine to Label

Asian cuisine, like Asia itself, is difficult to label. The world's largest continent, Asia's culinary hot spots include India, Pakistan and Sri Lanka; Nepal, Thailand, Burma, Cambodia, Laos and Vietnam; Malaysia and Indonesia; and China, Taiwan, the Philippines, Japan and Korea.

Asian cuisines are as diverse as the people: fiery Mogul dishes from India; fresh, intricate Thai flavors; a variety of styles from China; hot pots and fire pots from Korea; grills from Mongolia; and the simplicity and harmony of Japanese dishes.

Rice is a unifying element of the major Asian cuisines, as is the use of small amounts of protein in composite dishes containing starch and vegetables. Other hallmarks of Asian cuisines are noodles, chilies, curries, coconut, ginger and cilantro; bite-size meats and vegetables; whole, plate-size fish; bean curd; and dipping sauces.

The Stir-Fry Sensation

Stir-fry is one of the most immediately recognizable Asian influences on Western menus. According to the *R&I* Menu Census, 51% of all foodservice operations offer an Asian entree. Stir-fry was the dish most added to commercial menus, and it made the top five in commercial ethnic entree best-sellers. Stir-fried vegetables were the No. 2 commercial side dish and the side dish most added to menus in both commercial and institutional segments. Egg rolls made the top five on the institutional appetizer best-seller list.

Stir-fry is actually a cooking technique, but it has become a catchall name for various dishes. There are a few, simple stir-fry principles:

SCRUTINIZING THE SAUCES OF ASIA

Sweet, salty, spicy or piquant, Asian sauces hit all the flavor notes. The basic sauces listed below can go solo or be used in concert with other ingredients to create dipping sauces, marinades, dressings and condiments.

Chinese chili sauce: This adds fire to Asian dishes. It is often mixed with soy sauce and rice vinegar to make a dipping sauce.

Fish sauce: A pungent seasoning that resembles soy sauce, fish sauce is a favorite in Thai and Vietnamese cuisines. It is served as a condiment or dipping sauce.

Hoisin sauce: A thick, sweet, reddish-brown sauce, hoisin is spread on pancakes for mu shu pork. It can be used as a barbecue sauce base or to flavor stir-fry dishes.

Oyster sauce: This thick, rich, brown sauce is used to flavor and color braised and stir-fry dishes.

Plum sauce: This thick, sweet-and-sour condiment is most often served with meat and duck.

Sesame oil: This dark, thick, aromatic oil is used to season food. It generally is not used as a cooking oil because of its strong flavor and low burning point.

♦ Cut foods into small, uniform sizes to ensure quick, even cooking.

♦ Stir-fry foods over the highest heat possible.

♦ Cut all ingredients ahead of time and place them next to the wok in the order in which they will be cooked.

♦ Don't overload the wok; this causes a reduction in the cooking temperature. It's better to use a second wok.

♦ Be careful not to overcook. Stir-fried dishes are done sooner than you think.

With or Without a Wok

The wok is a multipurpose, round-bottom pan used most often for stir-fry dishes. Its high, sloping sides cause foods to slide to the bottom of the wok for quick, even cooking where the heat is highest. Wok cooking also requires less oil than conventional, flat-bottom pans. Wok accessories include dome tops, racks for deep-frying dishes such as tempura, long-handled utensils, and bamboo steamers and baskets for dishes such as dim sum and steamed, whole fish.

Plain, heavy, carbon-steel woks are considered the best, but require extra care. This includes adequate seasoning with cooking oil to develop the characteristic black, nonstick cooking surface, as well as careful cleaning without detergents or abrasives, which destroy the protective seasoned layer.

For stir-frying on a gas stove, use a round-bottom wok and set it directly on the burner ring. For electric stoves, use a flat-bottom wok.

Asian dishes can be prepared even without a wok. Andi Lester Minix, executive chef and foodservice director for the University of Charleston in Charleston, W.Va., cooks Japanese dishes using a spatula and flat-top grill. ♦

ASIAN ENLIGHTENMENT

New Asian Cooking

by Susan Gilleran

The mixing of cuisines from cultures isn't new. But the timing is right for Asian foods, flavors and methods of preparation to be totally assimilated into American cooking.

East-West merger mania has definitely spawned the success of Hugh Carpenter. He is the executive chef at Chopstix, a three-unit Los Angeles-based restaurant chain, and the author of two books on the subject of Asian foods. *Pacific Flavors* (New York: Stewart, Tabori & Chang, 1988), illustrated with photographs taken by his wife, Teri Sandison, is in its fifth printing. Carpenter's Cal-Asian innovations include won tons stuffed with a Southwestern-style mixture of chicken, water chestnuts and corn and served with guacamole; shredded chicken salad tossed with almonds, rice sticks and red ginger dressing; and fluffy white rice stir-fried with raisins, pine nuts and toasted sesame seeds. Carpenter foresees Occidental-Oriental marriages, such as those made at Chopstix, taking place on all types of menus for some time to come. This food trend will continue, he says, thanks to the influx of Asian populations into the United States; the wide variety of foodstuffs from the Orient now available to chefs; and the fact that Asian foods are flavorful and, for the most part, healthful. From a food-cost perspective, preparations with Asian twists also earn operators' popular vote.

"By integrating American and Pacific Rim ingredients and techniques in ways that are not typically found in traditional Asian restaurants, we are accomplishing at Chopstix what Wolfgang Puck is renowned for at Chinois on Main in Los Angeles," says Carpenter. "But by using common ingredients such as noodles, chicken and carrots, we are able to keep costs low, to appeal to those with sophisticated tastes who are on a budget."

John Berres of Cafe Flavors, the only restaurant in Charlotte, N.C., specializing in what he calls "an ethnic extravaganza," agrees that Asian items help hold down food costs, which offsets the high labor cost incurred by the amount of chopping and cooking-to-order that Asian dishes call for.

At Cafe Flavors, Oriental noodle and vegetarian dishes are extremely popular, Berres says. He also uses chicken thighs, which are one-third the price of breast meat, for grill items. "Thigh meat not only has more flavor, it tends to hold marinades and sauces better than the breast," he explains. (Thigh meat also has more fat than chicken breast.)

Since opening his doors in 1989, Berres has been turning out, to a packed house, yakitori-style chicken, Oriental lamb fajitas and stir-fried steak and onion sandwiches in addition to Mediterranean, Caribbean and regional American offerings. On weeknights, tables in the 88-seat dining room turn twice, on average. On weekends, they turn three times, which leads Berres to state another advantage of going the Oriental route.

"The great thing about these dishes is that they are quick. We get food out very fast," he says.

The ease with which Oriental flavors fuse into existing menus is a great asset to California Cafes, which caters to the tastes of individual markets, says Jim Benson, executive chef at the Corte Madera, Calif.-based chain. Benson oversees 11 units located primarily in the San Francisco Bay area. His most popular dishes include Southwest spring rolls, made with marinated shrimp, green chilies, cilantro and Jack cheese in a spring roll wrapper; chicken and basil pot stickers with Oriental pesto; and Taco Shimi.

"Visually, it's very exciting. People rave about

it," says Benson of Taco Shimi, which he describes as charred ahi tuna or poached prawns in crisp won ton skins, served on sushi rice with Chinese salsa and garnished with pickled ginger and wasabi. "It's got real Mexican-Chinese flair," he says.

Another big seller is lobster and mascarpone ravioli in lemon chardonnay sauce, which is prepared by stuffing a won ton skin with the seafood and cheese mixture.

"It's a different twist on Mediterranean, California and Oriental—a hodgepodge," Benson says.

"I don't do these dishes for the sake of being trendy," adds Benson. "The market out here demands it. Customers are attuned to what's happening, cuisine-wise. This food is very today."

Benson is convinced that foods prepared with local products—either steamed, sautéed, stir-fried, or grilled and enhanced with Asian twists—"will fly everywhere."

While woks are not a prerequisite for preparing Asian-flavored foods, they do add to the merchandising magic in operations where kitchens are part of the display.

"We paid an arm and a leg to designer Pat Kuleto to build us an auditorium where we could show different cultures coming together," says David Soohoo, chef-owner of Chinois East/West in Sacramento, Calif.

Customers seated around the kitchen counter can watch Soohoo, the son of immigrant Chinese parents, break from tradition and stir-fry with olive oil, or prepare his signature "Phoenix and Dragon," a dish combining chicken and shrimp, vegetables, Provençal herbs and cream.

But Soohoo admits to bending the rules ever since he was a boy, when his favorite meal consisted of stir-frying hot dogs and broccoli. ◆

Oriental Noodles Have It All

by Nancy Backas

A Northwestern Indiana group of Wendy's franchisees buys Oriental noodles for the salad bar from a Chinatown pasta manufacturer in Chicago. Chef Kelly Mills of the Four Seasons Clift Hotel, San Francisco, tosses Oriental noodles with scallops, Chinese broccoli, peanut oil, ginger and black beans to produce his updated version of Chinese stir-fried noodles. The secret is out—Chinese noodles are an ingredient of exceptional value and quality.

Chinese restaurants always have relied on dried egg noodles, and now other operations are discovering them. In addition, operators may choose noodles already prepped by the manufacturer. Fresh angel-hair strands are wheeled directly from cutting machines to a steamer, are cooked and oiled, then packaged in 5-pound bags. This means that a commercial kitchen can have fresh noodles, precooked, just three hours after egg, flour and water are formed into dough. In Chicago, operators pay only $3.60 per 5-pound bag for these.

Coupled with the volcanic temperature of the wok, these steamed, prepped noodles fit into a style of "flash cooking." A cook need only plunge steamed noodles into hot water while heating a sauce or stir-frying a topping. Then the noodles can be tossed with sauce in the wok, or seared in hot oil before being topped with the sauce, all within minutes.

Chinese noodle-making left home early in its history. Small noodle-makers would turn out a day's quota of noodles and wrappers. Other producers turned their ingenuity to creating dried egg noodles that tasted like fresh noodles and, because eggs were expensive, to inventing an eggless noodle. Because these cottage industries found sophisticated methods and recipes, the Chinese have dispensed with the distinction between factory-made and homemade noodles; to this day, everyone from peddlers to four-star chefs can buy ready-made, home-style noodles.

Continuing this tradition, Oriental noodle manufacturers in America purvey a large array of dried noodles, egg and eggless. The flour mixtures—usually a balance of hard and soft flours—are the well-kept secrets of each house. Machines knead, roll and cut the dough now, but because the noodles are still air dried, and the dough soft, the products preserve a handmade quality. The noodles generally range in size from No. 1 to No. 6; the former approximates the size of fettuccini and the latter the size of cappellini. They are sold in 10-pound boxes at about 50 cents a pound.

Machines also roll out sheets and sheets of fresh dough, then cut them precisely into squares—won ton and egg roll wrappers. Extra-fine wrappers come in a 45 to 50 count unit per pound. These produce a transparent dough, cousin to Italian stuffed noodles such as ravioli and tortellini.

Fresh noodles usually are sold in linguini sizes. Cooked, fresh egg noodles come either steamed or prefried. The latter, called "pillow noodles," have a rich taste and springy texture because the oil penetrates the dough. Both types crinkle up when blanched because of their light and porous quality. Fresh noodles also come in 4-inch won ton squares made of egg dough and 4-inch circles, made without egg.

Restaurants in large cities can buy Asian noodles through a specialty distributor. A quick search through the Yellow Pages under "Oriental food products" will unearth companies that trade in local as well as imported noodles.

A shopping trip to a large Asian supermarket will yield other noodle varieties. Entire aisles are crammed with local noodles, as well as those imported from China, Hong Kong, Taiwan, Thailand, the Philippines and Singapore. Japan and Korea produce a pure white, eggless noodle. Its chewy, dense character has a stick-to-the-ribs quality that satisfies hearty Northern appetites. In contrast, somen, the Japanese summer noodle, is extremely light and sized like spaghettini. (A word of caution: Japanese imports cost a great deal more because of the high value of the yen.) At any rate, supermarket proprietors of all nationalities will usually negotiate on prices.

Southern-style Chinese noodles are extremely diverse. The Chinese prefer an al dente noodle for which they use the term *suong*, translated as "crisp." It means a liveliness in texture rather than crackling crisp. The perfect noodle springs airily, but bites easily.

In searching for Oriental noodles, be guided only by what you read for the main ingredients (wheat flour, water, sometimes egg and salt) and the knowledge that there is no standard terminology used by the countries of origin. Any of these appellations will be found: alimentary paste, imitation noodles (i.e., imitation of egg noodles, but without egg), creamy noodles, Shanghai-style noodles. Weight ranges from 6 ounces to 1 pound, and color from pure white to a deep, eggy yellow.

Served as a first course, Oriental noodles have the advantage over Italian noodles of being more absorbent, so that they take to a lighter sauce or reduction, allowing flavors to penetrate. They also cook more quickly than Italian noodles because of the soft flour content. Chefs who experiment with won ton or gyoza wrappers will find that the heat reaches the filling faster, while the taste of the filling reaches the palate faster.

Asian noodles are cooked similarly to Italian varieties. Remember, however, that Asians generally do not add salt to the water, and they do plunge the cooked noodles into cold water to arrest cooking. The technique of reheating the noodles with sauce at serving time helps flavor penetration.

Noodles made of rice flour, bean starch, buckwheat (Japanese) and sweet potato flour also are found on the shelves of some Oriental supermarkets. These demand different culinary treatment than the wheat pastas, so check the package or some other reference for instruction. ◆

ASIAN ENLIGHTENMENT

Chino-Latino Dishes

by Karen Straus

On Eighth Avenue, near 18th Street in New York, La Chinita Linda, a Chinese-owned restaurant, lists Cuban pot roast, black beans and yellow rice on one side of the menu, and pork lo mein and fried rice on the other side. Patrons can choose a Mexican beer or a Chinese beer, and finish their meals with caramel flan and a fortune cookie.

In New York City, the fusion of Cuban with Asian cuisine goes by the name Chino-Latino. Several restaurants specialize in the cuisine, which has its roots in Chinese immigration to Cuba early in the 1900s. With the rise of Fidel Castro, many Chinese fled Cuba and came to the United States, bringing their unique brand of Cuban-Chinese cuisine with them.

Chino-Latino dishes easily translate to the mainstream menu. Ingredients are readily available and require only simple preparation techniques. Pork, common to both Latin and Asian cuisines, is found in Chino-Latino staples such as masita, deep-fried meat with garlic sauce and chopped raw onions. Served with rice and beans or plantanos (plantains), masita sells for $5.35 at La Caridad on Broadway and 78th. Another traditional dish is lechon, or roast pig with rice and beans and yuca, run as a weekend special for $6.50.

Pork Chops and Roasts

One of La Caridad's most popular dishes is pork chops. Two chops marinated in mojito, a traditional Cuban sauce of garlic, parsley, lime and oil, served with plantanos and salad sells for $5.75. Pork chops also are a staple at Manhattan's Bayamo, where Peruvian-born Chef Jorge Chang, after marinating the chops in garlic and cumin, panfries them in brown sauce. Served with rice and black beans, the dish sells for $10.95.

Other Bayamo specialties include Cuban roast pork with stir-fried lo mein noodles for $6.95; Miami-style Cuban torpedo sandwiches with roast pork for $6.95; and Bayamo's Grilled Chef Salad with spiced chicken breast, sliced steak, chorizo (a spicy pork sausage popular in Latin cuisines), Cuban roast pork and cheese for $9.95. Fried won tons filled with chorizo and Cuban hand rolls (nori seaweed leaves filled with spiced rice, crabmeat and avocado) served with spicy dipping sauce are other notable Bayamo offerings.

New Cuban Cuisine

Douglas Rodriguez, chef at Yuca, a Miami restaurant noted for its New Cuban cuisine, remembers his parents telling him about Cuban-Chinese restaurants in Havana's Chinatown. Rodriguez, born in New York, grew up eating Cuban rice and beans with Chinese pepper steak and lo mein noodles at neighborhood Chino-Latino cafes.

At Yuca, Chino-Latino is taken to a higher plane, with dishes such as spicy guava barbecue pork ribs with plantain-ginger flan, Oriental stir-fry vegetables and tangerine ponzu (Japanese citrus-vinegar dipping sauce), for $18. Another Rodriguez dish is pork tenderloin stuffed with house-made pork sausage flavored with Chinese five-spice powder. The roast is glazed with ginger, soy, honey and lime, and served with chili, coconut, hearts of palm, rice and spicy pork rinds for $23.

The beauty of Chino-Latino food, says La Caridad's Sam Lee, is choice. "You get more choices than you would at a regular Chinese or Spanish restaurant." And, he notes, some Chino-Latino restaurants are more Chinese or more Latin, depending on neighborhood preference. ♦

ABOUT PORK

- ♦ Approximately 48% of pork products consumed in the United States are distributed through food-service channels, a 25% increase since 1988.
- ♦ The majority of pork in the marketplace today is cured, such as bacon and ham. The remainder is marketed as fresh pork. Fresh pork should be grayish-pink in color. The darker pink the flesh, the older the animal. Cured pork is rose-colored. Pork fat is white.
- ♦ On average, trimmed, lean portions of pork cuts in 1992 were 31% lower in fat, 17% lower in calories and 10% lower in cholesterol than in comparable cuts listed in the USDA's 1983 handbook. In 1985 and 1991, grading standards were revised to account for the leaner hogs being produced today.
- ♦ A 3-ounce portion of lean, roasted pork tenderloin contains 133 calories, 24 g protein, 4 g fat and 67 mg cholesterol.
- ♦ During the War of 1812, the United States government got its nickname "Uncle Sam" from pork shipped to Americans in barrels stamped with the letters "US" and the name of the meat packer, Sam Wilson. Soldiers referred to the pork as "Uncle Sam's meat."
- ♦ Trichinosis, a disease caused by eating undercooked pork harboring a microscopic parasite, is virtually nonexistent in the United States as a result of widespread sanitary production conditions. Animals can acquire the parasite by feeding on uncooked garbage, but federal legislation now requires that all garbage be cooked before feeding to hogs.
- ♦ Safety precautions for handling fresh pork include washing hands, utensils and surfaces that come into contact with raw pork and never tasting uncooked pork. Cooking to an internal temperature of 137F kills trichinae parasites. Allowing for a margin of safety, experts recommend cooking to an internal temperature of 150F to 165F. The 170F to 185F recommended by many cookbooks results in overcooked meat.

MAINSTREAM MEDITERRANEAN

Food Gets Gusto

by Nancy Ryan

When Mediterranean-style dishes made their American menu debut in the 1980s, they were given a warm welcome by customers who had already read about the much-publicized "Mediterranean diet." (Doctors attribute the low rate of heart disease in Mediterranean countries to a traditional diet rich in unsaturated oils, low in cholesterol, high in fiber and carbohydrates, and low in fats and sugars.) The Mediterranean restaurant fare of the '80s depended heavily on the more expensive and familiar cuts of meat, fish and poultry (veal chops, tuna steak and chicken breast). It also tended to soft-pedal the flavors.

The continued popularity of Mediterranean fare has encouraged chefs and restaurateurs to shift their middle-of-the-road cooking style to dishes that are at once more exciting and more profitable. The emphasis is on no-holds-barred flavor, rich and gutsy. And the ingredients are down to earth and cost-effective. Following are three cornerstones of Mediterranean cookery: olive oil, grains and breads, which operators use to add value, flavor and interest to their menus.

Olive Oil

Olive oil, the Mediterranean's gift to the rest of the world, is used in tabbouleh, Veal Pasticciatta (Chef Aldo Saad uses olive oil in his signature tomato sauce for this dish), Grilled Rabbit with Fried Herbs on Lentil Baba Ghanoush, and Focaccia. But the innovative use of olive oil is not limited to Mediterranean-style restaurants, as the following examples from New York show.

At the Four Seasons, one of the best-selling appetizers is "the perfect baked potato," says General Manager Alex von Bidder. Chef Hitsch Albin bakes the potato at 350F for 45 minutes,

and allows it to rest at room temperature for 15. The potato then is quickly browned on a grill, cut open, squeezed lightly, and then drizzled with extra virgin olive oil.

At New Haven Pizza & Pasta Company, owner Louis Sica gives his customers extra virgin olive oil with red pepper flakes in it instead of cracked red pepper. The oil comes in small cola bottles with liquor-dispenser tops. Sica says customers shake the oil on both pizza and pasta.

Chef Jean-Georges Vongerichten, formerly chef at Lafayette and now at the new Jo Jo restaurant, creates a beautiful green, fragrant, basil-flavored oil. He blanches basil leaves for 10 seconds, shocks them in ice water, then drains them. The leaves are processed with extra virgin olive oil; the mixture is refrigerated, covered. After two days, he strains and refrigerates the basil-olive oil. The oil is drizzled on bread and used over salads and pastas. It also is used to deglaze pans, especially those in which lamb has been sautéed.

Mediterranean Grains

Polenta, bulgur and couscous, traditional Mediterranean grain products, have a twofold menu appeal: nutrition and variety.

Polenta, a cornmeal product with the texture of semolina, is a familiar Italian cold-weather entree and side dish with other uses. Executive Chef Leo Waldmeier, The Drake Hotel, Chicago, often combines polenta with a grated hard cheese such as Parmesan and pours it into a sheet pan to cool. He cuts the cooled polenta into diamond or crescent shapes and sautés it, and serves it with hearty meat entrees. At Cafe Tu Tu Tango, Coconut Grove, Fla., polenta is layered with ground seasoned lamb and baked in a casserole.

Bulgur wheat, another Mediterranean grain, appears most often on today's menus as tabbouleh salad. Bulgur has been steamed, dried, cracked or ground, and sieved into three sizes typically used in restaurants: fine (for tabbouleh and desserts), and medium and large (for salads, stuffings, pilaf and falafel).

A recipe for tabbouleh from the Olive Tree, Wichita, Kan., uses the fine-size bulgur. Chef Joumana Toubia also serves a cooked bulgur-onion-tomato-garlic pilaf as a side dish. At Actuelle in Dallas, chef-partner Victor Gielisse mixes bulgur, kasha and quinoa (each cooked separately) with pan-roasted hazelnuts, and serves this as a mixed-grain timbale ringed with pan-seared sea scallops in a red-wine sauce. Gielisse also serves a cacciotta cheese-stuffed polenta fritter with sirloin steak.

Tabbouleh lends itself to salad bars for another reason: holding power. As early as 1983, Chemical Bank Restaurant Services, New York, put tabbouleh on the employee dining salad bar, along with a selection of nontraditional options such as rice salad and barley salad.

Couscous, a semolina-like product of wheat, is popular in North Africa, where it is steamed and served with stews of lamb and vegetables. American restaurateurs, however, have found some broader uses for couscous: Joyce Goldstein, chef-proprietor, Square One restaurant, San Francisco, serves a Moroccan-style roast chicken stuffed with saffron-cinnamon couscous. Chef John Mountford of Houston's on the Plaza in Kansas City, Mo., serves a couscous salad as a side with any entree. And a signature couscous salad is served at Michela's restaurant in Cambridge, Mass.

The Mediterranean Bread Basket

The Mediterranean has hundreds of varieties of traditional bread. Recently, the more regional breads of Italy and the Middle East have found their niche on American menus.

Italian focaccia is a round, flat loaf brushed with olive oil and herbs before baking, and might be the early ancestor to pizza. Now operators are putting its familiarity to good use.

For example, at 3M Food Services, St. Paul, Minn., focaccia made fresh in the foodservice bakery is split, filled with meat, cheese and Romaine lettuce, then cut into eight wedges and served as part of a daily soup-and-sandwich special.

Focaccia can be used, day-old, in Italian bread salad: panzanella. Slightly stale bread is soaked in cold water; squeezed dry; added to ripe tomatoes, red onions and basil; and dressed with olive oil vinaigrette.

Pita, an ancient flatbread, lends itself to sandwich variety in both commercial and institutional operations. Greek and Middle Eastern restaurants stuff it with gyros or falafel. American operations stuff it with chicken, turkey or tuna salad; with fish or chicken breast fillets; and with meatless vegetable-cheese combinations.

Lahvosh, a thin cracker-like bread baked in large sheets, is making inroads into American bread baskets. It appears in fine-dining bread baskets of Pano's and Paul's in Atlanta and Actuelle in Dallas, where the kitchen now bakes its own. Lahvosh also is an ideal in casual restaurants, in institutional operations and on catering menus as an accompaniment to dips and hors d'oeuvres. ♦

MAINSTREAM MEDITERRANEAN

The New Wave

by Steve Weiss

Olives in Boston is on the itinerary. So is Philadelphia's 16th Street Bar & Grill and Naples' (the Florida version) Bayside Grill & Bar. The re-concepted L'Entrecote in Dallas is a definite must-see, and Eddie's Grill in Phoenix calls for a culinary layover-and-half.

Along the left coast, there's the preeminent Square One and the landmark Zuni, both of San Francisco, as well as the offshoot their staffs created, Portland's Zefiro's. In Seattle, one comes across Palomino, so successful that it has recently branched to Minneapolis as well. Also in the Midwest is Chicago's Tuttaposto, which is winning raves from restaurant and travel critics alike.

What bonds the establishments included in this restaurant tour is fairly recent enrollment and whole-hearted participation in the movement toward the expression of Mediterranean accents on the American menu. Each of these restaurants has opened or been re-concepted recently with a Mediterranean menu and each is under the culinary stewardship of an enthusiastic young American chef. Most would happily second the assessment of one critic, who calls Mediterranean cuisine "the gastronomic grail of the 90s: casual, healthy food packed with flavor and value."

Even so, the members of this new "Club Mediterranean" reflect about as much homogeneity—no less, no more—as can be found in the vast 16-nation region that their culinary repertoires represent. Some of the chefs involved here have their grounding in classical French technique, while others are restaurant family "lifers" who have sojourned in the Greek Isles. Still others have just gotten it out of books. Likewise, while rotisseries and wood-burning grills often are deemed de rigueur in this style of cuisine, there are cooks who manage to get by quite nicely with an old pizza oven and a sauté station.

The menus themselves are, well, all over the map. A restaurant such as Tuttaposto might feature the stinging heat of a Moroccan chermoula vinaigrette on grilled tuna, while that same piece of grilled fish is treated in a far more delicate Provence fashion with cherry tomatoes, basil, chopped egg and olives at Zuni, but both are certainly authentic Mediterranean dishes. Compounding this eclectic effect are regional American preferences, so that one finds an item like wood-grilled lobster served over gnocchi with toasted walnut butter and zucchini at Olives, while L'Entrecote offers a grilled bone-in rib-eye steak with ratatouille, sautéed leaf spinach and "smashed" potatoes.

Even in such widely available dishes as paella, ratatouille and seafood risotto, recipes vary immensely from establishment to establishment, depending as much on seasonal ingredient availability and good old leftovers as on specific flavor formulation. And then there's that Yankee ingenuity/weirdness that yields items such as 16th Street Bar & Grill's lahvosh-based "Mediterranean fajitas" (served with a build-it-yourself assortment of marinated grilled chicken strips, hummus, bean dip, fresh basil leaves and other assorted garnishes), and the sun-dried tomato and mozzarella "pizza salad" served with Caesar dressing at Eddie's Grill.

Ultimately, though, this is not a club entirely without a code. Interviews with chefs, managers and owners representing the establishments listed here do yield some strong consensus opinions about what matters if you're thinking about sending your menu on a trip to the Mediterranean. Following is some very useful insight and advice from operators who have already paid their dues.

It might not be the sexiest aspect of the Mediterranean menu, but many operators confess that attractive food costs and resultant low menu prices make today's most compelling argument for featuring the region's dishes. Much has already been written here and elsewhere about the cuisine's heavy reliance on vegetables, grains, starches, breads, legumes, poultry and less-expensive cuts of meat. More expensive ingredients, shellfish, cheeses, nuts, olive oil, are used moderately in multi-ingredient preparations such as salads, soups, casseroles, sausages, dips and pizzas.

Operators point out that many of their signature items fall in other-than-entree menu categories. At Tuttaposto, one of the most popular items is an appetizer of crisp Sardinian focaccia served with an assortment of taramasalata, eggplant caviar and hummus. At L'Entrecote, one of the best-sellers is a bowl of seafood raviolini in a bouillabaisse broth. 16th Street Bar & Grill customers go for the Grilled Eggplant Sandwich served on focaccia with mozzarella cheese, tomatoes and grilled onions. None of the preceding items is priced above $5.

Even upscale operations, which offer a lot of expensive ahi tuna, sea bass, shrimp and chops, benefit from the range of price options that they can make available to customers. Typical is L'Entrecote, which, until a year ago, operated as a gourmet French restaurant at the Loews Anatole Hotel in Dallas. Since the changeover, dinner check average has dropped from $35 to $26, but traffic and revenues have increased significantly, says Chef Lindell Mendoza.

Despite its extremely intricate flavor profiles, despite its occasionally esoteric ingredients and despite the sheer vastness of its origins, most successful merchandisers of Mediterranean cuisine regard it as a sort of cross-cultural soul food. "This is food that's not so much sophisticated as it is comfortable," offers Zefiro's Chef-owner Christopher Israel. As Palomino Chef Brad Komen wryly observes: "You can stuff it with pancetta, rub it with infused olive oil and spit-cook it over apple wood, and it's still roast chicken."

Indeed, most of the chefs doing Mediterranean in their kitchens are quick to point out that their core menus are not all that formal or esoteric. Judy Rodgers, chef-owner of Zuni, an

establishment that helped pioneer Southwestern cuisine before slicing itself a piece of the Mediterranean pie in the mid-'80s, is as earnest about her hamburgers (served on focaccia) and her Caesar salad as she is about her house-cured fresh anchovies. At Tony Mantuano's Tuttaposto, the Sunday night "family dinner," ordered by 50% of patrons, involves immense portions of pizza and starches inspired by "whatever's in the box."

"Whenever we become too fancy and not rustic enough we get rejected," says Palomino General Manager Roger Stillson. "The attraction of this food is that it's heartwarming. Whenever we survey our customers they tell us that our portions are ridiculously huge—but don't change a thing."

Everyone has a version of this story and not all have happy endings. Take the Denver debacle, for example. Three local award-winning Mediterranean restaurants—Bibelot, Majorca and Today's Gourmet—closed in the same year.

"I loved them all very much," says Bill St. John, restaurant critic of the *Rocky Mountain News*. "But the Denver people weren't ready. They weren't ready for Spanish sausages or anchovies on crusted bread or even marinated grilled shrimp."

Eddie Matney, chef-owner of Eddie's Grill, tells a similar tale. Of Arabic heritage himself, Matney originally opened his restaurant as KousKooz, and his extremely ambitious and authentically spiced "Ameriterranean" recipes simply proved too sophisticated for his market. Word-of-mouth publicity was awful, as even customers who showed enthusiasm for items such as tabbouleh and harissa were incapable of reporting what they had eaten to their friends.

Finally admitting to himself that "your peers don't make your salary, your customers do," Matney downscaled the concept to Eddie's Grill, in the process burying most of the overt Mediterranean menu references. Customers can still get tabbouleh and harissa, but they will have to ask for "parsley salad" and "red pepper salsa." Matney reports that customers are far more comfortable now that they no longer need a dictionary to get through the menu.

"What is perfect to a chef and what is perfect

to a customer can be miles apart," concurs Mendoza of L'Entrecote. "You must appreciate what your customer will understand," he explains. "If he feels like a fool he will not be back. The majority of our customers are not familiar with Mediterranean cuisine," Mendoza continues. "Dallas is a meat-and-potato town and we have to respect that. Maybe in the future we can be more aggressive, but right now our customer is going to be upset by creamy polenta if we don't serve it with a nice big chop."

Most of the Club Mediterranean crowd believe that they are on to something that is far more than fad. "It's a logical light and fresh extension of America's love affair with Italian cuisine," observes chef-consultant Charles Saunders, formerly of California's Sonoma Mission Inn. Stephen Poses of the 16th Street Bar & Grill describes the cuisine as "fundamental."

"This is not just a trend at all," summarizes Palomino's Komen. "It's a cuisine that lends itself perfectly to modern lifestyle concerns with health, low-risk dining-dollar investment and just having fun." Or as Zuni's Rodgers so succinctly puts it: "It's a culinary style that's been around for 700 years. It's probably not going away any time soon." ◆

Caribbean Currents

by Nancy Ross Ryan

Ever wonder where on earth to find those bold new menu winners? Items sure to add excitement—without sending food cost sky high or the sous chef into a nose dive? Dishes that might be destined for the same popularity as pizza and pasta, nachos and tacos, egg rolls and stir-fry—ethnic fare now part of the American menu mainstream?

The Caribbean is one place to look. And the dishes to bet on? Jerk, escovitch, curry, chicharrones, beef patties and a bevy of tropical beverages that can easily steal the show. Today's culinary barometer is giving high readings to Caribbean cookery. Four new cookbooks have been published in the past three years, and some mainstream Caribbean restaurants have opened with resounding success. One of the first is still successful: New York's Sugar Reef, opened in 1985 by American-born partners Zeet Peabody and Devra Dedeaux, who visit the Caribbean twice yearly in search of more good food. The opening chef, Dominican-born Pablo Rosado, still translates the recipes they find for Sugar Reef's menu, and creates his own as well.

Jerk: Jamaica's Pride and Joy

"Sugar Reef's No. 1 entree—drumroll, please—is Jerk Chicken," says Dedeaux. Jerk, the pride of Jamaica, is a method of spicing and barbecuing (first pork; today chicken, fish and beef) that dates from the mid-17th century, according to Helen Willinsky, Jamaican by birth and author of *Jerk: Barbecue from Jamaica.* She says the jerk method of pit-cooking meat was brought to the island by African hunters enslaved by the English. The Africans adapted seasoning methods of the native Arawak Indians, especially their use of chilies. In the mid-18th century, escaped ex-slaves waged guerrilla war on their former Eng-

lish captors. They camped in the bush, where their main food was little wild boars (harder to catch than the English), which they preserved by slathering with the aromatic spice-salt combination we now know as jerk. The preserved pork was grilled slowly, for up to 14 hours, over a fire of green wood. By the time the peace treaty between the English and the former slaves was signed, jerk was part of the Jamaican psyche.

"The taste of jerked foods is hot with peppers," writes Willinsky. "But, as you savor it, the variety of spices catches up with you, and it is like a carnival in your mouth. We have a saying in Jamaica, 'It is very morish.' You want more."

Customers often are confused by two similar names for different dishes: Jamaica's escovitch (also spelled escabeche), describes a pickled dish, usually fish or poultry, that has first been cooked, then marinated in the pickling mixture, usually using vinegar, and served hot or cold. Seviche (also spelled ceviche) refers to a dish of uncooked fish or shellfish that is marinated in citrus juice, usually lime.

Escovitch in the Caribbean islands is the culinary offspring of the Spanish colonizers and originally used fish as the main ingredient. As Dunstan A. Harris observes in *Island Cooking,* "A snack, full meal, or a finger food, pickled fish is found in all corners of the Caribbean." Today, escovitch preparations include onions, fish and poultry.

Pickled fish or poultry can be an appetizer, salad, or main dish accompanied by salad and bread. It can be served hot or cold to span the seasons.

Curry in the Caribbean Islands was brought by the East Indians, who were in turn imported to work in the British colonies. Today, Trinidad and Tobago, the furthest south of the islands, have the largest East Indian population, although curry traveled to Jamaica and French-speaking islands as well.

Caribbean curries are fragrant mixtures of island spices that differ depending on the island (and sometimes on the cook). For example, both Harris and Elisabeth Lambert Ortiz (*The Complete Book of Caribbean Cooking*) write about Colombo, the distinctive East Indian curry mix of the French Islands that calls for hot peppers, coriander, dry mustard, garlic cloves and turmeric pulverized to a paste. The curry paste is used to flavor fish, chicken, goat, pork, lamb or beef. And Dedeaux gives three recipes for curry in *Sugar Reef Caribbean Cooking:* from Jamaica, Trinidad/Guyana and the French Islands. These writers all caution that commercial curry powders should be the freshest possible.

The Spanish-speaking islands contributed a very famous snack to the Caribbean culinary repertoire: chicharrones, or pork cracklings. But a lesser-known dish, a speciality of Cuba and the Dominican Republic, chicharrones de pollo, is gaining popularity rapidly with Americans. Dedeaux says it's the second-most popular chicken dish on Sugar Reef's menu, where it comes with black beans, rice and tostones, which she calls "Puerto Rican french fries. They're delicious!" Tostones are green plantains, sliced, soaked, drained, and fried for about two minutes, then removed from the oil, flattened on both sides with a mallet, returned to the oil and fried until crisp.

Ortiz describes the Oriental influence in chicharrones de pollo: "The chicken is cut into small pieces, a technique that betrays the Chinese influence, which clearly belongs in the great family of stir-fry foods." In addition, soy sauce is used in the marinade. The bite-size chicken pieces are marinated in an appealing mixture of soy sauce, rum, lime juice, paprika and other spices; removed and dried; then floured and deep-fried.

Many of the Caribbean islands have their own versions of pastries or turnovers filled with meat, and often lobster or vegetables, but Caribbean connoisseurs all vote for the Jamaican beef patty as king. The Jamaican beef patty owes its ancestry to the Spanish empanada.

The basics for the filling are simple: ground

RECIPE RESOURCES

Caribbean Cooking, by John DeMers (Los Angeles: HPBooks, Price Stern Sloan, 1989); *Island Cooking: Recipes from the Caribbean,* by Dunstan A. Harris (Freedom, Calif.: The Crossing Press, 1988); *Jerk: Barbecue from Jamaica,* by Helen Willinsky (Freedom, Calif.: The Crossing Press, 1990); *Puerto Rican Cookery,* by Carmen Aboy Valldejúli (Gretna, La.: Pelican Publishing, 1987); *Sugar Reef Caribbean Cooking,* by Devra Dedeaux (New York: Roundtable Press, div. of McGraw-Hill, 1989); *The Complete Book of Caribbean Cooking,* by Elisabeth Lambert Ortiz, First Ballantine Books Edition (New York: Random House, 1986).

beef, onions, hot peppers, salt, pepper, thyme, turmeric, bread crumbs—with few variations (sometimes garlic, annatto, soy or other flavor accents). But when the moist, spicy filling is spooned into a flaky short crust, crimped and baked in a 400F oven, the resulting hot pastry is almost irresistible. Willinsky says that in Jamaica they are a way of life, eaten by rich and poor, young and old, at lunch, dinner or as a snack. They can be made large or small.

Although made by patty-shop vendors in the islands, beef patties are a natural for the American restaurant menu, and lobster and vegetable versions suggest variety. Although the pastry contains shortening, the cooking method of baking instead of deep-frying adds appeal.

Tropical Punch, With or Without

Rum is the spirit of the islands, and its classic drink is planter's punch. The recipe is a rhyme: "One of sour, two of sweet, three of strong and four of weak." This translates to: one part fresh lime juice, two parts sugar or syrup, three parts rum and four parts water or ice.

Some island drinks are already part of the American menu, for example, the daiquiri; rum collins; pina colada; rum rickey, sour and flip.

Still others await discovery and rediscovery:

Between the Sheets (a combination of rum, brandy, triple sec, lemon juice); Blue Mountain Cocktail (rum, vodka, coffee liqueur, orange and lime juice); Cuba Libre (rum, cola, and lime juice); Steel Band (rum, orange juice bitters and a twist); Scorpion (sugar, water, lime juice bitters and a potent amount of rum); Punch au Lait de Coco (rum and coconut milk punch). For cold winter days there is the Hot Rum Toddy, Hot Buttered Rum, and coffee and rum in endless variations. Willinsky has a recipe for Bloody Mary a la Jerk—made with rum and Dry Jerk Seasoning.

The fanciful names suggest marketing potential. For example, Sugar Reef's bar menu lists more than 30 tropical drinks. Despite its reputation for icy sophistication, the New York clientele loves them. The most popular drink, Dedeaux says, is the Surfsider, a blue punch made from white rum, blue Curacao and pineapple juice, served in a glass that sports a woman in a bikini and garnished with a miniature beach ball. It sells for $4, but for $7 customers can take the glass home.

The beauty of a tropical punch is that it doesn't have to pack one. Because of the variety of tropical fruit juices, nonalcoholic drinks are just as appealing.

Cooks' Caribbean Tour

The Caribbean dishes and ways of cooking previously described just skim the culinary surface of the 2,600-mile chain of islands stretching from the coast of Florida to Venezuela. The islands were discovered by Christopher Columbus in 1492, opening the way for successive waves of European colonizers: Spanish, French, Dutch, Portuguese, British, Danish and U.S. flags have flown over Caribbean islands, most of which now are self-governed countries.

The first European settlers wiped out the indigenous people, the Carib and Arawak Indians and over the centuries added European foodstuffs to the Caribbean larder, resulting in one of the world's most flamboyant flavor palettes. Spices range from allspice, nutmeg, mace, cinnamon and cilantro to curries. There's an Eden's garden of tropical fruits—avocado, pineapple, coconut, papaya, mango, guava, bananas, plantain and less familiar exotic fruit. Vegetables range from calabaza pumpkin, corn, true yam and sweet potato, to tomato, okra, garlic and onion. The cookery also uses legumes, rice, pork, beef, chicken and seafood.

The Europeans brought not only ingredients and cooking styles, but unwilling immigrants: African slaves, Chinese and Indian laborers who added their own cooking styles and ingredients to the Caribbean melting pot. The resulting cuisine is a sweet and spicy tropical style based on similar ingredients but with strong ethnic chords that reflect each island's history. ◆

South American Cuisines

by Nancy Ross Ryan

Empanadas, seviche, black beans and flan: That's the sum total of South American dishes likely to be found in America, except, that is, in the two dozen or so South American restaurants in major American cities. But on menus at large, the foods of the vast South American continent and its ten major nations are still waiting to be discovered.

Substantially different from the cooking of Mexico, many South American dishes recommend themselves to American menus for a variety of reasons: First, the food is just different enough, but not so different that it presents a challenge to the diner or a hurdle to the chef. Second, it is just spicy enough, but not incendiary. Third, dishes (many of them appetizers) range from complex and sophisticated to simple and savory. Most ingredients (many low-cost) are available, and the preparation techniques are accessible to American foodservice kitchens through South American cookbooks. (See "Recommended Reading" at the end of this chapter. The following introduction to South American cuisine, after an overview and suggested dishes adaptable to American menus, focuses on the cooking of Peru, considered by many food writers to be South America's best.

The food of South America, not the gold of the Inca empire, turned out to be the more lasting treasure. Chilies, corn, tomatoes and potatoes are all native to South America. (See sidebar, "Worth Their Weight in Gold: South American Foodstuffs.") It is hard to imagine the world's major European and Asian cuisines without one or more of those ingredients. Yet until the 16th century, these were unknown outside Central and South America.

Venezuela, Colombia, Ecuador, Peru, Chile, Argentina, Bolivia, Paraguay, Uruguay and Brazil have national cuisines and dishes that developed over the past four and a half centuries. Spanish colonizers imported traditional foods, adding to the indigenous larder with rice, wheat, barley, rye, coffee, olive oil, garlic, onions, pigs, chicken, cattle, lemons, oranges, sugar cane and okra. The result is dishes rich in flavor, spicy but few hot, ready for American menus.

The following cooks' tour of South America was adapted from the recently published *South American Cooking* by Barbara Karoff, which includes more than 200 authentic recipes.

Colombia

With two seacoasts, Pacific and Caribbean, it's no surprise that Colombians developed a talent for preparing seafood that includes many versions of mixed seafood casseroles, cazuela de mariscos. Sopa de pescado tunaco, a speciality of the Pacific coastal city of Tunaco, is a quickly cooked, freshly fragrant soup made from firm white fish (cod, bass or snapper), tomatoes, chilies, onions, olive oil and stock, and finished with coconut milk. Another specialty, soufflé de calabeza y camaron, an appealing shrimp and summer squash soufflé, translates into a light and agreeably different luncheon entree.

The national dish, ajiaco bogotano, is a hearty chicken, corn and potato soup that is remarkable for its variety of potatoes. While South Americans have varieties of corn unknown in the States (some with kernels as large as a thumb), and more than 200 varieties of potatoes, this stew can be made using domestic corn and a combination of russet, red, and yellow potatoes.

Empanadas, savory pastry turnovers with a variety of fillings, are popular all over South America.

Venezuela

Colombia's neighbor shares many of its dishes and cooking styles. It is famous for black beans, which Venezuelans call caviar criollo, native cav-

WORTH THEIR WEIGHT IN GOLD: SOUTH AMERICAN FOODSTUFFS

Tomatoes, potatoes, chilies—and many other foods that we today consider central to European and Asian cuisines—are indigenous to South America, writes Barbara Karoff (*South American Cooking*). They have enriched mankind far more than all the gold the Spanish conquistadors plundered from the Aztec and Inca civilizations in the 16th century, when the world was first circumnavigated and a great culinary exchange began. The following list of foodstuffs are native to South and Central America. Some (beans and corn) date from 2700 B.C., and some (avocados) as early as 8000 B.C.:

Allspice, avocado, Brazil nuts, chili peppers, corn, jicama, nasturtiums, papaya, peanuts, potatoes (sweet and white), tomatoes, arrowroot, beans, cashew nuts, chocolate, guavas, manioc (yuca, sweet cassava), passion fruit, pineapple, quinoa, squash, turkey, vanilla.

iar, a great side dish for chicken and grilled meats. Another preparation, frijoles negros con jamon, the Venezuelan version of ham and beans, includes chopped bananas, tomatoes and paprika. And the national dish, pabellon criollo, is beans, rice and shredded flank steak arranged in rows to resemble the Venezuelan flag.

Brazil

South America's largest country, and the only one with a Portuguese heritage, has three distinctly different cuisines. The cooking styles of Bahia, Sao Paulo, and Brazil in general are a culinary topic of their own. Brazil is also the only South American country where African cookery is a dominant force, a legacy from the slaves imported to work the sugar cane plantations.

The most famous Brazilian dish is feijoada completa, a main dish of fresh, smoked and cured meats with a tureen of black beans, a fiery fresh chili-garlic-lemon sauce, and side dishes of rice, cooked kale and toasted manioc.

Argentina and Uruguay

Where gauchos ride, meat is king. In Argentina, it's beef and in Uruguay both beef and lamb. Portions are enormous. Meat means grilled steaks, mixed grills, and carbonadas, or baked stews that combine meat and fruits. One example is pastel de carne y duranzo o albaricoque, or sliced sirloin with peaches or apricots, wine and raisins baked in a top and bottom crust. A sidelight: Thanks to a large Italian population, pastas are popular.

Matambre, the marinated, stuffed and rolled flank steak, can be served hot or cold, as an appetizer or entree. When sliced, the spiral layers show carrots, eggs and spinach.

Bolivia

In landlocked Bolivia, an empanada by any other name is a saltena, and it's the national favorite. Most are filled with mixtures of chopped beef, potatoes, raisins, olives, chopped hard-boiled eggs and enough chilies to deliver the heat Bolivians like.

One simple popular dish is lomo montado, steak topped with a fried egg. Another is a versatile corn pie with chicken, pastel de choclo con relleno de pollo. The casserole is lined with a corn-egg custard, filled with a mixture of chicken, tomatoes, eggs, garlic, onions and chilies, topped with corn custard and baked until brown. This unusual savory pie also can be made with pork and beef. Sopa de man is peanut dumpling soup: rich chicken stock with delicious little dumplings made from roasted, ground peanuts.

Paraguay

This other landlocked country is off the main tourist circuit and, says Karoff, maintains more of its Indian heritage. However, one of its most savory offerings is sopa paraguaya, not a soup but a cornbread, richer and more flavorful than Stateside versions, made with both cornmeal and puréed corn, and cottage and Muenster cheese.

Chile

Seafood is as central to Chileans' diet as meat is to Argentinians' and Uruguayans'—not surprising, considering its long, narrow Pacific coast. And in the moderate climate of central Chile, some of South America's best wines are produced. Although most Chilean seafood is not available in U.S. markets, the recipes for Chilean fish stews and shrimp chowders can be easily adapted. One of Chile's most interesting dishes is porotos granados, its national dish, a grand meatless vegetable stew of beans, onions, garlic, tomatoes, corn and winter squash. It is served with pebre, a delicious uncooked sauce of olive oil, vinegar, cilantro, garlic and chilies.

Ecuador

Both seafood and tropical fruits abound, including varieties of bananas unknown elsewhere. Seviche in Ecuador is sensational, being made with juice of Seville oranges. Locro de papas, a hearty, one-dish stew, is made with potatoes, fish and light cream, and finished with beaten eggs and cheese. It is a fine example of the locros of South America, which Karoff describes, exceptionally well-seasoned one-dish meals that always include at least one starch and/or grain along with one or more meats, fish or shellfish. Ecuadoran llapingachos give mashed potatoes a new dimension. Potatoes are peeled, boiled and mashed, then mixed with lots of sautéed onion, some butter and grated cheese. This can be fried in patties or baked in a gratin dish. In any event, accompaniments add excitement: The llapingachos can be topped with a fried egg and served with a sliced avocado, or served with fried plantains and a spicy peanut sauce. The simplest sauce is made from sautéed chopped tomatoes and onion.

One of the traditional delicacies that still has a following in Ecuador and Peru is not a likely candidate for American menus: cuyor guinea pig.

RECIPE RESOURCES

South American Cooking, by Barbara Karoff (New York: Aris Books, Addison-Wesley, 1989) and *South American Kitchen,* by Felipe Rojas-Lombardi (New York: Atheneum, 1991). See also the chapter "Chile" in *Sundays at Moosewood Restaurant* (New York: Simon and Schuster/Fireside, 1990).

Peru

Once the seat of the Inca empire, Peru has developed a distinctive cuisine generally considered South America's best. It has its own hallmarks and many striking dishes.

Corn and potatoes, staples of the Inca diet, have been transformed into dozens of dishes. Peru's potatoes—some 260 varieties—are legendary and their repertory seemingly endless.

In addition to papas rellenas, (stuffed potatoes), papas arequipena, potatoes Arequipa-style, are a simple but effective dish. Boiled potatoes, the perfect foil for other flavors, are halved, arranged cut-side down on a heated platter, then covered with a creamy but spicy peanut-cheese-chili sauce. Garnishing is another hallmark of Peruvian cuisine, and this dish is garnished with hard-boiled eggs, olives and parsley or cilantro.

A familiar Peruvian edible garnish popular throughout South America is choclo, attractive small cross-sections of corn on the cob. These also appear in soups and stews.

Although Peruvian food in general is not as spicy as that of Mexico, it is still the hottest in South America. In Peruvian, *ajo* means garlic and it is often paired with *aj,* or chili pepper. By aj, Peruvians usually mean the hot and heady mirasol, rarely available in the States. Serrano and hontaka chilies can be substituted. Garlic and chilies combined contribute to a famous chicken chili, aj de gallina.

Quinoa (pronounced "keen wa"), the ancient grain of Peru, is receiving its share of media attention today for its high protein content. Quinoa has been used since the time of the Incas, and appears on the menu of La Llama in Chicago, as Pollo Incaico: marinated breast of chicken, charcoal broiled and accompanied by a sauce of baby goat cheese, quinoa and spices.

Among Peruvian appetizers, the national favorite anticuchos de corazones, a small skewer of marinated charbroiled chunks, is perfectly suited to the American menu, with one slight modification. In Peru (and throughout South America), the short skewer is threaded with beef heart. In North America, the logical choice would be beef.

Peru's abundant seafood appears in several colorful preparations. In addition to seviche, chupe de camaron is a flavorful shrimp chowder that could challenge clam chowder on American menus. It combines shrimp and fish with potatoes, fish stock, milk, peas and tomatoes, and zesty accents of green onions, garlic and chilies.

These Peruvian dishes are only a small sample of the riches in store. And beyond Peru lies the rest of South America's culinary treasures waiting to be explored. ♦

Cookware for Ethnic Fare

by Beth Lorenzini

What makes ethnic cuisine ethnic? The food, seasonings and method of preparation. And while many ethnic foods are prepared on standard equipment, certain pieces, like the wok and the pasta machine, define ethnicity and set such restaurants apart. In the examples that follow, operators show how the proper piece of "ethnic" equipment can increase productivity and sales.

Modifications for Mexican

Since that heaping basket of warm tortilla chips is such an integral part of the Chi-Chi's experience, George Lask, director of restaurant and equipment design, helped improve the nacho-chip warmer. The Louisville, Ky.-based chain had a fabricator design a top-loading warmer without a door on the bottom. Instead of servers having to open a door to get warm chips, the access area is open. Chips are contained by a baffle and an air curtain retains heat. Servers can scoop chips with one hand and hold their trays with the another.

The warmer's heating system is unique as well. In many such units, the heating element is on the bottom. But often, chip crumbs can catch fire. So Lask had the chain's unit designed with the heating element on the top. A blower forces air downward and concentrates heat by the air curtain at the bottom opening. The design prevents fires and ensures that chips are warm when presented to patrons.

The fajita chargrill also was modified to ease preparation and improve presentation. Cooks used to warm fajita skillets in all sorts of ways on sauté burners and in cheese warmers, for example, says Lask. Today, the chargrill includes a rack atop one side of the grill that holds the fajitas skillets upright. It keeps the skillets hot and within easy reach.

Italian Ingenuity

All of the pasta at Pasta Al Dente in Hyde Park, Ohio, is made from scratch. But until March, the pasta machine, with its interchangeable dies, was working away out of sight in the kitchen. Management decided to begin making pasta in view of patrons, so it built a glass booth in the main dining room to house the large pasta machine, wood drying racks and a work table.

As soon as the pasta booth was up and running, sales of pasta dishes increased $3,000 to $4,000 a week, and show no sign of slowing. "It was amazing," says Rob Brindle, manager. "You can tell someone the pasta is fresh, but until they see it, it just doesn't have the same impact." Making the pasta in sight also has led to increased commercial sales. The restaurant not only bags pasta for patrons, but several other area restaurants now buy their pasta from Pasta Al Dente.

Expressly Oriental

Ann Arbor, Mich.-based Ho-Lee-Chow specializes in Oriental takeout, and that means speed is of the essence. For that reason, speed is of the essence in equipment design as well, according to Pam Burnham, vice president of operations.

One of the best speed-enhancing elements is the wok range. The range features two stir-fry woks and a blanching wok just behind the center. Cooks control the gas jets with a knee lever, so both hands are always free. Because all ingredients are precut and held in custom refrigerated bins directly behind the wok range, cooks merely turn, portion ingredients on counter scales, turn and drop ingredients into the blanching wok or the regular wok, depending on the entree.

Sauces for the entrees are held in a clip-on rack that hangs off the range between the stir-fry woks. Up to 12 sauces are contained in pump bottles that dispense exactly one ounce at a time. Since every entree takes either one, two or three ounces of sauce, cooks needn't worry about over- or under-saucing. Preparing entrees takes no more than 90 seconds, according to Burnham. And it's all done before customers' eyes.

The brick, inverted-cup-shaped Mongolian oven at Mai-Kai Polynesian restaurant, Fort Lauderdale, Fla., is heated by burning Australian pine. It is unique in the way it cooks and the flavors it produces. The oven cooks and smokes foods at high temperatures (650F to 750F), but the cooking process is actually slow because the heat source is indirect (located to the side of the oven). Steaks, Cornish hens and ducks are hung inside the oven cavity on hooks while the cavity draws smoke and heat over and up through a center hole.

When the oven was installed several years ago (it is one of only five in the country), sales of the entrees that were cooked in it accounted for only a small percentage of the total. Today, the smoky, savory flavors brought out in the food are in demand, according to Martin Yeung, manager. "People love the slow-cooked, smoky flavor; it's distinctive and delicious. Today, about 50% of sales come from Mongolian oven entrees. The oven makes us unique." ♦

Money-Making Menus

by Toni Lydecker

Does the menu thrill customers with tempting graphics and descriptions? That's one way to judge a menu. Or does the menu thrill the operator with spectacular profits? That's another, and it is the subject of this article.

Hands-on managers think they know which items make money and which do not. Often they're right. On the other hand, a computerized menu analysis might reveal a few surprises. The lunch special all the servers are promoting, for instance, might turn out to be less profitable than an item hidden away on the regular menu.

Identifying and promoting menu winners is the answer to this situation. Promoting low-cost items and increasing the contribution margin are other techniques for bringing more to the bottom line.

Better use of the menu offers the opportunity to create more win-win situations, where both customer satisfaction and profitability are increased. Tony Feicco, vice president of operations for the International House of Pancakes, became a believer after a redesign boosted profit margins at nine of ten test sites: "We need to handle menus like a blind person reads Braille. If you put your hands on the menu and really look at what's there, it will tell you what's going on in the business."

What's Profitable?

Many an operator brags about holding food costs to 25% of menu prices. Low percentages are used not only to measure how profitable menu items are, but how successfully the operation is managed.

That could be a mistake, on both counts. This kind of thinking is based on a widely used system of setting menu prices as a multiple of food costs.

If the cost of ingredients for a pasta dish is $2.50, that figure is tripled to yield a menu price of $7.50. What competing restaurants charge for similar items and the operator's best hunch on what customers will consider a fair price are then factored in to nudge that menu price up or down. The final figure goes on the menu, and the operator sits back to see what happens. The strategy might work, but some people think a roll of the dice might work equally well.

"The industry is trained to think that the lower the food cost, the more successful the restaurant. But food-cost formulas fail to take into account the volume, who the customers are, differences in labor costs, and the financial needs of the operation," observes Bill Paul, a consultant whose company, The Menu Advantage, is located in Cincinnati.

"Using a formula of cost times three is misguided," agrees Michael Kasavana, a professor in the Hotel, Restaurant and Institutional Management School at Michigan State University, East Lansing. Kasavana and Don Smith of Washington State University propose an alternate model for evaluating profitability.

Menu Engineering, a book by Kasavana and Smith, urges operators to calculate a "Menu Power Index" for each item on the menu. The MPI is a combination of two key pieces of information: (1) The average contribution the item makes to the profit margin, after deducting food costs; and (2) its menu mix percentage, based on the number of customers who ordered it.

The data are used to create a matrix that places items in four categories: Star (high contribution margin, high menu mix), Plowhorse (low CM, high MM), Puzzle (high CM, low MM) and Dog (low CM, low MM). An operator then

RESOURCES FOR PROFITABLE MENUS

Menu Engineering: A Practical Guide to Menu Analysis, Michael L. Kasavana and Donald I. Smith (Lansing, Mich.: Hospitality Publications, 1982)

Management by Menu, Lendal H. Kotschevar (Chicago: The Educational Foundation of the National Restaurant Association, 1987)

Marketing by Menu, Nancy Loman Scanlon (New York: Van Nostrand Reinhold, 1990)

has a sound basis for deciding whether to change an item's price, reposition it or eliminate it.

Under a food-multiple system, a steak dinner priced at $15 (food cost = $5, menu mix = 10%) might seem to be on equal ground with a chicken dinner priced at $9 (food cost = $3, menu mix = 10%). But as the Menu Engineering method shows, the steak dinner is actually more profitable, contributing $10 to the bottom line, compared to $6 for the chicken.

Although it is not practical for restaurants to do time and motion studies to determine production costs for each menu item, an operator can adjust the food-cost percentage a little, depending on the ease or difficulty of preparation, when calculating an item's power index.

Winners and Losers

Getting rid of the "dogs" identified in the profitability analysis will not only reduce menu clutter, but divert production time away from less profitable items and toward more profitable ones.

Losers can hide most easily in a large, rambling menu. Phyllis Ann Marshall, a consultant in Costa Mesa, Calif., remembers working with an Italian dinner-house menu that rambled on for several pages. "In every category, there were at least five items that were producing 3% of sales or less. The extra padding needed to be removed from the menu."

To prevent trauma to the minority of customers who like the losers, she suggests phasing

in changes gradually. Items prized by a few could go on the specials menu before fading away; the operation could let devotees of, say, liver and onions, know it will be served on Wednesday nights; or the item could be made in bulk, frozen in preportioned bags and served by request while the menu transition takes place.

Selling the winners is not just a matter of reorganizing a menu, but of giving marketing support to those items. It is common for servers to promote the Fresh Catch of the Day or other specials, but when some of the most profitable and popular items fall on the regular menu, servers need to be reminded to bring them to patrons' attention.

To make sure winners remain winners, be strict in enforcing specifications for quality, portion size and presentation. Customers count on finding consistency in these menu favorites.

Create More Winners

The operation has dealt effectively with menu winners and losers. But what about those problem items that showed up in the menu analysis, to use Kasavana and Smith's terminology, the Puzzles and Plowhorses?

The Puzzles, low-volume but high-profit items, might sell better if priced lower, or they might benefit from more aggressive marketing. If neither of these strategies increases customer appeal, the operator should consider taking them off the menu; even if they are pulling their weight, profit-wise, they are probably not enhancing the restaurant's image.

On the other hand, eliminating a high-volume, low-profit Plowhorse is usually a bad idea; unless an equally appealing substitute is offered, customers will miss it. But sometimes such an item can be turned into a winner, through increasing its profitability.

To increase the check average of a gourmet hamburger, pair onion rings, coleslaw or some other high-profit item with it to increase the check average. Or raise the price, but add extra ingredients such as bacon and avocado to increase the perceived value. Before the change becomes an official part of the menu, it should be tried as a special to test customers' reaction. If they show resistance to the new formulation or the price, the operation has the option of retreating to the original formulation and price.

Marshall approaches what she calls "middle-ground items" with the zeal of a private investigator. She follows the product from the time ingredients are received to the time it's served; interviewing prep staff, servers and customers along the way; and reviewing POS data and other records. These are some questions she asks: Who orders it and when? What menu niche does it fill: healthful, rich dessert, light entree? How does it function on the line? What about speed of service and consistency of preparation? How could the dish be improved?

Raise Profit Margins

Better control of food and labor costs can usually bring more to the bottom line.

Pointing out that the average table-service restaurant maintains an inventory of 750 ingredients, Kasavana recommends adopting a computerized "gold box" inventory model that meticulously tracks only expensive items such as steak.

Jon Persoff, a consultant who also owns a pizza restaurant in Los Angeles, suggests comparing food costs against sales data on a weekly basis for the 10 most cost-intensive products. That is, if each hamburger contains 1/4 pound of ground chuck and 400 hamburgers were sold, 100 pounds of beef should have been used.

Getting staff to be precise about portioning is also important in keeping costs in line. Persoff points out that an extra half-ounce of cheese on a pizza might seem trivial but, added to every pizza his restaurant sells, it would amount to $5,000 in the course of a year.

Weight the Menu Mix

Salads are not Persoff's favorite thing to sell in his pizza restaurant: The food cost runs 60%, compared to 22% for a pizza. Raising the price would not bring salads in line with other items, says Per-

soff. "How much am I going to charge for a salad? $3.50? A bean counter would do that, and not sell any. The salad is there not because I make money on it, but because it's an important part of my menu mix."

Every operation has menu items like this, desired by customers but only marginally profitable. They have to stay, but what operators can do is to weight the menu mix and their marketing efforts towards more lucrative items.

Rethink the Menu Niche

Sometimes a restaurant closes and reopens with the same management still in place, but a new look and new menu. Very often, that restaurant has decided it needs a different niche to please customers and succeed financially.

"Niche marketing is the price of entry these days," says Steve Weiss, a Scottsdale, Ariz.-based consultant. "Some restaurants have a tendency to put what they love on the menu, sometimes at the expense of loving their customer. You could be making the best hollandaise in town fail because no one wants hollandaise."

Weiss helped Boomer's, a hamburger chain based in Phoenix, come up with an image and menu after the company attempted, with disastrous results, to sell 99-cent hamburgers in competition with McDonald's and Wendy's. After consulting with Weiss, Boomer's management decided to maximize appeal to a more upscale clientele, in contrast to the many fine-dining restaurants that are downscaling these days. The chain stopped running newspaper coupons, and its "Charbroiled hamburgers and more" sign went down, replaced by one that promises "Fabulous fast food." A new menu also helps communicate what the food is all about.

New specialty items include the Monterey Chicken Sandwich, made with guacamole and chicken breast; the Deli Melt, consisting of smoked ham, turkey breast and two kinds of cheeses on sourdough; and a fajita chicken salad that includes black beans and charbroiled chicken. All sandwiches are priced under $4. And with 40% of its sales coming from deliveries to area businesses, Boomer's is also building its catering business more aggressively.

Following are two examples of restaurants that successfully redid their menus.

Menu Makeover: IHOP

The International House of Pancakes doesn't pay much attention to traditional menu categories anymore. Instead, the North Hollywood, Calif.-based chain groups its most popular and profitable items.

The winners fall in a V-shaped configuration on the menu because market research shows this is where the customer's eye goes first. In prime position in the middle of the V are such specialties as these: Huevos Rancheros, Pancake & Egg Combinations, International Burrito and Rooty Tooty Fresh 'n Fruity. Further down the page, International Omelette is boxed in.

The Rooty Tooty selection, which consists of two eggs, two strips of bacon, two sausage links and two buttermilk pancakes, not only has strong customer appeal, but is the most profitable item on the menu. Priced at $4.89, it costs only $1.79 to produce.

Omelets rank second. "They're a meal in themselves," says Tony Feicco, vice president of operations. "You can use broccoli, fish, anything as a filling, and sell them all day long."

He has worked with 10 IHOP operations to test variations on this menu approach, and in only one did it fail to increase profits. In Albuquerque, N.M., one of the test sites, the new menu resulted in additional profits of $9,800 over 10 weeks, compared to the same period the previous year. Based on experience in these operations, IHOP is finalizing menus for distribution to its approximately 460 operations nationwide.

IHOP will continue to offer less popular kinds of pancakes "because they're like the family jewels—the customer wants to see they're still there." Chicken sandwiches are there for the same reason, but in this case, management is trying to squeeze out more profit; chicken is being purchased in large quantities at a discount.

Close cooperation with food manufacturers is paying off, as well. Flavored butters, to serve with

blintzes, were labor intensive when made in-house and the quality varied. Now IHOP purchases scampi- and garlic-flavored butters made to its specifications. Although the custom-made butters cost a little more, the quality is now consistent and kitchen staff is free for other tasks.

Menu Makeover: Michela's

Grilled lamb chops, priced at $28, used to be a winner at Michela's.

Now they're off the menu. The new winner is a combination of half a lamb rack together with a stew made of lamb shoulder. The price? $19.50.

Hit by a severe business slump, Boston customers are spending less in restaurants, and white-tablecloth operations like Michela's are responding with lower prices. Whereas many entrees used to cost $25 or more, owner Michela Larson and her staff now work hard to keep prices under $20.

The average check has dropped from $50 to $42, but the restaurant has accomplished what it set out to do: keep the customer count equal to last year. To recoup some of the lost profits, Michela's has introduced new dishes that it hopes will become winners. At the same time, the restaurant holds down food and labor costs.

The restaurant has stopped serving expensive fish such as swordfish, which can run up to $7 a pound, except as weekend specials. Whole grilled lobster has been eliminated, as well. But there are new and equally appetizing seafood selections on the menu. Cod, a reasonably priced fish, is wrapped in pancetta with polenta and warm greens. Spicy Sicilian Fish Stew with couscous, on the lunch menu, is embellished with a few pieces of lobster to turn it into a more glamorous dinner dish.

Chef Jody Adams saves money by buying whole legs of lamb and butchering them in the kitchen. After steaks are cut from the middle section to be grilled for dinner, the top and shank ends are used in a Caramelized Lamb Stew with Black Olives and Pappardelle Noodles. She also economizes by adding the ends of a prosciutto to soups for flavor.

Customers who buy their lunches at the

restaurant's takeout shop often eat them in the atrium just outside. In the evening, those tables are covered with tablecloths, lights go on and the area becomes Michela's Caffe, a sit-down operation with more casual decor and a lower check average than Michela's. Some of the dishes are the same or similar to those on Michela's menu, however, allowing kitchen staff to do one prep for both operations. An example is ribollita, a Tuscan bean soup. Risotto, on the other hand, recently was eliminated from the cafe menu because it is so labor intensive.

Careful coordination between the lunch and dinner menus helps save labor costs, as well. Many salads are the same for both lunch and dinner, and one of the dinner pizzas is identical to that served at lunch except for the addition of caramelized onions and truffle oil which add $5 to the menu price. ♦

Build a Better Menu

by Monica Kass

Hand-held and read slowly, menus are one of the most intimate connections restaurateurs have with their customers. Ultimately, menus convey the personality of the restaurant they represent and clearly communicate information about the food it has to offer. Doing both is no easy task. Lots of color and big bold shapes go a long way in saying "This restaurant is a fun place to eat," but if the copy is a tangle of adjectives printed in too-small type, diners will be frustrated in their attempts to enjoy the dining experience. To help restaurateurs in their quest to produce more effective menus, *R&I* presents a piece-by-piece analysis of the parts that should make up the whole.

Graphic Impact

What's the first thing customers see when handed a menu? Color? Logo? Illustration? All three, in rapid succession. And the impression that is made is an important one. "It's called the 'last 30 seconds of marketing,'" says ad agency executive Rod Torrence, who worked with Denny's on their menus. "When a customer sits down at the restaurant table and picks up a menu, the situation is much the same as a customer approaching products in a supermarket aisle. Those last 30 seconds are when a lot of perceptions about a product are formed." For this reason, color choice, logo design and illustration—elements that determine a menu's graphic impact—require the majority of a designer's time in shaping a menu.

Color Choice

It's no accident that red appears on menus a lot, according to Leatrice Eiseman, executive director of the Pantone Color Institute in Los Angeles.

Because red is the color that advances forward in the human field of vision first, something printed in red is impossible to ignore. Physiologically, the body responds to the color red with a quickened heart beat, pulse rate and a shot of adrenalin. Primary blue, on the other hand, soothes and sedates. But brighten that blue to the electric color you often see on menus, and the effect is once again one of excitement. Says Eiseman: "The association of a blue flame being hotter than yellow flame applies here." While such basics of color theory help designers shape menus, most avoid a scientific approach, "I can't say 'intuitive' enough," says menu designer Dean Gerrie. Charged with the task of developing for Rusty Pelican a new menu concept that would help revitalize the restaurant, Gerrie designed a series of menu covers patterned in vibrant purples, greens, reds and blues. "We wanted to see how far we could go using color to communicate youth, vitality and tropical heat." says Gerrie. Judi Radice, author of a series of books on menu design, says her menu hues usually mirror, complement or accent colors found in the restaurant's architectural palette, or in the food the restaurant serves. Inspiration for the paper Radice chose for the Guaymas restaurant in Tiburon, Calif., for example, came from tortilla chips. "You've also got to take restaurant lighting into consideration when you're choosing colors," she says. Monica Banks, a Manhattan designer, says she uses colors to communicate the feeling of the restaurant in a subtle way. The menus she did for Golden Temple restaurant in Brookline, Mass., combine traditional Chinese formality with a whimsical contemporary approach. Borrowing from the ancient art of fish printing in which a fish is coated with pigment and pressed on paper, Banks decorated the menu covers with fictional animals printed from actual food items used in Chinese cooking. To help the prints stand out, Banks designed backgrounds in "the most luscious, mouthwatering colors I could."

Logo Design

An effective logo condenses the character of a restaurant into one symbol. Because so much goes into its development, many restaurants choose to use the logo as the chief design element on their menu. The approach is a cost-effective one, and works well to reinforce the restaurant's identity. The logo also can be duplicated on napkins, matchbooks, point-of-purchase displays and employee uniforms. "It's the one thing you can take with you," says Bruce Yelaska of Bruce Yelaska Design in San Francisco. "If used in an ad, it's even more important." Yelaska suggests that a logo should be simple, but not too abstract. "You don't want people asking, 'What does this mean?' every time they see it outside of the restaurant, on a book of matches, say, or in an ad. Large corporations can afford to use an abstract logo because they can back it up with lots of ad dollars. Restaurants can't." Yelaska adds that problems in creating a logo design can be an early warning signal for an underdeveloped concept. "If you can't communicate through an image what the restaurant wants to be, you haven't thought the concept through enough." The logo Banks designed for Malvasia restaurant in New York reflects the restaurant's Mediterranean/Italian theme and architecture. "The main motif in all of the wrought-iron work in the restaurant is right angles, which is very Mediterranean," says Banks. "So I developed a logotype that spells the restaurant's name entirely in right angles."

Photographs: Yes or No?

Beyond choice of color and logo design, the method of menu illustration plays a significant role in displaying information about a restaurant's personality and food. Denny's used food photographs of its entire product lineup as the basis for its new menu. Rod Torrence explains: "Denny's previous menu was very functional, but we felt the menu could play a much bigger role in shaping customer perceptions about food quality, quantity, value and variety." As an ad expert, Torrence knew that just as print ads draw more attention on different parts of the page, food items placed in certain positions sell better. To avoid the look of a 1960s coffee-shop menu, Denny's avoided boxed pictures with strict linear formats. Instead, Denny's shot each spread of the menu as one large photograph, with food items positioned randomly throughout. To avoid clutter and establish dayparts, Denny's used electric-blue section headers in oversize, easy-to-read type across each spread. In addition to affecting customer perceptions about food, the use of photography aids sales staffs. A Bombay Bicycle Club executive explains the company's restaurants use photographic inserts to promote specials. "In the casual-dining segment, the wait staff is usually long on enthusiasm and energy, but short on sales expertise. The pictures help sell our product when words fail the staff." While photography works well in some instances, it's not the answer for everyone. Drawings can have the same graphic impact and convey just as much about a restaurant's personality as photographs, at less cost. Irvine, Calif.-based Red Robin, for example, has switched from menus that combined illustration and photography to menus illustrated exclusively with whimsical paintings. Their reason: "We feel the illustrations are much more in keeping with the fun image we want to convey. The former photographs were too formal."

Communication

Once the initial impact of color, logo and illustration has passed, the "meat" of the menu, its print content, comes into play. "This is where designers have to exercise a lot of constraint," says designer Yelaska. "What looks wonderful might not be very legible or readable." Legibility and readability are two different things. According to *Upper and Lower Case*, a periodical for typographers, "legibility is the ability to distinguish one letter from another in a particular typeface design. Readability, on the other hand, is the degree of ease with which typography can be read." Legible type is characterized by large, open spaces in letters such as "e" and "b." They are medium in weight and do not have excessive downstrokes on "p" or upstrokes on letters such as "b" or "h." Because the most legible typefaces are those that don't call attention to themselves (Century Schoolbook, Excelsior, ITC Bookman, ITC Franklin Gothic and Univers are examples cited by *Upper and Lower Case*), the attempt to convey a restaurant's personality by choosing an ornate typeface is not advisable. Readability is most affected by the size of the type. The smaller it is, the harder it is to read. Line lengths also affect readability. If a line of copy extends too far across the page, customers' eyes will tire before they reach the end. Because restaurants are often noisy, full of visual distractions and dimly lit, making a menu readable and legible is doubly difficult. For this reason, just as a restaurateur has to make a marinade much stronger than a vinaigrette for the flavor to carry, designers have to print menus that are simpler to follow than typical printed matter. The menu Lydia Shire shaped for her restaurant, Biba, in Boston, (with the help of designer Monica Banks) is a good example of a menu that is both readable and legible. "Lydia was very creative in terms of the wording of her menu selections, very literary," says Banks. In keeping with that feeling, and "to be friendly to the customer," Banks printed menus in Century Schoolbook type in an ample size.

Copywriting Clarity

The same "simple is better" guideline that makes menus kind to customers' eyes helps make copywriting easy to understand. But simple does not necessarily mean bland. Lydia Shire's straightforward menu descriptions still have appetite appeal. "Citrus salmon with crackling skin, parsley cakes," a line full of alliteration, is fun to say. As part of its menu redesign, Denny's rewrote food descriptions to add appetite appeal without becoming too wordy. The old description for Nachos Supreme, for example, sagged: "Tortilla chips covered with taco meat, refried beans and Cheddar cheese, then topped with tomatoes, green onions, olives, salsa, guacamole and sour cream." Its succinct replacement is zippier: "Crispy tortilla chips piled high on a large platter. With spicy ground beef. Mexican-style beans. Cheddar cheese, salsa, tomato, black olives, guacamole and sour cream."

Physical Attributes

Remaining elements of menu design—materials selection, size and shape—are largely dictated by operational and cost considerations. For independent restaurateurs, who have menus that change often, the typical focus is flexibility. For chain operators, durability is key. But there is a lot of crossover. Menus for decidedly chic restaurants, including Malvasia in New York, ParkSide in Atlanta and Golden Temple in Brookline, Mass., are plastic-laminated shells with printed paper inserts, a menu format long thought of as a dinner-house hallmark. Meanwhile, the casual/theme Rusty Pelican chain just switched to cafe-style menus: clear, cloth-edged folders with poster-like front cover inserts and computer-generated menu listings. This approach gives the chain the same menu flexibility that independent restaurateurs enjoy. Red Robin replaced its 8-page booklet format with a tri-panel foldout, primarily to save on binding and paper and reduce menu cost from $4.25 to $2.65.

Red Robin also added an insert to the first panel of its new menu, giving units in different regions the chance to feature local specialties. Beyond functional and cost considerations, a menu's physical attributes also communicate restaurant personality. Die cutting menus into unusual shapes is a design choice that gives menus custom appeal, but adds to their wear and tear. "Die cutting creates extra surfaces," says designer David Bartels of Bartels & Carstens, St. Louis, but it weakens the menu. Hand people a die-cut menu with lots of edges and they'll automatically bend them." Using unusual materials is another way to establish a restaurant's unique character through menu design. Minneapolis-based Duffy Design Group shaped menus from metal for Azur, a D'Amico and Partners' restaurant. According to senior project designer Sharon Werner, the painted aluminum menus are a reflection of the restaurant's interior. "It's French-Deco," says Werner. "A lot of metals and leather." Azur's lunch menu is of copper-painted alu-minum with a leather hinge. The dinner menu is aluminum coated in an aubergine paint. Printed paper menu inserts are held in place by the leather hinges. ◆

Computerize Your Menu

by Monica Kass

Afternoons used to find Michela Larson hunched over her desk, hand lettering menus for Michela's Restaurant in Cambridge, Mass. As the restaurant grew, there was no time to labor in longhand, and Larson took to late-night sessions with her Macintosh computer. "That was better than handwriting," says Larson. "It gave me flexibility to change things and got me into the habit of using the computer, but I couldn't get to it until 12:30 at night, when I got home from the restaurant, which made for mistakes in the menu. Plus, I had a lot more than menus to work up."

Larson hired a designer to typeset the extra work, invitations and menus for Michela's many parties, wine tastings and promotional events, "but that got very expensive."

Finally, says Larson, "It just seemed to make more sense to print everything here, not to worry about sending things back and forth across town."

One year after opening Michela's, Larson bought a desktop-publishing system (computer hardware, software, and laser printer) to print the menus herself. To make sure the menus wouldn't look impersonal or "computer-techie," Larson worked with the Boston design firm of Sametz Blackstone Associates to develop the marbled paper sheets that provide a background for Michela's computer-generated type.

John Kane, senior designer at Sametz Blackstone, looked at a lot of marble before he found the right slab. Kane's use of organic materials in putting together a computer menu helped soften what could otherwise have been too high-tech looking for Michela's homey setting.

Larson estimates that she spent about $16,000 for her desktop-publishing system (plus high-quality photocopier and design services), an amount "I

very easily could have spent on design and printing in two year's time." Larson spent $4,000 for her laser printer, $3,000 for the computer, $1,000 each for the software and hard drive, $3,000 for the photocopier and $4,000 for designer services.

"In the two and a half years we've been using it, the system has paid for itself," says Larson. "Not only do we use it for lunch, dinner, cafe and dessert menus, and wine list, but we print invitations and menus for special functions and wine tastings, do in-house public relations materials with it and use it for our budget spreadsheets."

Flexible and Fast

The purchase or rental of a desktop-publishing system for menu production is an option that many restaurateurs, both chains and independents, are considering. Benefits are many. Beyond streamlining menu production costs, computers allow operators to change menus quickly, as food costs fluctuate or new items are introduced.

Souper Salad, a Boston-area chain, rented desktop-publishing services from a printer in the area. Larry Reinstein, vice president of operations, explains, "We made the decision to switch from a laminated menu that we made up every six months, to one printed on a desktop-publishing system. Printing the menu this way allows us to change the inside of the menu very rapidly at a minimal cost. With the way prices fluctuate so much these days, this really helps. You can only raise prices so much on an item before a customer gets angry. Now, if our suppliers are charging more for an item, chicken say, instead of having four chicken items, we'll list maybe two. This also gives us the flexibility to buy in on something when the market price is good, and to hold back when it isn't."

Reinstein says Souper Salad initially rented desktop-publishing services to see if the system was feasible. Based on its experience, the company plans to purchase its own system.

Any restaurateur's decision to purchase equipment comes with the caution that he work with a menu designer to come up with a finished product that isn't "MacUgly." Gregg Rapp, president of the Menu Workshop in Seattle, says, "We get so many calls from restaurants who have this equipment and try to do a menu without any art direction. The result is something we call MacUgly. They want us to come in and help them fix it. Well, I believe most designers would rather be approached from the start instead of having to turn french fries into mashed potatoes."

Equipment Options

That caution in mind, equipment purchase should be tailored to fit individual needs. According to Stephen G. Miller, associate professor in hotel/food administration at Boston University and former director of education for the National Restaurant Association, "If a restaurant has already invested in a certain kind of computer hardware, it makes sense to use it to create menus. If restaurateurs own a personal computer but not a laser printer, they can find a service company (e.g., design firm, copy services such as Kinko's, and some dealers) that will rent time on their laser printer. Or, they can take their computer diskette to a commercial typesetting house and have them compose a menu from what is programmed on the diskette."

Starting from scratch and purchasing an entire system offers a restaurateur the greatest flexibility. According to Bob Jones, president of Professional Publishing Associates, Chicago, a desktop-publishing consulting firm, "A complete package, including computer hardware, software and laser printer, can be put together for under $20,000; some go as low as $10,000."

Required hardware includes the computer,

display monitor, keyboard, built-in hard drive (20 megabyte minimum), connective cables and, for easy text manipulation, a mouse (a graphic pointing device used with menu-driven systems). The computer software used to shape and print menus includes word-processing, page-layout and graphics packages. Word-processing programs ($150 to $500) are the most basic of the three, with a function Steve Miller describes as "a typewriter with a few bells and whistles." There are two widely used word-processing programs for Macintosh computers: Microsoft Word and Claris MacWrite. For IBM and IBM-compatibles, Wordperfect is the standard.

Page-layout programs ($130 to $900) require a bit more computer expertise to master, but allow users to manipulate multiple columns and insert windows where graphics will be. For Macintosh and IBM, Aldus Pagemaker is the most widely used page-layout program. Letraset Ready, Set, Go and Quark Express are other Macintosh-compatible programs.

Graphics packages go beyond page-layout programs, allowing users to design and select pictures and symbols to fit into the layout. For Macintosh, Miller recommends Macintosh Superpaint; for IBM, Jones recommends Corel Draw.

The final major piece of equipment in a desktop-publishing system is a laser printer. Laser printers produce copy that is much higher quality and easier to read. Restaurateurs might wish to laser-print all of their menu sheets, or they can create a master and photo copy the original onto the menu sheets.

Battling Computer Phobia

With equipment in hand, most restaurateurs initially suffer from computer phobia. Says Michela Larson, "It took me three or four months to make the decision to invest in the equipment and then it was, 'I've put this big beast in here, nobody touch it or it'll crash.'"

Larson gradually overcame her fears through experience with the machine. Other new users might look into joining a local computer-user group. User groups, located in major cities around the country, are nonprofit organizations that share computer information.

For a $25 to $40 annual membership fee, new members can ask questions of more experienced members and, often times, have access to other services. (To find groups, check listings in computer trade magazines or ask equipment and software vendors for group information.) Another support for new computer users is the growing network of desktop-publishing consulting firms, listed in the Yellow Pages under "Typesetting." These companies offer training classes to new computer users, and the best come with free phone support. ◆

2

THE STAFF
MANAGEMENT AND TRAINING

At *R&I*, we believe that "service is the product of the '90s." While menu options and food quality are usually number one on a diner's list of demands, getting (and giving) good service is becoming *the* most important part of the eating-out experience. In research with our readers, no single subject generated more response than "Ways to Improve Service." Thus, the second of our Core Four topics is service, which can be looked at from both a management and staff perspective.

In the '90s, corporate cultures are changing. Management is trying to "empower" staff people to do their jobs better. In a restaurant, this means, for example, that servers have discretion to correct situations on the spot without getting a manager's approval. As the management culture changes, techniques for hiring, training and retaining foodservice employees are undergoing significant modification.

In both areas, *R&I* reports on the human and technical side of these personnel areas. Our opening selections highlight the need for management to understand a changing work force and its attitudes. We also include proven service training techniques from expert Bill Marvin. Finally, we highlight staff incentive programs that drive successful companies. ♦

The Changing Faces of Foodservice

by Susie Stephenson

It's late morning in Chicago, and the foodservice employees at O'Hare International are making pizza after pizza for the airport's restaurants. At the front of the line, a Mexican employee pulls dough crusts from a mobile cart and places them on the assembly line. A Polish worker spreads tomato sauce on the crusts. Further down the line, Indian workers scatter cheese on the pizzas, and finally, Chinese-Hawaiian helpers scatter on the sausage, pepperoni, onions, mushrooms and green peppers.

It's an odd foodservice kitchen that doesn't look like the one at O'Hare—a mix of old-line Eastern and Western European immigrants and the immigrants of the moment, those from Asia, and Central and South America. And the waves will keep coming: Congress recently increased the number of immigrant visas to 700,000 from 500,000, with preferential treatment going to those with families already in the United States. By the end of the century, the work force will be about 12% black (not just African-Americans), 11% Hispanic, and 8% Asian-American. In one respect, the ethnic jumble is nothing new. Opening a restaurant is a time-honored tradition for immigrants, a tradition that has given rise to many a foodservice success story. Anthony Athanas of Boston's Pier 4 is one example; Cecilia Sun Yun Chiang of the Mandarin in San Francisco is another.

But from another perspective, this group is different. For one, few have white skin; quiet assimilation is not possible, as it was for European immigrants. Second, while some dream of becoming "Americanized," many want to preserve the cultures of the countries they left by wearing their own clothes and eating their own food and practicing their own religion. Furthermore, their clothes, food and religions differ markedly from anything American or European. Indian saris, Thai spices and Hinduism are just three examples.

The Impact on Menus

Since institutions get new immigrants as customers en masse, the new immigrants are having the strongest impact on hospital and school menus. The challenge is not to provide Americanized versions of ethnic food, but the real thing.

"We have so many people of Hispanic descent that we have to prepare authentic Mexican food," says Joe Martinez, manager of foodservices at the R.E. Thomason General Hospital in El Paso, Texas, a city bordering Mexico. "We do a lot of from-scratch preparation because our customers know what real Mexican food should taste like." For example, the department marinates its own skirt steaks for fajitas.

Fred Luberto, vice president of Luberto's Caterers, a regional company based in Moonachie, N.J., has faced similar problems. Many of the 1,800 employees at a Teterboro, N.J., MetPath facility serviced by Luberto's are Indian, Filipino and Pakistani. This is particularly true of the groups working the second and third shifts at this medical testing laboratory. Although Luberto has satisfied most of the dayshift customers by adding vegetarian dishes and expanding salad bar selections, he hasn't had as much luck with the two night shifts (of about 350 employees each).

"A lot of these people brown-bag it," he says. "We've haven't been as successful offering them items that they will eat." To help solve that problem, Luberto has solicited recipes from the employees, which the company's chefs are now adapting.

Making authentic mainstream

The changes in immigration patterns (coupled with a more well-traveled population in general) also have meant more sophisticated customers, ethnic or U.S.-born.

"What we serve is kind of a reflection of Sacramento since that's our market," says Russell

Leverenz, head of foodservice on the California State University campus in California's capital. "We've got everybody here—Asian, Hispanic, African-American, Indian, you name it.

"The range of choices when it comes to food is much better known than it used to be," Leverenz continues. "Customers today know a quality tortilla. The ones from some of the distributors, well, they're just like wallpaper. That just doesn't make it here. Customers today know what's good."

Leverenz says that in his operations, customers know the difference between boiled chicken and pulled chicken, between chili salsa and salsa brava, between paanang (Thai curry) and Indian curry. "In each case, it's like the difference between a Ford and a Toyota," he explains. "They're both cars but you've got to know the difference. If you put the wrong salsa on a quesadilla, the customer will know it."

Introducing "new" ethnic foods

But if your customers aren't sophisticated, how do you educate them?

Gary Beitch, director of dining services at the University of California/International House in Berkeley, has had the most success offering special ethnic nights, when the department gets a specific cultural group involved with the production of a menu and the evening.

"With any luck, students have friends who aren't of their background, and they'll be able to convince these other students to try the food," says Beitch. "We've found this process a lot more effective than just sticking a new dish on the menu, calling it Thai Noodles and expecting anyone 'different' to try it." Having ethnics cook the dish also prevents bland versions of ethnic favorites from creeping onto the steamtable, which might alienate more sophisticated customers.

The foodservice employees at Carson International, which operates O'Hare airport's foodservice, also get an opportunity to taste authentic ethnic dishes at an end-of-the-year holiday party. For the past two years, each ethnic group on the

staff has prepared some of its own food for the celebration. The individual members choose recipes and provide the company's purchasing agent with a list of needed ingredients (which Carson orders and pays for). The employees prepare and serve the food.

"We had foods from our Polish employees, our Afro-American employees, our Chinese-Hawaiian, Mexican, Italian and Indian employees," explains Betsy Marlow, assistant to the divisional vice president. "The employees put the names of the items next to the serving dishes; they dressed in their native clothing and they served the food. They explained how it was cooked, what was in it, whatever someone wanted to know.

"The first year we held the celebration, it was good," she says. "This last year it was superb."

The efforts seem to be paying off. Institutions are not just adding more sophisticated ethnic selections to menus; they're opening a more diverse selection of eating places. California State University/Sacramento, for example, plans to open an Asian restaurant that will include a Thai section.

Changes in Hiring and Training

Circumstances have added "teacher" and "immigration patrol" to restaurateurs' job descriptions. How do they handle it?

The language barrier

Many immigrants to the United States must take entry-level foodservice jobs because they're not proficient enough in English to be hired in positions for which they are trained. Some take English classes on their own; others participate in institutionally sponsored English as a second language (ESL) programs.

At R.E. Thomason hospital in El Paso, for example, a professor from the local branch of the University of Texas teaches four language classes each week. During two classes, she teaches English to the Spanish-speaking population; during the other two, she teaches Spanish to the English-speaking employees. The hospital pays for the courses. Employees attend free of charge and need only purchase their textbooks.

Carmen's Pizza in Evanston, Ill., implemented a ESL program several years ago. Owner Jose Venzor helped start an adult learning center in Evanston that provides an instructor and all course material for $30 an hour. He covers the

---

WHAT PEOPLE FROM OTHER COUNTRIES THINK OF US

Just as foreign cultures have become identified with certain habits, so has the American culture to those seeing it from the outside. Below are some impressions gathered from foreign visitors to the United States:

INDIA: "Americans seem to be in a perpetual hurry. Just watch the way they walk down the street. They never allow themselves the leisure to enjoy life; there are too many things to do."

KENYA: "Americans appear to us rather distant. They are not really as close to other people, even fellow Americans, as Americans overseas tend to portray. It's almost as if an American says, 'I won't let you get too close to me.' It's like building a wall."

TURKEY: "Once we were out in a rural area in the middle of nowhere and saw an American come to a stop sign. Though he could see in both directions for miles and no traffic was coming, he still stopped!"

INDONESIA: "In the United States everything has to be talked about and analyzed. Even the littlest things have to be 'Why, Why, Why?' I get a headache from such persistent questions."

ETHIOPIA: "The American is very explicit; he wants a yes or no. If someone tries to speak figuratively, the American is confused."

Source: *International Dimension of Organizational Behavior*, Nancy J. Adler (Boston: Kent International Business Series, 1986)

---

expenses for employees and their families.

The need for such programs is great. At Thomason, all dietitians are bilingual, and when a person calls the hospital, the recorded message (to help people direct their calls) is given in English and then Spanish.

Yet not all facilities can provide language training. "We're suffering the budget crunch just like everyone else," says the foodservice director at a college on the West Coast. "The college just isn't about to put up the money for any kind of language or diversity programs for the employees."

This director notes that ethnic students tend to be the children of wealthy foreigners and are already adept at the English language. That's less the case with ethnic foodservice employees. "Not very many of the refugees from El Salvador are trained as chefs. Or in English for that matter," he says. "They're coming in at entry-level positions and, unfortunately, they're channeled and trained to stay right there."

Making do

But a lot of foodservice employers just make do. They've been dealing with immigrants for years and know employees will find ways to talk to one another even if they don't speak the same language.

"If someone doesn't understand our Chinese manager, he just asks her to repeat what she is saying, or to draw a picture or to get a translator," says a college foodservice director. "It works out in the end. The message gets across. We just don't make a big deal about it. We've all just got to learn to be a bit more patient, a bit more flexible."

"Our substitute foodservice employees come 'off the street,'" says Richard Farrar, director of student nutrition services for the San Francisco public schools. "They work a couple of hours a day, no benefits. Many come without English language skills. But the jobs that they're doing require a minimum amount of understanding, a minimum amount of conversation. That's acceptable to us. And if there is a problem, there's usually somebody in the area who can translate."

Legal versus illegal aliens

Although not many restaurateurs ever talked about it, illegal aliens were the backbone of the restaurant industry for many years. (Few, if any, were hired by institutions due to more formal and stringent hiring procedures.) These immigrants worked hard, fearful of exposure. Most were underpaid, since they had no recourse.

But restaurateurs who took advantage of this dedicated and cheap source of labor often paid a price. "You don't know what it was like to have the immigration department show up at your place at 11 in the morning and you stood there and watched all your help either flee or be taken away by the authorities," says one New York restaurant owner who acknowledges there were illegals in his operation. "It created chaos in the kitchen."

To some degree, this situation changed in 1986, when a new immigration law sought to curtail the flow of illegal aliens by prohibiting their employment (shifting the onus to the employer), thus cutting off the supply of jobs that pulled many aliens to this country. This approach has worked, except the market in forged papers now flourishes.

Quotas

As the 1990s move forward and more immigrants come to this land, more whites might begin to believe that they have the disadvantage; that affirmative action doesn't work and isn't fair to them. Recession will only exacerbate the problem.

Yet experts agree that a diverse group of people makes for a more dynamic workplace. "Some managers describe multicultural organizations as more flexible and open to new ideas," writes international business author Nancy J. Adler in her book *International Dimensions of Organizational Behavior*. "Others stress the ability of multicultural organizations to understand customers' needs better, for example, to tailor their marketing campaigns to the nationality of their clients. Others note the multiple perspectives brought to problem solving and the increased ability to avoid 'groupthink.'"

Those in foodservice echo the author's opinions, reveling in the new ideas, the different views that come from a culturally diverse group of employees. And finding someone who knows not only what authentic Korean food should taste like but also how to cook it is never a problem.

Workplace Problems, Solutions

Because of differences in culture and customs, a more culturally diverse work force holds more potential for misunderstandings and uncertainties.

In one California operation, for example, the foodservice manager could not convince two male Hispanic employees to take direction from a female supervisor. "I tried to explain to these two men that the fact that the supervisor was female should have no bearing on their attitude towards her; she was their boss regardless. But I guess they had been raised in a family where men just didn't have to take orders from women, and these two just seemed unable to make the adjustment." The manager ended up firing the two employees and feeling he had failed.

A manager in the Midwest says her office had a Puerto Rican employee who dressed with much more flair than others in the office. While other men in the office wore pinstriped suits, white shirts and rep ties, "this guy wore dark patterned shirts, suits with wide shoulders and really thin ties," she recalls. "I thought it was great. We were so white, so suburban. We needed some diversity. But this guy made a lot of the rest of the management staff very uncomfortable. They branded the person as 'a Puerto Rican' rather than a peer because Ricardo fit their image of how a Puerto Rican would dress. They just didn't have very high expectations of him. I'm sure he was aware of that. It was easy to sense."

To prevent such problems and create a cohesive, productive group of employees, take the following measures:

◆ **Acknowledge a problem exists.** A quick survey could provide some useful statistics. The predominantly white (95%) University of Richmond has set up a diversity committee, a move directed by the school's new president.

"We want to take a look at a whole range of services and programs and the ethos of the campus to understand better what a minority experiences on a predominantly white campus," explains Len Goldberg, director of student affairs. "We're doing some of the very obvious counts of how many minority students, faculty and administrators we have, for example, and what they do at the university. Now there's a large proportion in foodservice, maintenance and custodial, and those aren't bad jobs. But the experience must be supplemented by prominent minority faculty and administrators."

But the university also is studying the more subtle messages that it sends out. "One of the subcommittees has gone around to see what kind of art and paintings we have, what music is coming out of the public-address systems," Goldberg says. "What we're discovering is that we're sending out a very homogeneous message and it's white and male."

♦ **Form interethnic groups.** Cooperative groups reduce prejudice by undercutting the categories that lead to stereotyped thinking.

"Once you categorize people into groups in any way, you tend to like people in your own group more than those in others," says Dr. Samuel Gaertner, a psychologist at the University of Delaware, Newark. "Cooperation widens your sense of who's in your group. It changes your thinking from 'us and them' to 'we.' People you once saw as part of some other group now are part of your own. That's why team learning groups can reduce bias."

♦ **Create the right climate.** Managers, supervisors and owners of foodservice establishments must show that there is no room for any kind of racial stereotyping or putdown.

♦ **Appoint an ombudsman.** Some corporations and institutions also are creating an ombudsman position, where those who feel harassed can lodge a complaint that will be acted on, not covered up.

♦ **Require sensitivity training.** Beginning with next year's freshman class, undergraduates at Stanford University will be required to take courses that address the issue of cultural diversity in the United States. The University of Michigan will implement a similar program this fall.

Part of the sensitivity process is helping people and institutions rethink the ways they evaluate people and unlearn habits that can alienate or confuse employees from different backgrounds. For example, because many Asians come from cultures that place a premium on humility, they often have trouble competing with American workers. While Asians view personal assertiveness as impolite, their white competitors (who are still usually men) see it as the normal way of getting ahead and use it to their advantage.

It also helps to let employees be themselves when possible. At the MetPath operation in New Jersey, for example, employees are, where possible, allowed to wear their native clothing. And they must speak English only when they are actually working. "It just doesn't matter to me if everyone is speaking their native language during their breaks or in the dining areas," says Denise Stephenson, director of human resources for the company's eastern division.

However, not everyone thinks all this diversity awareness and training will do any good. "Look, I tried doing stuff like put together a baseball team of foodservice people who would play the custodial people to give us a common sense of purpose," says one foodservice director. "But that stuff is better for the theory of business schools. People feel more comfortable hanging out with people who are like them. The Latinos want to hang out with other Latinos, the Indians with the Indians. And nothing I do is going to change that."

Goldberg, from the University of Richmond, agrees in principle. "With the economy the way it is now, people are more defensive and more aggressive," he says. "They're more hostile; their future is more uncertain. You can be magnanimous when you're holding all the cards. It's a test of values to see if you can be more sensitive and understanding of others who are not like yourself when you're in more direct competition."

Will the United States, specifically the foodservice industry, rise to the challenge? Given the changing faces of foodservice, we have no choice.

Facts and Figures

The Hispanic population grew at an average annual rate of 3.4% from 1980 to 1988. Between 1975 and 1985, the number of Hispanic workers in the United States nearly doubled, to 7.7 million from 4.2 million, according to a Department of Labor study. The population of blacks increased at a rate of 1.8% a year in the 1980s. Immigration from Haiti, Jamaica, and a number of African countries such as Nigeria fueled that growth, as did a higher fertility rate in this country among blacks. The number of black Americans in the work force increased from approximately 8 million in 1965 to 12.4 million in 1985. In 1990, there were 6.5 million Asian-Americans, 30.5 million black and 20 million Hispanic people in the United States. While it is expected that the labor force will grow slowly over the next decade, two-thirds of the increase will be women starting or returning to work; minority males and immigrants will account for much of the rest. Only 9.3% of the new workers will represent the population from which nearly all top corporate managers have sprung: white, non-Hispanic, U.S.-born men. According to the Department of Labor, native white men now account for 45% of America's 117.8 million workers. Over the next few years, that share will decline to 39%. ♦

An Open Letter:
Workers Tell It Like It Is

by the Editors of R&I

Dear Foodservice Executives and Managers:

We are the hourly workers, the grunts, the sergeant majors of the foodservice industry. We are seven million strong, one of the largest employee groups in America.

Many of us have families and work two jobs just to pay the bills. Some of us are minorities who have been discriminated against. Some are middle-aged mothers who have raised families and only know how to be good servers. We haven't had much education or training. We come to you with few skills, but a big need to survive.

The editors of *Restaurants & Institutions* have asked us to tell you how we really feel about our jobs. We'd like to say we think this is a great industry, but the work conditions often aren't very good. We complain a lot, but then, we have a lot to complain about. The fact is that foodservice for most hourly wage earners means an endless round of tough, exhausting work.

Some of you understand, because you've been here. You know what it's like in the trenches, when the rush starts, the kitchen heats up and tempers rise and equipment breaks down and someone walks or gets fired on the spot. You know that our pay and benefits are lousy, and too often we are treated like our feelings don't count. Most of us are moving from job to job, hoping to get ahead or, better, get out and go on to a real career.

Careers are one of the things this letter is about. You need to improve career paths, so more of us can move up to become supervisors or managers. We want the kind of rewards we can put in the bank. Better wages, health benefits and a few days of paid vacation would go a long way towards making us feel appreciated. We told *R&I* what we like about our jobs—working with food,

the constant contact with people, the flexible hours. Give us more reasons to stay. You can start by treating us as valued employees, not cheap labor.

Sincerely,
Hourly Foodservice Workers

Here are the top issues among hourly workers.

Wages: At the top of almost every hourly's list. Everyone from fast-food workers to busers and servers agrees that they're too low. Servers say their hourly wage barely covers taxes on tips and doesn't cut the muster on slow nights. Busers, in turn, complain that some servers pocket a portion of the tips they're entitled to. And cooks are forced to jump from job to job to make a respectable living.

Benefits: Almost nonexistent for hourly workers and becoming nearly cost-prohibitive for those given the option to enroll in partially paid health-insurance programs. Insurance, paid vacation and sick leave are a reality only for workers in institutional settings and hotels—in many commercial operations, workers don't get so much as a free meal.

Training: Many hourly workers say training falls short of the mark. Full-service operators do better, but young fast-food workers complain about being thrown into the fray before they understand how to perform their jobs. Trainers tend to be co-workers as opposed to experts with teaching skills. Also, busy and understaffed operators don't have the time to train properly.

Management: Hourlies point out that some managers don't seem to like their own jobs much. Who pays the price for their discontent? The sweat hogs. Managers overlook scheduling requests, play favorites and ignore their needs. And trust between managers and hourlies tends to be a rare commodity.

Career Paths: The restaurant industry hails itself as the land of opportunity. Yet many hourlies complain that the wait for advancement is too long. Others don't possess the necessary skills to get ahead—and their employers don't help them gain those skills. Women and minorities complain about discrimination. The end result is disgruntled workers who lose hope that they can better their lives.

Position-by-position, here is what workers have to say, in their own words.

Servers

Although tips in a busy white-tablecloth restaurant can be lucrative, the reality for most servers is an uncertain income plagued by slow periods in the restaurant and poor tippers. The job requires lugging trays and being friendly to every customer—even the lousy tippers. Nonetheless, servers grit their teeth and bear the load because they enjoy the instant monetary gratification of a successful shift or flexible schedules that allow them to pursue studies or other interests.

Doreen, 32, full-time server for almost three years in casual-dining restaurants: "For all the running around we do, and for all of the times we have to bus our own tables, we should be paid at least the minimum wage."

Wendy, 37, server for ten years at a family-style restaurant and currently with multiconcept, full-service operator: "I get virtually no paycheck. It is very unfair. By the time I pay my taxes there is nothing left. We also pay a lot to the busers, so the company doesn't pay them a decent wage either. The owner is getting away really cheap."

Brenda, 38, server for 15 years in family-style restaurants: "We should be able to eat for free; some sort of hospitalization would be nice, too. We have a very risky job. We carry hot plates all the time and could fall down at any time. And we do all this with no insurance. I have been thinking about talking with a union to get some help."

Laura, 26, college student: "I had some insurance options but had to pay for all of them. I don't consider it much of a benefit when I have to pay for it. After a minimum amount of employee service, say one year, the employer should pay at least half of the insurance costs."

Holly: "Training was not sufficient. I watched a video about selling wine with food but they never showed me how to carry a tray. Then they put me out on the floor for my first time and told me to 'go to it.' "

Wendy: "They train wonderfully here. Any bad habits picked up somewhere else diminished in a hurry. Also, the busers were retrained recently and that has been a big help. They never break anything, and it doesn't bother me to give them good tips because the training makes them great at turning tables."

Brenda: "Management is OK. It is the cooks I have a hard time with. They will botch your order if they are mad at you. Then we hear it from the customers and end up with lousy tips. The cooks yell at the waitresses for other reasons beyond our control. We don't need to be talked to like that, and when we tell the boss about it, he only replies, 'Consider the source.' They won't fire the cooks because they need them."

Laura: "I want a manager who is real upfront about the situation at the restaurant and my personal financial potential. I want someone who doesn't play favorites and has real people skills to deal with frenzied situations that always come up on crazy Saturday night shifts. I would also like someone who knows how to deal with inexperienced employees like myself."

Sheryl, 18, server for one year in 20-seat delicatessen: "If I could tell my manager one thing, it would be to trust us more. Whenever a customer leaves, he'll say, 'What did you do?' instead of 'What happened?' It puts us on the automatic defensive."

Cashiers and Hosts

They do the seating, the greeting and the tallying at a restaurant, not to mention the soothing and smoothing of customers' ruffled feathers for an average hourly salary of around $5.

Hosts' duties include everything from washing windows and keeping reservation books to appeasing and assisting servers. Cashiers not only make change, but also track customer counts and how many menu items are served. While most feel they are treated with respect by management, hosts and cashiers complain about low pay, servers' demands and cramped quarters. On the up side, they all enjoy the daily face-to-face contact with the public and their colleagues.

Heather, 21, hostess for two months at dinner-house chain: "Hostesses get all the pressure from customers and waitresses. Everybody yells at you. What I'm paid is not worth it."

Heather: "I watched a video about how the job is supposed to work but, in reality, it is nothing like that. The video showed seven hosts on duty. The most I've ever seen is two. And there have been times when it was just me."

Flora, 42, cashier for two months at nursing home: "Training was good. I spent a day or two on every aspect of the job, side by side with someone who knew the position very well."

Heather: "Managers don't cover for us well enough. A manager was standing right next to me when a customer was yelling at me about bad service. I looked to him for help, but he just walked away. Later, when I asked him why he did that, he replied, 'I had better things to do.'"

Alicia, 18, hostess for eight months with full-service chain restaurant: "Managers try their hardest. My manager talks to me or has dinner with me. He's more like a buddy. I would tell the general manager to be a little more outgoing. He portrays the upper-class manager too much. He should take time to help us out and make us feel a little more important."

Betty, 62, cashier for six years at department-store restaurant: "I'm treated very well. The only thing I don't like is that my work space has been cut down to 3 feet since a candy counter was added."

Cooks

The tough job of taking the heat and keeping a cool head can pay off.

Technically, a line cook works the line. More

often than not, it means working the broiler or sauté stations. Some kitchens place line cooks in the pantry to make salads and sandwiches. Others are forced to do their own prep work in the smallest of kitchens.

Prep cooks cut, chop, portion food and perform any other preliminary tasks for line cooks.

Pay and benefit gripes aside, cooks complain mostly about not being promoted, not working enough hours to make ends meet and a lack of adequate training. Often they take on kitchen management responsibilities such as purchasing without receiving a manager's paycheck.

Line and prep cooks find that high turnover works both for and against them. When it comes to looking for a new job, it is fairly easy to find one. But when the sous chef quits, they are overlooked for promotion and the job is usually filled from the outside.

Most cooks work at one restaurant for one year or less because they have aspirations of moving up in the kitchen hierarchy, eventually becoming sous chefs and, ultimately, executive chefs. But at this lower level, few are happy with the pay or benefits. However, this is clearly a group of foodservice employees that are in the business because they want to be. They love cooking and learning about food. They are willing to put up with conditions less than ideal, but only because they don't expect to be at any one place for long.

Here is what some line and prep cooks say about their jobs:

Frank, 27, line cook in upscale Italian restaurant for past 1-1/2 years: "I work 35 to 40 hours a week at $6.25 an hour. I also work 20 hours a week managing a pizzeria to supplement my income. I recently asked for a raise, and when the restaurant is renovated, I will be making $7 an hour. But I don't get health benefits or paid vacation. I've learned that is just the way it is in the restaurant business."

Giovanni, 20, cooking since age 10, has spent the past year as a line cook for midscale seafood restaurant: "Foodservice is definitely a lot of hard work. I have duties and responsibilities of a manager without the title, pay or benefits. I work 40 to 50 hours a week and make $9 an hour, plus overtime pay. But there is a catch with overtime pay. I can work a 12-hour day without being paid overtime unless I work at least a 40-hour week. I think that is unfair. When I put in a 12-hour day, I should get more than a regular day's pay."

Liz, 26, line cook for six months in upscale Italian restaurant: "I've been told I can move onto another job but in reality I don't think I can. There just seems to be a lot of chauvinism. I don't know if that's the way it is in other kitchens, but that's the way it is here. I expect to be a line cook three or four years and get ahead as much as possible. I originally thought I would be at this place a couple of years, but now I'll have to see how it goes. If the chef persists in his rampant chauvinism, I might have to reconsider."

Giovanni: "There was no training program when I came. The chef did not really spend time with me when I started. I had to bump my head quite a few times until I learned on my own. The previous sous chef was a real jerk. He just didn't want anyone to excel. He pulled little tricks to make you look bad. But now I have developed my own training program for pantry and prep cooks. I've moved up two pantry cooks to line cooks and these guys are as good or better than I am simply because I taught them the ropes. I'm not afraid to do anything in the kitchen that is needed. Everyone else sees that and tries to do the same or better."

Brenda, 35, prep person, hospital foodservice operation: "For the most part, management listens to us. Sometimes with the daily stress, you'd think management doesn't care about us. But in the long run they do care and have my respect."

Dishwashers and Busers

Dishwashers—or stewards, as they're called— typically begin as potwashers and, if they're lucky, rise to the station of dishroom supervisor. It's hard, greasy work often relegated to black or Hispanic workers. Breaking down trays in a hospital or keeping up with the flow of dishes from a restaurant dining room requires not only stamina but manual dexterity and a keen sense of timing.

Duties of a buser range from filling water glasses and clearing tables to setting up buffet tables. Although some hope to become servers, others lose interest in that job after seeing it at close range. Here's what several dishwashers and busers had to say:

Victor, 50, full-time hospital dishwasher and part-time steakhouse waiter who has been in the United States five years: "I'll do any kind of work with pleasure. Some people don't feel the way I do, though. A Mexican guy who works in the dishroom says, 'Mucho trabajo, poco dinero. Much work, little money.' The benefits are good—dental, health, life insurance, retirement. A steakhouse wanted me to come to work full-time to do maintenance. But I decided to stay with the hospital because of the benefits."

Manuel, 43, floor supervisor in steward department of hotel banquet kitchen: "The highest wage here is $6.80 an hour. We should get more money. Also, the captains should split the tips they get for banquets after all the headaches we go through for them. But they never do."

Manuel: "The hotel requires workers to know English, but some of the hardest workers I know can't speak it and don't get hired. Once we are on the job, mostly we speak Spanish anyway."

Neal, 19, buser for three years at country club: "My managers yelled a lot about the little things. I know this is a country club and everything has to be perfect, but they yelled and embarrassed me too often. A lot of the waitresses felt the same way. I'm planning a career in the foodservice industry and would like to be a food and beverage manager or own my own restaurant. I hope I don't repeat some of the management mistakes I've experienced in the past three years."

Fast-Food Workers

Called upon by management to be the most versatile of all hourly workers, fast-food employees do it all. They take the orders, prepare the food and clean up the messes. Fast-food workers face the wrath of inexperienced young managers, yet sometimes grow through the praise of thoughtful ones. Some juggle a job and schoolwork, while others have to support a family. Wages and benefits are less than inspiring but as a first job, a fast-food environment can teach basic responsibilities such as getting to work on time, handling money and dealing with the public.

A group of fast-food workers told *R&I* what could be done to make their jobs more fulfilling:

Angel, 19, high-school dropout working for large hamburger chain for one year: "I'm making $4.25 an hour but would like $6 an hour. I have a wife and child to support and could use some overtime work, but the manager only gives it to me when it's absolutely necessary."

Lisa, 20, returning to college in fall while working 20 hours a week at large hamburger chain: "I really didn't get any training. I watched a video about how they operate, put on my uniform and was sent behind the counter. Another girl at my level showed me how to work the cash register. But that was it. Management should take more time to train us. Too many people get frustrated right off the bat because they don't know what they are doing. They learn only when something goes wrong. Maybe management figures it's a waste of time because the employees don't stay long enough and there is always a steady stream of applicants. But it's just a vicious circle."

Lisa: "I wish the managers would get together on policy and operate under the same rules. We get so many new managers that have different ways of doing things. For example, one manager, a woman, was real big on cleaning and always pushed it. Another manager thought that if you were cleaning, it meant you had nothing better to do and should just go home. These are two radically different approaches! They even differ on how much to fill cups. It is confusing for employees. What is the right way?"

Roberta, 17, worked at large hamburger chain for two years until parents made her quit to spend more time on schoolwork: "I was always busy and enjoyed the job because of the friends I made. But the managers kept changing my schedule, and I could never plan important events like a special rock concert. I felt like I didn't have control of my life. And if you were a 'good kid' and worked whenever asked, managers took advantage and asked you to change your schedule all the time."

Call to Action

To learn how your own hourly employees feel about their jobs, consider conducting a survey that asks workers what they think about wages, benefits, scheduling, career opportunities, training, role models and treatment by management.

If turnover is high, find out which competitors are doing a good job with retention. Ask your employees to check with their friends who work for competitors to find out what they're doing right.

Stretch the budget to provide a few more dollars for efficient and reliable workers. You'll be repaid many times over by their gratitude and improved productivity.

Explore alternatives for health coverage and other kinds of insurance. A group insurance plan sponsored by the state restaurant association might be an option that costs less; Wisconsin has a model worth checking out.

Consider providing flexible scheduling, paid vacations, monetary incentive programs or, at the very least, free meals.

Take a close look at training programs to make sure they are properly administered at the unit level.

Require managers to undergo human-relations training. More honest and open meetings will help create a better sense of understanding between labor and management. Give stressed-out managers a break from the job occasionally, in order to recharge their mental and emotional batteries.

Most of all, learn to listen to what hourly workers have to say about their jobs. Certainly, most operators cannot offer their employees the moon, but compromises can be reached. And sometimes just some honest concern can go a long way. ◆

In Praise of Waiting:
Exceptional Essays Celebrating
the Art and Craft of the Waiter

by Michael Bartlett

Hemingway's definition of courage as "grace under pressure" is one any waiter would understand. Hemingway believed you had to experience something to write about it. His particular arenas were war and blood sports, but he also appreciated a good meal and how it tasted and how it was served when it was good, as he might have put it in his own self-conscious prose. If he were here to read the essays following, he would want to shake the hands of the authors, because they had been there and had found words to express their experience.

These essays are the result of one of the best ideas authored in foodservice: The Year of the Waiter, a unique and long overdue search for men and women who can express their feelings—for themselves and on behalf of all those who cannot be so articulate—about the craft and art of serving tables in restaurants. As one winner said, "In the course of writing this essay, I spent an afternoon scouring the library for information on my profession. I found next to nothing—no biographies, no memoirs, no histories." The writing that follows is the first installment on a new literary category—the Literature of Service.

The waiter-authors come from all over America and all kinds of restaurants. They have loads of experience and in a variety of formats and viewpoints, they capture the alternate agony and ecstasy of serving food to others. For most, it is a career, spanning 30 years in some cases, not just a job, and definitely not something servile or temporary. The ideas, plans and proposals contained in the following pages form a combination Manifesto and Declaration of Independence for Wait-

ers. They are a historic first step toward educating an often ignorant and unappreciative American public to the fact that in our emerging Service Age more people will devote their lives to making others comfortable in leisure environments.

There are recurrent themes in these essays. First, there is the question of dignity, both that which should attach to the job and the self-doubt many experience about their station in life in a society that still looks down on service jobs. Second, waiters wrestle with identity. Many feel like nonpersons; some use analogies to robots, because they see diners treating them this way. Third, there is, on a positive note, pride. The best of them relish the challenge of satisfying the patron no matter what the situation. Finally, all waiters love to list the many roles they play in the course of a meal—diplomat, salesperson, arbitrator, motivator, nutritionist, psychologist, accountant, host, actor, choreographer, acrobat and counselor on food and drink.

If *Restaurants & Institutions* has anything to say about it, every year will be "The Year of the Waiter." Our own editorial agenda aims at encouraging more people to combine Hemingway's passion for challenging experience and another American Nobel Laureate's insight into the real nature of the waiting profession. As John Steinbeck put it, "Service is a position of power, even of love. I can't understand why more intelligent people don't take it as a career—learn to do it well."

Amen.

Following are just some of the essays contributed by waiters across America.

Dinner with Walter, Mae and Mikhail
Anne Tylar, Union Square Cafe, New York, N.Y.

A recipe exists for the perfect waiter just as one exists for the perfect sauteed plaice with *beurre rouge* and *haricots verts*. Just as seasonings vary from chef to chef, the balance of ingredients for the perfect waiter may differ, but there is a general consensus on the basic mixture. After five years in the restaurant business waiting tables myself, I feel qualified to disclose this carefully guarded recipe. It is two parts Walter Cronkite to one part Mae West, carefully blended with a cup of Mikhail Baryshnikov and a liberal sprinkling of Mother Teresa.

As the primary ingredient, Walter Cronkite encompasses a number of necessary qualities for the perfect waiter. He exudes an air of confidence and knowledgeability. Imagine, if you will, Walter approaching a table in a bustling restaurant. He would incline his head slightly or gently clear his throat and suddenly command attention while announcing the evening specials. No question a diner could ask would render him speechless for he would know exactly how the medallions of venison with celery root gratin are prepared and whether or not the papardelle of zucchini has garlic in it. Walter Cronkite is learned and well informed. He seeks answers to questions and is constantly increasing his knowledge. A diner on a low-cholesterol diet would feel confident allowing Mr. Cronkite to guide his selections, and the timid diner on his first date would gratefully permit him to choose a moderately priced Chardonnay. The American public *trusts* Walter Cronkite, just as one should be able to trust the perfect waiter. The vast knowledge, quiet dignity and aura of trust found in the Walter Cronkite ingredient are qualities all waiters should strive to attain.

Despite my admiration for the Walter Cronkite ingredient, an entire meal of him might be a little bland, which is why my recipe includes one part Mae West. The effervescent Mae possessed a whole spectrum of attributes valuable to the perfect waiter. Primarily, it is the air of temptress that is important. She could attract a diner's attention to the magnificent *coupe maron* dessert or to the deep-fried calamari with graham cracker crumbs and anchovy aioli. By varying the usual shrimp cocktail and sirloin steak routine, she would have shown a diner a "really good time." Mae also took great notice of physical appearances and would have certainly purred her appreciation of a clean-shaven face and neatly combed hair. Any good waiter (and certainly a perfect one), would also improve any dining experience by possessing a light-hearted sense of humor and adventure. The Mae West ingredient helps restaurant-goers enjoy themselves. She makes them feel catered to and that they have her undivided attention. Let's not overlook the delight any diner would experience hearing Mae say, "Come back and see me sometime."

Our perfect waiter recipe thus far has knowledge and personality but lacks finesse. The cup of Mikhail Baryshnikov includes all the physical demands of any waiting job. As any waiter knows, the job requires an extraordinary amount of endurance. There are long hours on one's feet constantly walking, carrying, bending and French serving. Although serving tables does not require the painful years of practice required of an intricate *pas de deux*, it does require a good deal of learned grace, agility and strength. Nothing alarms a diner more than a clumsily handled cocktail tray laden with frosty drinks, or, worse yet, hot coffee. The Baryshnikov ingredient is one of physical assurance. It is arm-carrying four dinners and side dishes simultaneously or maneuvering a tray with eight dinners in one hand and a tray stand in the other with grace and confidence. A constant sense of readiness is another important attribute of this ingredient. In order to execute his amazing leaps, Misha is always centered and prepared. In the same way, a waiter must be always at the ready, poised to change an ashtray, refill a water glass or to carry hot food. Lastly, a ballet is not a solo performance, it is a corps working together. So, too, a perfect waiter should be part of a team helping the whole restaurant put on a good show.

To complete the perfect waiter recipe, sprinkle the Mother Teresa ingredient liberally and fold in. In a word, Mother Teresa is altruistic. She does not bring her own problems to work but is there to serve others. She is not disdainful or haughty, but is giving and willing to help others. The perfect waiter must suspend his outside life and focus on the customers at hand. One must be sympathetic to those who need their menus explained in minute detail. And saintly forgiveness must be shown to those who never learned that it is impolite to snap fingers at a waiter or to blot lipstick on linen napkins. Patience is another mandatory virtue in the waiting profession. It is necessary to be patient with the hard-working kitchen staff during prime-time rushes. The perfect waiter must have the ultimate faith that the food is being prepared just as quickly as possible. Every waiter would also benefit if he could perfect Mother Teresa's benevolent expression and soothing tone of voice. They would help on that occasion when a customer's filet mignon with bernaise is overdone.

The recipe for the perfect waiter includes many diverse ingredients. Knowledge, trust, personality, agility, grace, teamwork and patience highlight just a few. Naturally, the recipe could be seasoned to taste depending on the locale; a pinch of Louis Jourdain for a restarant featuring French *haute cuisine*, a dash of Cindy Lauper in a trendy club or a dollop of Jane Fonda in a health food bar. However, the basic recipe is universal.

If waiters across America instill themselves with the confidence and skills exhibited by my recipe's ingredients, the waiting profession would gain in stature, self-assurance and worthy recognition. Waiters need to take more pride in their jobs because waiting requires a great many intricate skills and great waiters are often hard to find. Personifying this recipe wouldn't hurt our incomes either. Wouldn't you feel honored and delighted to be served by Walter Cronkite, Mae West, Mikhail Baryshnikov and Mother Teresa? That's how our customers deserve to feel—that's why they leave a tip.

Something to Sing About
David Deschamps, Jasper's Restaurant, Boston, Mass.

"Judging by the virtues expected of a servant, does your Excellency know many masters who would be worthy valets?"—Pierre De Beaumarchais, Le Barbier de Seville (1775)

When people ask me what I do for a living, I am often tempted to reply that I work as a psychologist, interpreter, instructor, salesman and stress manager. But I have a penchant for conciseness, so I tell them instead that I am a waiter.

I am a trained professional with seven years of experience at some of America's finest dining establishments. Yet many friends and acquaintances insist that my chosen profession is a last resort suitable only for vagabonds and transients. This is a fallacy, every bit as shallow as the notion that athletes are unintelligent or that philosophers are impractical. Fine waiters are artists: They exhibit poise, imagination, insight. It is time that America's waiters receive the respect they deserve.

Why is the waiter's profession maligned in this country? Part of the explanation is historical. Whereas the earliest French restaurants stressed variety and meticulous preparation, American restaurants circa 1800 followed the less inspired British tradition, offering meals that were "heavy and greasy, cooked and served indifferently." Given these roots, it is not surprising that France has produced not only a long line of first-class restaurants and master chefs, but also a consciousness that food is to be savored and that those who work with food are worthy of esteem. Americans, in contrast, have tended to view eating as a chore to be rushed through. This attitude is clearly documented by the popularity of fast food in the United States.

During the last 10 years, however, this situation has changed. With the establishment of scores of fine new restaurants, American cuisine has finally emerged from the shadow of French cuisine. Americans, reaping the benefits of this development, are gaining a new appreciation of food—and, gradually, a corresponding appreciation of waiters.

Although this heightened regard for food is gratifying to waiters, we would be even happier if the new American diner recognized that our seemingly simple job often presents colossal demands. Let me illustrate with an incident that occurred while I was serving breakfast at a four-and-a-half star restaurant in a posh Boston Hotel. A well-dressed businessman joined three of his colleagues at 8:30 one morning, told me that he had a 9 A.M. meeting, and requested two soft-boiled eggs out of the shell with pumpernickel toast and decaffeinated coffee. Because the man was running late, I had to cut in front of my frazzled co-workers to plead with the equally frazzled cook to give this order priority. Next, I attempted to locate the bread—only to find that we had "86'd" the pumpernickel. I called receiving to check if the day's shipment had arrived from the bakery, but it had not. As a last resort, I phoned room service. Victory! I dashed down to the third floor, grabbed the forlorn-looking loaf and headed for the toaster. As I inserted the bread, I uttered a quick prayer to the Lord of Toast, hoping he would keep the rebellious machine in check.

I went to attend to my other customers, who must have thought I was lounging on a coffee break, and upon returning to the kitchen I found not golden toast but blazing bread. At this point my manager entered the kitchen, asking, "So where is table 50's toast?" When I pointed to the wreckage, she sent out a distress call to the hotel engineer. He ambled in about 10 minutes later, carrying an old toaster that had been replaced by the new "labor-saving" model. Meantime, I picked up the man's eggs, dunked them in ice water, peeled off the shells, and discovered that they were raw. (I should have known that the Lord of Eggs would conspire with the Lord of Toast.)

Finally, around 9:10 I entered the dining room with a second round of eggs, perfect toast, an assortment of jams and steaming coffee. I raced over to table 50, rehearsing my apology as I ran, but when I arrived, I found empty chairs, not hungry executives. The men were gone.

Not all days are this harried, but many come close. It would make a tremendous difference if my customers knew that when I disappear, I am working for them. Furthermore, the fact that those of us in the service industry smile politely does not mean that we are dolts. For three summers, I worked as a singing waiter at a vacation resort. When patrons discovered that I could sing, their attitude toward me changed markedly: They began to treat me as an interesting individual instead of an automaton. What I wanted desperately to tell them was that every waiter and waitress—even the ones who are tone deaf—has talents and ideas. Why do we have to get up on stage before this becomes apparent?

It is unfortunate that waiters have been taken for granted. It is downright lamentable that we have allowed ourselves to be taken for granted. In the course of writing this essay, I spent an afternoon scouring the library for information on my profession. I found next to nothing—no biographies, no memoirs, no histories. Yet if we want to change, we must speak up. It's up to us to get involved in professional associations and contribute to trade journals; it's up to us to lobby for formal training schools for ourselves and better pay for our overworked managers; and it's up to us to convince the public that an automatic gratuity would elevate service here to the European level of excellence.

The bottom line is self-respect. How can we expect the public to recognize our contributions if we do not recognize our own contributions? The time for such recognition has come. As far as I am concerned, waiters have been an invisible lot for too long.

Suuuperwaiter!
Celeste Fraser, Savory's, Ann Arbor, Mich.

Years ago, when Ozzie whisked Harriet out of the kitchen for a fancy meal, little could recommend a restaurant higher than: "Home Cooking. Just like Grandma Used to Make." These days, Harriet's more likely to meet Ozzie after the office to relax over a dinner Grandma never dreamed of.

When Granny packed up her skillet, she also packed up Cousin Madge, the clumsy waitress who used to stand gum-chomping and grinning, scribbling down orders out front.

A new pride has emerged in American cuisine—a pride that has transformed the American waiter. No longer can a waiter suffice with more or less competence in serving from the left and removing from the right. Diners today cross the restaurant threshold into a new frontier, where the waiter must serve as a guide through forests of endive, over jalapeño hillsides, to shimmering chutney shores.

These new adventures in eating require of waiters a certain aplomb—an artistry if you will—in educating and encouraging modern pilgrims of the palate. Every master of the table acquires this art, in part, from the masters of the kitchen: Talking and tasting with the chefs make up an essential part of daily pre-table training. Well-fed, the best waiters then become as well acquainted with the wine as they do the chef; after all, how else to know whether to recommend cayenne pepper oysters with Chardonnay or Pouilly Fuisse? The best waiters bravely increase their waistlines in order to increase both their knowledge and their clients' enjoyment.

In fact, smart waiters find so much satisfaction in sharing their smarts in food and wine that they keep all talk of future vacations and former lovers to themselves. For diners who appreciate great food and great service also appreciate great conversation: their own. When not needed, the waiter retires back beyond ear shot, keeping well within sight, ready to reappear at the drop of a napkin, the nod of a head, or the emptying of a wine glass.

With the removal of a glass, great waiters can transform themselves into Superwaiters, ready in an instant to confront their greatest nemesis: the rush. Able to keep six tables happy in a single round. Possessing an intellect stronger than a locomotive, the Superwaiter can remember table five's second martini, table three's extra fork, and the lovely foil-wrapped steak for table seven's Pekinese. Order-typing fingers fly across keyboards. Near X-ray vision keeps contact with every client's eye. All the while the Superwaiter glides through the restaurant with the unobtrusive calm of a Clark Kent. No matter how busy, Superwaiter will never leave a customer hungry, thirsty or waiting for the check.

Professional service demands a high level of skill and with that skill comes a great deal of pride. I discovered that pride when I began waiting tables as the traditional "in-betweener," working my way through school. To my surprise, I soon began studying the menus as assiduously as I studied 18th Century Lit. Contrary to my former idea of the career waiter—poor Madge, who could do little else—I found my professional co-workers intelligent, talented and happy with their careers. Yes, careers, a new word in waiting and one that will take on a great new meaning.

Not all waiters have achieved "Superwaiter" status. I still trip over my cape sometimes. Still, as diners grow to expect professional service, the talent of waiters will grow to meet those expectations. Finally we shall have the American waiter at best: something of an artist, a little of a superhero, a bit of a pioneer.

Yankee Ingenuity
Lorel Nazzare, The Twenty Two Lincoln Restaurant, Brunswick, Maine

I work as a waiter at an expensive restaurant in a poor state. It is 15 minutes before opening. Tonight will be busy. I'll be responsible for about 15 people. My challenge will be to provide superb and appropriate service to a clientele ranging from fishermen and military personnel to L.L. Bean executives and language professors.

We are sitting down to "class" with Sid, the extremely demanding owner-chef. He explains how he assembles a chartreuse of salmon, asks a waiter what is in a dodine and lists the wild mushrooms in the feuilletee. There are nine desserts to memorize, including the almond genoise with a mousseline of mandarin, strawberries and raspberries. I try to organize them alphabetically.

My first table is seated by the hostess. Ice water in hand, I go to greet them. They are two well-dressed middle-aged couples who will be attending a musical at the local summer stock theater after dinner.

"Do you have Stolychnaya in Maine?" asks one of the men.

"It helps get us through the winter," I reply and win an approving chuckle.

I take drink orders in my head (no writing at tables for parties of four or less) and return to my station trying to remember some of the tunes from the show they'll be attending.

My second table is seated as I am delivering the show-goers cocktails. They are old acquaintances—both language professors at the small, elite college in town. I hug them, say "Hi," in Italian and French, and bring them a bottle of house wine I've recommended.

I notice that my show-goers are warming to each other's company and are obviously in no rush. I need to remind them gracefully that they must be out by 7:45 p.m. so I go up to them humming, "Get Me to the Show on Time." The vodka lover winds and nods. Message received.

My linguists inquire about the food. Sabayon comes from the Italian zabaglione. Pistou is French for pesto, and I endorse their decision to go for the monkfish.

The show-goers are ready to order and want a full Cabernet. I recommend the '78 Ridge Napa Valley and remove the white wine glasses. I clean their ashtrays (no more than two butts allowed). I pour fresh water.

I greet two Navy couples celebrating reunions after six months of deployment in Spain. They order strawberry daiquiries and ask what's good. I don't introduce myself because I sense they don't care about that. I recommend steak and seafood.

I serve up five-course meals and pour wine for the show-goers and take the Navy's order for steak, veal and squid. While clearing away my linguists' table, they start talking about a costume party we attended five years ago. "You two made a

fabulous octopus," I laughed, while noticing the hostess seating my fourth table of the evening, a couple of young executives from the nearby L.L. Bean company.

I dash back to the kitchen, deposit dirty dishes, order desserts, get coffee and remember to write down the Navy's order (octopus . . . no, squid).

Topinambours are more commonly known as Jerusalem artichokes, Dodine refers to the roasting of the rabbit meat before it is finely chopped and pressed into a baking pan. I could go on all night. Some tables demand that I do. Others don't care. Adjusting. Always adjusting.

I serve the Navy its dinner and the ensigns frown at the portions. I tell them my husband does, too. My show-goers get their coffee and get off to the show on time.

My yuppies are finally done quizzing me and are ready to order, and I see the hostess bring new folks to table five. Damn. A walk-in. And they look like low rollers. Smiling, I go greet the fisherman and his wife. He asks about the fish, and I ask him how the shrimp had run last season. They order champagne for their anniversary celebration, and I run to polish and frost the glasses and try to remember the story about the three-legged lobster.

The Navy asks for its check in a slow, Southern drawl, and I deliver it with a warm "Welcome back to Brunswick."

I bring elaborate dinners to my yuppies and they want to know how anybody could ever eat the entire six-course degustation on the menu. I said that my husband and I skied 20 miles (on Bean equipment) the day we came in for our complimentary degustation (a Christmas present from Sid).

The cork on the bottle of Schramsberg won't budge and the fisherman promptly pops it with a strong grasp. His wife and I exchange knowing smiles. After six hours, my work is done. I've made good wages for a poor state and I feel I've earned it all.

Stewards of Service

Charles A. Taormina, Rudolph's Bar-B-Que, Akron, Ohio

Service. Waiters serve as salespeople for managers, as employees for owners, as delivery personnel for patrons, as distraught cohorts for chefs, as celebrities for dishwashers and as egoists for themselves: struggling with the challenges of speed and space, timing and finesse, stamina and strategy, psychology and finance. Waiters, waitresses, servers, girls, guys, boy, man, ma'am, Sir, hey! . . . the titles vary with all the emotions colored by perfection or failure, the joking table rapport or the tense.

A waiter is the most essential focus of any restaurant and at the same moment the most expendable. He becomes the last arbiter of quality between the chef's hand and the customer's. At the table the server must act the friend and servant, mentor and expert, entertainer and host. He must deliver and attend the diners with promptness, accuracy and grace. Such concentration requires 110% of effort each working second. The performance demands quick wits and energy, but usually no formal preparation—so the employment pool remains forever large. Anyone can wait on tables, yet few excel at serving, and even fewer endure.

Cuisine as we know it in the West has evolved from the Florentine masters brought into France by Catherine de Medici. The extensive table routines hail from Czarist Russia. Our idea of public dining grew from vistas of the French Revolution where soup kitchens might *restore* us, in a restaurant: and the concept of gratuities began with small boxes placed at the exit of English coffee houses, where there was a sign above the coin offerings: "To Insure Promptness." This mixture of European sources has created our varied heritage: speed and quality. We are Americans now, cooking for and serving to, Americans; and naturally, we value our own experience. There is in this development a coming of age, I believe, which fine New World recipes and even our more popular foodstuffs indicate. We should hold a professional pride that there will evolve a truly American Cuisine as well as a particularly American form of elegant dining. This will complement other reputable types of faster, or more abbreviated, styles of restaurants. The waiter, of course, is decisive in this process.

The danger lies in forgetting that we are human. There is pressure here, as everywhere else, on increasing the volume and profitability of our food businesses, on efficiency and the glamour of technology. We forever forget that we created such tools and techniques, for our own use, as people first. That characteristic of each meal, the factor beyond the actual food dish and inviting decor, the all-nebulous or vague "emotional" quality or total atmosphere appreciated by the customer, is created mostly by the waiter. This will never be measured and should always be valued as a surprising, and usually alluring, component, which forms a diner's total satisfaction and therefore a business's real success. People serving people. But the manner of the server is an integral part of one's overall business format: Faster places display more harried and impersonal workers; the leisurely allow for the more relaxed and intimate. As businesses grant more attention to the numbers game outside, we must observe how easy it is to avoid the people scene inside. Each of our "bottom-line" considerations should become the same: excellence.

A waiter's role also serves our total outlook as a nation, as consumers and entrepreneurs, as workers and citizens. The waiter must work as part of a larger project, viewing the task as more than isolated table encounters for immediate cash. Along with the server who learns to appreciate the diversity of customers—new faces and stories and jokes and sorrows; the public, too, must perceive the complexity and drive of people employed in service trade. Restaurants have become a haven for society's gentler outcasts as well as artisans, musicians, actors, unemployable multiple Ph.D.'s and even our share of professionals. In the end, one can discern a nobility in this varied contact with others, attending to so many people's needs with a kind of stewardship feeling should leave one finally, humbled and inspired. Service. ♦

FIVE STEPS TO EXEMPLARY SERVICE

by Bill Marvin

Our primary job in the foodservice industry is to give our guests a wonderful experience. If our guests do not enjoy themselves, nothing else really matters. Think about that for a minute. Many operators spend too much time concerned with hiring, cost controls, financial decisions and marketing. They spend five times the effort trying to reduce food cost 0.5% than they do finding ways to increase sales and have guests return more frequently. In my experience, if you take care of your guests, sales will take care of themselves. If you take care of sales, the costs will take care of themselves. ♦

FIVE STEPS TO EXEMPLARY SERVICE

Why Guests Come Back

by Bill Marvin

To paraphrase service guru Peter Glen, good service is just finding out what people want, determining how they want it . . . and giving it to them just that way.

Good service is, simply, satisfying your guests. Exemplary service is delighting your guests by totally exceeding their expectations. For example, two teenage girls recently sat in a Spokane, Wash., restaurant waiting for their dates to take them to the senior prom. When it became obvious that the dates were not coming, their plight touched Beth Sayers, dinner manager at Clinkerdagger's Restaurant. She asked the girls if they would mind being escorted to the prom by two waiters she recruited to be Prince Charmings. With the requisite approval from the girls' parents (and one waiter's wife), they were off. The restaurant not only supplied the dates, but paid for the hors d'oeuvres the girls ate while they waited. Sayers even gave the waiters money to pay for pictures and other expenses at the prom. Commenting to the local media, Sayers said, "Sure it was a nice thing, but what the girls did was far more courageous. We had the easy part. In the face of embarrassment and humiliation, these girls went to their prom." That is exemplary service.

At the outset, be warned that the word "service" is dangerous because it can be too easily defined just from the perspective of the provider ("I can't understand why Table 6 is complaining. I gave them good service!"). Good service can only be described and understood from the guest's point of view. Even "satisfaction" isn't powerful enough. It only means the guests got what they expected, and simply meeting expectations is not enough to make you an example in today's market. Doubletree Hotels, for example, wants to provide service that "astounds" you. Play the game of semantics. Focus on "gratifying" or "delighting" your guests and see what happens.

There are many different types of foodservice, and we can easily get caught up in the differences between fine dining and fast food, or cafes and cafeterias. To understand guest gratification, however, it helps to understand how all types of foodservice are similar.

Monumental Trivialities

Hotelier James Nassikas coined the term "monumentally magnificent trivialities" to reflect his obsession with details. He built one of the most respected hotel experiences in the world, the Stanford Court in San Francisco, on his passion for attending to the little points that he knew were important to his guests.

Industry observers note that the distinguishing feature between exemplary operators and mediocre managers lies in their absolute belief in mastering the details. Many failed restaurateurs have learned this lesson the hard way. What they thought was trivial turned out to be monumental in the minds of guests who didn't come back.

Details, Details

To understand how minutiae can destroy your business, you must understand why people have a good time and why they don't. The answer is not as obvious as it might appear. It is, however, surprisingly simple.

You know from personal experience that when you are having a bad day, everything is a disaster. Conversely, when you feel wonderful, the whole world just works more easily for you. The events of the day don't change, but their impact changes significantly.

It works the same way for businesses. If you enter a business that has a depressing environment, it affects your mood and starts to bring you down. In your lower mood, minor events take on more significance. You are less trusting of people. You are more likely to find fault and complain. You are harder to please.

Because they are unaware of the importance of the atmosphere they create, many businesses foster an environment that almost guarantees their customers cannot have a pleasant experience. Just think of the mood you were in the last time you had to go to a typical post office or bank. These are operations that have traditionally focused on their own needs rather than on the needs of their customers. In doing so, they create an expectation of general inefficiency and lack of concern that places their clientele in a state of mind where they are less likely to experience good service.

Fortunately, restaurants have a natural advantage over many other businesses. Because people go to restaurants expecting to have a good time, they usually arrive in a pleasant mood. A higher state of mind predisposes them to enjoy themselves. People will have a good time any time they are in a high state of mind; any time they feel good. For example, just try to have a bad day when you're in love. When guests are in good moods, they are more forgiving and more generous. They spend more. The food tastes better. They are more open to your recommendations. They tip better. They are more likely to tell their friends what an exciting restaurant you have. All we have to do is create and maintain an atmosphere where people will stay in a good mood, and they will always have an enjoyable experience.

Here is where minutiae become momentous. People enter your restaurant focused on having a good time. Anything that catches your guests' minds can divert their attention from a good time and be a distraction. Distractions change a person's mood. Every distraction is like tying a small weight onto the helium balloon of their higher states of mind. As these little annoyances add up,

they create more weight, pulling your guests' mood down. As your guests' mood drops, their thoughts become more negative. They are more critical and abrupt with your staff. Your staff, in turn, can easily become less responsive to these suddenly impolite people. The experience can spiral down quickly for everyone. When a guest is in a lower mood, even the finest food and service will draw complaints. You can't fix it. It is just the way people view the world when they are in a low state of mind.

The things that kill you are seemingly insignificant items—momentous minutiae—that can distract your guests and affect their mood. No one who has ever been in the business would deny that foodservice is a game of details. Still, the price of success in our industry is attention to the small points.

Missing some points means obvious sudden death. For example, if you send guests to the hospital with food poisoning, don't expect to see them back as patrons. If your staff embarrasses a businessperson in front of clients during an important luncheon, that guest is history. Most of the points are not as terminal as that. They are just distractions and petty annoyances. But remember the idea of weights on the balloon.

Why Guests Don't Come Back

It might help to think of the quality of your guests' dining experience as a game. Because people want to have a good time in restaurants, you start this game with a perfect score, say 100 points. As guests approach the restaurant and progress through their meal, you gain or lose points.

How you handle the details of the business can raise or lower your score. Most service lapses are things for which you will lose points when they happen, but you won't necessarily gain points if they don't. On the plus side, there are a few unexpected touches for which you can gain points and improve your score.

There is no particular point value to anything other than the value arbitrarily given by the guest. For example, something one person might not even notice could cause someone else to walk out in a rage.

Your guests are not aware of it, but they keep a mental score. As they leave the restaurant, they assign a subconscious point total to their experience. The more positive their experience, the higher your score. Your point total also has relevance in comparison to your competition. If, for example, you receive 75 points and your competitors are scoring 70, you will be the restaurant of choice. Let a competitor get 80 points, and you will be in trouble.

One other consideration: The higher the check average, the higher the necessary point total to satisfy your guests. People have higher expectations of a $50 dinner than they do of a fast-food lunch . . . and they should!

If you score higher than people expected, they will love you, at least for now. If you score less than they expected, no matter how good a job you do, you won't be on their "A" list. Worse yet, if you are inconsistent, up one time and down the next, your guests will not trust you. When people mistrust your restaurant, you must score higher to reach the same level of guest satisfaction. For every person (in relation to every individual restaurant), there is a score so low it will cause them never to patronize the place again.

What You Can Do About It

It is hardly reasonable to expect that errors will never happen in your restaurant. Nonetheless, you can significantly reduce minor irritations through awareness, careful staff selection, continual training and passionate attention to detail. It is important that your guests sense how important the details are to you and your staff. It is critical that your guests see that your entire operation focuses on their satisfaction, and that you are making a sincere effort to correct any lapses. This level of focus and caring creates and maintains an environment where guests will have a high sense of well-being.

Personally, I appreciate when an error is swiftly and skillfully corrected. It often shows me more than if the mistake never happened. Perhaps it is the human frailty and personal concern shown. If your heart is in the right place, you will not usually lose points for occasional oversights.

Keep Your Priorities Straight

Any time you are serving your own interests to the detriment of the interests of your guests, you are working against yourself. Repeat as necessary: "This restaurant is run for the enjoyment and pleasure of our guests, not for the convenience of the staff or owners."

Service is not what you do, it is a state of mind. But don't overcomplicate it by turning it into an intellectual exercise.

If you start to think of your operation differently, if your priorities shift a bit so that every decision you make is driven by a concern for guest gratification, if you see a few new ways to become more responsive to the needs of your guests, then you are on the path to exemplary service.

Guest Service Checklist

To assess your level of guest service, answer the following questions honestly. Avoid wishful thinking. Mark "Y" if the results are always achieved, "N" if the results are not regularly obtained and "?" if the outcome varies. For a more accurate picture, have all your staff members complete the checklist anonymously. It might be revealing to ask some of your regular guests for their opinions as well.

☐ The company has a written philosophy of guest gratification that is integral to all orientation/training activities.

☐ All company procedures and decisions are based on what is best for the guest.

☐ Management has developed an effective, well-conceived strategy for guest service that is consistently delivered.

☐ Staff members consistently focus on delighting the guests.

☐ Top management consistently demonstrates its commitment to guest gratification in words and actions.

☐ Managers actively determine what their

guests want and how the organization can meet or exceed guest expectations.

☐ Staff members consistently behave in a friendly and courteous manner toward guests.

☐ Staff members consistently reinforce the guests' feelings of self-worth.

☐ Staff members consistently and effectively convey their genuine interest in helping the guests.

☐ Staff members consistently provide proper meal pacing.

☐ Staff members consistently observe teamwork practices that focus on the needs of the guests.

☐ Staff members have a feeling of being professionals and of being important to the organization and the guests.

☐ Staff members consistently anticipate problems rather than wait until the guests complain.

☐ Staff members know how their work should be done and consistently meet job-related standards.

☐ Staff members provide proper answers to all guest questions or alert their supervisor when additional information is necessary.

☐ Staff members consistently wear the appropriate uniform, which is kept neat and clean.

☐ Staff members consistently contact their supervisor about potential conflict situations involving guests.

☐ Staff members consistently treat guests the way the guests want to be treated.

☐ Staff members consistently provide an equal level of service to all guests.

☐ Staff members consistently give their undivided attention when interacting with guests.

☐ Staff members consistently demonstrate the politeness and respect due all persons.

☐ Staff members consistently observe the proper procedures for resolving guests' complaints.

☐ Staff members never make excuses and promptly resolve complaints in favor of the guest.

☐ Staff members consistently maintain "smiling eye contact" when speaking with guests.

☐ Staff members consistently go out of their way to accommodate special guest needs.

☐ Staff members consistently acknowledge guests' arrival immediately and indicate how long it will be until service can be rendered.

☐ Staff members consistently observe proper telephone etiquette.

☐ Staff members thank guests for their patronage as they arrive and again as they leave.

☐ Staff members consistently address regular guests by name.

☐ Staff members consistently pay attention to details regarding all work that they do.

Source for checklist: adapted from *Food Service Management by Checklist*, by Brother Herman E. Zaccarelli with permission of John Wiley & Sons, Inc. ◆

Finding the Right Staff

by Bill Marvin

You wouldn't serve a sandwich on moldy bread, would you? Would you be famous for your chili if you made it with spoiled beef? Of course not. These questions sound silly because you know that you can't produce quality food with substandard ingredients.

On a similar tack, who could deny that foodservice is a people business? In a people business, people are your principal ingredients. The quality of your staff determines your level of guest service and produces your sales volume. The quality of your staff also determines all your principal operating costs. Yet many operators still try to produce a quality dining experience with substandard staff. It will not work with people any more than it will work with chili. Operators certainly do not intentionally assemble a substandard staff, but few would deny they could do a better job when it comes to hiring.

"My guest is the most important asset I have," says W.C. Wells, partner in the new Taylor Vaughn's Old Fashioned Dinner House in Portland, Ore. "I won't risk their patronage by placing them in the hands of just anyone. 'Warm bodies' are an injustice to me and my staff and a disservice to my guests."

Wells, who has been a restaurateur in the Northwest for more than 20 years, is proud of the fact that it is difficult to qualify as a member of his staff. "We screen applicants thoroughly, check all references carefully and conduct at least three interviews to be sure we get the best people. It takes time, but it is well worth it. The real value to our operation is that we create stability and consistent high standards in our company culture, and we think this helps good workers become excellent workers." Is all this concern worth it? Wells reports that sales in his 150-seat restaurant have increased by 10% every week since he opened.

In the real world of foodservice, it seems that there is seldom enough time to spend on the hiring process, largely because managers have to spend too much time cleaning up the messes made by the marginal workers who are there because there wasn't enough time to spend in the hiring process! Does this sound familiar?

You know that warm bodies make for lukewarm business, but how can you break the cycle? It seems that you have to be a human resources expert, but who has the time to study personnel theory when there are meals to serve and a business to operate? These days, simply staying current on labor laws and regulations can be a career in itself! No matter how well-written, personnel books are seldom specific to the needs of the hospitality industry and all require the operator to interpret and adapt the information before it can be used. I can't speak for you, but I always had more pressing issues to deal with.

Years of frustration (30 in the foodservice industry, to be exact) led me to develop the Foolproof Foodservice Selection System. The system is a plan for creating a quality foodservice staff. Without a plan, you are just making things up, and you run the risk of making mistakes, either by hiring the wrong person or by violating employment laws. Without a plan, hiring takes more time and produces more stress. Worse than that, you don't get the best people, and that is the greatest loss of all.

The Role of Tests

Some companies have elevated pre-employment testing to an art form. Armed with a battery of personality profiles, honesty tests and psychological probes into every imaginable corner of a person's psyche, they attempt to determine the best candidates for a job opening. Structured tests are clearly preferable to the typical "chemistry test" (the "do I like you?" judgment) that defines the hiring process in many operations. Still, structured tests can be expensive, and they do not eliminate the need for a complete interview and background check. For most foodservice operations, structured industrial tests are overkill.

The Foolproof Foodservice Selection System uses four general types of tests:

Screening tests identify candidates most likely to be successful in various positions. Screening tests help you quickly separate applicants with good potential from those who are unlikely to be as productive. In this way, interview time is only spent with qualified prospects.

Professional tests for management staff, production staff, service staff and beverage staff identify professional knowledge. The first professional test is a screening test to identify those applicants who obviously have no familiarity with the technical basics of the position. This does not automatically eliminate someone with no prior knowledge, but alerts you to those whose aspirations exceed their qualifications. The second professional test is a lengthy (150-question) examination of technical and professional knowledge. The second test in particular provides an excellent outline for future staff training.

Demonstration tests identify proficiency in specific job-related skills and measure the practical aspects of job performance. Demonstration tests also verify the candidate's ability to meet physical requirements of the job, such as lifting.

Situation tests are plausible foodservice scenarios that place applicants in a sticky situation and ask them how they would handle it. Situation tests indicate how the candidate's mind works, give an insight into their professional perspective and help gauge their priorities under stress.

The Screening Interview

Within this space, it is not possible to deal with all of these elements. (For more information, see *The Foolproof Foodservice Selection System* by Bill Marvin. New York: John Wiley & Sons, 1993.) Here is a simple first step that will start improving your odds of selecting from a more qualified pool of applicants: Before spending your scarce time conducting full-blown interviews, give all applicants a Screening Interview that will measure general foodservice success potential.

The screening interview measures the four characteristics that describe every individual who is a successful, productive staff member: extroverted, proud, responsible and energetic. Screening for these attributes will help you find candidates who will make every effort to satisfy your guests and are appropriately sales- and results-oriented.

Extroversion: Extroverts are people-oriented individuals. Their behavior indicates a sincere desire to be liked by others. This is particularly important for guest-contact staff because these people need to be very outgoing and interact positively with people. An outgoing nature may be less critical in production positions, but it certainly makes for a more pleasant working environment. Extroverts are generally positive people with good social skills. Extroverts are assertive enough to state their opinions clearly and concisely without stepping on anyone's toes.

Pride: People with a high degree of pride view their work and other areas of their life as very important. They have a high need to be a part of successful activities. People with high levels of pride are particular about doing their job not only correctly, but the best possible way. Proud individuals are significant contributors to the overall success of any work setting or project. Proud people take a personal investment in your restaurant not only being successful, but also being viewed as one of the best restaurants in your community.

Responsibility: A responsible individual follows through on commitments within a defined time frame. Responsible people feel accountable for producing a quality effort while they are "on the clock" and are likely to provide a quality dining experience and value-added service to every guest and in every job-related task they do.

Energy: Foodservice is extremely fast-paced and requires people who demonstrate high energy levels and the ability to move quickly and appropriately under pressure. People with high energy levels often have varied interests and are involved in a number of outside activities. They usually divide their time and energy among a number of interests. With proper direction and guidance, highly active people are likely to accomplish much more in shorter time frames and be more accurate in their work than inactive people.

These qualities are important success factors for all foodservice positions. You may choose to give different weight to certain factors. For example, extroversion may be less of an issue in production positions where there is no guest contact. Still, the Screening Interview is extremely effective. Let me relate a personal example to illustrate what I mean.

I was the foodservice director for the U.S. Olympic Training Center when the World Cycling Championships, one of the world's largest sporting events, were held in Colorado Springs. This event had never been held in the United States before, so there were no precedents and no idea what to expect. The event organizers asked me to handle the concessions, catering and hospitality tents for the two weeks of competition. Of course, during the time the event was in progress, we would have a full house at the Training Center, so I could not use any of my regular foodservice staff.

The challenge was to create an organization of about 150 people from scratch, run it at full speed for two weeks and then send everyone home. There would be just one opportunity to get the right people, and if they didn't work out, there would be no time to find replacements. I expected about 250 people to apply for jobs, but had no

idea how to go about selecting the people it would take. As fortune would have it, I attended a conference two weeks before the event and found my answer.

A major full-service restaurant chain noticed that some of its staff members did a much better job than others, even though all had been hired the same way and should have been more equally qualified. In trying to uncover the reason, the chain's managers found that the exceptional performers tended to answer interview questions differently than the mediocre employees, even though the lackluster ones gave basically correct replies. The chain researched this discovery and developed a list of 14 simple questions along with the desired type of answers.

Interviewers score the answers on an all-or-nothing basis: an applicant either received a point or not depending on whether their response matched the "positive" answer expected from outstanding workers. At the time, I really didn't care if the system was accurate or not! I just wanted a way, any way, to make staff selections without spending a lot of time doing interviews!

As expected, we had a huge response to our newspaper ad. After giving a presentation to the entire group on the available jobs, the foodservice organization and the hiring process, we had everyone fill out an application and talk with an interviewer. The interviewer simply asked the 14 questions on the Screening Interview. Six people asked the questions and we screened 265 people in just over an hour.

The Screening Interview was the extent of our selection process. After totaling the individual scores, we began assigning shifts starting with those who scored highest, working our way down the list until our schedule was filled. The last people assigned were a few who had scored in the middle of the point scale. Once the staff was in place, we promptly forgot about the scores and went to work.

The first week of racing started fast and got busier, but my rookie crew handled it in stride. Only two people failed to report for work, and everyone did a tremendous job, performing their tasks well and keeping a sense of humor in the middle of what was frequently an improvised situation. I couldn't have been more pleased!

At the end of that first week, we had a few days off before the final races. Since we didn't need as many staff for the rest of the events, we decided to give the extra hours to our very best workers. My supervisors selected their "star performers" based on work performance. When I pulled their applications, I was shocked! All of our exceptional workers had scored in the top third on the Screening Interview!

Scoring the Screening Interview

The Foolproof Foodservice Selection System scoring allows for answers that are not clearly positive or negative. The possible interviewer responses are "yes," "no" and "maybe," where "yes" is worth two points, "maybe" is worth one point and no points are awarded for a "no." The highest possible score is 28 points. Scores over 22 on the Screening Interview indicate prime candidates, while scores of 18 to 22 suggest marginal applicants. Different interviewers could interpret a particular answer differently, but personal interpretations are unlikely to yield a score that will materially misrepresent a candidate's potential.

Administering the Interview

A member of your staff asks the candidates the questions; the applicants does not see the Screening Interview. The process is most effective when the questions are asked without lengthy conversation. Remember, this is a quick way to identify those candidates worthy of more attention, and the idea is to keep it quick. After greeting the applicants and establishing rapport, inform them that you have a few quick questions that will help you get a better idea of how they view the foodservice industry. Ask them the questions and check off your opinion of how their answers meet the scoring criteria.

The form is designed to allow the interviewer to concentrate on the applicants and not be distracted by the need to make notes as they speak.

Remember that you are only trying to determine how the applicants' response compares with the desired answers. At this stage of the selection process, you are not conducting an interview. Keep the meeting short and focused. Once the questions have been answered, thank the candidates for their time, tell them what to expect next and end the session.

If you need the position filled immediately, you might ask the candidates to wait in the dining room while you score their response and determine if you wish to conduct an interview. Otherwise, make your general observations of the candidates' punctuality, appearance and general interest level, and tell them you will call them later in the day if you want to explore the position further.

All other things being equal, candidates with the highest scores on the Screening Interview are most likely to be successful on the job. It is important to keep in mind, however, that the actual test score is less important than what the answers reveal about applicants' attitude and approach. Except in extreme circumstances, I do not recommend that operators use the Screening Interview as the sole hiring criteria. It is important to check references to see if the applicants are truly who they represent themselves to be. Several interviews, particularly if conducted by different people, will give a better idea of motives and patterns in the candidates' history and an idea of how well they will fit in your operation.

Professional tests will help you determine the level of skills a person brings to the job. Lifting tests will demonstrate the physical ability to do the work required. Situation tests will show you how the applicant's mind works. All are appropriate steps in conscientious staff selection.

Still, if you ever face a deadline while trying to identify the people who want to work from the ones who just want a job, the Screening Interview can help immeasurably. If you changed nothing else about your hiring procedure other than to start with the Screening Interview and talk to only those who score in the top third, you would be selecting from a more highly qualified group of applicants. ♦

Training for Exemplary Service

by Bill Marvin

"The most expensive training is no training at all," asserts Randy Thurman, vice president of Azteca Mexican Restaurants in Seattle. "When you don't train, you only guarantee dissatisfied guests, high turnover and low productivity."

The previous article acknowledged that just as you need quality ingredients to make quality dishes, you must start with quality people as the primary ingredient in exemplary guest service. To continue the analogy, even the highest-quality ingredients will not satisfy your guests until they are combined and modified by following a good recipe. Left alone, top-quality ingredients will eventually just become top-quality compost.

It's the same with foodservice workers. Left alone, they spoil. Think of training as the recipe for getting the best from your staff.

For smart operators, training is a logical extension of their guest-focused service mentality. But the prospect of creating an effective training program can seem intimidating. However, the following six points will provide a clearer understanding of the fundamental steps of training.

1. **Define positions.** Position descriptions are like a road map of your organization. Properly constructed, they help workers better understand the route you want them to take.

   Describe positions in terms of results instead of activities. If you call someone a server, they may think they have done the job if they simply serve. Defining results allows people to interpret their jobs in a way that works for them.

   My favorite example of the power of focusing on results happened 15 years ago at my first restaurant in San Francisco. I had the accidental good sense to tell my dining room staff to be certain that every guest had a good time and forgot to specify just how they should go about it. Walking through the dining room one evening, I was stunned to watch Sam, one of my best waiters, sit down at the table to take a guest's order.

   Despite my initial apprehension, it worked. As the party left, they were raving about the restaurant and particularly about Sam's unorthodox approach to service.

2. **Have a plan.** A successful training program is organized to impart proficiency in those areas that can be taught. Job skills, professional knowledge, company procedures and work priorities all are valid topics. In setting up a training program, ask yourself the following questions:

   What does new (and present) staff have to know to be successful?

   How are they going to learn it?

   Who is going to help them learn it?

   How can you tell if the training was successful?

   When you have answered these questions, reduce your plan to writing. Briefly outline the content, goals, materials and audience for each session. Be realistic. Limit each training period to one or two points that can be handled in 20 to 45 minutes.

   Develop your training program with the needs of your guests in mind. But don't automatically assume you know what they want. Many operators reasonably assume that a friendly, outgoing staff is an important factor in guest gratification and in most operations it is. However, a Taco Bell study determined that their customers primarily want food served correctly, hot and fast. The smiles and extra touches that are so important in full-service restaurants aren't as important.

On-the-job training is perhaps the most common industry learning format. Industry consultant Jim Moffa of Food for Thought in Grosse Pointe, Mich., suggests having the new server wait on the staff and serve them the employee meal. The apprentice follows the restaurant's guest service sequence, and the staff members offer their comments and critique after the meal.

3. **Impart perspective.** Truly effective training gives the trainees perspective on their job and the operation. People must understand how their job relates to the overall goal of the operation: making every guest happy.

Sandi Spivey, manager of field training for KFC, points out that responsive "front counter" service cannot happen unless the people at the front counter know how everything works in the back of the house. "If there is a problem or service snag, they will then know exactly who to talk to or what to do," she notes.

At the Watermark in Cleveland, owner Hap Gray makes sure that his staff understands all aspects of the operation. He requires new hires to work in other departments of the restaurant for seven to ten days before settling into their final jobs.

4. **Set a personal example.** To get the crew excited about learning, top managers must show that they are seriously (and eagerly) pursuing their own professional advancement. To keep their staff open to new ideas, managers should realize they do not know everything and that it is permissible (and positive) to learn from their workers.

I also recommend that managers take part in local and national trade associations, attend industry shows and participate in educational programs. Trainers, too, may have to look outside the organization for professional development.

The implication is that the best way to change your staff's behavior is to change your own. "I couldn't understand why everybody in the organization seemed to resist learning anything new," confesses Dan DeGrace, owner of Benjamin's Restaurant in Durham, N.H. "Then it occurred to me that it had been several years since I had done anything to improve my own understanding of the business. As soon as I started attending seminars offered by the state restaurant association, my restaurant's staff turned their attitudes around totally." DeGrace says turnover is down and sales for the first quarter of the year are up 30%.

5. **Involve your staff.** Ray Lindstrom, president of Seattle-based Restaurants Unlimited, notes that today's work force grew up in an environment where they had a voice in how things were done. "If their parents continually asked for their input at home, what expectations do you think they have when they come to work?" he points out.

Lindstrom and his partners quickly realized that the work force of the '80s and '90s requires a different work environment to really be effective. "We work very hard to provide a climate where our staff really is involved in the daily decisions. It doesn't work if you only try to make them think their opinions are important."

When designing training programs, consider the idea that people usually like to learn, but they don't always like to be taught. This supports Lindstrom's contention that trainees should have some input into their training. It also suggests that a lecture will be more effective when followed by a discussion. Discussion allows everyone in the group to participate and helps workers reach their own understanding of the material.

6. **Monitor your results.** A training program should be designed to produce measurable results. You do not have to beat anyone over the head with statistics. Simply posting the measurements without comment is the most effective way to deliver the message.

After measurement, it is important that you recognize and reward any progress that moves you in the direction you want to go.

This article might raise more questions than it answers. However, if it has started you thinking more about training, it has accomplished its purpose. Exemplary service does not happen by accident. It is fueled by a driving passion for guest gratification that starts at the top of the organization. ◆

FIVE STEPS TO EXEMPLARY SERVICE

Exemplary Service Guaranteed

by Bill Marvin

Jeff Kimmel recently bit the bullet and implemented a service guarantee in his 120-seat Poppyseed Restaurant in Buffalo, N. Y. "I realized that if someone has a bad time in my restaurant, no matter what the reason, it will affect how they remember their meal. I am going to take the hit for it anyway, so I might as well accept responsibility for everything that happens and make it right if necessary," he explains. "Once I thought about it, I saw the danger of thinking that because something was 'not my fault,' I could somehow avoid responsibility for its impact on the well-being of my guests."

The Battlefield of the '90s

Service guarantees. Some operators embrace the idea, some are apprehensive, but like it or not, service is the foodservice battlefield of the '90s. If you don't put your money where your mouth is, one of your competitors surely will. Those who thought that service guarantees applied only to fine dining were brought back to earth when McDonald's began advertising a systemwide service guarantee. Executives at the Oak Brook, Ill.-based chain say that if a customer is disappointed with the food, speed or manner of service, or receives an incorrect order from a drive-thru window, the company will make it up with a free meal on the next visit.

Executives insist that the policy is not a short-term promotion but a permanent part of their operating philosophy, supported by a major advertising campaign.

Is Big Mac on to something here? To find out, we will look at service guarantees in the foodservice industry: what they are, why they help, how

they work and what it takes to put a guarantee into practice.

The phrase "service guarantee" might be slightly misleading because the guarantee relates more to guest satisfaction than it does to guest service. A service guarantee is simply a policy, advertised or unadvertised, that unconditionally commits the operation to making its guests happy. It states that if the guest is not completely satisfied with anything, the company will make it right or it will not take the guest's money. A service guarantee recognizes the important difference between activities (staff actions) and results (happy guests) and focuses on the latter.

To the extent that they address their guests' complaints, most operations already have a toe in the water of service guarantees. Still, there is an important difference between reacting to the events of the day and actively taking full responsibility to make sure that guests have a great time every time they dine. It helps to understand that people don't go out to eat just because they are hungry. They can handle hunger with a candy bar. People go out to eat to have a good time, and if they don't have a good time, they have not received what they paid for. This situation would merit a refund or at least an adjustment in any other industry. Why should it be any different in foodservice?

The Cost of Carelessness

In my "Building Repeat Business" seminar, I use the following example to underscore the importance of making sure that every guest has a great time every time: Let's say a restaurant really blows it with a party of four. Let's also say that a typical guest dines in the establishment three times a month and rings up an average check of $20.

What is the cost of this incident over the next five years? I say five years because I think people have an attention span of about that long when it comes to most restaurants. The immediate loss per person is $60 per month, $3,600 over five years. If one person at the table has a bad time, everyone at the table has a bad time, so all four diners are a loss. The direct cost in lost business from this party is four times $3,600 or $14,400 over five years.

This is bad enough, but it is just the start. Statistics show that a dissatisfied customer will tell eight to ten people of the problem (one in five will tell 20 others), so there is a significant indirect cost. Let's give the operator a break and say that of the eight to ten people that each of the four diners tells of their disaster, only five decide not to visit the restaurant. This represents another 20 lost diners or an additional $72,000 in lost business during the term. In this case, a momentary lapse of service will eventually cost the operation $86,400 over five years.

Looking at the cost of guest dissatisfaction in these terms, the idea of making a commitment to assuring that every guest has a great experience makes perfect sense. It might be unrealistic to expect to satisfy every guest every time. Guests understand that perfection rarely happens. However, it is important that they sense that your foremost concern is their satisfaction.

A Potent Tool

Implementing a service guarantee can be a potent way to market and to achieve exemplary service. Here are just a few of the reasons why:

A service guarantee requires that operators focus on results. The only reason a foodservice operation exists is to make its guests happy. If that is not happening, it doesn't matter how tight its control systems, how clever its advertising or how large a profit the operation made—big trouble is on the way.

To commit an operation to ensuring the gratification of its guests requires the operator to find

out what patrons expect and that they have a way to be sure their guests get it every time they dine. This passionate focus on the needs of the guest becomes a driving force that will naturally raise the level of service and repeat business.

The average restaurant spends six times more to attract new guests than it does to keep old ones. Yet guest loyalty is worth many times the price of a single purchase.

A service guarantee forces operators to set clear standards. "Do the best you can," does not give workers much guidance. Compare this with "your meal served in 10 minutes or less" or "a great time every time." An effective service guarantee will establish measurable criteria against which the operation can internally measure and adjust its performance. Standards will vary with the operation, but common measurements could include the following:

♦ The guest will be welcomed to the restaurant with a smile within 30 seconds of walking in the door.
♦ Guests will be greeted by the server within one minute of being seated at the table.
♦ Drink orders will be served within three minutes after being ordered.

And so on. Committed operators will then adjust their staffing and operating systems to make sure that these standards are maintained. Exemplary guest service requires that the standards can be consistently met without making excuses for factors such as the day of the week, volume of business, unplanned absences and similar events.

A service guarantee compels operators to solicit feedback from their guests. As I noted in the first part of this series, the goal of exemplary service is to go beyond mere satisfaction and really delight the guest. This goal forces operators to go to the source (the guest) to find out how they are doing.

Looking for feedback means more than asking, "Was everything all right?" A mindless question like this will only bring an equally mindless answer. Operating under a service guarantee is an active process rather than a passive one. Studies have determined that only 4% of dissatisfied guests will tell you when they have a problem. The rest will just go away quietly and most will never return. While a service guarantee might make guests more likely to let you know when there is a problem, smart operators will not wait for their guests to make the first move.

A service guarantee requires that an operator focus on the basics. If an operation obligated itself to make things right every time a guest was dissatisfied or experienced a service error, how would it conduct business? Would you expect them to hire anyone less than the very best applicants they could find? Would they allow their crew to start work without extensive training or without clearly understanding the company's service standards? Would they fail to coach and counsel their crew? You get the idea.

A service guarantee obliges operators to understand their failures. One of the first objections many operators have to the idea of a service guarantee is that it is going to cost a lot of money. After all, free meals and drinks can add up quickly. The fact is that if the guests are not having a good time, it is already costing a lot of money represented by guests who never return; the operator just doesn't know the total. Putting a price on service failures creates a powerful incentive to identify the causes and solve the problem.

Seattle restaurateur Tim Firnstahl, who believes in the concept so much he even named his company Satisfaction Guaranteed Eateries, points out that spending money is really the goal of implementing a service guarantee. "The guarantee brings out a true, hard-dollars picture of company failures and forces us to assume full responsibility for our output. The cost of keeping a company's promises is not just the price tag on the guarantee, it is the cost of system failure." He notes that the costs of breakdowns in the system are not the same as the costs of employee failures. "System-failure costs measure the extent of the confusion for which management alone is to blame," he observes. "By welcoming every guarantee payoff as an otherwise lost insight, you can make every problem pay a dividend."

Successful Guarantees

A service guarantee has several important properties. First, it must be easy to understand. Your guests (and your staff) must immediately understand what you are guaranteeing without having to struggle through long explanations. The shorter and more unambiguous the guarantee, the more impact it will have in the market. To be most effective, the guarantee should be unconditional. Any condition will only irritate your guest.

Remember that guest satisfaction is the reason for offering a service guarantee in the first place. Conditions are often a feeble attempt to keep guests from taking advantage of the terms of the guarantee. The risk pales when compared to the cost of alienating a party of diners over the fine print. There is more to gain from the 98% who will be delighted by your concern than there is to lose from the 2% who might take advantage of the guarantee to get something for nothing.

An effective service guarantee should involve meaningful compensation. What you offer in the event of a service breakdown must be enough of an incentive to cause your guests to tell you when they are dissatisfied. Going overboard is almost as bad. The measure of meaningful compensation is whether the guests feel that what you offer represents a reasonable value for their inconvenience.

For example, initially Domino's offered pizza at no charge if it wasn't delivered within 30 minutes. The chain found that customers felt that free pizza was inappropriate compensation for a driver being a few minutes late. Domino's changed its guarantee to offer $3 off the cost of a late delivery, and discovered that customers found the offer more reasonable and easier to accept.

Effective guarantees are hassle-free. This means they are easy and painless for guests to invoke and collect on. If the process of collecting on the guarantee is complicated, it will further irritate the guest and actually be counterproductive. Payoffs should be handled on the spot, ideally by the staff member involved. Surveys reveal that seven out of ten complaining guests will do business with you again if you resolve the complaint in their favor. If you resolve it on the spot, 95% of dissatisfied guests will do business with you again. Beware of systems that require management approval of every guarantee payout because they only allow a disgruntled guest more time to stew. Unlike fine wine, complaints do not improve with age. In fact, if a guest complaint is allowed to linger unresolved for too long, an otherwise appropriate solution will only prove a further annoyance.

The very best time to deal with complaints is before they are made. Take the initiative to invoke the guarantee if your internal standards have not been met. Do not wait for the guest to complain before taking action. Exemplary service means identifying and solving potential problems before the guest even becomes aware of them. A final point to remember is that an effective service guarantee must compensate for the inconvenience the guest experienced as a result of the problem.

To make sure that exercising the guarantee actually results in happy guests, always replace plus one. "Of course there is no charge for the soup and please accept dessert with our compliments." "There will be no charge for your meal this evening and please use this gift certificate to come back as our guest so we can show you that we can get it right." Exceeding your guests' expectations in this way helps salvage patrons who might otherwise take their business elsewhere, spreading horror stories of your operation as they go.

Implementing a Guarantee

A service guarantee is not a gimmick or a marketing technique and, if implemented as such, is doomed to fail. To be effective, a service guarantee must accurately reflect a deep and passionate commitment to guest gratification on the part of owners and managers. Sincerity counts. Staff and management who are truly grateful for opportunities to pay off on the guarantee make the guest feel appreciated. It helps to understand that every cause of complaint identified is an opportunity to improve the overall level of service in the operation. Toward this end, it is important to see failures in the system, not in people.

Paying off on the service guarantee reveals exactly where you are falling down on the job. As long as you focus on system failures and not people failures, your staff will be willing to find solutions to operating problems.

But take heed: The first time you discipline a member of your crew for pointing out an operating problem, you will lose the cooperation and input of all your staff, perhaps forever. Even when individuals appear to be at the center of an issue, they are never the real problem.

For example, suppose that a restaurant has had to comp several meals because food was slow coming out of the pantry. One reason might be that the menu is overloaded with pantry items. Perhaps there is an item on the menu that is too complicated and time consuming to prepare and no one could keep up. It might be that a critical piece of equipment is out of order or missing. Another possible reason is that the orders are not being relayed properly or legibly to this station. Production delays could indicate a lack of training or it could be that the staff-selection system needs revision. Dealing with the system rather than personalities makes it safe for your staff to become part of the solution.

You might want to reorganize your company around the guarantee. Every element of your business should work in favor of guest gratification. This could mean new job descriptions where performance is evaluated on results rather than activities. It might require a thorough review of the company's policies and procedures to eliminate those that evolved to serve the needs of the staff rather than the needs of the guest. Repeat as necessary: "This operation is run for the enjoyment and pleasure of our guests, not the convenience of the staff or owners."

Most of your staff might find the authority to make things right to be an intimidating new power. While many operators fear their crew will abuse this right, the crew's initial tendency is more likely to under-use the responsibility. To effectively exercise their new roles, your staff needs suggestions and guidance as to what might constitute appropriate payoffs under the guarantee. I am certainly not suggesting that you establish a strict set of rules, only that you help your staff grasp what might be proper under different circumstances.

It is important that service staff in particular be trained how to respond to guest complaints when they arise. They should understand that never paying off is unrealistic, contrary to policy and makes a sham of the service guarantee. Be sure, too, that your staff understands that paying off on the guarantee is not a substitute for delivering exemplary service the first time.

What Have You Got to Lose?

Jeff Kimmel found that implementing a service guarantee is helping him get what he always wanted from running his restaurant. "I'm a small operation with a lot of loyal patrons. I didn't quite know what to expect when I made the commitment to a service guarantee. I was delighted to see that our repeat business was up noticeably after only a few months. Despite taking every opportunity to make things right for our guests, we can barely give away $100 a month."

He also has noticed that the power granted under the service guarantee has his staff more involved in the daily restaurant operations. "My waitresses really like the fact that we care enough about our guests to stand behind a service guarantee," he reports. "The volume increase may be due as much to an improved staff attitude as it is to the guarantee. I wish I had done this years ago!" ◆

Keeping Score on Service

by Bill Marvin

"I am convinced that the key to success in this business is to find out the truth from your guests and then act on it immediately," declares Carl Essert, general manager of Christopher's and Christopher's Bistro in Phoenix. "What counts is the results that we get, not our actions or our intentions. I cannot play the game to win if I don't know how we are doing with our guests." That is, you have to keep score.

Don't underestimate the power of keeping score. Scoring provides the feedback that keeps operators and their staff members involved in the quest for exemplary service, tells them if their efforts are having the desired results and gives a way to show progress toward company and individual goals.

It is dangerous to think that you are delivering a high level of guest satisfaction just because you have not heard any complaints. Statistically, a typical restaurant only hears from 4% of its dissatisfied guests. The other 96% just quietly go away, and 91% of them never come back. This means that for every complaint you hear, there are another 24 that got away. As Jeff Jacobs, co-owner of Carrol's Creek Cafe in Annapolis, Md., so neatly puts it, "No news is only bad news you haven't heard yet!"

Because scoring service requires input from people (our guests) and because people are all different, it takes a multipronged approach to be sure the picture we develop is accurate. In the next few pages, we will look at three primary ways of keeping score in foodservice: mystery shoppers, comment cards and guest surveys.

Mystery Shoppers

Mystery shoppers provide an impartial "guest's-eye view" of the operation. A mystery shopper is not a critic. The shopper's proper role is to be objective and observational rather than judgmental.

"We are reporters, not consultants, and it is not our role to tell management what should be happening in their operation," reports Howard Troxel, president of J&K Shopping Service in Denver and chief executive manager of the National Shopping Service Network. "We do our most effective work when we know what management wants to happen so that we know what to look for."

Troxel recommends that there be a standard format for the evaluation. The format should list the points of evaluation and assign a value to each based on its impact on the guest's enjoyment of the dining experience.

Troxel suggests that reports be scored by management, not the shopper. This way, the company determines how to interpret the observations of the shopper. If the shopper's report is to be used as part of a bonus program or evaluation, he suggests that the management and the person involved score the report separately and then mutually agree on the score that will become part of the permanent record. If the shopping service scores the reports, be sure both sides understand the standards and measurement criteria. Troxel also suggests posting a blank copy of the shopping form so that everyone on the staff knows what management considers important.

Sam Arnold, owner of the Fort in Morrison, Colo., has an interesting variation on the mystery-shopper idea. Periodically he chooses 20 people who he believes will be bright and impartial, typically friends and regular guests. He sends each a letter containing $100 along with a request to spend $50 in the restaurant and give the other

$50 to the person on the staff who gives the most responsive service. The staff does not know who these people are or when they will appear.

"It's not as expensive as it may seem," Arnold notes. "First of all, half the money gets spent in the restaurant so I don't count that as a cost. The money that goes to my staff to reward exceptional caring is insignificant when compared to the cost of not providing that level of service."

Comment Cards

Many people are more inclined to express themselves in writing than they are in person, making comment cards a valuable tool to solicit their feedback.

Stephanie Telesco, owner of Brick Oven Beanery in Boise, Idaho, has been using comment cards ever since she opened her restaurant seven years ago. "We've had great luck with comment cards," she reports. "Our card is really simple. We give one to every guest who comes through the line and ask them for their opinions. We get a high return and a lot of helpful information to help us do a better job."

Steve Madenberg, director of organizational research for Morehead Associates in Charlotte, N.C., has designed operational surveys for restaurants and other businesses for several years, including a detailed guest analysis system using comment cards. "In designing comment cards, we found that most people would not spend more than two minutes to complete one," he reports. "By keeping the questions simple and easy to answer, we have been able to ask as many as 17 questions without losing guest interest."

Here are a few suggestions for comment cards:

Limit the number of questions to those that can be answered in two minutes. If you have more questions to ask, have a selection of different cards that include the additional questions.

In addition to a locked box at the entry for comment cards, the cards should be postage-paid and addressed to the owner or general manager at an address other than the restaurant. Many people are more inclined to complete the cards away from the restaurant (remember they have other reasons for dining out). Using an outside address helps ensure that cards containing negative comments will not be screened by the unit staff before you see them.

Keep the questions clear and simple. Questions that lend themselves to a yes or no response work best.

Even though a question can be answered yes or no, use a response scale; things are seldom black or white.

Your measurement scale must be obvious. Be sure the scale includes a choice of N/A (not applicable). A scale from "Poor" to "Excellent" is common, although the terms themselves might have different meanings to different people. Asking guests to grade an item on a scale of 1 to 5 tells you nothing unless it is clear whether 1 stands for best or worst.

Avoid negative questions. For example, it is difficult to find a good way to ask people their opinion of the smell in the restrooms.

Ask for information that you can use. Asking if your restaurant is conveniently located is a waste of time unless you can move the building if the answers are negative.

Allow a place for the guests to provide specific comments or express themselves.

Provide a space for respondents to give their names, phone numbers and addresses if they wish. This information is essential if you are to respond to their comments, and can provide valuable information for marketing and direct-mail campaigns. If you intend to use the information for a mailing, provide a place for the writers to give you permission to add their names to your mailing list. This way, your material will not be regarded as junk mail.

Offer an incentive for guests to complete the card. Drawings for free dinners are a popular prize. It is even more potent if every entry wins something like a coupon for a free dessert or a glass of wine. Redeeming the prize will usually lead to the sale of a meal and, because respondents must include their names and addresses to receive the prize, you gain valuable marketing information as well.

Interestingly, it seems that the key to getting information from comment cards is to conscientiously respond to all comments, whether positive or negative.

I do not recommend that comment cards be tied to staff rewards or punishment. Rewards might encourage your staff to "stack the deck" with fictitious comments, while punishment will only make sure that negative comments never reach you. Use the feedback from comment cards to gain additional perspective on your service system.

Guest Surveys

The idea of keeping score is to find out how the guests feel about the food and service, so what better way than to go directly to the source? Statistics suggest that seven out of ten complaining guests will do business with you again if you resolve the complaint in their favor. If you resolve it on the spot, 95% will dine with you again.

One way to get the word is to conduct telephone surveys of past guests. This approach is a regular exercise for Tim Firnstahl of Satisfaction Guaranteed Eateries. The idea developed as an extension of his commitment to guaranteed guest service. "Once a month, using reservations lists and credit-card charges, groups of employees call several hundred customers and ask them to rate their experience," he explains. "We want to know if the food and service was lousy, OK, good, very good or excellent. If they say 'OK,' that means 'lousy' to us and they get a letter of apology, a certificate for a free meal and a follow-up phone call."

Firnstahl reports that comments from his guest surveys have led to new training procedures, recipe and menu changes, restaurant redesign, equipment purchases, and whatever else it took to put things right and keep them that way.

Since time is of the essence when identifying potential sources of guest dissatisfaction, Essert of Christopher's selects six guests every day for telephone follow-up the next day. Essert typically chooses large parties or groups celebrating a special occasion. "We don't call parties of two

because we can never be sure that we won't unintentionally embarrass someone," he cautions.

To shorten the time lag even more, many operators make it a point to talk with their guests while they are in the restaurant. One excellent measurement of service quality is repeat patronage. A good opening question might be "Is this your first visit to our restaurant?"

If they are first-timers, ask how they heard of the restaurant. Reinforce the wisdom of their decision to dine with you and notify the manager for a personal follow-up. It is an especially good sign if new diners were referred by past guests. If they have dined with you before, ask them how long it has been since they were here last. After the guests are seated, make a quick note of status, dining frequency, means of introduction, etc., for management purposes.

The best way to be sure that irritations are resolved before they become problems is through direct guest contact at the table. W.C. Wells, co-owner of Taylor Vaughn's Old-Fashioned Dinner House in Portland, Ore., has made this an operating standard of his restaurant. It is part of the job requirement for the manager on duty to talk with the guests at every table in the restaurant.

Keeping Score

While much of service is a subjective judgment by the guest, there are items that can be measured and tracked. Human nature being what it is, the things that get measured are the things that get done. There are no real standards in these areas other than those you develop yourself. To help provide a perspective, however, here are a few thoughts:

Repeat business: This is simply a statistic estimating what percentage of the patrons are repeat guests. Personally, I like to see 80% to 85% of a restaurant's patronage composed of returning guests. A certain percentage of first-timers is necessary to replace patrons who leave town and to provide for future growth. If first-timers are a high percentage of the total patronage, it might mean that guests are not returning and should trigger an investigation. You can get the information from small talk on the way to the table, use of frequent-diner cards, comment cards and manager visits.

Frequency: It is safe to assume that the more often guests return, the more pleased they are with your operation. Increasing the dining frequency is probably the most powerful way to build sales volume, even in a slow economy, because it does not require you to expand your customer base. If your guests normally come in twice a month and you can make them dine with you just one more time a month, that can represent a 50% sales increase. Frequency can be estimated by the same means used to project repeat patronage.

Satisfaction: Using the feedback provided by shopper's reports and comment cards, it is possible to grade guest satisfaction with the various

elements of your service program (taste, timing, quality, cleanliness, hospitality, safety, value, etc.). Converting this information to graph form and posting it will keep your staff informed and interested. A word of caution when dealing with satisfaction statistics: Beware of complacency. While a 95% satisfaction rating in an area might seem commendable, it still represents a 5% dissatisfaction. For example, if you serve 100,000 meals a year, a 95% favorable rating still suggests that there are 5,000 dissatisfied guests spreading negative stories about your operation!

So, once you internalize that the primary job is to make your guests happy, it will start to color the way you look at everything in the operation. When you reach this point, you will understand. Exemplary service is not what you do, it is a state of mind. ◆

Personnel Success

by Jeff Weinstein

With annual turnover rates reaching 300%, apparently the foodservice industry's problem is not finding employees, it's keeping them.

Some operators, however, do not consider rampant turnover a fact of life. Companies such as Wendy's, Chevys, Chi-Chi's and the Peasant Restaurants continually develop benefit and incentive programs, morale boosters, empowerment practices and hiring systems that help make their turnover rates the envy of the industry.

"Over the last three years, we have made retention the major focal point for our company," says Joe Talarico, vice president of training and development for Chi-Chi's, Louisville, Ky. "We talk about it daily. And our people understand that we focus on personal as well as professional development. We always try to develop programs around people, not professionals."

Because Chi-Chi's focuses on people, management turnover has dropped to as low as 21% early in 1992, down from 36% in 1989. Talarico says turnover at the general manager level is approximately 10%. For hourlies, turnover dropped to 120% by the end of 1991, down from 150% in 1989.

Other companies also can boast about their turnover statistics:

Chevys, San Francisco, has a management turnover rate of 25%; approximately 96% for hourlies.

Turnover at the Peasant Restaurants, Atlanta, stands at 20% for management and 40% for hourly workers.

At Wendy's, Columbus, Ohio, the ranks of general managers turns over at a rate of 20% a year, down from 40% in 1991, while crew turnover has dropped to less than 200%, down from approximately 250% in 1989.

What are their secrets to success? After talking to these companies and independent operators with a reputation for holding on to people, it seems simple. Treat employees with respect, praise and recognize, and give them a chance to develop, both personally and professionally. Those who fail pay a hefty price. Every time the Peasant Restaurants loses an employee, it costs conservatively $1,000 to hire and train a replacement, according to Director of Training Mary Reynolds.

Before you can keep employees, you have to catch them. "I'm constantly interviewing because you have to throw out a lot of hooks to catch a good fish," explains Danny Meyer of Union Square Cafe, New York.

Smart operators always are willing to interview a prospective employee, and they are making the process much more elaborate. For instance, at Union Square Cafe, prospective employees must go through five interviews with five different staff members who make recommendations to management. "It creates a stronger unit because management hasn't forced a candidate down the staff's throat," says Meyer. Fewer than half make it through the process, but Meyer says servers stay an average of three and a half years.

At Chi-Chi's, if a unit has a star server, he or she is asked to conduct a second interview with a job applicant. "The servers seem to know whether or not the candidate has the traits to become a team player," says Talarico.

Managers for the Peasant Restaurants are trained to look for service-oriented people, according to Reynolds. Candidates are asked a lot of situational questions to see how they think on their feet. For example, "How would you react if you dropped a glass of wine at a table?"

Peasant's management-interview process also includes a three-hour management assessment test, which evaluates overall reasoning ability, drive and energy level, leadership skills, social skills, objectivity, adaptation to stress and analytical thinking.

From restaurant to restaurant, the leading reason for crew turnover is an adversarial relationship with management. Companies that are improving their retention rates have refocused management training to emphasize softer supervisory skills instead of technical skills.

Last fall, Wendy's devised a system to evaluate multiunit managers' potential and developmental needs. As part of the process, each manager builds a development plan with training that focuses more on communication style and ability to delegate and less on how to control food costs and create profit-and-loss statements.

Wendy's manager-in-training program also emphasizes supervisory skills. Training takes place at Wendy's role-model stores. Managers are motivated to reach training-store status because there they are paid about 4% more than regular store managers. Every training store is recertified every six months.

To avoid promoting hourlies to managers too soon, another turnover-making error, Chi-Chi's has developed a 12-week stepping stone promotion system. Hourlies train at all nine restaurant positions and each week learn one facet of management, such as scheduling. Chi-Chi's graduated 22 people from the program last year, all of whom are still managers today. The program is administered by the unit general manager and supervised by a regional manager.

At the hourly level, cross-training appears to be one of the most effective retention tactics. Employees learn how to handle numerous tasks, as well as develop an understanding of the pressures involved in performing other functions.

"Cross-training ultimately results in a loyal staff because they understand the restaurant's system and are aware of what is happening in each facet of the operation," says Michael McCarty of Michael's in New York and Santa Monica, Calif.

McCarty's cross-training program works with incentives. Either a server, cook or buser will start at a training wage and receive a raise for learning each function. For example, servers start at $6 an hour as busers. They advance to runners and, finally, head runners at a higher salary.

Then they work in the kitchen for a week at yet a higher salary to see how it operates, learn the computer system and observe how management handles relationships between front- and back-of-the-house personnel. Finally, servers start waiting on tables at $11 an hour and progress to $14 as they master the wine list and learn how to interact with regular customers.

"The willingness of an employee to go through this process tells us about the character of the individual," says McCarty. "If a person can't hack it as a buser for a week or learn how to make cappuccino, what kind of server will he or she make? This way we don't waste time, and the person can quickly judge whether or not they want to work here."

McCarty is one of the few operators in the United States who adds a service charge to the bill in lieu of tipping. He says it helps keep employees because kitchen workers don't get upset about servers who work four-hour shifts and make twice as much as they make in eight hours. Hourly turnover at Michael's is approximately 10%, and even lower for managers.

Wendy's also stresses cross-training. Each unit has an orientation guide for each job function, along with a training video to supplement the 5-inch-thick training manual. Hourly workers are awarded movie passes for each function they learn beyond what is required for the job.

Hourly staffers also benefit from Peasant's intensive training program. Training programs vary because of the uniqueness of the company's 21 restaurants, but common training threads include:

- Intense wine, menu and plate presentation training, and kitchen experience.
- Learning how performance impacts Peasant's five-part formula of quality, value, service, decor and consistency.
- Familiarity with manners, service etiquette and key Peasant phrases.

Tests are given during the training period, which lasts seven days for wait, bar and kitchen staff, and three days for bus, host and cocktail service positions.

A practice that goes hand in hand with training is scheduling. But no matter how good a scheduling system an operator devises, foodservice employees must work when everyone else plays: weekends. To try to work around that fact of life, progressive operators schedule a maximum five-day work week for their managers. "If managers have time to take care of their home lives, they will be in a better frame of mind to make good business decisions," says Talarico.

So not only does Chi-Chi's stress a five-day work week, but the chain wants managers to take two days off in a row. The same is true at Chevys, where five or six managers are on staff to provide the needed scheduling flexibility. The five-day week is so important at Peasant that managers are not required to attend meetings if one is scheduled on a day off.

At Conti's Cross Keys Inn, Doylestown, Pa., owner Walter Conti tries to eliminate "dead hours" so employees don't have to report too early or stay too late. Conti's now stays open until 10 P.M. instead of 1 A.M. "The business generated during those hours didn't pay, especially when you take into account drunk-driving problems," says Conti. To save managers from burnout, Conti delegates some additional chores to the cooks and chefs so the manager can come in later in the afternoon.

Once managers and hourlies are properly trained, they must be given the responsibility to make instant decisions and a vote in operational changes. This creates a sense of ownership in the operation, a valuable retention tactic.

"The key is to push responsibility and authority to the lowest level," says Fred Parkin, vice president of human resources for Chevys.

Chevys unit managers used to report directly to the president. But company growth recently led to the addition of one layer of management. These regional managers operate as coaches to develop both store managers and hourly employees.

Most of the operational changes made at Chevys have come from sessions held at units on Saturday mornings. Over breakfast, senior management discusses with the staff companywide and unit performance, and listens to employees'

problems and ideas. Past sessions have led to the addition of a children's menu, new to-go containers, the removal of lard from most menu items, a free-refill policy and a variety of menu additions and deletions, according to Parkin.

Chevys also holds monthly meetings for all general managers and kitchen managers to discuss other operational policies. Parkin says some managers are demoted because they can't handle the participation. They'd rather be told what to do.

"But our system is not built on telling people what to do," says Parkin. "We give them responsibility, guidelines, and let them run within the corridors of constraint. I don't care how much money you give managers or how you structure your business, responsibility is the single greatest motivator in business."

Peasant also has found that making managers feel included also keeps them from leaving. Quarterly meetings with all managers cover sales, company direction and developments. Managers are given an opportunity to offer input, and a motivational speaker addresses a particular topic. The meetings also have a social aspect to allow exchange between managers.

Some Peasant units have employee councils that meet to discuss projects and solutions to problems in the restaurant. For instance, the council, not the general manager, will devise a game plan to fix a problem with housekeeping and cleanliness. "That creates a great sense of ownership," says Reynolds.

At the Hard Rock Cafe, Los Angeles, policy dictates that hourly employees have the right and ability to call senior management if they object to a decision made by a manager. "Managers know that every decision they make is as if President Peter Morton or myself were standing right next to them," says Vice President of Operations James Rees. "This open-door policy solves more problems than anything else we do."

While hiring, scheduling, training and empowerment tactics go a long way to improve retention rates, nothing carries more weight than salary and benefits.

148

The companies featured in this article are competitive with salaries and try to offer attractive benefits not available everywhere.

One of the most unique benefits is provided at Wendy's. In addition to a medical plan that includes dental coverage, Wendy's offers adoption benefits. Employees who adopt a child are reimbursed for medical and legal expenses and receive time off with pay when the adoption takes place.

In 1990, Wendy's "We Share" stock-option program was conceived to help management personnel see the long-term benefits of staying with the company. Each August, the program takes 10% of a manager's entire compensation from the prior year and gives stock at a designated price. Managers have 10 years to exercise the stock at that price. They also can use the profits to buy more shares.

"I hear store managers talk about the stock and how meaningful the money could be in a couple of years," says Reynolds. "When they start to talk like that, it helps pull people together and get them to act like owners who are dedicated to the bottom line."

Among the perks at Chi-Chi's is medical insurance for part-timers who work at least 20 hours a week. "A lot of part-time employees stay with us because of the medical benefits," says Talarico.

Many restaurant companies also give their managers a monthly food allowance. At Peasant, trainers get $100 a month to eat at company restaurants, managers get $110, senior managers get $150 and general managers receive $200. General managers also get $100 a month outside allowance to dine at the competition.

Meyer gives everyone on staff at the Union Square Cafe a $50 per month dining credit. But when cashed in, each employee must write a critique of the experience. "It helps us manage and shows the employees that we care what they think," says Meyer.

Incentives That Work

From quarterly bonuses to an impromptu reward of a trip to Hawaii, award programs are the most popular form of motivation and recognition today.

Here is a sampling of creative bonus and award programs that industry retention leaders use:

- **Wendy's:** Quarterly cash bonus program for managers who meet certain criteria, such as top-line sales, bottom-line profits and controllable costs such as food and labor.

- **Chi-Chi's:** Awards 22 trips to Cancun to field managers who increase liquor sales during Cinco de Mayo festivities.

  Five Employees of the Year win $1,000, a getaway trip for two worth up to $1,000, electronic equipment worth $400, a trophy and a trip to Louisville, Ky., for their awards and dinner with vice presidents. Employees of the Quarter get $100 and an embroidered Chi-Chi's baseball jacket and a $50 gift certificate. Employees of the Month at each unit receive $25 and dinner for two at Chi-Chi's.

- **Chevys:** The "Kitchen Hat" program recognizes continuous service by kitchen personnel with special Chevys hats, coded by length of service, and a check, ranging from $100 for one year of service to $500 for five years on the job. At five years, each kitchen worker receives a Chevys satin jacket.

  The "250 Point Club" rewards everyone on a Chevys staff with a embroidered polo shirt when a unit receives a perfect shopper's score. The "No Sweat" award is a Chevys sweatshirt for every employee who completes 18 months with the company.

- **The Peasant Restaurants:** The General Manager of the Year receives a trip for two to Europe. To win, the manager must live up to the company's five part formula, have the five highest scores overall on regional inspections, have the highest scores on dining experience as rated by the corporate staff, have a superior training program rated by Reynolds, have an accurate and timely administrative record, and post positive sales growth.

  Crystal items from a specialty store in Atlanta are given as Christmas gifts to all Peasant first-line managers. Hourly employees with at least five years of service can also pick a crystal gift, presented during the holiday by the general manager.

♦ **The Hard Rock Cafe**: On a spontaneous basis, as many as three times a year, President Peter Morton will walk into a unit and ask the managers to nominate and the staff to vote for the best employee of the quarter. The winner will receive, for example, an all-expenses paid, one-week trip to Hawaii.

"A lot of what we do is not planned," says Rees. "We give out club memberships to managers, allow spouses to come along on business trips or just hand out $100 to a buser who is doing a great job. The unexpected reward feels the best."

And then there are morale boosters and personal growth programs, which go a long way to make employees glad to be with their company and not the restaurant down the block.

Chi-Chi's distributes a pamphlet to managers' spouses that educates them about the long hours and pressures of being a restaurant manager. A video library is available to employees that includes personal-improvement subjects such as active parenting and weight loss. The chain awards ten $1,000 college scholarships to employees.

Chevys restaurants organize summer picnics and Christmas parties for all employees and guests. Management also is encouraged to organize and fund athletic teams.

The Peasant Restaurants read and post positive letters from customers. It offers a continuing education series, which includes a doctor-taught series on job stress and how to deal with burnout.

Wendy's inner-city stores form basketball teams to play at local YMCAs.

"Involvement" best sums up the key to retention. Owners and managers must communicate that attitude from minute to minute and year to year to create the culture that breaks the vicious cycle of turnover.

Make sure employees are told about company goals and visions, and their role in the dream. Develop employees with potential. Recognize and reward employees who meet or exceed expectations. Do whatever it takes to create that sense of belonging, trust and, most important, loyalty. ♦

3

THE CUSTOMER
MARKETING AND MERCHANDISING

The customer is the third factor in the restaurant equation. In the last 20 years, the average diner has become much more sophisticated about eating out. Boomers weaned on fast food graduated to theme restaurants and are now prime targets for new cafe concepts and fine dining. Customers want choice above all, and each group has its own set of choices. Smart operators are doing more micro-research in order to pinpoint their core customer base.

Once identified, restaurant customers must be wooed. Media campaigns, promotions, and discounting are three important tools. As we become more "wired" together via phone, FAX, computer and television, there is need to understand how to use these vehicles to capture diners.

Keeping them depends on how well they are treated during their time in the restaurant. For example, the all-important "first impression" is often overlooked. Operators who don't know how to market and serve kids cannot compete for Boomers with young children. Handling a difficult customer with aplomb can insure his or her return.

Finally, dealing with external influences, such as the media, can make or break a restaurant. When a crisis occurs, there are rules to follow. When a restaurant critic calls, what are the criteria used to judge an operation? These are some of the concerns addressed in this section on the customer. ♦

The New Demographics

by Karen Cheney

If Norman Rockwell were alive today, he would paint a very different picture of the quintessential American household. Just take a glimpse inside your nearest McDonald's. Two playful youngsters are choosing their own dinner, with little guidance from a rumpled-looking father. A Hispanic woman skims the *Wall Street Journal* as she eats a quick meal by herself. Four elderly people sit together, sharing their opinions on our president.

Understanding the finer hues of today's sociological palette is the only way to produce successful advertising campaigns. It's also the only way to keep costs down, says Kyle Craig, president of KFC USA. "I predict that dollars will go down in marketing because we're going to be targeting markets and reducing expenditures," he says.

Restaurateurs, then, must keep a constant eye on the patterns that define our society. To get started, take a look at the top trends *Restaurants & Institutions* has sketched:

The number of people over 65 continues to rise. In just one decade, the number of adults 65 and over rose a phenomenal 20.5%. No restaurant could ignore the attitudes and demands of this important consumer segment, but few restaurants or chains offer more than a token "senior discount."

Restaurants need to understand and address the demands of this group, which responds to specific values, including personal growth and revitalization, autonomy and self-sufficiency, and altruism and social connectedness, according to studies by *American Demographics* magazine. Marketing images that invoke such values will score well with older people.

Other important trends include increasing levels of education among the elderly, more grandparents caring for their grandchildren (5% of children live with their grandparents) and a rising number of elderly living alone.

More adults age 35 and older are going to college. Growth in the number of college students tapered off in the 1980s to 21.4%. The largest drop has been in full-time students 34 and under, whose college enrollment declined from 78% in 1970 to 71% in 1989.

The good news is that more adults age 35 and over are hitting the books again. Their numbers jumped from 8.6% of all college students in 1972 to 16%, or 2.1 million, in 1989. This increase in part-time, older students is leading to more convenience food on campuses, including kiosks and takeout for eating on the run. As the number of older students rises, college menus will become more sophisticated. For example, schools with large older populations might consider supermarket-style take-home dinners for students' families.

Children grab the purse strings. Between 1989 and 1991, while the economy suffered a marked downturn and the country went to war, children watched their income increase 82%, according to *American Demographics*. In 1991, children ages 4 to 12 controlled $14.4 billion, up from $8.5 billion in 1989.

As more mothers continue to join the labor force, children are making more decisions regarding household expenditures. The number of single-parent families continues to grow. Households with a single parent accounted for 28% of the 34.7 million families with children under 18 in 1990, according to the U.S. Census Bureau. In fact, studies show that only 30% of children live in a "traditional" family—that is, one with a mom at home and a dad at work.

Nontraditional families eat out more often, and children certainly influence where the family decides to eat. As a result, children have become a more important target in advertising campaigns.

Through 2000, the key target group in the echo boom (children of baby boomers, who today range from newborn to 20-something years old) will be children ages 6 to 12.

Fast food's marketing campaigns always have targeted children, but more and more full-service restaurants will join them. Approximately 25% of full-service restaurants reported an increase in the number of child patrons in 1990, according to the National Restaurant Association. Finally, school foodservice will have to accommodate even more kids, as the youngest echo-boom members enter first grade in 1995.

More people are living alone. The number of singles has jumped dramatically to 12% of all adults, or 23 million, in 1990 from 7% in 1970, reports the U.S. Census Bureau. Women make up the largest portion of adults who live alone (61%), but the rate of one-person households is growing fastest among men.

Unlike the 1980s, when women over 65 and men under 30 comprised the majority of singles, divorce and an aging baby-boom population is producing a greater number of middle-age singles today. In fact, the number of single women ages 35 to 54 will increase 30% to 3.4 million by 2000. Similarly, the number of middle-age men who live alone should rise 27% by the end of the '90s.

This is a windfall for restaurants, because singles, especially those under 45, tend to dine out more frequently. During 1990, 42% of singles under 45 dined out at least once a week at a full-service restaurant, according to a report by the NRA. Compare that to only 28% of married persons in the same age bracket and 35% of older singles who dined out at least once a week.

"We've seen a tremendous increase in singles in certain markets," says Karen Willison, director of marketing, On the Border, Dallas. "About a third of our marketing efforts go toward that group."

There are more jobs for the highly educated. True, unemployment has risen over the past few years, putting a strain on the business and industry segment of foodservice. But consider the gains in specific job categories. From 1985 to 1990, the fol-

lowing grew rapidly, according to the U.S. Census Bureau: executive, administrative and managerial occupations (21.5%); technicians and related support occupations (18.1%); professional specialties (16.1%); and protective service jobs (15.8%).

The middle class (defined as adults ages 25 to 55 with incomes of $18,500 to $55,000) keeps shrinking. This group lost ground between 1978 and 1986, falling from 75% to 67% of the adult population. This would mean less-than-good news for midscale restaurants were it not for another trend: The baby-boom generation (now age 28 to 48) has hit its peak earning years, and most boomer families are two-income households. Consequently, this generation will demand more convenience goods such as takeout and fast food.

Women pour into the labor pool. Women will account for the largest percentage of growth in the labor force until 2005. Twenty-six million people are expected to join the labor force between 1990 and 2005, and women will make up 62% of that number. That means women will be 47% of the total work force in 2005, up 2% over 1990.

Partly because of the recession, the growth rate of women in the labor force has slowed somewhat. However, the rate for men actually has declined.

Hispanics will be the country's largest minority group. From 1980 to 1990, the black population grew 13% to nearly 30 million. Hispanics, however, posted a colossal 53% increase over the same period, and now number 22.3 million.

Signs of Hispanic influence are everywhere. Just turn the dial of a radio, or spend a few minutes flipping television stations, to hear the change. Every major city has a large Hispanic neighborhood, and Hispanic restaurants are cropping up everywhere. And look for this increase to affect menus: Cuban, Puerto Rican, Peruvian and Argentinian dishes could become just as popular as tacos and enchiladas.

Chains such as Anaheim, Calif.-based Carl's Jr. are looking into ways to target Hispanics in their marketing campaigns. "We've used a lot of Spanish-language radio to reach the Hispanic market," says Patty Parks, spokeswoman. She adds that the chain also uses bilingual posters to promote community relations.

Although they represent a shade less than 3% of the total population today, Asians or Pacific Islanders make up the fastest-growing minority. Their numbers increased 107.8% from 1980 to 1990, and they now account for nearly 7.3 million of the population. ◆

Winning Promotions!

by the Editors of R&I

What makes a promotion a winner? It's a matter of perspective. Did sales and traffic increase? Did the new item sell? Was the charity donation goal met? Is the community more aware of your presence in town? The motivation behind promotions varies, and the success of a promotion cannot be gauged on a general scale. These winning promotions make the customer step back and say, "Now that's a good idea!"

GOLD COAST DOGS
Promotion: Taxi Rides

Gold Coast Dogs, a three-unit hot dog and hamburger chain owned by Chicago's Potekin family (father Irv, and sons Barry and Fred), has more than great hot dogs and hamburgers to thank for good business. When starting out in 1985, Barry Potekin came up with a few promotional ideas that built his clientele into a permanent, and devoted, entity. "In the first months, I used to go out several times a day and hail a cab," says Potekin. "I'd give an arbitrary address and, during the ride, bend the cabbie's ear about the restaurant." At the end of the ride, he would give the driver a $5 tip and tell him to use it toward a meal at Gold Coast Dogs. Potekin would then hail a cab back and repeat the process. Not only did his cab driver business increase, but, as hoped, cab drivers spread the word to passengers and the business grew. In another approach, Potekin would call a local office, ask how many employees were there, and send up a tray filled with hamburgers, hot dogs, fries, shakes and soft drinks. "The trick was in the timing," says Potekin. "We had to get it there by 11:30, just when everyone was thinking about heading out to eat." The stir that was created by the rumor of free food at the receptionist's desk was unbelievable, according to Potekin. "They thought it was great fun, and then they'd come into the store the next day to say

thanks and would end up buying lunch. I made new customers and all my money back."

CARL KARCHER ENTERPRISES
Promotion: Carl's Jr.
"Olé Guacamole" Sweepstakes

Even in the sunny west, where patrons of Anaheim, Calif.-based Carl's Jr. restaurants abide, the chance to get away from it all on a luxurious cruise is still a draw. The burger chain made the possibility a reality for 20 lucky winners of its four-week "Olé Guacamole" contest. The prize from the drawing (no purchase necessary) was a four-day, three-night cruise for two aboard a Norwegian Cruise Lines Southward ship. Included was transportation to and from the point of departure, all meals and entertainment on board, and $100 cash spending money (all donated by the cruise line, so promotion costs for Carl's Jr. were minimal). More than 420,000 entries were received, reflecting a 5% participation rate. And, most important, Guacamole Bacon Cheeseburger sales peaked during the promotion with an average of more than 85 burgers sold each day per store. Olé.

MICHAEL STUART'S RESTAURANT
Promotion: Chef for the Day

What connoisseur of fine food hasn't dreamed of donning the toque and manning the range of a fine-dining establishment? Michael Stuart's owner, Michael Lieberman, started his Chef for the Day program to offer customers a chance to make the dream a reality. It allows anyone interested to apprentice for a day in the kitchen of the 172-seat Chicago restaurant, experiencing firsthand what goes on behind the scenes. The guest chef joins the culinary staff for a day of menu planning, making fish and meat stocks and basic sauces, trimming meat and fish, and preparing vegetables and salads. Given his or her individual knowledge and ability, the guest chef also might be offered a fling on the cooking line, steaming a vegetable, grilling the main course or plating dishes for the servers. The neophyte also gets an instant course in cleanup. The cost: $175, which includes a complete set of chefs' whites (jacket, pants, toque), and dinner and wine for two after the guest's shift is over.

MORRISON
Promotions: Secretaries Week and Seafood Days

During Secretaries Week (observed in April), Morrison decided that florist shops should not have a monopoly on rewarding hard-working assistants. In its Ruby Tuesday restaurants, posters featuring a sheet filled with shorthand announced that anyone who could read it deserved a free dessert on the next visit (actually, all secretaries were eligible, whether shorthand was their forte or not). In addition to the dessert offer, kind-hearted bosses who had taken their secretaries out to lunch were rewarded with a $5 gift certificate, good toward the next meal at the restaurant. Sales during the week increased substantially.

Seafood Days, created to move six new seafood entrees, used colorful posters, banners and mobiles to promote the entree, two vegetables, bread and butter. The promotion resulted in a 4% increase in customer counts and an average increase of 15 cents a check.

BOB EVANS FARMS
Promotion: Biscuit 'n Gravy Children's Menu

Biscuit, a lovable, cream-colored shaggy mutt, and Gravy, his long-haired canine partner, are the official spokeshounds for Bob Evans' children's

menu rolled out by the Columbus, Ohio-based chain.

The menu, tailored to the 8-years-old-and-under crowd, spotlighted classic kindergarten cuisine such as "Squiggles and Sauce (spaghetti), "Cock-a-doodle Noodles" (chicken and noodles), and "Chocolate or Strawberry Tummy Yummies" (sundaes). Initial cost of the promotion was $60,000. Children coming into the restaurants are handed "fun packs" containing bibs, Biscuit 'n Gravy stickers, crayons, and placemat menus illustrated with puzzles and figure outlines that can be colored in. The promotion also features costumed characters of Biscuit 'n Gravy, who visit units for special occasions and participate in seasonal and holiday promotions, parades and other related events.

STREETS OF NEW YORK RESTAURANTS
Promotion: Pizza Passion Deal

Billing itself as "The Place Where Pizza Is a Passion," Phoenix's Streets of New York Restaurants launched a red-hot campaign that increased sales dramatically in all of its nine units and—something that cannot be said of all promos—promises to last.

Instead of planning the promo to coincide with low-traffic periods, Streets targeted Phoenix's peak pizza-eating month: January. The campaign zeroed in on the 24-to-49-year-old pizza consumer with a newspaper, radio and TV campaign, a logo design of a red lip print (courtesy of a lip-print search) on box labels, seals, menus, T-shirts and buttons. Signature "passion" pizzas were delivered to local media personalities.

LEVY RESTAURANTS
Promotion: Two-for-One Movie Tickets

Getting into the team spirit when pondering promotional possibilities can lead to great success, as shown when Chicago's multi-concept Levy Restaurants joined with M&R/Loews Theaters and American Express to make patrons a deal they could not refuse. During a three-month period, customers dining at any of the ten Levy restaurants in Chicago who used American Express to pay for the meal could redeem a direct-mail coupon and receive admission at two for the price of one at any M&R/Loews movie theater in Chicago. Response was tremendous, with thousands of coupons redeemed.

DOMINO'S PIZZA
Promotion: Bubble Gum

In one of its promotion programs, Domino's put its highly recognizable logo to good use: The Ann Arbor, Mich.-based pizza chain raised money for the National Committee for Prevention of Child Abuse with the sale of pizza-shaped bubble gum. The pizza delivery king signed its first licensing agreement with a Chicago-based chewing-gum manufacturer to produce and sell the brand-name bubble gum, along with the manufacturer's regular brands of gum, in 700,000 retail stores. The agreement called for the donation of 1% of wholesale sales to the National Committee to Prevent Child Abuse and a royalty fee to be paid to Domino's. The thin, round pieces of gum, cut into pizza-slice wedges, were packaged in miniature Domino's pizza boxes. Aside from an initial $5,000 donation to the NCPCA, it didn't cost Domino's a thing to set the promotion in motion.

THE HERITAGE RESTAURANT
Promotion: Wild Game Month

More than ten years ago, The Heritage restaurant in Cincinnati, Ohio, initiated a wild game promotion to offset November's traditionally sluggish traffic counts. The result? A 27% increase in sales. Today, the 250-seat restaurant features a "Wild Game Month" twice a year, in February and November. Two or three specials are listed nightly, along with an $8 appetizer platter offer-

ing such things as pheasant jambalaya, elk sausage and alligator fritters (deep-fried tails). The appetizer allows people to be adventuresome without risking their entire dinner. Orders average between 30 and 50 a night.

FOUR SEASONS CLIFT HOTEL
Promotion: VIP Treatment for Kids

One might think that this elegant San Francisco hotel caters only to a most elegant guest, often in town on business, and so it does. What hotel managers quickly realized was that the corporate guest was arriving more often on weekends, to take in the sights of the scenic city, and that the guest was often accompanied by spouse and children.

The Kids and Families program includes keeping a VIK (Very Important Kid) list that lets hotel staff know that a child is staying at the hotel. (The child's name and age are duly noted and a personalized welcome made up for the room.) A brochure listing available amenities (baby supplies, comic books, toys, diapers, strollers, baseball cards and more), baby-sitting services, children's activities, city sights for the family, parks, children's clothing and toy stores, is available at the concierge desk. The hotel invested in a popular TV video-game system that can be set up in the room and offers movie rentals tailored to children, which are delivered with popcorn and balloons. A cookies and milk tuck-in service is standard and all of these amenities are available at no extra charge to the visiting families.

TGI FRIDAY'S
Promotion: Summer Drinks and Sunglasses

Beverage sales jumped 10% to 15% at TGI Friday's units participating in the Dallas-based chain's specialty drink promotion for summer. More than 460,000 pairs of red and white novelty sunglasses

HOW TO DO A
SUCCESSFUL PROMOTION

GETTING THE WORD OUT

So you've got a great promotion. Question is, what's the best way to get the word out? Apart from paid advertising mailers and in-store merchandising, the best idea is to get the media behind you. Here are a few tips on how it's done. Jane Aldrich, anchorwoman for WLNS-TV, Channel 6 in Lansing, Mich., says that, to attract their attention, tell the media:

♦ **Why They Sould Care:** Ask yourself what makes your promotion different than the rest? Outline this in your cover letter.

♦ **What's in It for Them:** List photo opportunities. Offer food. Make it easy for the media by inquiring about power supply needs and lighting needs. Be helpful, not fawning. When contacting print media, apply similar principles, but keep in mind that unusual mailers attract attention. Two examples: Dakota's Restaurant in Boston is named for the Dakota mahogany granite that is used throughout the restaurant. To announce its opening, the restaurant sent out chunks of granite to the media. Carlucci Riverway in Rosemont, Ill., decorated its opening announcements with fava beans, underscoring the restaurant's Tuscan cuisine.

RESOURCES AT HAND

Why reinvent the wheel when there might be an ideal helper for your promotion just down the block or in your own kitchen? What latent talents abide in your own staff? Some employees might be artists, dancers, singers, travelers, collecters, or might just have an innate talent for flower arrangement. Or they might know some talented people. Ask around. Here are some other resources that can help: local college art or theater departments, community theaters, ethnic grocers, Chambers of Commerce, charitable organizations, local chefs, libraries, museums, trade commissions, historical societies, antique shops, thrift stores, elementary and secondary schools, art communities, travel agencies, specialty restaurants, societies for the arts, manufacturers and distributors.

HOW TO AVOID PROBLEMS

Here are just a few common-sense tips on how to avoid problems when putting a promotion together.

♦ When doing a promotion in a joint venture with another party (be it a charity, another restaurant, community organization or another business), be sure to sit down well in advance and find out what each party wants out of the promotion, both in terms of money and publicity. Also, decide who is picking up costs for promotion elements.

♦ If the promotion involves any unusual equipment, large decorating items or extra seating, for example, get out the tape measure and make sure getting the items on site and set up can be done. Go through the actual logistics—power supply, labor needs for setup and space requirements—well in advance.

♦ If the promotion is an outdoor event, make alternative plans for inclement weather. If banners or large, attention-getting signs, inflatables or other unusual outdoor promotion elements are being used in public, check with city hall to find out if a permit is required.

were doled out to customers ordering one of four specialty drinks (two of them nonalcoholic) that were being highlighted from Memorial Day weekend to the end of July. So successful was the promotion that all 125 participating units were out of sunglasses within the first week.

THE SEILER CORP.
Promotion: Around the World in Seven Days

The arrival of Wednesday often provokes a midweek culinary crisis in college and university dining, where monotony is the enemy of a well-run foodservice operation. Chris Lambertson, Seiler's foodservice manager at Eastern Mennonite College in Harrisonburg, Va., confronted the problem with his promotion: Around the World in Seven Days, a presentation of cuisine from seven selected countries (yes—including the United States) on seven selected Wednesday evenings in the fall semester. The dinners were open to students on meal plans and a carefully targeted market of 260 cash customers that included staff, faculty and friends of the college. Lambertson publicized the promotion in the available campus information channels (newsletters, two student papers, bulletin boards, mail and the radio station), right before the school year. The seven special dinners were free to meal-plan holders, $4 for adults, $2.50 for children, and advance tickets were offered at a 50-cent discount. The cuisines selected were: Indonesian, Filipino, German, Chinese, Japanese, Spanish and Cajun-Creole. Each event had its own menu and handouts with interesting information about the country featured.

ZINGERMAN'S DELICATESSEN
Promotion: British Foods Festival

"The British are coming!" was the call all through the month of March at Zingerman's Delicatessen in Ann Arbor, Mich. The restaurant/specialty-foods store promotes the cuisine of a different country every month. Every day, British-oriented tastings, history talks, cooking lessons and more were offered. Featured foods included authentic farmhouse-made cheeses, biscuits, jams, meat pies, chutneys, kippers, teas, sauces from India (from the days of the British Empire) and more. Almost life-size cutouts of double-decker buses were suspended from the ceiling and had likenesses of famous Brits (the Beatles, Margaret Thatcher) looking out of the windows. Union Jacks and lots of red, white and blue adorned the store.

JUNIOR'S
Promotion: Deli Survival Kit

Junior's, the Westwood-based deli in the heart of Los Angeles, has realized a 15% to 20% response to a Deli Survival Kit for Two sent to newcomers just moving into the area. Approximately 700 gift certificates have been mailed out every six weeks since November 1988. As of mid-April, an estimated 600 people had visited Junior's to pick up and take home a free deli dinner for two. The gift box, valued at $10, contains a large chunk of beef salami, two types of cheese, a loaf of freshly baked rye bread, and a dessert item such as rugallah. Also included are condiments, utensils and napkins. The Survival Kit is an offshoot of Junior's ongoing complimentary Cheesecake and Coffee promotion, an invitation to residents in the area to come in and get acquainted (or re-acquainted) with the restaurant.

SCHLOTZSKY'S
Promotion: BUN RUN Race

On April 1, 1989, 6,000 registered participants gathered in Austin, Texas, to run their buns off for charity. The 7th annual Schlotzsky's BUN RUN Race, the largest sanctioned 5K race in the United States, raised more than $60,000 to benefit the Austin Sunshine Camp, a camp for underprivileged children in central Texas. The race was organized by the Young Men's Business League of Austin and was co-sponsored by the Stripling Blake Lumber Co. in Austin. The race drew runners from all walks of life, from near Olympian to jogging pet owner.

SPAGHETTI WAREHOUSE
Promotion: Octoberfeast

Just wait until Germany, where Octoberfest started, or Milwaukee, where it flourishes, hears about this: The Old Spaghetti Warehouse (Garland, Texas) staged its own Octoberfeast featuring three "feasts"—combination platters. Customers were tempted to try the Ultimate Italian Feast for Two platter (a $15.95 extravaganza with meatballs, Italian sausage, cannelloni, chicken Parmigiana and spaghetti). Media ads also entic-ed customers to dine on the Spaghetti Feast or the Fettuccini Feast, both under $8. No spur-of-the-moment event, it took four months' advance planning, and cost $45,000 in print and radio media, and another $7,000 in production. But the proof of the promo is the payoff: Check averages increased when customers traded up to the promo's higher ticket items.

JACK IN THE BOX
Promotion: Put the Bite on Illiteracy Book Drop

Old books have a great deal of value, especially when proceeds from their sale and auction go to help public libraries and adult literacy programs. In this promotion, customers of the 70 Jack in The Box units in the Phoenix, Ariz., area were encouraged to drop off their old books and received a $1.00-off coupon toward a Grilled Chicken Fillet, the newest product introduced by the San Diego-based fast-food chain.

On March 11, one of the chain's units hosted the book sale, and many autographed books (George Burns' and Bill Cosby's among them) were auctioned at a celebration that lasted from 10 A.M. to 1 P.M. Free sodas and cheesecake were offered, and local celebrities stopped by to support the promotion. Some 5,000 to 6,000 books were gathered in the two-week drop-off period; those not sold were donated to the Phoenix Pub-

lic Library. In addition to the book-sale proceeds, Jack in The Box donated $2,000 to local libraries and several area literacy programs.

DOUBLETREE INN
Promotion: Key Lime Pie Contest

The first day the ad appeared announcing its first key lime pie recipe contest, the Doubletree Inn in Coconut Grove, Fla., was inundated with several hundred phone calls. The public's response was so great that the hotel had to cancel all further advertising and limit the entries to the first 40 recipes received. Participants were notified by phone and instructed to bake their pies at home and bring them to the hotel on the appointed day. Contestants were required to submit pies using original personal or family recipes. The winning entry was featured as the signature dessert in the hotel's Brasserie restaurant. The winner received a dinner for two once a week for a year "to ensure that the restaurant is keeping the quality standards of the original recipe." All other contestants were given a dinner for two.

G.D. RITZY'S
Promotion: Guess the Lightweight Celebrity

G.D. Ritzy's, the Columbus, Ohio, casual-dining chain specializing in American food favorites, kicked off a year's involvement with the Special Olympics by asking local celebrities to contribute their images (torsos only, no heads), which appeared in a newspaper ad asking: "Do you know a great body when you see one?" Participants were asked to fill out entry forms identifying the five celebrity torsos.

Entries that correctly identified the celebrities qualified for the prize drawing. The ad also offered coupons to redeem at Ritzy's: 50 cents off on both the Chicken Grill Sandwich and the Lightweight Plate; 25 cents off on steamed vegetables. Ritzy's matched the amount of redeemed coupons with a donation to the Special Olympics.

RICHARD'S OF HYDE PARK
Promotion: Christmas in February

The original owners of Cincinnati's Winter Garden started "Christmas in February" in the '30s because they closed the restaurant during the holiday season. Richard and Mary Cay Werner, who bought the restaurant two years ago and changed the name to Richard's of Hyde Park, have opted to continue that tradition, even though they do not vacation during Christmas and New Year's. "The Christmas-in-February promotion has been a real shot in the arm because February is a short, slow, drab, cold month," says Rick Werner. The restaurant is decorated with Christmas lights, trees, wreaths, and holly. Employees, who dress up as elves, bring back the restaurant's Christmas poinsettias, which they took home and nurtured through January just for the occasion. (Poinsettias are hard to find in February.) Also, in keeping with the spirit of Christmas, the Werners take a dollar off the dinner of every customer who comes in with a canned-good item for the Free Store, an organization that feeds the city's poor and homeless.

SAN FRANCISCO SCHOOLS
Promotion: Celebrity Waiter Luncheon

A Celebrity Waiter Luncheon has raised more than $100,000 for San Francisco School Sports, an organization that raises funds for beleaguered middle- and high-school sports programs. The $100-a-plate luncheon, sponsored by several top Bay Area corporations, was staffed by more than 150 sports celebrities and students from San Francisco City College Hotel and Restaurant Department.

MELANGE RESTAURANT
Promotion: Shore Party

One way to jolt dedicated couch potatoes out of their winter ennui, and increase foot traffic by 15% to 20% in the middle of February, is to throw a "Shore Party" such as the annual weekend affair hosted by Cindy and David Jarvis of Melange Restaurant on Chicago's North Shore.

For the event, the Jarvises decked out the restaurant with surfboards, beach balls, balloons and even a wading pool for children. The wait staff donned brightly colored beach wear, Hawaiian leis and sunglasses and came to work equipped with bottles of suntan lotion and zinc oxide. Door prizes included everything from dinner for two to sun visors with the restaurant's logo and inflatable kiddie life preservers.

LINCOLN HIGH SCHOOL
Promotion: Burrito Blowout

Lincoln High School in Portland, Ore., created the "Burrito Blowout," the world's largest and longest burrito, for two reasons: to heighten student awareness on the homeless and hunger issues, and to gain a place in the "Guinness Book of World Records." The event was a cooperative effort between food vendors, who donated nearly all of the food supplies, and the school's students and cafeteria staff. The event was held in the school gym, where tables were set up in serpentine fashion from one end of the room to the other.

Four hundred students, working in teams of ten, took 27 minutes to construct the 1,492-foot-long burrito. After the judges confirmed the length, the burrito was disassembled and distributed to local shelters and community agencies that provide food to the poor and homeless. As for the Guinness Book? Alas, the students received a polite letter informing them the world-record category for food had been dropped.

JACK'S CRAB HOUSE
Promotion: Louie the Crab

Initially, Louie the Crab, a 50-foot inflated crustacean, was "hired" to attract customers to Trader Jack's Crab House & Pub's first annual Super Bowl of Crabs. Perched atop the West Palm Beach, Fla., restaurant, Louie did indeed attract the attention of customers. He also attracted local politicians, a city codes administrator, the police, radio and television stations and a mad slasher. The promotion stunt, which began mid-November and lasted until mid-December last year, started to get exciting when the city codes administrator issued a citation ordering owners Jeff Kukes, Liz Whelan and Jack Palumbo to pay a $250 fine for every day Louie was up. They chose to pay the fine because sales were going through the roof. The police finally issued a permit, and "Save the Crab" T-shirts were selling out. Eventually, city commissioners gave in and declared Louie an honorary citizen. By the end of the month-long event, sales had increased by 40% and profits were up 250%.

CANTEEN CORP.
Promotion: Creative Juices
Chicago-based Canteen Corp., the foodservice management contractor, knows the value of a promotion as well, so much so that it created an entire program for its managers. Entitled Creative Juices, the program featured a brochure and starter kit with a promotion theme for every month of the year. Each monthly promotion brochure included a focus summary; Thru-Put opportunities such as takeout for the Chinese New Year, or blood pressure and weight checks for March's Healthy Appetites theme to increase sales and participation; Canteen file recipes that fit the promo; community resource suggestions; decorating and costume ideas; trivia tips about the promotion theme; supplier information and daily promotion ideas to keep interest up throughout the month. According to Canteen's manager of marketing services, the cost of the program to managers is far less than they would pay if doing a promotion from scratch. Manufacturers often donate foods for promotions, and this keeps cost down.

BLUE CROSS/BLUE SHIELD
Promotion: Chinese New Year Celebration
The Marriott Corp. crew at the Blue Cross/Blue Shield employee cafeteria in Eagan, Minn., whisked away the February blahs with a colorful Chinese New Year Celebration. "Our foodservice employees really got involved," says Sue Grouws, general manager. "One of them has a friend who traveled extensively in the Orient and he brought in posters, tea chests, dolls in traditional costume and a tea set that we used on our displays." A dragon kite was hung from the cafeteria ceiling. Oriental fans and hats set off the Chinese entrees and salads. Servers, dressed in red kimonos and Oriental hats, carried the theme as well. Grouws considered the promo an excellent opportunity to expose employees to different stations within the cafeteria, and so worked with her distributor to offer products that fit the salad bar and soup area. For two days, the salad bar featured such items as bamboo shoots, chow mein and cellophane noodles, Mandarin spinach salad and several varieties of rice.

KNOX COUNTY SCHOOLS
Promotion: Grandparents Day
Once a year, sometime between January and May, about half of Knox County's 55 elementary schools invite grandparents in for a day. "It is a huge, orchestrated event," says Phil Clear, director of foodservices for the Knoxville, Tenn.-based system. "And you would not believe the response." Everybody from principals to teachers to cafeteria staff gets involved. Paper tablecloths, banners, flowers on the table, colorful streamers waving from the air conditioner all add to the festive atmosphere of the cafeteria. Clear says they have to make sure there is enough help to accommodate what can add up to 300 to 400 guests in any school, including parking, hall guides, help in the kitchen, dining room (principals walk around refilling tea and coffee), and line service.

VANDERBILT UNIVERSITY
Promotion: Vandy Lean
During the month of March—Nutrition Month —Vanderbilt foodservices launched its Vandy Lean promotion, which called upon students at the Nashville, Tenn., university to sign a "declara-

tion of participation," an agreement to eat lean for three weeks.

Dr. Martin Katahn, author of *The Rotation Diet* and *The T-Factor Diet*, worked with Frank Gladu, director of dining services, on the promotion and gave the kickoff speech on February 27. Printed materials got the word out to the 5,000-student population and included banners and fliers with the Vandy Lean message, a series of five table tents for dining halls, and three menu planners (one for each week) listing dining options for breakfast, lunch and dinner as well as health and nutrition facts. A Fat Gram Counter listing 400 foods also was part of the program, and Vandy Lean notepads and pencils were distributed throughout the promotion.

Registered dietitians from the university dining and health services departments weighed in the students, performed body-fat analyses and checked cholesterol levels. Students then were given their menus. Throughout the program, added incentives like T-shirts, a $100 gift certificate to a sporting goods store, and a free round-trip ticket for two to Denver or anywhere in California (donated by American Airlines) were awarded in drawings for students who saw the program through the full three weeks (60% did so). Manufacturers and distributors underwrote 30% of the promotion cost.

MICHIGAN STATE UNIVERSITY
Promotion: Exams Are in the Bag

Foodservices at MSU, East Lansing, helped to dispel the dreaded exam-week tremors by offering parents a chance to send their kids a care package. For $13, parents have a choice of three "Exams are in the Bag" care packages. The three include such items as cheese and crackers, candy bars, granola bars, nuts, fruit, raisins, gum, juice and lollipops. Two of the packs include coupons for pizza and snack shop cookies. A bluebook and school pen also are part of the packages.

In addition to snack items, the Spartan Mug Bag includes a 22-ounce insulated mug that is refilled for free at campus operations during exams week. The Spartan Popcorn Bag version

has a souvenir popcorn container good for free popcorn refills while students hit the books. Finally, there is the Spartan Basket, which has more snack items in lieu of pizza and cookie coupons for those students in halls that lack a snack shop.

SUBWAY
Promotion: Movie Role Giveaway

The scene in Warner Bros.' *Lethal Weapon II* shows Mel Gibson, Danny Glover and Joe Pesci driving to a Subway sandwich shop. One of the actors gets a tuna sandwich, not what he ordered. Ensuing comic dialogue pokes fun at the perils of fast-food eating, but the marketing department at Milford, Conn.-based Subway doesn't mind at all. "There's no way of knowing how much product placement in a major film does to improve your company's image, but we do know it has a significant positive effect—no matter what gets said about the product in the film," said Subway spokespeople. In addition to the fee Subway paid Warner Bros. for appearing in the film, Subway launched a Lethal Weapon II contest chainwide to publicize the film. Winners in the two-pronged contest (one customer and one employee winner were chosen) won walk-on roles and all-expenses-paid trips to appear in comedian Steve Martin's film *My Blue Heaven*.

RESTAURANTS IN BOSTON, CHICAGO AND LONDON
Promotion: Monet's Table

In the search for promotional inspiration, don't overlook the local art museum. Dozens of hotels and restaurants have had success with promotions that tie in to art exhibits. Take for example, the Claude Monet exhibit, which traveled from Boston to Chicago to London. The exhibit spawned a plethora of restaurant and hotel promotions, capitalizing not only on Monet's artistic talent, but on his culinary exploits as well. Welcoming the exhibit, The Art Institute of Chicago, hosted the Artistic Chefs Table Awards. Ten

Chicago chefs were invited to compete, recreating menus and table settings from Monet's book. Various chef competitors featured Monet specials at their restaurants during the exhibit's Chicago show.

PIZZA PIT
Promotion: The Great Pizza Pit Treasure Hunt

Marketing Director Tom Hartl estimates that Pizza Pit gained $12,000 worth of free advertising from its participation in Madison, Wisconsin's Fourth Annual Downtown Winter Carnival. Pizza Pit (for the fourth year running) organized the treasure hunt that caps the two-week January festival. Starting on the first day of the carnival and continuing for a total of 12 days, Pizza Pit broadcasts clues from ten Madison radio stations to help treasure hunters find the carnival treasure: a brass commemorative medallion and $1,000 check. The clues, geographic and historical references familiar to Madisonites, were given in verse. According to Hartl, near the end of the treasure hunt, Pizza Pit received an average of 100 calls a day from hunters looking for more clues. Sales were up 20% during the promotion, which cost Pizza Pit $1,012.60. "$1,000 for the winner's check, $12.60 for the medallion," says Hartl. Area radio stations donated air time for the clues.

BACINO'S PIZZA
Promotion: Pizza Dough Spinning Contest

What makes a great pizza spinner? "He's got to be able to keep the dough up for a long time, stay in control and not poke any holes," says Dan Bacin, owner of Bacino's Pizza in Chicago. Announcing the contest, Bacin attached fliers to all pizza boxes going out for delivery. Sixty potential spinners showed up for classes, which were held on consecutive Saturdays leading up to the contest. Once their training was complete, 45 felt

confident enough of their spinning skills to compete: the youngest, age 6; the oldest, 63. Prizes (bicycles, cash, gift certificates) were awarded to winners in four age categories. The events, free to all participants, were covered by Chicago newspapers and a television station. Total cost: $1,000, not including prizes.

INTERNATIONAL HOUSE OF PANCAKES
Promotion: Marathon Breakfast

Something about a 15-foot-high by 12-foot-wide inflated stack of pancakes says breakfast is served. Los Angeles-based IHOP rounded up 200 volunteers to cook breakfast for 3,000 people on the morning of the Los Angeles Marathon, March 4. Proceeds from the hearty breakfast, which cost diners $3, went to the City of Los Angeles Foundation, a nonprofit organization set up to raise funds for city-operated human service programs. Donations from the event totaled $55,000 plus $3,000 in services. Vendors donated 56% of the $18,000 the promotion cost to put on.

DOC DAMMER'S SALOON
Promotion: Celebrity Bartender

One night each month, patrons ordering a drink at Doc Dammer's in the Colonnade Hotel, Coral Gables, Fla., will find themselves served by a local celebrity. For more than a year, professional athletes, television and radio personalities, patrons of the arts and other famous folk have served up cocktails and donated the tips to their favorite charity. On celebrity nights, bar sales increase an average of 15% and dinner sales increase 3% to 6%. "What's great about the promotion is that each celebrity draws a different crowd," says Marie Correa, a spokeswoman for the hotel's public relations agency. "For instance, an athlete will attract different people than a radio personality. We're getting all kinds of people through the doors."

BLACK-EYED PEA RESTAURANTS
Promotion: Get Lucky at the Black-eyed Pea

Printed in true tabloid fashion, three issues of Black-eyed Pea restaurant's *Truly Lucky News* featured screaming headlines: "Man Sees Elvis' Likeness in a Bowl of Black-eyed Peas!!!"; "Family Eats Magical Peas, is Transported to Australia!" The tabloids, and the tales they told, teed up Dallas-based Black-eyed Pea's Get Lucky sweepstakes, a promotion based on Southern folklore that says anyone who eats black-eyed peas on New Year's Day will be lucky. Sweepstakes prizes included a trip to Australia, nine trips to various destinations in the continental United States, and $30,000 in cash prizes. Customers visiting any one of Prufrock Restaurant's 70 Black-eyed Pea restaurants during January were handed a copy of the *Truly Lucky News*, detailing the contest. "It gave them something fun to read while they were waiting for their food," says Black-eyed Pea's Julie Brunson, a public relations representative. "And it was a creative way to make sure customers filled out the entry form, printed on the back page of the tabloid." To encourage repeat visits, Black-eyed Pea issued a new *Truly Lucky News* each week. And, fostering employee involvement, Black-eyed Pea employees posed for the pictures that illustrate the tabloid. "Because they knew the people in the pictures, the servers loved talking to customers about the promotion," says Brunson. Several television and radio stations and newspapers covered the promotion, contributing to an 18% sales increase during January. Total cost: $100,000.

PREMIER VENTURES
Promotion: T-Shirts Around the World

The photographs show Russian gymnasts wearing Beach Grill T-shirts in Red Square. Mickey Mouse dons his T-shirt in front of the Magic Kingdom. A fan from Berlin wears his on the Wall. All are included in one of Denver-based Premier Ventures' Around the World collages.

The concept is a simple one. Hostesses at four Premier Ventures restaurants are trained to spot visitors from other cities and countries. When visitors buy the restaurants' signature T-shirts to take home, hostesses tell them to have a picture of themselves in the T-shirts taken in front of a landmark in their respective cities or countries. "They send us the picture, we put it up on the collage at whichever restaurant they visited and send them a free T-shirt for their effort," explains Leeny Harrington, marketing coordinator. So far, photos have come in from all over the United States and such countries as Holland, Switzerland, Australia, Spain, Italy, France and Great Britain. "It's good word-of-mouth publicity," she says. "Each visitor who does the T-shirt thing goes back and tells his friends to visit us when they come." T-shirt sales have doubled since Premier started the collages in 1988.

SCHWARTZ BROTHERS RESTAURANTS
Promotion: Pickle Mania

What's the best way to get the word out about a new Seattle deli? Plaster the city with pickles. That's what Schwartz Brothers Restaurants, owner of 20 restaurants, did when it replaced its Cafe Casino restaurant with Schwartz Brothers Restaurant & Delicatessen. Before the opening, the company rented space on bus billboards to run posters of giant pickles floating over the Seattle skyline captioned, "Start spreading the news." Then, when it closed Cafe Casino to transform it into the deli, Schwartz hired the fourth- and fifth-grade classes from Seattle's Montlake School to draw giant posters of pickles to paper the windows. (Schwartz Brothers liked the post-ers so well, it later used them to paper the walls in the restaurant.)

On opening day, Schwartz Brothers sent out "pickle patrols," teams of employees in pickle-stamped aprons to hand out 10,000 pickle slices at Seattle's busiest intersections. Newsletters full of pickle trivia and facts about Schwartz Brothers also were passed out. Deliveries to radio stations meant more exposure for Schwartz Brothers, as did a giant inflatable pickle tied onto the restaurant's delivery van.

Total cost: $25,000.

MAMA LEONE'S
Promotion: Circus at Leone's

New York-based Mama Leone's promoted special recipes from the Togni family, who were in town with Ringling Bros. and Barnum & Bailey Circus for the American premiere of their European circus act featuring elephants, horses and rare animals. The Togni family supplied Mama Leone's with four favorite recipes: Spaghetti a la Ubriacon (spaghetti with sautéed sweet sausage, cream and brandy), Gypsy Chicken (chicken with white wine, tomato and mustard), Flavio Penne Arabbiata (quill-shape pasta with pancetta and tomatoes) and Lasagna primavera.

Mama Leone's built five-course, $29.95 *prix-fixe* dinners around these main dishes. To play up the circus theme, the restaurant borrowed a large collection of old circus costumes and banners from Ringling Bros.' archives for decoration. Newspaper ads told people about the promotion, as did a story in the *Daily News*. Located ten blocks from Madison Square Garden, where the circus was performed, Mama Leone's promotion attracted families to the restaurant for meals after matinee performances and for dinner before evening performances. Total cost: $10,000.◆

First Impressions

by Monica Kass

People don't complain about waiting for tables at Lou Mitchell's, Chicago. They're too busy eating doughnuts, Milk Duds and bananas. "Doughnuts are for everybody, Milk Duds for the ladies and bananas for the kids," explains co-owner Nick Noble, working the door on a busy Saturday. "I'd say we hand out 3,000 boxes of Milk Duds in a week. Who knows? I never keep close count. The whole formula is to have fun and appreciate the customer."

Mitchell's sweet reception has a nice kickback: a measurable forgiveness quotient that keeps customers smiling despite cramped communal tables, high noise levels and busy aisles. "It's the power of the first impression," says Noble. "Don't underestimate it."

If some restaurateurs do, it is because impressions are the sum total of many elements, and can seem hard to define and harder to control. But by examining the parts that make up the whole, operators can find practical ways to improve first impressions.

"It starts with the phone voice." says Arthur Schwartz, restaurant critic for the New York *Daily News.* "It's my job to dine out every night, and I've often said I can tell a good restaurant by the way they answer the phone. If they put me on hold and then fumble for a pencil when they come back on, I know this can't be a great restaurant."

"There are several things you can do to stay on top of it with reservations," says Michael Hurst, owner of 15th Street Fisheries in Fort Lauderdale, Fla. "You need to be pleasant and friendly, but you have to stay in control of the conversation. Otherwise, people will ask you to spend all this time reading through the menu and giving them directions, without committing to a reservation."

In addition to sticking with a script and not letting customer conversations wander, Hurst says being willing to take reservations at least five days in advance can alleviate pressure.

Extremely high-volume restaurants such as Joe Baum and Michael Whiteman's Windows on the World, New York, have to rely on banks of reservation clerks and a sophisticated proprietary phone system to handle the 3,000 to 4,000 calls that come in each day. But the same rules apply. "No matter how busy we get, there are never more than three rings before you get a human voice," says Baum, "and while we have to use operators, there is a backup network of management always ready to take the call. We recognize the customer's need for security and want everyone to know we can be had—in the right sense of the word."

After the initial phone call, the rest of the elements that form first impressions are packed into the flurry of moments that take customers from door to dinner table.

"A lot of it is visual," says John Buchanan, a managing partner at Lettuce Entertain You Enterprises. "The cleanliness of the street, the design of the restaurant, the appearance of your people. But what you do when customers walk in, that's the thing that sticks."

Restaurant critic Schwartz agrees, "My first impression after the reservation is the greeting I get at the door. I don't want to be left standing there wondering what to do with myself. I want to feel like I'm being taken care of. Think about it: If you feel like you're in good hands, you relax. Then if something goes wrong later, you're much more forgiving."

Well-organized independents do their best to welcome guests by name—especially when it's their first visit. Says Hurst: "Name recognition is very helpful in making a good impression. I take notes when a party calls to make a reservation so that when they come in, I have a good idea who they are."

Similarly, Commander's Palace in New Orleans color codes reservation cards (orange for VIPs, blue for birthdays guests and green for smokers) to make it as easy as possible for management to strike up a personalized conversation when guests come in.

Restaurants that do not take reservations face an even bigger challenge: how to help customers weather waits for tables.

Upscale restaurants with bars have a built-in solution of a sort—especially if food is served at the bar—but it is still a good idea to communicate with customers as they wait. Says Jeanne Delia, restaurant critic for the *Sun News* in Myrtle Beach, S.C., "If the maitre d' just gives you a hopeless look and sends you off to spend money at the bar, you're off on the wrong foot. It's nice to have someone look you in the eye and tell you they are doing everything they can to get you in soon."

Telling customers how long the wait is, instead of waffling, also is a good idea, says Denise Minchella, principal of the Hospitality Group, a service-training consulting firm in Los Angeles. "Never apologize for the wait. It's better to make eye contact and say, 'Our wait is 15 minutes,' than to shift your eyes and mutter something."

Another big factor in shaping customers' first impressions is the equitability of service. Is everyone treated alike? Restaurant carryovers from the '30s and '40s, such as the haughty headwaiter loath to notice ordinary citizens, are still in evidence, but not as prevalent. Says Charles Britton, food editor for several Copley newspapers in Los Angeles, "What's happened is that most restau-

rants' clientele is too broad to succeed at the snooty thing. When the ability to spend money becomes more widespread, suddenly it becomes very silly to be so exclusive."

So while the "ketchup room"—*Women's Wear Daily*'s phrase for undesirable seating areas in upscale restaurants—might still exist, service from wait staffs is increasingly equitable.

"The biggest trend in service is toward sophistication and subtlety," says Minchella. "Servers are getting away from the cutesy thing." Whiteman agrees, "There's a fine line between being friendly and being familiar that should not be crossed. And there's a certain finesse to what you say. If you approach a table and ask, 'Can I get you something from the bar?' you get dead air and an awkward pause. If instead you greet your table with, 'Good evening, these are our wines for the day,' you give customers information and direction."

If all goes right—the phone voice is pleasant, the reservation clerk helpful, the maitre d' welcoming and the waiter professional—before the food ever arrives, customers will be inclined to come back. Baum sums up: "We like to think the first impression is the last impression: a significant indicator of the personality of the place that confirms customers' judgment of choice. Truthfully, with so many people eating out so often, it's no longer an innocent experience. We have to transcend our own interests to reinforce customers' reasons for coming and then, for coming back." ◆

When Customers Won't Pay the Bill

by Jeff Weinstein

An enterprising customer in Southern California got four free pizzas from California Pizza Kitchen restaurants before anyone caught on. Each time a new manager took over at any of the four units in her area, the woman came in with a story about how the previous manager offered her a free pizza on her next visit. She would start to create a scene as she explained how she didn't get enough pineapple on her last pizza. Of course, the manager relented just to get her out of the restaurant.

Because the Beverly Hills, Calif.-based chain documents each complaint, Vice President of Operations John Kaufman detected a pattern. As it turned out, the woman used the same first name in each case, changing only her last name. The pineapple pizza caper was solved.

Customers can use hundreds of tricks to avoid paying the bill—everything from planting a foreign object in their food to registering a false complaint. Kaufman recalls how one customer went as far as to put a pet frog in his salad. And there is the popular "dine and dash" technique, where customers eat, then leave before the bill arrives.

Whenever a customer can't, or won't, pay the check, the best approach is to keep cool and work out any arrangement possible for payment. For instance, most operators who usually don't accept personal checks will do so with proper identification as the last available option.

Whatever the outcome, don't let the customer get the best of you. If you can't work out payment, and the customer refuses to leave identification, let him or her walk, says Vincent Liuzza Jr., president of Cucos, Metairie, La. "It's not worth the manager's time and effort," says Liuzza. "The manager could be saving the restaurant more money by attending to customer needs."

Hope for the Best

Every operator should have policies for dealing with intentional or unintentional check dodgers. But different types of clientele demand different policies.

If a guest doesn't have any means to pay the check at the upscale Chasen's restaurant, Los Angeles, the manager has the customer fill out a credit voucher, mails the bill and "hopes for the best," according to Chief Operating Officer Ralph Woodworth. If a customer's credit card doesn't verify, Chasen's allows disgruntled guests to call the card's customer service representative to talk it over.

Woodworth says he receives most complaints about the bill a day or so after the event because upscale customers don't want to cause a scene in front of their party. If they call the next day to complain about finding a foreign object in the food, the manager tries to verify the facts with servers and the kitchen. While the response varies based on the restaurant's relationship with individual customers, Woodworth says if the allegation cannot be verified, he apologizes and asks the customer to try the restaurant again.

If a customer can't pay at a midscale operation such as Cucos, the manager first asks for a telephone number and identification such as a driver's license, then asks the customer to mail payment or return with the money as soon as possible. On the customer's second visit with an empty wallet, Liuzza says the manager follows the same procedure but with a very stern tone, intimating that the customer is not particularly welcome at the restaurant.

If a Cucos customer gets hostile, the manager continues the conversation in the office. "If the customer refuses to step into an office, we just ask

HOW TO REDUCE CREDIT-CARD FRAUD

Credit-card fraud is a $6.7 million problem in the restaurant industry, according to MasterCard risk-management expert James D'Amelio.

D'Amelio offers restaurateurs the following suggestions on how to train cashiers and servers to recognize authentic and fraudulent credit cards.

Holograms: Most bank cards such as MasterCard have three-dimensional holograms that display side-to-side motion when moved.

Signature panels: Bank-card signature panels have repetitive designs, incorporating the bank-card name. These panels are tamper-evident, making erasures of a signature more obvious. A cashier shouldn't process a transaction if the signature panel appears to have been erased, discolored, glued or painted.

Account-number embossing: All embossed account numbers should be the same size, height and style—and should be in alignment. All MasterCard cards should have 16-digit account numbers beginning with the number 5. Visa cards have 13- or 16-digit account numbers beginning with the number 4.

Embossed security characters: Increasingly, bank cards have security characters embossed on the front of the card next to the expiration date. There might be "MC" on a MasterCard card, or "CV," "BV" or "PV" on Visa cards. "MC" appears on cards bearing the indent-printed account number on the signature panel; cards with the Visa security characters should have a bank identification number matching the first four digits of the embossed account number printed directly above it.

If a card doesn't measure up to any of these features, or if it appears the card has been tampered with in any other way, immediately call the card authorization center for instructions on how to proceed. Some companies offer rewards for holding such cards.

them to leave," says Liuzza. "Unless the situation turns violent, it's not worth calling the police. And no matter what the circumstances, we try not to let any customer leave mad—even if we think he is wrong."

When faced with the old "dine and dash" situation, the operation generally eats the cost. At the 35-unit Italian Oven chain, Latrobe, Pa., managers sit down to discuss "dine and dash" incidents with the servers. They rehash the event, and the manager points out how the incident could have been detected and what to look for next time.

While outward appearance usually doesn't reveal a guest's intention to leave the check on the house, there are a few signs to watch for.

Kaufman at California Pizza Kitchen says servers are taught to keep a closer eye on teenagers; customers who are poorly dressed, extremely fidgety or intoxicated; or those who specifically request a seat close to the front door. Woodworth warns to watch couples who, at the end of their meal, go to the restroom at the same time.

To deter potential troublemakers, managers should make their presence known by walking past the table several times during the course of the meal.

And just who covers the bill when a guest leaves without paying? Most companies cover the loss themselves.

However, incidents at California Pizza Kitchen operations are recorded in servers' files. After three occurrences, servers receive "serious counseling" from the manager, according to Kaufman. Three episodes also could result in firing, especially if they happen within a four- to six-week period. Repeated incidents could be a sign of a server who isn't paying enough attention to guests or is giving free meals to friends. ◆

Whining and Dining

by Rajan Chaudhry

Ron Magruder, president of The Olive Garden, sat in the chain's guest relations department, fielding calls from customers. "I want to talk to the president of the company," said one woman, incensed by an overcooked eggplant parmagiana. "Well, that can certainly be arranged," responded Magruder, who had identified himself only as "Ron in guest relations," "because you're speaking to him."

"Of course, at first she didn't believe me," Magruder recalls, "so I had to explain how we all spend time in the guest relations area, that she just happened to call in on the day when I was there, and that I was glad she had.

"She went back to the restaurant and wrote me a nice letter, telling me that the eggplant was much better since she had talked to me," he says.

The Olive Garden, Orlando, Fla., is at the forefront of a revolution among foodservice organizations determined not to let size or layers of management muffle the voices of their customers and willing to devote dollars to systems that keep them tuned in.

Today, such direct links between corner stores and corner offices are enhancing reaction time and improving customer satisfaction. They give top management the unfiltered feedback it needs to quickly judge the effect of its programs and to spot trends early. They also offer a precious second chance to satisfy an unhappy customer who might otherwise be lost forever.

Launched in 1990, The Olive Garden's guest relations department employs five full-time staffers and boasts a customized computer system, a fax machine for guest comment cards and a toll-free phone number. Headquarters personnel rotate regularly through the department. "It brings you face to face with the guest, which you don't often get to do in the administrative environment," says Magruder.

The purpose of the department is not to shift responsibility for guest satisfaction away from store managers and staff, but rather to support them in their efforts, says Charles Tate, vice president of consumer and community affairs. Summaries of guest comments go from the guest relations area to store managers twice weekly.

With the department now handling several thousand customer contacts per month, The Olive Garden has taken service to a new plane: "We believe that a good dining experience doesn't necessarily begin or end at the door of the restaurant," says Tate.

Almost half of all contacts come from guests who want to commend a server or relate a positive experience, says Tate. Customers have requested everything from recipes to the names of the manufacturers of the restaurant's carpeting. The No. 1 complaint is that the lines are too long, he says. In response, the chain has begun exploring ways of making the wait for a table more pleasant, including passing out appetizers in the lobby. "It's something that our people find refreshing," he says. "It's real and it's human and it's immediate."

Although The Olive Garden has invested heavily in its customer center, feedback systems need not be high-tech or expensive in order to work.

At Vanderbilt University, Nashville, Tenn., Frank Gladu, director of dining services, introduced a customer comment card program in 1988 that has become a model for other university feedback efforts.

Under the program, guest complaints, comments and questions are tacked on bulletin boards outside each of the school's three dining facilities. General managers write responses on the cards within 24 hours, and cards remain posted for at least a week, Gladu says. Afterward, Gladu himself reviews the cards and passes them to the department's advisory board. "No question about it, it's a great barometer," he says.

The bulletin board has proved to be fertile ground for new ideas. This year, for example, guests suggested that the university offer a breakfast bar at night. When the school tried the evening breakfast bar in March, 83% of diners ate from it, says Gladu. "I'd say it's our most popular bar," he says. "And we never would've conceived that idea; it never would've occurred to us."

Gladu refers to his card program as a "safety valve": "Customers, instead of walking out feeling like they didn't have an opportunity to voice their opinion, get it off their chests, and hopefully something positive will come from it."

Since he initiated the forum, Gladu says he's seen a fundamental shift in guest attitudes. Four years ago, he says, 96% of cards carried complaints. At his most recent count, about 50% were complaints, 35% were requests for new products or services, and 15% were compliments.

The "reach" of the bulletin boards gives the program its punch, he says. "You're not just responding to that customer, you're responding to hundreds of people who read the board every day. It's your opportunity to turn a potential negative into a positive."

For more involved discussions, Gladu often turns to his advisory committee, which is composed of students, staff and faculty—in short, customers.

Like the comment card program, the advisory committee has produced offbeat suggestions that work. For example, Gladu this year bucked college-feeding trends by converting his dining program from a la carte service to an old-fashioned board plan for dinner. "The dinner plan was not the brainchild of the dining administration; that really was a product of months of discussions with the advisory committee," he says.

In addition, Gladu regularly visits student groups, a crucial part of his customer base, both to educate them and to answer their questions. He also conducts short customer surveys on very focused topics, and he employs a marketing intern from Vanderbilt's business school to hold focus groups.

Vanderbilt's Nashville neighbor, Shoney's Inc., is another organization that is being transformed in its quest to listen better and respond faster to its customers.

The keystone of the company's strategy is a mystery shopper program in which guests rate their dining experiences at various restaurants. Earlier this year, the company invested $400,000 in a computer system to help digest feedback from its shoppers more quickly.

To build responsiveness into its culture, Shoney's has begun linking managers' bonuses with their units' scores. And it has set a company-wide goal of 80% customer satisfaction in 1992 and 85% in 1993.

At Shoney's, the impact of listening to guests is measurable in dollars. "There is an incredible correlation between same-store sales increases and shoppers' scores: The stores that made the customers the most satisfied had the best sales in 1991," says Ty Hasty, Shoney's senior vice president of marketing. "The stores with the best customer satisfaction also ran the highest profit percentage," he adds.

Like The Olive Garden's guest relations center, Shoney's shopper program is designed to support store-level management. But both systems also provide a wealth of marketing and trend information for top executives. "In one respect, you're taking care of customers and finding what their problems are," says The Olive Garden's Magruder. "You're also building some information bases."

The Olive Garden used its new database during its latest major limited-time event, the Italian Discovery menu, to mail promotional pieces to customers and to track reaction to the new items.

At Shoney's, trend information from in-store surveys is providing the platform for a restaging of the Shoney's concept. "You've got to stay on top of your business and look towards the future if you want to protect it," says Hasty, who heads the company's concept development team. Over the past few months, Shoney's has built on its consumer research with focus groups, listening both to customers who prefer Shoney's and to those who prefer its competitors. "Focus groups are qualitative by nature, so to really get good direction, you need to do a lot of them, in a lot of different markets, with a lot of different types of people," says Hasty. He has also talked to franchisees, store managers and hourly employees, involving all those who interact with guests every day.

Based on the feedback, Hasty plans to target a niche that is somewhere between Shoney's current family-restaurant positioning and the more upscale casual-dining segment. "You can listen to your customers or you can go out of business," he says. "Our customers are telling us things they think will make us better, and now's the time to act on them."

Those who have created customer-driven operations seem to agree that, to be truly responsive, an organization must give its listeners the authority to act, and act rapidly, on behalf of guests. "The common wisdom is that we managers have to learn how to better motivate our people," says Len Roberts, Shoney's chairman and CEO. "I think that's a bunch of nonsense. Our people bring their own motivation. What people need is to be liberated from us. They need to be involved, they need to be accountable, and they need to be trusted."

Shoney's organizational changes are aimed at giving unit managers more decision-making authority while opening communications with top management. The company has thus eliminated a layer of management that was impeding its store-level employees from taking action.

Similarly, at Seattle-based Restaurants Unlimited, which operates 22 dinner houses, a flatter supervisory structure is bringing top executives within earshot of front-line employees and its customers.

Until it cut a layer of management, the company had been slow in reacting to the changing needs of its guests, says President Ray Lindstrom.

"Since the mid-1970s, we have given responsibility to our service people to do what was right for the guest to take the food back, fix it, or say 'You know what, this has not been acceptable; you're not going to pay for this,' " says Lindstrom. "Because our people take responsibility in that way, they have a lot of information about the guests. The problem was that we had to get that information up to a level where larger decisions could be made, to those who had the authority to say 'Let's write a new menu.' "

Restaurants Unlimited relies on guest surveys to generate feedback and uses restaurant staff as sounding boards. "We don't ever do a menu without sitting down with crew members," says Lindstrom. "Today, both our guests and crew have been raised in an environment where they were encouraged at school and home to have an opinion. 'Lunch salad prices are too high. You took off my favorite item. You're too slow at lunch.' There isn't anything they don't tell us. They want you to know. All you have to do is ask."

At The Olive Garden, guest relations staff are empowered to take whatever action they think is proper to turn an unhappy customer into a loyal one. That might include giving out gift certificates in the amount they feel is correct, or even cutting a reimbursement check on the spot.

Tate tells of one recent incident in which a lunch-hour customer carried out a meal and returned to his office, only to discover that his order had been filled incorrectly. The customer wasted no time faxing the comment card packed with the order to Olive Garden headquarters. The guest relations specialist who received the card could easily have offered an apology and called the case closed. Instead, the representative called the general manager of the restaurant, who within 15 minutes had redone the order and personally delivered it to the customer's office. "There was no rule that told that either employee had to do it," says Tate. "It happened for the best possible reason—attitude." ♦

Menu Merchandising

by Monica Kass

When people go to the Rainbow Room in New York, they expect to be entertained by the music, the dancing and the food. Spectacular dishes like Arctic Halibut Baked in a Golden Balloon and Bouillabaisse for One Crowned with Lobster are shows in themselves. The halibut is baked in a massive gold foil pouch for its theatrical effect. The bouillabaisse is served in an oversize lion's head bowl with long croutons standing erect to enhance the presentation. Paraded across the room, they are a classic example of the, "I want what she had" menu-merchandising technique. But gorgeous as they might be, beautiful platters of food can't talk or walk out of the restaurant to flag people down. That's the marketer's job. Foodservice marketers have three chances to send food messages to their customers: in the home, on the street and in the restaurant. Methods used to reach customers in their homes include broadcast and print media, direct-mail pieces and newsletters. To reach them on the street, marketers use signage and promotions. In the restaurant, point-of-purchase materials, the physical menu and the staff work together to relay the food message.

Broadcast and Print Ads

Historically, television, radio and print ads have been used primarily to drive home a restaurant's name and image. The food message often is secondary, highlighted in three situations: when it offers a point of difference from the competition (witness Burger King's persistent emphasis on flame-broiled burgers), when it is a product introduction, or when it is a limited-time promotion.

Because of the current focus on value among chain restaurants, many of today's commercials are selling "product at a price;" such ads are a safer technique than heartwarming image-building ads.

"Because we're a small chain, we can't afford to do image advertising," says one marketing executive. "It takes a long time to build and sometimes doesn't work." He explains that sales generated by a "product at a price" commercial, on the other hand, generally pay for the commercial during its run. "If we're running a two-month $8.95 prime rib special and spending $200,000 on the ad, we are able to pay back the $200,000 in the two-month span."

Comments from marketing experts at Bob Evans, Columbus, Ohio, are similar. "We've tried to do some image-building, slice-of-life kinds of things in the past and will continue to do some of that. But our coming commercials will be a little more skewed to food, because the best ad campaigns we've had thus far have been 'news' and the only real news at a family restaurant is the product."

For the chains that can afford TV campaigns, the downside to bargain-food commercials is that they are not as memorable as image marketing. For example, McDonald's "Good Time, Great Taste" commercials were the most popular in the country in 1989, according to an annual ranking done by Video Storyboard Tests, a New York advertising research firm. McDonald's 1990 shift to a bargain-food focus dropped the company to the ranking's No. 5 spot. Conversely, Little Caesars rose from No. 17 to No. 6 in the 1990 ranking, all on the strength of an inspired commercial starring a dog that barked "I love you."

And while "beautiful food" advertising on TV can be an effective food-merchandising technique, especially for product-specific chains like Red Lobster, industry segments where menus vary little find this technique is less effective. "Television is not a great medium to showcase food," says one agency that handles national advertising for Denny's. "Food takes on a sameness and is not differentiated enough from one restaurant to the next."

Direct-Mail Marketing

Direct-mail pieces and newsletters focus more specifically on food and can work well as menu merchandising tools for all segments of the food-service industry.

For instance, American Restaurant Group's 18-unit Spoons Grill and Bar chain has built a remarkably effective direct-mail strategy in California over the last few years. The chain has a 4% to 6% redemption rate for each coupon sent out with its mailers, compared with the overall industry's 1.5% coupon redemption rate. By monitoring the response to each of the mailers Spoons sends out each year and refining its mailing list, the chain has been able to reduce the size of each mailing and still enjoys increases in redemption rates.

In 1990, Spoons sent out four direct-mail pieces, each selling one specific food product. The mailer promoting Spoons' Great Tex-Mex Fajita Cookoff is a good example. A one-fold mailer, the cover was done in bold colors and graphics surrounding the words "The Great Tex-Mex Fajita Cookoff." Inside was a brilliant color photograph of the food, with a coupon attached. The marketing director for the chain explained the strategy, "We truly believe that you need to have a one-product focus on each mailer. It's more direct. And because you have a nanosecond to get the customers' attention with the piece as they rummage through the barrage of junk mail, you need impactful colors and a hard-hitting message. Then, 'wham!' they open it up and there's the food, bigger than life."

Spoons includes a coupon in the mailer to track the progress and success of the piece. "It's *not* a discount," says a representative. "That would cheapen your image. You don't say 'save four dollars,' or, 'eat free for the next month,' on the coupon. You just print the product title and price."

Spoons also started radio ads that complement its direct-mail campaign. The radio spots are used to get the name out and then tee up the current food promo.

Newsletters

Newsletters are another focused home-marketing technique for small, regional chains and independent operators. If done with a food focus, a well-designed newsletter can communicate a restaurant's image as well as pique customer curiosity in a restaurant's menu.

The slick color newsletter Brennan's of Houston has been publishing quarterly since spring 1988 is a case in point. The restaurant's efforts to keep the newsletter food-oriented without being too hard-sell on the Brennan's name has generated a lot of feedback from customers. Owner Alex Brennan-Martin believes that has been "a much more effective use of our marketing dollars than an ad."

The front page features food events in the restaurant. A feature article on the middle spread might focus on service or give fun food facts. Because Brennan's is a special-occasion place, Brennan-Martin also includes upcoming holiday menus in the newsletter to help people plan ahead. Initially, he hesitated in committing to the newsletter when faced with the $9,000 cost per issue. "It takes a while to get feedback, to see what effect a newsletter has on your business, but we decided to stick it out and the investment is more than paying off," he says.

On the Street

Reaching customers on the street with food messages is an underutilized merchandising technique. It can be as simple as posting a menu in the window, using costumed characters to hand out samples and menus on street corners, or sending those characters to schools and hospital rooms to cheer children and patients.

A more involved method is to host a street festival like the Oktoberfest Chicago's Berghoff restaurant celebrates annually. Food-specific signage, temporary or permanent, can also be effective. Participation in local "Taste of . . . " city events and charities are other valuable street-marketing methods.

As with any promotion, the more unusual or clever the approach, the more memorable it will be. Two examples: Trader Jack's Crab House and Pub, West Palm Beach, Fla., used a 50-foot inflated crustacean to promote the restaurant's first annual Super Bowl of Crabs and increased sales by 40% and profits 250% in one month. Schwartz Brothers Restaurants in Seattle plastered the city with pickles pictured on billboards and buses, handed out by "pickle patrols" on street corners, and attracted lots of media attention and customers to the new delicatessen it was opening.

Point of Purchase

Every smart marketer uses point-of-sale materials to encourage impulse buying. Posters, mobiles and table tents call attention to limited-run specials or new items often in support of broadcast or print ad campaigns. They can also be used to move high-profit menu items such as desserts and drinks.

Because limited-service establishments don't have hand-held menus to detail food offerings, they rely on point-of-purchase materials more heavily than full-service restaurants. Fortunately, because their ordering areas are separate from seating areas, quick-service restaurants and cafeterias can take on the clutter of a retail environment more safely than full-service restaurants.

Full-service restaurants might be tempted to use point-of-purchase materials just as extensively, but one expert cautions them to be selective, "It's best to use point-of-purchase materials sparingly in a full-service restaurant. Because the customer has a limited attention span, it's better to send one strong message than many competitive messages. Try not to let your salesmanship encroach on the pleasure of their dining experience."

The Physical Menu

Of the two broad menu types—menu boards and hand-held menus—menu boards have the least merchandising capability. Without much room for description, menu boards must rely on supporting illustrations and photographs to tell the food story. Those that do their job the best are easy for the customer to follow and highlight higher-profit items. Miami-based Burger King, for example, recently redesigned its menu boards to make them easier to read and to distinguish between dayparts. Menu boards are now color-coded, with different colors for breakfast items, lunch and dinner items, side dishes and drinks.

Hand-held menus communicate on many more levels. The way a menu looks conveys information about the restaurant's image, style and products. The way a menu reads dictates what sells and what doesn't.

La Mirada, Calif.-based Denny's used food photographs of its entire product lineup as the basis for a series of new menus. Denny's previous menu was functional, but didn't play a big enough role in shaping customer perceptions about food quality, portion sizes, value and variety.

Explains a Denny's representative, "The menu is really a showcase for all of our products, similar to a supermarket aisle or a mail-order catalog. Showing each product heightens appetite appeal and has given us the opportunity to change people's impression of Denny's from a breakfast place to a restaurant with wide variety for each meal."

Menu Copywriting

Volumes have been written to help restaurateurs do a better job with the copy portions of their menus. Basically, the "simple is better" guideline that makes menu boards kind to customers' eyes applies with hand-held menus.

Design expert Nancy Loman Scanlon encourages restaurateurs to describe items clearly and cleanly, "Use as few words as possible, making each one count and keep sentences short so customers can read through the menu quickly."

She also suggests that they stick with one grammatical style. "If one ingredient is capitalized, all ingredients should be capitalized. This consistency in presentation makes for an easier-to-read menu, which will help the customer order more quickly," says Scanlon. Consistency also gives an impression of thoroughness and exactness, which goes far when customers sum up their overall impression of a restaurant.

Finally, she says, "Avoid superlatives." They won't enhance sales, they'll take away from them. Customers appreciate truth in copy.

The Role of the Server

The spoken word is the last and sometimes most important chance a restaurant has to sell its menu. But suggestive selling must be done gently. In the same way that too much point-of-sale material adds confusion to a restaurant's interior, too much talk from a waiter is a major customer turn-off.

Instead of encouraging wait staff to hard-sell customers, restaurants should emphasize an unobtrusive but informed style.

Kathryn Robinson, restaurant critic for the *Seattle Weekly*, offers an inspired list of suggestive-selling techniques. Among her ideas: Sell according to the weather. On a hot day, a waiter should ask customers if they want a cold, refreshing drink. When it's cold out, suggest a hot cappuccino. Another check-building method: Sell up. When someone asks for a gin and tonic, counter with, "Will that be a (insert brand name) and tonic?" And another wine-service tip: Pour less wine in the host's glass than in the other guests' glasses. The host will run out faster and be that much more inclined to order another bottle.

Jim Sullivan, president of Pencom, a Denver-based consulting firm, suggests drawing the entire staff into the selling process. His suggestions range from training the phone-answering staff to be polite and helpful to showing hostesses how they can make a 20-minute wait a pleasant one for guests. "The smart restaurateur realizes that servers aren't our only salespeople," writes Sullivan in his book, *Service That Sells* (Denver: Pencom Press, 1990). "Seeing all your front-line employees as salespeople means you have a daily obligation to teach and train everyone to use service that sells." ◆

Hot Type: How to Do a Winning Restaurant Newsletter

by Jeff Weinstein

When it comes to producing a restaurant newsletter, heed the advice of a renowned athletic-shoe manufacturer: "Just do it."

Restaurateurs from coast to coast love their newsletters. In fact, most say they would be lost without them. "I would feel out of touch with ways to maintain and build a client base," says Scott Carney, general manager of Gotham Bar & Grill, New York.

"When you compare newsletters to other advertising options, it is the most in-touch, personal form of communication," Carney adds. "It helps customers recall fond memories of the restaurant and lets them know you haven't forgotten about them. As E.M. Forster wrote in *Howards End*, 'Only connect.' "

Restaurateurs can connect with a newsletter, for as little as 25 cents each. The options on length, style, paper, printing, circulation and mailing determine the cost.

Words of Wisdom

The first step in producing a newsletter is determining the contents. Put yourself in the readers' shoes. What would they want to read?

"Our readers look for a mix of fun and informative stories with a warm, conversational tone that promotes a sense of being an insider member of a club," says Alfred Thimm, chief operating officer of the Palm restaurants, Washington.

Deann Bayless, co-owner of the Frontera Grill, Chicago, suggests, "Make it personal to reflect the restaurant's personality and the owners' individuality."

For example, the Frontera Grill newsletter promotes the restaurant's earthy approach to food and cooking. The latest issue featured an article on a small, unknown supplier. Bayless says such stories let customers know how truly close the owners are to their products.

Among the 100-plus newsletters collected for this story, several items stood out as regular features:

♦ **Coming events**: The newsletter's main purpose is to inform customers about events such as winemaker dinners and special holiday menus. But don't go overboard with announcements, or the letter will start to look and read like an advertisement flier.

♦ **Coupons and promotions**: Operators in the mood to deal might consider putting a coupon in the newsletter. F. McLintocks Saloon & Dining House, Shell Beach, Calif., promoted a dinner package that included theater tickets and hotel accommodations. The Palm offered a free T-shirt with any purchase. The coupon created an interactive component and helped build names for the Palm's mailing list.

♦ **Recipes**: Including them enables customers to cook their restaurant favorites at home. The Gotham Bar & Grill is closed on Thanksgiving, but runs a complete dinner recipe in its fall letter.

♦ **Food, menu trends**: Add a column on hot menu items from across the country, nutrition facts or popular restaurants in another cities for customers who travel.

♦ **Owner or chef column**: A must for that personal touch. Topics range from new menu plans, service upgrades and food trips taken by the staff to community involvement.

♦ **Celebrity news**: Not all restaurateurs believe a newsletter is the place to gossip about celebrity sightings, but such columns are common.

Buckhead Life Restaurant Group, Atlanta, publishes sightings on the front page of its newsletters. In fact, managers at each of the group's eight restaurants must keep a log of celebrity diners.

♦ **Mailing-list signup:** Signups help build the mailing list and ensure correct addresses for regular customers. Leave space on a signup form to ask if customers are interested in other services such as banquets.

♦ **Trivia, puzzles, contests and jokes:** Add variety and elements of fun to the letter. In a take-off of television's *Late Night with David Letterman*, the Cypress Club, San Francisco, publishes owner John Cunin's Top Ten list. In March, he featured the top ten descriptions a winemaker hates to hear. The No. 1 description: old running shorts.

♦ **Maps, other locations:** Not everyone has a sense of direction and not everyone knows you might have more than one location.

♦ **Business tips:** Because it attracts a lot of business professionals, The Palm runs management tips from Fortune 500 executives.

♦ **Customer comments and testimonials:** A great way to toot your own horn with sincere feedback. Along with testimonials, The Palm features caricatures of famous customers such as Billy Crystal.

♦ **Employee profiles:** Here's your chance to parade the service side of the business and a great way to show employees they are valued and important. Goose Island Brewing Co., Chicago, recently featured its sales director, which also created an opportunity to promote its private party rooms.

The Write Stuff

Once decisions are made about the newsletter's content, creating the product generally is farmed out to writing, design and publishing professionals. With few exceptions, restaurateurs don't have the time or talent to handle the job.

Unless you have an in-house marketing department, working with a public relations agency or a freelance writer is recommended to translate good ideas into crisply written copy. Make sure the writer has access to a computer. All copy should be created on a computer disk so it can be easily turned over to designers and printers for the next steps.

If possible, hire a writer who is familiar with the goings-on at the restaurant. There are newsletter-writing companies with good writers and artists, but unless they can tap into what is important to the restaurant, they won't know what is best for the letter.

Designed for Success

Well-written copy deserves a stylish, eye-catching design. Most restaurateurs consult or retain a graphic designer to create a look that captures the appearance and feel of the restaurant.

Designers often choose a paper color that complements the restaurant's decor or logo. White or off-white is a safe bet and the cheapest option. Recyclable paper is popular because it shows the restaurant's environmental awareness.

Two Guys from Italy, White Bear Lake, Minn., uses oversize paper so it stands out when the newsletter arrives in the mail.

F. McLintocks publishes 50,000 newsletters quarterly. It uses newspaper stock and prints at the local newspaper press to keep costs down. The length generally ranges from a two-sided sheet to eight pages.

Don't forget to include some computer-generated graphics, photographs or cartoons. Readers tend to lose interest if the pages are crammed with nothing but deadly gray type.

Find a reliable photographer to take shots of noteworthy staff members and willing celebrity guests, and at special events or food trips.

The designer enters the production process when copy is delivered on a computer disk. Taking direction from someone with the restaurant, the designer creates the layout and sends back a proof so the restaurateur can approve the design and check spellings, event dates and menu prices.

NEWSLETTER TIPS

- An owner's or chef's column adds a personal touch.
- Hire a writer who is familiar with your restaurant.
- Buy a mailing list to jump-start your newsletter.
- Celebrity columns add a touch of pizazz to newsletters.
- Recipes should be a staple for every newsletter.
- A column by the owners on the front page adds an immediate personal touch to any newsletter.
- Take the opportunity to state your service philosophy.
- Trends give readers fodder for party conversation.
- Use your newsletter to promote special events.
- Give staff members a pat on the back by writing employee profiles.
- Offer discounts or specially priced meals to give newsletters a value-added component.
- Include jokes, puzzles and games for variety.
- Announce seasonal events at least six to eight weeks in advance of the event.
- Include a map of your restaurant. Not every reader knows how to get there.
- Offer customers a chance to join the mailing list and offer feedback.
- Create a handsome logo and a catchy name for the newsletter to catch customers' attention.

Printing and Mailing

Once the copy and design are set, it's time to visit the printer. Best advice is to decide on a printer during the planning stage. Ask for a discount based on volume, promising regular business.

Finding one reliable printer also should ensure a consistent product. Most cities have a number of printing plants, both big and small, so it pays to shop around for the best price. And unless you and your staff want to spend hours affixing address labels and stamps, find a printer who has the staff and facilities to do the mailing, as well.

F. McLintocks lets its designer broker the printing because of the pickup and delivery involved. The designer picks up the finished product and delivers half of the 50,000 pieces to a mailing service. About 15,000 go to a local workshop for shut-ins for mailing, and 10,000 go back to the four restaurants to use as pass-outs. The quarterly publication costs about $12,000 a year to print, according to Director of Marketing Vicki Conner.

If the printer does the mailing, it will be up to the restaurateur to provide the mailing labels. Computer software is available to build and print out a mailing list.

Because it is expensive and time-consuming to build or buy a mailing list, it is important to keep the list clean. This involves two steps: uncovering duplicate mailings and making address changes.

Duplicate mailings can happen when names are submitted more than once, when a name or address is misspelled, or when a list has multiple sources. Look over the list regularly for such problems, and include a message to readers to inform you of duplicate copies.

Newsletters mailed at a flat bulk rate are not forwarded or returned if the recipient has moved or if the address is incorrect. A restaurateur could continue to mail the letter for months or years without knowing it has not reached its intended destination. For an additional fee, however, the post office will make address corrections on bulk-rate mail. According to Conner, it is worth the price.

"We get 2,500 back each mailing and make corrections with the new addresses," says Conner. "And we know the others have arrived. That is a secure feeling."

Some restaurateurs with smaller mailings of 3,000 or fewer mail newsletters on their own, using first-class postage to make sure they don't get lost.

Using first-class postage also helps the letter get delivered faster and avoids potential headaches for the restaurateur. "Some customers get mad when they call about promotions the day they receive the newsletter bulk mail, only to find out that the event is sold out," says Bayless of Frontera Grill.

Managing the Mail

Based on the number of newsletters you can afford to print and mail, there are several ways to build a mailing list and distribute the letter.

The Palm sent its last issue to 45,000, but has a goal of reaching 120,000 for its 12 units. To jump-start the program and bolster its in-house mailing list, it bought one-time use of Palm customer addresses from American Express. Each restaurant gets an additional 2,000 copies to leave at the front door, and valet parkers place a copy on car seats. The corporate office also follows up to make sure the letters are distributed.

Two Guys from Italy's initial mailing to the 20,000 customers on its database was too expensive and time consuming, according to Public Relations Coordinator Colleen Murphy. On the second go-round, management singled out zip codes in the immediate vicinity of its two units and cut its mailing to a manageable 10,000 customers. With each new mailing, management plans to expand by adding another zip code.

When the Italian Village, Chicago, mailed its first newsletter this winter, it used a local business daily newspaper to expand its circulation. For $2,000, the restaurant had the newsletter poly-bagged with *Crain's Chicago Business* and delivered to 7,600 *Crain's* subscribers.

The final decision to make about a newsletter is how often to publish. Again, it depends on the workload and how much a restaurant can afford. ♦

Showtime!
How to Open a Restaurant

by Jeff Weinstein

The stage is set. Crew members know their places. The cast of characters is lined up at the door ready to take center stage. The most important and exciting event in the life of a restaurant is about to take place—opening night.

Early reviews from critics and local opinion makers can make or break a restaurant. You have only one shot at a successful opening, so it's imperative to set priorities carefully. These include training the staff properly, inviting and entertaining luminaries, and working with the press to secure media exposure.

With all the adrenalin going, you might be tempted to fly from one planning session to the next. But in your hurry, don't be hasty.

Skimming over the details to rush an opening in the name of cash flow can be deadly. "Opening too quickly is the biggest mistake a restaurateur can make," says Ned Grace, president of Phelps-Grace Company, East Providence, R.I. "You damage your customer base if you're not prepared on Day One. And unfortunately, I see it happen all the time."

Training Camp

Operators agree that the success of a restaurant opening hinges on the staff's performance, which means proper training is essential. The general rule of thumb is two weeks' training before any opening event, according to Michael Colacchio, vice president of marketing for Il Fornaio America Corp., San Francisco, which operates 24 restaurants in California.

Training for Il Fornaio concepts starts with a two-day orientation. Company President Larry Mindel spends the first day speaking about the company history, his vision and expectations for

the unit preparing to open, and what support employees can expect from the company.

On following days, front- and back-of-the-house employees split up for seminars on computer systems and the menu. They also take part in role-playing sessions that impart service philosophies. The entire staff reassembles a few days later to watch and ask questions as the chef prepares every dish on the menu.

On the sixth day, the staff begins trial runs for each of the three meal periods. Much of the practice is done internally—servers serving each other. The menu for the first training period generally is limited to a handful of side dishes and entrees. Items are added to subsequent periods until the entire menu is made available.

On the last three days of training, Il Fornaio management produces full-blown dinner trials with one turn for each table to intentionally overload the kitchen, servers and the system.

To fill the restaurant on the first of three trial nights, operators usually invite the contractors who built the unit. The following night, staff from other units or close friends of management act as friendly guinea pigs. A third night often is connected to a charitable organization whose membership matches the restaurant's target audience.

Although two weeks of preopening training is considered the norm, some operators advocate getting the doors open as soon as possible. "The best experience is live experience," says Tom Kaplan, general manager of the newly opened Spago in Las Vegas. "The staff's attention span diminishes after a few days of training, so we put some pressure on by giving them real customers in a hurry. Most rise to the occasion."

Kaplan says his staff is ready to open two or three days after the building passes final inspection. To ease the process, however, he overstaffs throughout the operation to start. For example, servers wait on two tables instead of the usual five for the first few weeks.

Of course, it doesn't hurt that experienced personnel want to work at an eatery owned by the famed Wolfgang Puck. And it also doesn't hurt that Puck brings in experienced staff from his other restaurants to assist.

"One of the most obvious but overlooked training techniques is to draw from staff at existing units," says Kaplan. "Many restaurants bring in a chef and a manager for an opening, but we use experienced staff from all areas of operation, including busers. It's like an all-star game." (Many chains, including Hard Rock Cafe and Cooker, have special teams responsible for opening new units and training staff.)

Spago's quick opening keeps preopening costs at less than 1% of first-year sales, says Kaplan. That compares with 3.5% spent by Il Fornaio, according to Colacchio.

The PR Machine

Even before the training starts, management should crank up the public relations machine to make sure the right invitations go to the right people. They will help get word-of-mouth advertising going for you.

If you can afford it, hire a public relations firm to handle the distracting details of coordinating opening events. The company should build a mailing list that targets a microcosm of customers the restaurant wants to attract on a regular basis. The VIP list also should include government officials; retail and advertising executives, who do a lot of business entertaining; leaders from the visual and performing arts fields; and representatives of the medical and legal communities.

In addition, make sure the PR firm has a track record for effectively placing restaurant news within the local print and broadcast media.

For smaller operations or institutions, limited budgets often mean managing public relations efforts in-house. If you can't afford to hire a public relations firm to handle your opening party,

take note of the advice public relations specialists offer later in this article.

How Many Parties?

The first decision to make is how many and what type of opening parties you want to throw. In addition to a grand-opening party, many operators like to invite small groups to more intimate gatherings to get a better feel for what the restaurant is all about.

"Grand openings don't present your restaurant in its intended light," says Earl Geer, who opened Hi-Life Restaurant & Lounge, a 135-seat operation in New York. "To avoid firing all our guns on the first-night grand-opening party, we invite smaller groups of 30 to 50 people on subsequent nights and introduce them to the real restaurant."

The small parties at Hi-Life go on for two weeks, Tuesday through Friday. Friends of management and good customers from Geer's Hi-Life Bar & Grill, also in New York, are invited to come in on specific nights. These guests pay for their dinner, but they receive a drink and an appetizer and/or dessert on the house.

Geer creates good will with these parties, but on top of that, when passersby peek through the window, the restaurant looks busy during the first few weeks of operation.

Charity Involvement

Another option to consider when opening a restaurant is making it a charity event.

South Miami Beach, Fla., public relations specialist Susan Brustman says tying an opening to a fund-raiser makes more of an impact. "You immediately bond with the community and develop a loyal following from the organization that benefits," she says.

Brustman also points out that fund-raisers lead to potential exposure in the living and society sections of the newspaper. "There is plenty of time to get into the food and restaurant review sections," she says.

However, many restaurateurs resist a charity tie-in. Some say it overshadows the restaurant's opening. Others don't want their guests to feel an obligation. "If I invite the assistant to the mayor, I don't want to force her to make a $10 donation," says Grace.

Attention Grabbers

Once the number and style of parties is clear, it is time to create invitations. Try to integrate the restaurant's concept into the design of the invitation. For instance, it should be consistent with the restaurant's color sensibilities and typefaces in the logo and menu.

"Direct-mail invitations provide a brief, magical opportunity to grab the attention of the invitee," says Tom Doody, owner of Tom Doody Public Relations, Chicago. "It becomes part of your direct-marketing campaign because 75% of the people who can't attend the party will log it as interesting and worth further investigation."

Media and VIP invitations should be mailed about two weeks in advance of a grand-opening celebration. Tab 35 to 50 high-profile guests for follow-up telephone calls about a week later.

Party Time

Monday is the best night to throw an opening gala because it normally is a slow business night.

To avoid overcrowding, tier events over the course of a night or two days. It is standard practice to invite media and VIPs from 6 p.m. until 8 p.m. Then invite the influential party crowd from 8 p.m. until 10 p.m.

Stay away from sit-down dinners at grand openings—a crowd of 200 to 400 that shows up at the same time overtaxes the kitchen and the service staff. Most PR pros recommend two hours of passed hors d'oeuvres or buffet stations featuring menu samples and an open bar. Some operators switch to a cash bar after two hours to help pay for the party costs or persuade guests to leave.

When guests enter a big stand-up party, they have a tendency to gravitate toward the bar. To avoid overcrowding in one area of the restaurant, plan the route the guests will travel, suggests Matthew Rovner, partner, Ward/Rovner Public Relations, Boston.

A FULL BAG OF OPENING-NIGHT PARTY TRICKS

Boston public relations expert Matthew Rovner offers tricks to keep opening parties flowing and guests happy.

- ♦ **Hand out name tags**. Nothing is worse for an owner than forgetting a guest's name ten minutes after being introduced.
- ♦ **Overstaff**. Make sure you have enough people parking cars and checking coats. Waiting in lines to get in or out leaves guests with a bad impression.
- ♦ **Assign people to circulate through the room**. Make sure someone on staff is available to answer questions about parties and catering, help clear dishes that pile up, and give tours of the kitchen to meet the chef.
- ♦ **Create events within the event**. The owner should offer a toast or say a few words to mark the occasion and break up the evening.
- ♦ **Bring in the band**. A string quartet playing background music is a classy touch for an upscale event, especially at the beginning of the party when the room isn't full.
- ♦ **Make sure someone stays at the front door**. Owners get involved in the party, leave the door area and don't say goodbye. Make sure someone is at the door to shake hands, ask if the guests had a good time and make sure no one leaves drunk.
- ♦ **Give guests something to take home**. Gifts can get expensive. A memorable but inexpensive option is a copy of the menu tied with a ribbon.

"We direct guests to meet with the owner in the front of the dining room, where we have removed some tables and chairs and set up three or four food stations," says Rovner. "People get caught up eating, we provide cocktail service and most guests never make it to the bar area. We can get a lot more people in the door and improve traffic flow."

Rovner also recommends using just one entrance area to keep control of the party. "You run into problems with the flow if people come and go from different doors. It also helps keep freeloaders away," he says.

Another problem during private parties: customers who arrive, see lights on and think the restaurant is open for business. To avoid losing a potential customer, Grace keeps envelopes at the door with a takeout menu, a card for a free dessert, and a note explaining that the restaurant staff is training and the operation will open soon.

Post-Party Media Plan

A restaurant opening doesn't end after the parties are over.

Restaurateurs and public relations representatives should follow up with the working press to see whether they need an interview, photographs or a dinner reservation, or if they want to come back for private tastings. Within the first six weeks, some PR people try to create media-only dinners or interview sessions to learn about the menu or meet the chef. Don't push it, though. Many media representatives prefer to come back on their own after the opening.

Photographs taken during opening events should be forwarded to local columnists with a post-party press release that mentions names of important attendees. Send trade-press editors a press kit that includes a menu, an explanation of the concept, and background on the owners and chefs. If you have a photography budget, food photos usually are preferred over interior and exterior shots.

Getting Down to Business

Once the initial excitement dies down, it's time to tend to the daily chores of running a successful restaurant. After months of hard work and anticipation, the atmosphere will never be quite the same.

"An opening is the most exciting thing you do in this business," says Il Fornaio's Colacchio. "It draws on all your training and experience, and if you've done a good job you reap the greatest reward. It's like launching a ship. It's better than the last one you built, and you know you can do it again." ♦

Restaurants That Market to Kids

by Brenda McCarthy

Nothing adds to the atmosphere of a dining experience like the wail of a hungry, antsy toddler. Parents, patrons and restaurant staff will agree, however, that it's not the most pleasant addition. Consequently, parents flock to kid-friendly restaurants where they know kids are welcome.

What makes a restaurant kid-friendly? The right mix of atmosphere, service, menu and pricing, say several parents *R&I* talked to. Here are some of their comments on what lures them, children in tow, to their favorite kid-proof eating spots.

Atmospheric Pressure

The atmosphere, from concept to seating capacity, is a major influence on where parents choose to dine with their children. Julie DeRoin, mother of a 20-month-old son, approves of restaurants that modify seating for families.

"They know how it is! So they have a section in the back where they put you. It doesn't matter if your kid isn't staying put," says DeRoin.

Restaurants that offer play areas for kids also fall in favor with parents. Other musts are adequate supplies of clean booster seats and high chairs.

Even lighting affects kids. "One time we went to a nicer restaurant that was really dark when Joe was a year old. He wasn't happy there. I think the atmosphere turned him off," says Stephen Rohr, father of two.

"You also don't want to go into a restaurant where there are no other kids," Rohr adds. "If the kids get a little too loud, we feel like the world is tunneling in on us."

Child-Liking Servers

In a kid-friendly restaurant, the servers help dining parents when that tunneling starts. Or they stop the tunneling before it starts by keeping kids occupied and happy.

"The wait staff is very important, and so is the management and how they train them to treat you," says DeRoin. "If they see you with kids and seat you before they seat others, for instance, that's wonderful."

Other touches don't require a lot of effort on the part of the server, just some attention to detail. DeRoin relates how some servers bring extra napkins to the table without her even asking for them. Another server once brought each child at her lunch table a cup of ice to chew on while waiting for their meals.

"It's the smallest thing, but it makes the biggest difference in the world," says DeRoin. "You'll intentionally go back to a restaurant because of things like that."

Doreen Saltzman, mother of three, likes when the servers give something extra to kids. One restaurant her family frequents gives each child a mini candy bar on a kiddie plate. Another gives balloons to the kids.

Plain Fare

For very young children, menu is not an issue. As children age, however, they develop food preferences, albeit limited ones. A restaurant that wants to court kids and their parents is smart to offer items kids will eat.

"Not every menu carries grilled cheese or hot dogs, which are what kids like," says DeRoin.

According to parents, kids tend to veer away from ethnic foods. Debbie Ford, mother of a 21-month-old son, says she and her husband will avoid ethnic restaurants for this reason.

"We would not go out for Chinese. He's not interested in the food, and the atmosphere doesn't grab him either," says Ford.

Some restaurants compromise by offering a

kids' menu that appeals to kids' tastes and does not necessarily reflect the cuisine of the restaurant. The Italian Oven, Latrobe, Pa., offers items like grilled cheese and french fries for kids.

Food that is served cafeteria-style or on a buffet appeals to some kids because they are in charge of choosing what they eat.

"It makes them feel more independent," says Saltzman, who sees in buffet service the added benefit of getting kids to try new foods without parental prodding.

"My oldest likes the make-your-own-omelet section and will go up and order one with everything from olives to broccoli," she says.

Pricing

Some parents think that a restaurant that can get a child to willingly try new foods is worth any price. If it also excels in atmosphere, service and menu, they will become repeat customers, even if it means paying a little more.

"For a nicer meal, we wouldn't be adverse to spending a lot," says Rohr.

Other parents don't want to spend a lot of money on a meal that might not be finished by a picky eater. Many take advantage of the value promotions restaurants offer parents.

"Absolutely. We go to restaurants where kids eat free on Sunday," says Saltzman.

Beyond price, however, is a less-tangible draw for parents, which Saltzman summarizes: "We'll go to the restaurants we're more comfortable with, where we feel welcome and wanted." ◆

TRAINING STAFFERS TO SERVE KIDS

Training staff members to be kid-friendly can help make a restaurant experience pleasant for everyone involved: parents, kids, staffers and other patrons.

Seat and serve diners accompanied by kids first to help children from getting antsy.

Get creative in your gifts for kids. Chevys stores have a display area where tortillas are made, which also distributes balls of tortilla dough for kids to play with. The Italian Oven, Latrobe, Pa., gives kids kits for making pasta necklaces and bracelets.

At Chevys, servers greet kids first, kneel down so they are speaking on the kids' level, and ask the child, not the parents, what he or she would like to order.

Train servers to distribute distraction devices to kids as soon as they are seated.

Children of different ages have different seating needs, and the staff should be flexible in modifying the standard table. The Italian Oven keeps different sizes of booster seats and highchairs, and servers are trained to eye children to determine their fit.

Servers at the Italian Oven are trained to look for signs that children are fidgeting. When they do, they bring animal crackers or a breadstick.

Managing a Foodborne Illness Crisis

by Karen Cheney

Robert Nugent, president of Jack in The Box, leans tensely toward a microphone. It's unlikely that he has ever before had to deal with such a ceaseless barrage of questions from the press, health officials, his employees, customers and, most painfully, the parents of the child who died from eating an E. coli-tainted burger. Under the glare of television lights, he wipes his brow and proceeds to update a wary audience.

Who could forget his image of distress? Certainly no one in the foodservice industry. For any restaurant owner, manager or CEO could easily transpose his or her own face over Nugent's. The fact is, no one is invulnerable to crisis. Even those who follow the most rigorous food-safety guidelines are very likely to have a foodborne-illness case occur sometime during their years of business. One day, a cook will fail to heat up a grill sufficiently. A refrigerator will go on the blink between regular audits, causing sensitive products to spoil. Employees will neglect to wash their hands before cutting meat or produce. A supplier will ship contaminated product.

Still feel immune to foodborne-illness outbreaks? Just consider a few of these not uncommon headlines: "E. Coli Victim Leaves Legacy of Awareness," (*Seattle Times*); "Colorado Faces New Outbreak of Hepatitis-A" (*Chicago Tribune*); "Florida Issues Surf 'N' Turf Warning for Foodborne Illness" (United Press International); "Salmonella Outbreak Prompts Health Warning" (*San Francisco Chronicle*); "Mayonnaise Blamed for Illnesses in Oregon" (Associated Press).

And these are just the cases that received national attention.

Deaths caused by foodborne illness are infrequent. In most cases, a brief hospital stay and medication will cure patients. The restaurant, however, might suffer permanent losses, even closing its doors for good if it fails to regain public trust.

Enter the Crisis Experts

Since the famous Tylenol incident in 1982, when a terrorist poisoned Johnson & Johnson's pain-relief capsules with cyanide, crisis management has become a booming industry. Companies took note of the public support that occurred when that crisis was dealt with well, and, in the case of the Union Carbide/Bhopal disaster or the Exxon/Valdez spill, the negative reverberations of mishandling a tragedy.

Amazingly, however, some still failed to put plans in place in anticipation of a catastrophe. When timing and initial response matter so much, this could be fatal for a company. "The first round of coverage will determine whether you're the villain or the victim," warns Lynn Sokler, a crisis-management expert and vice president at Manning, Selvage & Lee, Atlanta.

Gerald C. Meyers, former chairman of American Motors Corporation and author of *When it Hits the Fan* (New York: Houghton Mifflin Co., 1986), says that most executives don't like to think about or discuss crises. They are bred to think success. The most effective way to approach crisis management, however, is to assume that you are always in a "precrisis" mode.

Assemble a Response Team

"There are probably eight people who I would go to and alert in a crisis," says Michael Evans, vice president of public relations for Miami-based Burger King and coordinator for that company's crisis-response team. Those individuals include someone from operations, the legal department, quality control, risk and safety, and human resources, as well as appropriate field staff. "It's not necessarily a war-room mentality, but these are the people I would consult," he adds.

Any team should be small enough to allow members to make decisions quickly, but large enough to include key players. A researcher or quality assurance person, for instance, will gather facts about what might have gone wrong in the restaurant's food storing, preparing or serving procedures. Meanwhile, a lawyer determines the possible legal implications of the crisis. One crucial team member is the designated spokesperson, the only one who should make public statements. This will help avoid the release of contradictory information.

The response team also should hold periodic sessions to anticipate every possible problem. "What is it that wakes you up in the middle of the night in a cold sweat?" asks Sokler. "You have to sit down and come up with all the things that could occur."

"With nine million people coming through your door every day, the exposure is great," says Evans. "If you can anticipate potential dangers, you're minimizing your exposure. . . .We have about ten areas that we anticipate things could happen, and we outline strategies."

Take the Right Steps

In March, Arby's corporate headquarters received a call from one of its units. A woman and three children had gotten sick and notified the restaurant that it could have been from eating Arby's roast beef sandwiches. "Our unit manager alerted us immediately that there may be a problem," recounts Jack Mason, director of quality assurance and regulatory affairs for the Miami-based chain. "Then the first thing we did was to make sure that the family was fine, that they'd been taken care of and had been to the doctor."

Mason warns that it's important not to admit guilt until you have all of the facts: What did the customer eat? When? How many people were involved? (See "Receiving a Complaint" sidebar.)

"What's really critical is what happened to the product from the time that they bought it. Did they buy it at a drive-thru? Did they take it back to the office?" he asks, pointing out that many people buy several sandwiches when there is a special and store them in their own refrigerators for later consumption.

RECEIVING A COMPLAINT

When someone complains of foodborne illness, it's a good idea to use a standardized form to record the incident. This will ensure that you ask all of the right questions, even during those times when business is hectic.

Get all of the pertinent information, including the names and addresses of all party members, the staff person who served the meal, the date and time of the customer's visit, the suspect meal and unit location.

Remain concerned and polite, but don't admit liability or offer to pay medical bills. For instance, do say: "I'm sorry that you're feeling sick." Don't say: "I'm sorry that our food made you sick."

Never suggest symptoms, but let the complainant tell his own story.

Record the time that the symptoms started. This will help in identifying the disease and determining the restaurant's responsibility.

If possible, try to get a food history of all of the meals and snacks eaten, before and after the person was at your restaurant.

Never offer medical advice. Gather information, but don't interpret symptoms.

Source: Educational Foundation of the National Restaurant Association, Applied Foodservice Sanitation, 4th Edition (John Wiley & Sons, 1992)

Joel Simpson, vice president of quality assurance for Dobbs International, says whenever the company receives a complaint, "We operate under the assumption that we have a potential problem. We don't take the attitude that this is simply an allegation."

When should you alert health officials? Most restaurant managers follow the rule that when two or more unrelated people complain of illness, you've got a problem. At this point, it would be wise to notify your state's local health department.

Meanwhile, the restaurant should begin its

TOP FOUR FOODBORNE ILLNESSES

Salmonellosis
 Latency period: Five to 72 hours. **Symptoms**: Stomach pain, diarrhea, nausea, chills, fever, headache. **Major food vehicles**: Beef, other meats, dairy products, baked goods and potato salad. **Control**: Thorough cooking.

Staph Intoxication
 Latency period: thirty minutes to eight hours. **Symptoms**: Abdominal pain or nausea, followed by vomiting; occasionally fever, weakness and dizziness. **Major food vehicles**: Ham (28.6%), all meats, potato salad and eggs. **Control**: Prompt refrigeration of cooked food; thorough cooking.

Botulism
 Latency period: Usually 12 to 48 hours; sometimes up to eight days. **Symptoms**: Dry mouth, double vision and difficulty swallowing; also nausea, diarrhea, sore throat. **Major food vehicles**: Peppers, asparagus, beans, salmon and fish eggs, tomatoes, beets, pickles, baked potatoes and potato salad. **Control**: Thorough heating and rapid cooling of foods.

Ciguatera Poisoning
 Latency period: Three to 18 hours. **Symptoms**: Diarrhea, nausea, vomiting, abdominal pain; sometimes taste and vision aberrations. **Major food vehicles**: "Reef and island" fish. **Control**: Eat only small fish.
 Source: Centers for Disease Control, Atlanta; USDA

puts the time and date on it and sends it out for microbial analysis. "Then we would hope that if a person was admitted to a hospital, there would be a stool sample and a vomit sample," Mason says.

In this particular case, seven people turned up with confirmed cases of staph infection, soon attributed to a faulty oven. "It was holding product at 80 degrees to 90 degrees instead of 150 degrees," says Mason. Two elderly women were hospitalized, but both are well now.

Although health officials did not require the restaurant to shut down temporarily, Mason took extra precautions and closed at 2:30 P.M., reopening at 10 the next morning. "We completely sanitized the place," he says. In the end, Arby's handled the incident so smoothly that it never made it to the general media.

Communicate to the Public

"While most companies have an operations crisis plan, they don't have a communications crisis plan," says Clarke Caywood, director of the graduate program in corporate public relations at Northwestern University's Medill School of Journalism, Evanston, Ill. Caywood collaborated with Jack Gottschalk on a book called *Crisis Response: Inside Stories on Managing Image Under Siege* (Detroit: Gale Press, 1993).

When the image you project could save or shatter your business, it's extremely important to deal effectively with your customers, employees and the press, emphasizes Caywood.

According to most experts, Jack in The Box went wrong in its initial dealings with the public. "I'd give them a C, maybe a C+," says Caywood. "Their communications system wasn't in place. . . . The public's assumptions about what was going on were running rampant—and being behind the public is very dangerous."

There is only one reality—what the public thinks is happening, says Sokler, not what is happening. "Unless you bridge that gap quickly, you'll have a perception vacuum." It's a good idea to set up a toll-free number where concerned customers can ask questions regarding an outbreak.

In dealing with the media, give regular press

own investigation. "We go back and check all the procedures we've taken in our system. We want to make sure that the roast beef is cooked thoroughly," says Mason. "We document the temperature of the roast and the weight of the roast."

If there is any leftover product, the restaurant

DEALING WITH THE PRESS

Begin each press conference or interview with a well-defined message in mind. Also, make it clear that the welfare of the victims is your top concern.

Try to answer questions directly, but never speculate when you're unsure of the answer. Instead of saying "No comment," say, "I'll try to get back to you when I know the answer." Keep track of all questions and answer them when the facts become clear.

Don't assign blame or possible causes of the crisis until you have all of the facts.

Don't use technical jargon, but be sure that every statement you release is free of ambiguity.

Never speak "off the record."

Let the public know about your safety record and the precautions that you take to provide wholesome food.

Consult with experts when appropriate. Testimony from a medical expert, for instance, could allay fears and clarify misinformation.

Source: NRA; *When It Hits the Fan*, by Gerald C. Meyers (New York: Houghton Mifflin, 1986)

WHERE TO LOOK FOR HELP

The following organizations offer publications with advice on preventing food-safety problems.

Charles Felix Associates, P.O. Box 1581, Leesburg, Va. 22075; (703) 777-7448. Subscribe to *Food Talk*, a food-safety newsletter.

Restaurants & Institutions, 1350 E. Touhy Ave., P.O. Box 5080, Des Plaines, Ill. 60017-5080; (708) 635-8800. Ask for copies of the 1991 "Clean Restaurant" series.

American Council on Science and Health, 1995 Broadway, Second floor, New York, N.Y. 10023-5860; (212) 362-7044. Order the handbook, *Eating Safely: Avoiding Foodborne Illness.*

National Restaurant Association, 311 First Street, NW, Washington, D.C. 20001; (800) 526-6662; from New York state, (516) 674-3250. Request a copy of the *Crisis Management Manual* (order code: MG600).

conferences—even if you don't have all the facts yet. "The first thing you can do is be extremely frank and forthcoming. Communicate as clearly as possible that there has been a problem, and don't look like you're dodging criticism," says Caywood.

"If it's a large-scale crisis, you probably should have a single communications person who is in charge of all the inquiries," says Sokler. "You should have daily news briefings. . . . A smaller crisis may require only one meeting with the media, depending whether there is more to the crisis that unfolds."

Don't Neglect Employees

Some companies are better at communicating with the general public than they are with their own employees. These are the people who have firsthand contact with your customers. Also, their own fears during a foodborne-illness outbreak might drive them to leave the company for good.

"In some instances, inoculations will be required of all employees," says Denny Lynch, vice president of public relations, Wendy's International, Dublin, Ohio. "Some health departments will require employees to wear gloves; in other markets, they'll say that they don't want those." Someone must communicate all of this information to the staff.

And don't forget the parents of young employees. "They help decide whether or not the employee will stay," says Lynch.

Manage Your Image

Remember that companies like McDonald's that have built up a bank of good will in the community will weather crises better. "The more people know who you are and what you stand for, the more they will believe that you are going to do what's right," says Sokler.

The National Restaurant Association recommends that restaurant owners make humane gestures to people who become ill in their restaurants. Take care of all medical expenses and send flowers. Maintain good relations with health officials, too, by inviting them to a reopening celebration. While these gestures won't make you immune to crisis, they will help your recovery be as speedy as possible. ◆

Restaurant Critics' Rules

by Wendy Rohr

Although they are anonymous while they eat, what they write about the food becomes well-known. Wouldn't it be nice to know what critics are considering when they're sitting at your table? To find out what makes the typical critic tick, *R&I* asked ten reviewers from cities across the country to name the factors they look at most closely. The results prove that critics from coast to coast are as different as the dishes that they sample from day to day. Some are food fanatics, placing taste at the top of their lists. Others say they prefer to look at the big picture, weighing every dining element. A few favor fresh flowers while others loathe loud music.

But no matter how widely their personal preferences vary, most critics agree that food, service, value and comfort are key.

Following are summaries of what the critics had to say about how they do their jobs.

MOLLY ABRAHAM
Detroit Free Press

"A restaurant is a combination of everything," notes Abraham. "I'm not one of those critics who goes in and stares at the food."

One of the things that Abraham likes best in a restaurant is the use of fresh flowers. "A gorgeous flower arrangement that gives me a good feeling," she says. Among the things that give her bad feelings: "If you see a layer of dust on the green plants, or if the staff doesn't look well-groomed."

Freshness—the use of fresh ingredients as often as possible—tops the list of what Abraham looks for in restaurant food. Creativity also counts. "I look for something I haven't seen 1,000 times before," she says. "Obviously, I don't expect every restaurant to come up with a new fantastic dish. But I look for imagination in how they present something. Even if it's a hamburger."

Service is another crucial factor. Abraham looks for a good level of service, not one that is either overbearing or invisible: "A good server seems to realize when you want to speak with him and when he should step back."

The "level of comfort" to diners also figures prominently in Abraham's reviews. That comfort level includes everything from furnishings to lighting to noise. "I hate going into a restaurant where the lights beat down on you," she says. "And I don't mind noise, but when it gets to the decibel levels where it bothers you, it ruins the comfort level."

Another item that Abraham notes is what she calls the level of expertise. "It's a certain spirit—a feeling that the people who run the restaurant are professional and really care about doing a good job," observes Abraham. "I admire people who do a good job of running a restaurant. It's one of the hardest jobs around."

GAEL GREENE
New York Magazine

"It's great to walk into a place that has the smell of garlic cooking in olive oil," says Greene. She also likes to be greeted by other pleasant smells such as butter or apples and thinks "extraordinary flowers" are a plus.

Among those items that currently bother Greene are useless "confetti on the edge of plate" such as parsley, sugar, cocoa, ground cumin and chili. "Somebody did it, and now everyone is doing it," says Greene. "It's ridiculous and it gets on your sleeve."

When reviewing a restaurant, Greene first weighs the quality of the food. "Food is the first thing that rings my bell," she says. "It can be seriously great or amusingly good, complicated or simple."

Then there is the "feel of the room." Greene asks herself if it is comfortable, beautiful, appropriate, fun or great for people-watching. She adds that service, price, and lighting figure into how the room feels. Greene thinks the service should be attentive but unobtrusive. "I hate the waiter who introduces himself or the one who tells you you did a good job of ordering," says Greene. "I also hate when a waiter clears the table before everyone is done."

Greene says she thinks lighting and sound should be well-modulated. "Lighting is incredibly important, and people tend to leave it to amateurs," she says. "I'm grateful when the light makes me look 23."

Greene notes that not all of the factors she considers have to earn high marks for a restaurant to earn a good review. "I always look for balance," says Greene. "If the food is OK, the price is right and the crowd is great, that's a place I would probably recommend."

ELLIOTT MACKLE
Atlanta Journal/Constitution

"That a restaurant has palm trees and a waterfall is unimportant if the pupu platter is a cat-litter box," says Mackle. "The food is the most important thing."

In general, Mackle looks for fresh, well-prepared, attractive food. But he also keeps his eyes open for menus that lie. "If what comes to the table is not what the menu promises, I take points off," he notes. Just recently, Mackle ordered an entree that appeared in French on the menu as mussels in herb sauce. Instead, he was served mussels in tomato sauce. "I'm seeing this kind of thing a lot and it's very sloppy," he says.

Other factors that matter are value and service. "A $23 hamburger is probably not a good value," says Mackle on pricing. And he feels the service should be well-paced and servers should be informative. "I don't need to know their names as much as I need to know what they are doing,"

he says. "And if something is special, I want to know why it is special and how much it costs."

Physical comfort and ambience also play a role. "I ask myself, 'Does my back hurt when I leave?'" says Mackle. The critic particularly dislikes seats that are designed to make you finish eating as quickly as possible. "That's fine for McDonald's but not for a white-tablecloth," he says. In terms of ambience, Mackle asks, "Does it feel nice? Does it make you want to stay there?"

RUTH REICHL
Los Angeles Times

"Each restaurant is different," notes Reichl. "I do not judge a restaurant on my standards but on the restaurant's standards." Reichl criticizes critics who judge restaurants by their personal standards. She says she tries to put her preferences aside when working as a critic.

In other words, Reichl educates herself on what the restaurant is trying to do before she decides if it is good or bad. She says this is particularly important in the Los Angeles market, where ethnic diversity is vast.

"A lot of critics judge cuisine that they don't know," says Reichl. "I even read a review where the critic said he didn't like the jellyfish at a Chinese restaurant because it was bland. The Chinese don't judge jellyfish on flavor but on texture. You have to know that if you're going to write a review."

Reichl says the factors she focuses on vary from place to place. "You would think the most important thing is food, but that's not always true," says Reichl. "Some people go to places because they are comfortable. Sometimes it's because they are cheap. Sometimes it's because they are quick."

The important thing in Reichl's mind is that restaurateurs know who they are, who their clientele is, and what they want to do. She tries to tell her readers what the restaurant is trying to accomplish and where it doesn't achieve its goals.

PHYLLIS RICHMAN
The Washington Post

"The basic thing is that the food should be delicious in what it sets out to be," says Richman, who lists her five top criteria as "food, food, food, service and environment."

"Great food has a magic that takes it beyond its ingredients and makes it hard to dissect," she continues. "You feel as if you're eating a personal expression or someone's art."

In terms of service and environment, Richman says the importance of those factors varies from place to place. "For the Hard Rock Cafe, environment is a good part of its reason for being," she says. "But we have a Thai restaurant here in Washington, for example, that people go to for the service and well-prepared food."

Ranking at the top of Richman's dislike list is dishonesty in a restaurant. "I don't like when a restaurant makes claims that it can't deliver," says Richman. Among those claims, she says, are calling something "homemade" when it's not, or saying something is "fresh" when the discerning critic can tell it most certainly isn't.

CHRIS SHERMAN
St. Petersburg (Fla.) Times

"There is no reason to sprinkle dehydrated parsley on a dish," observes Sherman. He says he looks for freshness first as the mark of a good restaurant.

And although he considers it to be basic, value matters to Sherman. "Most of us are aware that turning out a great meal for $45 is no great accomplishment," he says. "If you can't do that, you ought to get out of the business."

Imagination is another important element. "You've got to think a little bit beyond what everyone else is doing," says Sherman. "That might even mean putting a slightly different hot sauce on the table."

The one place most restaurateurs can improve the appeal of their meal? Through imaginative choices in the bread department, says Sherman.

"Baking is a way to turn the cheapest ingredients into something good," he says. "It's an inexpensive way to dress up a restaurant." He recalls a seafood restaurant where servers dish house-made biscuits out of heavy black baking tins.

Service is next. For example, Sherman looks for a quick greeting at the door. "If I have to stand there for five minutes, it's as aggravating as hell." He adds, "The hostess job is usually given to the most air-headed, least trained of the servers. It should be the opposite."

Wine prices also are on Sherman's checklist. He is impressed by restaurants that cut the markup, which he says averages three times retail. "It's a rarity when you can find a place that keeps the markup down," he says. "Most of us would rather find a place that doesn't have a liquor license yet so you could bring your own."

PHIL VETTEL
Chicago Tribune

"Culinary excellence" tops Vettel's list of positive restaurant qualities. He looks for basic good food and for people doing outstanding things with the simplest of ingredients.

His list of negatives includes orally delivered specials sans the prices and poorly trained servers. "A special should never be more expensive than the most expensive entree on the menu, and if it is, they should tell you up front," says Vettel. "You feel really small if you have to interrupt to ask the price." Vettel says he looks for six basic things when reviewing a restaurant. A good greeting is among them—Vettel likes to see someone competent at the front door. Cleanliness is another. He makes simple observations such as whether things are new or old, if light bulbs work and if the menus are worn.

The selection on the menu is another factor. "It should have a selection that looks inviting and makes sense in terms of what the restaurant is trying to be," says Vettel. He also checks the wine list to see if it is in line with the restaurant's goals.

In addition, Vettel considers what he calls

"basic creature comforts" such as lighting, temperature, comfortable seating and table size. "You shouldn't have to be a contortionist to get into the place," he says. "And some restaurants that offer three- and four-course dining have these itty-bitty tables. Where are they supposed to put all the food?"

Another element is how the restaurant is running overall. "I look for a lack of anxiety on the faces of the people who are running the show," says Vettel. "If you see servers rushing about like there is some sort of fire drill, it makes it very difficult to relax."

GEOFFREY TOMB
The Miami Herald

"Strolling guitarists annoy the hell out of me," says Tomb when assessing the things he likes least about restaurants. Loud music for "the sake of music" is another mistake. And like many other critics, good food is what Tomb likes best.

"Whatever the philosophy is, it has to be conveyed by the food," says Tomb. "If it is a mom-and-pop-type place, are they doing wonderful things with home-style vegetables or are they opening a can and using a microwave? And if it is a five-star restaurant, does their theme come across in their food? Does it deliver the message it is supposed to convey?"

Next on the list is taste. "In Miami, in particular, we have a lot of bright wonderful chefs who go for an extra dimension in a dish just to give it embellishment, and I think they sometimes go one step too far," says Tomb. "There is no sense in clouding it up just to give it a mango sauce. Food should taste like food."

The third factor is presentation. "I'm keen on how food looks," says Tomb. "My mom was a good cook, and she always said the plate should balance in terms of color. It should be inviting to look at."

Service and atmosphere are the final two elements Tomb examines. He says he's not a stickler in the service department: "If something takes 20 minutes, maybe there's a reason for it."

WALTRINA STOVALL
Dallas Morning News

For Stovall, spotting a winner is simple: "If they can allow you to enjoy the company you're with and provide you with good food, then that's a good restaurant."

Among Stovall's personal dislikes are loud music and servers who hover. "Music should be in the background," she observes. "And I hate when the waiter enters into your conversation."

For her reviews, food is most important. She explores how fresh it is and if it is cleanly prepared. "I look for basic good cooking," says Stovall. "And I love finding a new dish or a new way of preparing an old dish."

Stovall also considers the personality of the place. "I look for something that they're doing that makes them different and gives the restaurant its personality. It could be in the decor as well as the food."

"Attitude" and "price" also make a difference. To judge attitude, Stovall focuses on the service. She thinks the staff should be helpful and friendly. For price, Stovall says she looks for value. "An inexpensive restaurant can also be over-priced."

Then there's the comfort factor. "Is the music too loud? Is the music inappropriate?," Stovall asks herself. "Is the air-conditioning turned up too high? All this makes a difference in terms of comfort."

JIM WOOD
San Francisco Examiner

"I do not like places where they put their customers down," Wood comments. "Some places have a snob value. They try to make their customers feel ill at ease. That is intolerable." What Wood does like is "low-priced restaurants where the food is outstanding."

When reviewing a restaurant, Wood first considers the food. He looks for fresh ingredients and food that "tastes like what it is."

After that, Wood surveys the service. Ironically, he does not use the service he receives as a benchmark. "I'm often recognized," notes Wood of his frequent visits to San Francisco eateries. "As a result, I pay almost no attention to the service I get but to what is happening at the other tables."

Price also matters. "I like places that give good value—they can be inexpensive or sometimes quite expensive," he says. "The important thing is that by the end of the meal, the customer has to feel it is worth it."

Finally, Wood keeps in mind what he groups as "outside" factors. He asks a number of questions that include: Is the restaurant easy to get to? If you have to drive there, is it easy to park? If you have to walk a considerable distance to get there, is the neighborhood safe?

"In San Francisco, some of the best restaurants are in places where the cops don't even go," says Wood. "In those cases, I recommend going in a group." ◆

4

THE KITCHEN
OPERATIONS

When we use the word "kitchen" to describe our final Core Four element, we mean much more than that. As our lead story explains, the making of a restaurant begins with a business plan and money to implement it. In other words, the entire physical plant, from design to maintenance has to begin with an integrated concept that ties together the name, colors, menu design, wait staff uniforms, back- and front-of-the-house materials, operational systems from computers to storage facilities.

For example, more attention is being paid to the relationship between menu items and equipment. Operators are looking for multi-use cooking equipment so they can make menu changes without buying a new piece of equipment, or they are acquiring specialty items for specific cuisines.

Food safety is one of an operator's top three worries. One bad incident can kill a restaurant. Our award-winning series, "The Clean Restaurant," looks at cleanliness from three angles, which add up to a complete primer ready to use. Complementary to food safety is safety in general, both for employees and customers. And if there is need to build or retrofit for the disabled, our ADA series shows how. Looking to the future, we offer ideas and solutions on the environmental challenge facing us all. ◆

How to Finance a Restaurant

by Lisa Bertagnoli and Monica Kass

Independent restaurateurs say they'd have better luck finding El Dorado than obtaining financial backing for a restaurant. The myths surrounding restaurant finance are nearly as outlandish as those about the legendary city of gold: Banks never give loans for start-ups. The Small Business Administration only helps minorities and women. Investors won't open their wallets unless your name is Baum or Melman. The truth of the matter is that hundreds of restaurants have been opened by people loaded not with cash, but with ideas and management expertise.

Sources for capital fall into two basic categories: individuals and institutions. The former usually are friends, relatives or business associates. The latter encompasses banks and the Small Business Administration, both of which will lend restaurant money if the circumstances are right. In fact, most operators finance their businesses with funds from both sources.

Partnerships

The advantages of going into business with a partner are clear. In a general partnership, the work is split, as are any profits or losses. In the best partnerships, a synergy exists to balance talents; each partner focuses on his or her area of expertise.

That's what happened with Stephen Pyles and John Dayton, the duo who owns Baby Routh in Dallas and Goodfellows and Tejas in Minneapolis. The two met in 1982 when Pyles catered a party at Dayton's house. The timing was perfect: Dayton, then a lawyer with considerable business acumen, was looking for a new career, and Pyles, a French-trained chef, needed backing for a new restaurant.

The two opened Routh Street in 1983, operating as a general partnership. Dayton, who entered the partnership as an investor, not an operator, bought the property on which the restaurant sits. He leased it to the partnership for a rent in excess of the monthly mortgage payment. Opening costs were covered with a bank loan, easily obtained thanks to adequate collateral that included Dayton's property.

As the restaurant flourished, Dayton says he quickly shed the pretense of being "only" an investor. "The only way to be involved in a restaurant is to be totally involved," he maintains, adding that his new career as a restaurateur is more demanding than his law practice ever was.

Because both Dayton and Pyles believe that running a restaurant requires a total commitment, they decided to keep the partnership to themselves, and not open it to more investors, or what would be called limited partners. "Most limited partners invest capital thinking only of their return," he explains. What's more, Dayton did not want to deal with investors only interested in buying bragging rights and preferential treatment at the restaurants.

There's a simpler reason Dayton and Pyle do not court additional investors: they do not need the money. But for budding restaurateurs without ample cash reserves, opening up the partnership is a good, relatively risk-free way to finance a restaurant.

Limited partners invest a certain amount of money in the restaurant in exchange for a priority share of the profits (i.e., limited partners get their portion first, and any remaining funds are then divided among the general partners). They do not receive interest on their investment, and have no say in the operation of the restaurant.

After the limited partners' investments are repaid, the profit priority usually returns to the general partners. Ensuing profits are split between the general partners and the limited partners as two groups, not as individuals, on a percentage basis determined before the restaurant opens.

Most limited-partnership agreements enable the general partners to buy out the limited partners after the latter have received their investments and some profit.

A possible hitch lies in the distribution of profits to the limited partners. For example, if a restaurant posts a $100,000 profit, and the general partners decide to reinvest that money in the restaurant, the limited partners must pay taxes on their share, even if they never actually see the money. To avoid this, the general partnership should distribute enough of the profits to enable investors to cover taxes, and reinvest the remainder.

If the limited partnership meets certain requirements, it can be organized as an S corporation. S corporations can have no more than 35 partners, none of which are foreign nationals, and make their money from businesses that create a product or provide a service (those that make money solely from royalties or rental property do not qualify).

S corporation shareholders have voting rights and receive profits. The difference between an S corporation and a "regular," or C corporation, is that taxes are paid by each shareholder, not by the corporation. This saves the company from double taxation, first on the corporate level and then on the level of each shareholder.

No matter how you choose to organize investors, the key to finding them is a solid business plan, says Michael Dellar, who with Bradley Odgen opened the Lark Creek Inn, Larkspur, Calif. According to Dellar, an investor-friendly business plan has several earmarks: conservative projections, favorable lease arrangements, reasonable rent and fair salaries for the general partners.

"It's pretty basic: Develop your business plan as if you're the investor, and you'll be able to get people in," advises Dellar, adding that Lark Creek Inn has 34 investors, "each one personally and diligently nurtured."

Risk Management

These 34 partners will be with the pair indefinitely because Dellar and Ogden do not believe in buy-back provisions. "A lot of restaurateurs put forced buy-back provisions in their plans," explains Dellar. "Why is that right? I feel that if people risk their money on us, what right do I have to cut them out of the profits later on?"

Dellar's view is extremely generous in the eyes of some restaurateurs. While they are grateful to investors for taking a risk at the start, the feeling is that the short-term dividends a successful restaurant brings investors are enough to compensate for that risk. "Savvy investors want to get as much as possible from the deal with as little risk and in as short a time as possible," says John Terczak, owner of Terczak's restaurant in Chicago. "They're not interested in hanging on forever."

Another Chicago restaurateur, Gordon Sinclair, says not including a buy-back clause in the investor agreement was the one mistake he made when he opened Gordon in 1976. "Gordon took off so quickly, it was the only show in town," he recalls. "The investors were so into the prestige of being part owners, they wouldn't budge."

When Sinclair persisted in trying to buy back the shares in his restaurant from the investors, each became "an individual negotiator, a free agent," he says. He ended up paying one woman $25,000 for a $3,000 equity. In the end, he acquired all the shares, terminated the original corporation and rolled it over into a new corporation, in which he is the only shareholder and president.

California Pizza Kitchen principals Rick Rosenfield and Larry Flax also converted their partnership into a corporation after their first two restaurants, located in Los Angeles, proved wildly successful. But instead of making themselves the only shareholders, the duo made a private offering of CPK stock to friends and business associates.

Just like investors in public companies, private companies' shareholders have voting rights and receive dividends. If they want out, investors simply sell their shares back to the company. Most private companies print annual reports, and they are required to supply shareholders with a tax statement. They are not, however, as public companies are, required to file any documents with the Securities and Exchange Commission. "It's all

FINANCIAL PHRASES

General Partnership:
A partnership between two (or sometimes three) people. General partners are active partners, meaning they have control over the restaurant's operation and finances.

Limited Partnership: General partnerships can open up the partnership to investors, called limited partners. Limited partners invest in a restaurant in exchange for a priority claim on profits. They are passive partners and have no part in running the business.

Buy-Back Provision: Allows the general partnership to buy back limited partners' shares after the investors have received a certain profit on their investments.

S Corporation: Limited partnerships with fewer than 35 investors, none of whom are foreign nationals, can organize as an S corporation. They differ from "regular," or C corporations, in that they are not taxed on the corporate level. Therefore, any losses incurred can be deducted as personal losses. Like C corporations, S corporations have officers, and shareholders have voting rights.

SBA 7a Loan: A Small Business Administration loan backed by a guarantee to the bank that if the restaurant defaults, the bank will get a percentage of the loan from the government. The maximum guarantee is $750,000.

Equity Injection: The money that lenders require restaurant owners to put into their projects. Can be cash, a certificate of deposit or stock, anything equal to at least 20% of the total cost of opening the restaurant.

the benefits of a public company without the pressures," remarks Rosenfield.

Making "Concessions"

Yet another kind of "partner" is coming into fashion as the industry matures and restaurateurs find themselves with a dearth of good freestanding sites. These new partners are the developers of office buildings and retail complexes who are starting to view restaurants as viable traffic-builders.

Agreements with developers can be quite beneficial. San Francisco-based O! Deli Corp., which operates about 15 delicatessens in office buildings, says that developers pay anywhere from 25% to 100% of buildout costs. O! Deli picks up furniture, supplies and equipment costs.

In retail developments, landlords provide tenants with finish allowances, which cover outfitting and decorating costs. Dayton and Pyles of Routh Street received such allowances when they opened Goodfellows and Tejas in the Conservatory, a Minneapolis retail complex.

The best lease agreement, according to both Dayton and O! Deli President Joe Sanfellipo, is one in which the landlord takes a certain percentage of monthly gross sales, provided it amounts to more than a predetermined base rent. "The landlord recaptures his investment, and it makes it profitable for him to help you do business," explains Sanfellipo. Such rent structures also discourage landlords from putting competing restaurants in the office complex, he adds.

Restaurateurs should do some research, however, before signing a lease with a developer. Sanfellipo suggests comparing the amount of space leased with the actual occupancy. For instance, a building can be 78% leased, but if only half those tenants have moved in, traffic counts will not live up to projections. Sanfellipo also strongly suggests obtaining necessary permits, for instance, health department and liquor licenses, before signing the lease.

Operating restrictions should also be reviewed before signing a lease deal. Some developers do not allow tenants to advertise in the lobbies. Others restrict the size and color of signage, hours of operation and supplier access to the restaurant. And finally, just as with a freestanding restaurant, location is everything: "You don't want to be on the 10th floor," warns Sanfellipo.

A Borrower Be?

Ask independent restaurateurs about getting a bank loan and they will roll their eyes, talk about impossibilities or say flat out, "You can't get loans from banks for a start-up."

Banks concede that there is almost no way they'll finance 100% of the project, but if the restaurateur has an affluent friend willing to guarantee the loan, or has a 25% to 30% chunk of money to start with, the situation brightens considerably. Gordon Sinclair opened his second restaurant with the help of Chicago retail mogul Marshall Field. "My bank loan was fully collateralized by Marshall Field," says Sinclair. "He was very generous and supportive."

Amy and Patrick Kerr raised more than half of the money needed for their restaurant, Mirador, through a limited partnership offering. The rest came from a personal bank loan. "Our investors are reputable people, so that helped us get the loan," says Kerr.

Odessa Piper, who owns L'Etoile in Madison, Wis., managed to get a bank loan after putting up her life savings as collateral and persuading her father to act as cosigner. Her experience as a manager at a popular Madison restaurant helped her credibility in the eyes of the bank, she adds.

Another way to get a bank loan is with the help of the U.S. Small Business Administration's guaranteed loan program (7a). Unlike conventional loans, for which banks are completely liable, SBA's 7a loans guarantee that if the restaurant defaults, the lender gets a percentage back from the government. (The maximum guarantee is for $750,000.)

"It's not cheap money and it's not easy money," says Juanita Weaver, media director for

the U.S. SBA in Washington, D.C. SBA-loan hopefuls have to go through the same procedures to get a guaranteed loan as they do for a conventional bank loan.

The big advantage is in cash flow, Weaver explains. The average term of repayment for a guaranteed loan is 8 to 9 years—up to 25 years if the restaurateur is buying the property. Compare that with the two- to three-year average repay-

---

COSTS TO COUNT ON

Food and labor costs combined account for most of the cost of doing business, as much as 60% of a restaurant's sales. The remaining costs encompass all the details, including:

Other Costs of Sales: Paper, supplies, linen, uniforms, china, tableware, glassware, menu and check printing, entertainment charges, flowers and plants.

Utilities: Water, gas, electric.

Gross Payroll: Salaries for full-and part-time workers.

Payroll Costs: Payroll taxes, bonuses and other financial incentives.

General and Administrative Costs: Office expenses and supplies, telephone, health department permits and liquor licenses, legal and accounting fees, travel expenses, employee benefits.

Occupancy Costs: Rent or mortgage payment, cleaning services and supplies, equipment repairs and maintenance, garbage pickup, exterminators, security services, property taxes.

Insurance: Property insurance, general liability, product liability, liquor liability (not required in all states), plate glass and boiler insurance, workers compensation and disability, fire (both contents and value, i.e. for a wine cellar).

Advertising: Advertising, public relations, cost of designing menu, promotions, any coupons. Be sure to include the cost of redeeming coupons and promotions.

HOW TO WRITE A BUSINESS PLAN

The key to gathering investors, or convincing a bank that you are an attractive risk, lies in a good business plan. According to the Small Business Administration, a complete business plan comprises seven sections:

Cover Letter: Include the dollar amount you are requesting, terms and a time frame.

Business Summary: Give the name and location of the restaurant, a brief description of the menu, the target market and any competition, and brief profiles of management. Include business goals, financial needs and earnings projections.

Market Analysis: Discuss in detail your industry segment (e.g., casual, family dining, fine dining), industry trends, target customers and competitors.

Description of Products, Services: Include the entire menu, pointing out any signature items or trademarked names. Also, compare your menu to the competition's.

Marketing Strategy: Here, explain menu price points and the markups on each item, advertising strategies and planned promotions.

Management Plan: Include an organization chart and description of responsibilities for the officers and operating partners. Also detail staffing requirements, and include resumes for key personnel.

Financial Data: Include your financial history, plus a three-year financial projection for the restaurant and the logic behind the projections. The SBA suggests covering the first year by months, the second year by quarters, and the third year as a whole. Explain key ratios (food and liquor percentages and food and labor costs as a percentage of sales, for instance), and returns to investors compared to the industry and the competition.

ment term banks require for most conventional business loans and the benefits are obvious.

"Under one scenario—the conventional bank loan—you wouldn't be credit worthy. The guaranteed loan makes you credit worthy," Weaver concludes.

She recommends that prospective restaurateurs start with their bank of record. If that bank doesn't handle SBA loans, restaurateurs can call the SBA's Washington hotline—(800) 365-5855—and ask for a list of lenders in their district.

According to Charles Anderson, deputy director of the U.S. SBA, Illinois district, there are three tiers of lenders: preferred, certified and regular. Preferred lenders have the authority from the SBA to approve a guaranteed loan immediately without notifying the SBA. Certified lenders are guaranteed a three-day turnaround on paperwork. Regular lenders can expect to wait slightly longer.

The three-tier program is meant to make the

guaranteed-loan program more attractive to banks, explains Anderson. "For a long time, banks didn't want to participate because they thought there was too much paperwork and red tape involved. This cuts through that."

Before contacting the lender, SBA advises restaurateurs to work through their business plans, either with the help of volunteers at SBA's business-development offices or with private attorneys.

Once that is done, restaurateurs can expect several requirements. "We like them to have at least three years of management experience in the type of restaurant they want to open," says Patti Wilson, vice president of the United Illinois Bank of Benton, Benton, Ill. Then comes "equity injection": the money the restaurateur puts into the project. Wilson says this can be cash, a certificate of deposit, blue-chip stock, anything equal to at least one-fifth the total cost of the project.

She also emphasizes the need for a solid business plan, one complete with information about the competition as well as income and expense projections. She adds that the numbers in the plan must be verifiable.

Seller Financing: Is It for You?

If you want to buy a restaurant that is already in operation, you might be able to obtain financing from the seller. In fact, seller financing will become more popular if the real estate market stays soft: "If there are 300 restaurants in a town and 295 are for sale, the sellers that offer financing will be the winners," observes John Seidl, a Westchester, N.Y., restaurant broker.

This is how it works: After the seller and the buyer agree on a price, the buyer will be asked for a down payment of anywhere from one-quarter to one-half the sale price. The buyer then will take a personal money mortgage from the seller for the balance, agreeing to repay it in monthly installments equal to the amount of the loan divided by the number of months on the loan, plus interest. The loans usually are repaid over ten years. In cases where the buyer is purchasing a business and not property, the repayment period should not be longer than the lease on the restaurant building. Seidl says interest rates for seller financing have hovered around 10% for the past several years.

There are two hitches to these kinds of deals, says Seidl. The first is that the buyer is usually advised not to personally guarantee the loan. The reason is simple: If the buyer guarantees the loan and then defaults, the person holding the mortgage can take possession of anything the buyer owns to make good the loan. The second hitch is, in Seidl's words, the "highly contingent" character of these loans. The agreements need to be accepted by local licensing authorities. In the case of sales of businesses, the landlord must agree to a sublease.

Going Public: Ark's Story

Although offering public stock in a company might yield a lot of capital, the move also subjects a

company to intense scrutiny. But for Michael Weinstein, chief executive of New York's Ark Restaurants, the trade-off was worth it. Ark's management took the casual-restaurant company public in December 1985 for two main reasons. Weinstein says he and his partners wanted to stop depending on bank loans, which they personally guaranteed, for expansion capital. They also wanted to give employees a chance to share in Ark's growth through stock purchases and options.

Ark accomplished both objectives, Weinstein says. During the first public offering, at $7.50 per share, the company raised more than $7 million for 29% of the company: That cash influx has enabled Ark to open nine restaurants during the past four years. Employees indeed are sharing in Ark's growth: About 40 chefs and managers own stock in the company. Weinstein says his dilemma is making investors understand why Ark does not open cookie-cutter restaurants. "From a technical point of view, it makes sense," Weinstein explains. "Our concepts aren't diluted by 12 others like it in the area." He adds that 100% pretax returns on equity are not unusual for successful Ark restaurants, such as the Museum Cafe in New York. The company has opened its share of duds, however, including New York's Big Kahuna, which was replaced by K-Paul's New York. "The company is too young a public company to measure returns over a long period of time," he remarks, "but we bet they'll be good."

Staying Afloat

Once financing is secured and the restaurant is open, the trick is to stay open. "Sales tend to dip after six months of operation," says Baby Routh's Dayton. The blush of good initial reviews wears off; the restaurant is no longer a novelty, he explains. Rick Rosenfield of California Pizza Kitchen agrees. "Even if you have good food and are well managed, it takes time to turn a profit," he says. A good rule of thumb is this: Open with enough money to cover food, labor, rent and administrative costs for six months without touching any of the restaurant's profits.

Sometimes restaurateurs learn this lesson the

hard way. "You tend to lose money as long as you can afford to," recalls Odessa Piper. She covered initial blunders, including hiring an expensive jazz band to entertain late-night diners, by selling stock she held in a small Madison-based chain, but quickly learned how to manage the restaurant's finances.

L'Etoile since has proven very successful, and Piper's star in Madison has risen as well. Piper says about a dozen people have approached her with serious investment offers since she went public with plans to open a casual restaurant in the turn-of-the-century building that now houses L'Etoile.

George Jackson's money problems were not as easy to resolve. Jackson, who helped open Houston's popular Cadillac Bar, recently closed Palacio Tzintzuntzan in the same city. The restaurant,

backed by some of Houston's best-known businesspeople, started with a bang, but turned out to have a few fatal flaws.

"I thought operating capital would be the least of our worries," says Jackson, who opened Palacio with only $20,000 in reserves. But the restaurant's valet-parking deal fell through at the last minute, and the food, an East-meets-Southwest hybrid, proved too sophisticated in Jackson's view for Houston diners. The operating capital Jackson expected to build in the first few months never materialized and the restaurant closed four months after opening.

A bigger stash of operating capital might have saved Palacio Tzintzuntzan's life, Jackson believes. "I opened with $20,000," he laments. "I should have had $200,000." ◆

THE CLEAN RESTAURANT

by Jeff Weinstein

Restaurants need to be the cleanest places on earth. If not, the potential for the transmission of disease is great. Public health officials estimate that about 80% of stomachaches, digestive upsets and "24-hour flu bugs" are, in reality, caused by inadequate sanitation and unsafe food-handling practices, both at home and at foodservice establishments.

A dirty restaurant eventually will lead to an empty restaurant. The 1990 *R&I* Tastes of America Survey points decisively to lack of cleanliness as the leading customer irritant, leaping from No. 8 on the 1989 hit list.

The following three articles focus on how to keep restaurants clean. The first article covers the physical restaurant, from the initial design of the facility to daily maintenance schedules. We also include tips on how to survive a visit from the health inspector. The second article covers employee hygiene, and the third covers safe food-handling practices.

For the physical restaurant, no computer program can replace a broom, a mop, some detergent and water, a scrub brush, a pair of hands and some old-fashioned elbow grease for cleaning and sanitation. ♦

THE CLEAN RESTAURANT

Clean by Design

Facilities designers keep cleanliness in mind from the moment planning begins—both in new structures and remodeling jobs. All areas of the restaurant must be accessible for cleaning and sanitizing. In addition, the choice of surface coverings, the kind of ventilation and placement of electrical outlets are crucial to successful sanitation practices.

During construction: Avoid leaving openings in ceilings, walls and raised floors during the construction phase, says Chicago-based designer Jordan Mozer. He also advises clients to employ a pest prevention system. For instance, during a renovation, open up the floors, clean them out, spray an insecticide and fill any voids so nothing can grow below the floor once it is resealed.

Cold storage: In back-of-the-house areas, shelving in refrigerators and freezers should be portable, says designer Paul Hysen, The Hysen Group, Livonia, Mich. If shelves can be wheeled out, the area can be hosed down and properly cleansed in the battle against food acid buildup resulting from constant spillage. The humid atmosphere in refrigerated areas also speeds corrosion of materials. When designing cold-storage areas, Hysen suggests specifying either stainless-steel shelving or shelving coated with an epoxy material to inhibit corrosion.

If shelving is not portable, it should be installed at least 10 to 12 inches off the floor to create easy access.

Avoid storing product, especially perishable items, in the original crates or cardboard boxes because these permit leakage onto storage-area surfaces. Since spoiled product inside the original crates or boxes can ruin the entire load, shipments must be inspected, cleaned out and repacked in other containers. Excellent alternative containers are those made of transparent plastic, polystyrene or polycarbonate materials.

Floor and wall surfaces: "If you don't spend money for substantial surfaces at the beginning of the project, you'll continually pay to keep them in good repair," says Hysen. He recommends a hard quarry tile, or an unglazed but baked tile for the best traction and durability. Grout should be an epoxy, preferably in a dark color because the grout in tile discolors quickly.

Coved floors in which the floor covering curves up to cover the first 6 to 8 inches of the wall enable employees to mop without damaging wall surfaces. In addition, the curve doesn't provide a hiding place for debris and germs, as would an angled corner. Floors also should be sloped to drains for easy drainage of water.

Other wet environments, such as the trash room, should have tile or plastic wallboard surfaces impervious to moisture; painted drywall will not last in wet surroundings. In the dishroom, fiberglass-paneled walls are imperative, according to Hysen. Both floors and ceilings should be tiled to prevent seepage of water and water vapor.

To make ceilings easy to clean, use a plastic-coated, lay-in tile or a gypsum board that has been coated with epoxy paint.

When considering wall colors, avoid sheer white because employees do not like the clinical look, according to Hysen. Eggshell, cream and pastel colors are more attractive than white, and still show soil.

Prep areas: Equipment should be portable whenever possible, unless it needs electrical or water lines attached. Water and electrical lines should come out of the wall 12 to 18 inches above the floor instead of up through the floor: Designers suggest as few penetrations of floor surfaces as possible so operators do not have to mop around a lot of pipes.

Plating area: Good lighting allows easier detection of dirt. Fluorescent lights with a high foot-candle level are fine, according to Hysen.

Also, since this is a high-traffic area, a durable quarry tile is preferred for the floor.

Production areas and dishrooms: Operators must pay particular attention to the allotment of aisle space. How will people turn with a cart? Do they have to make a lot of acute angular movements? Is there enough room in wait pickup areas for people to come in with trays and carts? If there's not enough room, wall surfaces and doors will be subject to added abuse.

Front-of-the-House Design

Public areas, open to staff and customer traffic, must not only be sanitary, they must look good, too.

Host area: This is the first thing a customer sees, so it should always look neat and clean. Host stations should be movable so maintenance crews can clean underneath them, says Mozer. Charles Morris Mount, principal with Silver & Ziskind/Mount, New York, makes the point that controlling clutter at the host stand also is important. The stand should be designed so the telephone is kept below the desk top or mounted on a side wall.

Bathrooms: Perhaps the best indication of a clean restaurant is its bathrooms. Mozer says it is important to recognize that water will be splashed all around. For that reason, he recommends a sturdy scrubbable surface such as tile for the floors. He also recommends running the tile up the wall about five feet.

Server pickup area: Counter material should be seamless, according to Mount. Granite looks great, but is expensive. Laminated, heat-resistant plastic surfaces are more affordable and easy to clean. Avoid a counter tile because the grout can be a harbinger of germs.

The pickup area will be easier to clean if sufficient room is designed. Mount suggests that operators picture three waiters crossing each other's path at any point in the area. He says that requires a minimum of a six-foot passageway.

Since waiters' areas get a lot of hard use, avoid expensive wood materials. Water spills, for instance, will soak into wood; the wood will expand and push away a plastic veneer, explains Mount. At American Cafe in Washington, D.C., Mount installed a plastic top, but ended up switching to stainless steel after the restaurant opened.

Aisles: An often overlooked element of front-of-the-house design, aisles are rarely wide enough. Waiters are constantly bumping and spilling. Mount shoots for an aisle width of at least 44 inches wide and preferably 54 inches. "In New York, where the cost per square foot is so high, operators tend to shrink aisle space," says Mount. "But they pay the price in the long run because of the undue wear and tear on materials and finishes."

Tables and chairs: Mount likes to use "the truck driver test." He looks for tables and chairs that will hold up to the largest, roughest people in the world. He also believes practicality is sometimes more important than style and looks for materials that will last.

Floors: Perhaps the toughest front-of-the-house area to keep clean is the floor. If carpet is desired, Mount suggests a nylon material because it best resists kitchen grease. Mozer prefers materials that are woven through the back and more dense. He says these withstand heavier traffic and stand up to intensive cleaning. Mozer avoids carpeting high traffic areas, however: "It may help deaden the sound, but it starts to look bad in a hurry."

Wood floors also are tough to maintain. Mount says his clients usually want dark stained-wood floors. But he says stains wear off quickly and patterns of wear and tear start to show. Mount suggests choosing woods that are inherently dark, such as cherry. They are more expensive, but in the long run, the restaurant will not be shut down as often to refinish the floors.

Tile works well on floors and is more economical, says Mount. The only problem is noise, which must be compensated for by putting more money into acoustical ceiling tiles.

Ceilings: Even though operators might expect otherwise, ceilings are impossible to keep clean, according to Mount. As grease absorbs into the tiles, they change colors, begin to smell and start to lose their acoustical properties.

Mount says the best ceiling he ever installed was composed of formed seaweed pieces. He claims such material is inherently fireproof and can be painted without losing its sound absorbency. "It looks like shredded wheat, but it's excellent and inexpensive," says Mount. "If it gets dirty, you spray it with paint."

The most common ceiling materials are acoustical gypsum and dry wall. Although they don't absorb sound as well, they are easy to care for if painted with a high-gloss oil, according to Mount.

Walls: Budget dictates that walls are almost always gypsum board. Gypsum is tough to take care of, so Mount always installs chair rails so tables or chairs do not bump the walls. Gypsum can be painted, and mirrors applied, as well. The best way to clean gypsum board with an oil-based finish is a spray cleaner.

Laminated plastic can be used on walls, too, says Mount. It is more expensive, but gives a different feel and look. This material also is durable and easy to clean

Organizing a Cleaning Plan

Since the human element is the key ingredient in cleaning a restaurant, motivational management and schedules are required to ensure jobs get done as often as needed.

Responsibility: First, it is important to communicate the importance of the maintenance function. Stress that every guest uses cleanliness to judge a restaurant and to decide whether to return. If one particular person is assigned to cleaning duties, make sure that person is recognized as important and compensated accordingly. Dee Clingman, vice president of quality control at General Mills Restaurants in Orlando, Fla., says the person whose job it is to clean and sanitize the physical plant should be the highest-paid hourly employee on staff.

At Dublin, Ohio-based Wendy's, the dining-room coordinator is responsible for keeping clean areas that come in contact with guests, says spokesman Denny Lynch. This includes the dining tables. Wendy's policy is for staff to bus tables after every use to facilitate cleaning up. The coordinator also patrols the self-service salad bar area, which is prone to excessive spills.

Generally speaking, it is the unit manager's responsibility to list an inventory of cleaning activities and to make sure cleaning supplies are adequate. This person then designs a cleaning schedule that includes specifically what is to be cleaned, when it is to be cleaned, and who cleans it. The Culinary Institute of America's (CIA) sanitation training manual suggests that employees take care of their own areas and that large jobs should be rotated. According to the CIA handbook, the schedule also should say when cleaning should take place and how often. Although most cleaning can be done during off-peak hours, bathrooms should be checked as often as every 15 minutes during rush periods.

At all times, it is important to apply common sense. If there is a minor spill at the condiment stand during a lunch rush, wipe it up. But don't bring out the mop and bucket because it will most likely become a hindrance to customers.

Enforcement: In order to make sure employees understand what clean really means, Clingman suggests managers show workers exactly what is required for each cleaning function. For example, in the bathroom, show the worker how to get a reflection in the porcelain in the toilet bowl and avoid water marks on the handles. "Be detailed in your demands or it might not occur to the employee to do certain tasks," says Clingman. Post cleaning instructions near each item or machine.

Cleaning services that work during the night must be as well-trained as the in-house crew. For instance, says Mount, "They always place the base of the chairs on the tables. That practice damages the table and makes it twice as hard to clean. Chairs should be stacked upside down."

General Guidelines

To keep a foodservice operation pristine, take the following steps:

- Either as the last task at night or first thing in the morning, thoroughly clean all bathrooms —that includes fixtures, walls, bowls, floors and vents.
- If any dirty dishes are left over from the previous evening, wash them as soon as possible.
- Do not forget to clean underneath heat lamps in the kitchen or on buffet tables every day.
- Vacuum carpets, mop and scrub lobby-area surfaces, and clean and polish doorknobs and handles.
- Check outside the unit to make sure the parking lot is free of garbage. Weather permitting, hose down the dumpster area daily.
- Throughout the day, clean and sanitize equipment to prevent cross-contamination of food. Utensils such as cutting boards and tableware have been identified as leading sources of cross-contamination. Even utensils in constant use should be cleaned at least every four hours, according to guidelines set by the Educational Foundation of the National Restaurant Association. Also, use separate wiping cloths for food- and non-food surfaces. When not in use, store cloths in a sanitizing solution used only for that purpose.
- Clean the food-contact surfaces of grills, griddles and similar cooking devices with a grill brush and cleaning solution at least once a day. Non-food-contact surfaces of equipment should be cleaned once a day to free them of accumulation of dust, dirt, food particles and other debris.
- An often overlooked back-of-the-house area is the heating and air conditioning system. Change filters frequently to avoid blowing dust into cooking areas where high grease and moisture contents already exist.
- Hose down and scrub floors after the kitchen shuts down every night. Hot-water connections for high-speed hoses are recommended. The hotter the water, the easier it is to break down grease buildups. Hose down floor mats at cooking lines and at the expediter's stand after each meal period.

Surviving the Inspection

The trend in health inspections is changing from concern about floors, walls and ceilings to analysis of hazards that cause foodborne illness. Inspectors are more interested in the food-preparation process, where food might become contaminated. But make no mistake, violations of physical plant codes still lead to fines.

Ken Pannaralla, chief sanitarian with the Chicago Department of Health, offers tips on how to keep your operation in top shape for the inspector.

- **Nonsmoking sections:** Inspectors are on a big kick to make sure operators have required nonsmoking section signs.
- **Broken refrigerator seals:** This typical problem causes cold air to seep out, meaning the unit fails to keep products at the appropriate temperature.
- **Steam tables:** Check them often to make sure there is enough water to reach the bottom of pans so food stays at the proper serving temperature. Steam reduces water levels, which often go unchecked by staff.
- **In-line dishwasher thermometers:** Check dishwashers regularly to make sure the final sanitizing rinse temperature reaches 180F.
- **Cutting boards:** Make sure they are in good shape. If cutting boards are decimated from use and can no longer be satisfactorily cleaned and sanitized, it is time for new ones, says Pannaralla.
- **Floors, walls and ceilings:** These are secondary to inspectors, says Pannaralla. If they are excessively dirty, the inspector will make a note and tell the operator to clean up.
- **Flatware:** Often stored inappropriately, flatware should be stored "business end" down, handles up. Pannaralla says many employees just throw the utensils into a bin.
- **Outdoor dumpsters:** If neighbors (residents and businesses) are going to complain about something, it's most likely an improperly maintained or uncovered dumpster. Pannaralla sug-

gests going as far as locking the dumpsters shut. Better yet, some operators enclose dumpsters with a fence (shielding it from the neighbors and from vandals) and install a water connection so the area can be hosed down every day.

♦ **Parking lots:** Keep lots clean of glass, litter and, to avoid critical insect and rodent problems, food waste. If a problem is spotted, inspectors will come down hard on the operator and require complete compliance within 48 hours, according to Pannaralla.

Designing for Cleanliness

The following design details make the cleaning process easier:

♦ Install air screens (which blow air continuously) over doors of storage areas to keep flies out.
♦ Install wall bumpers, edge-corner protectors and bumper rails along walls in storage areas to protect surfaces from supply carts and portable shelves.
♦ Install nonskid abrasive quarry floor tile in all areas, especially frying and grilling areas in which grease builds up quickly.
♦ Make sure floor drains are installed in wet areas near kettles and steamers.
♦ Install proper lighting in storage and prep areas so hard-to-see dirt is visible.
♦ Back-of-the-house should have hot-water connections for high-pressure spray units.
♦ Designate areas for trash containers, especially in cooking areas.
♦ Install rubber safety mats in cooking areas. Pick up mats and spray them clean between meal periods.

Cleaning Food-Prep Areas

♦ **Floors:** Wipe spills as soon as possible. Damp mop once per shift or between rushes. Scrub floors with brushes once a week. Strip and reseal twice a year.
♦ **Walls and Ceilings:** Wipe splashes and smud-

ges as soon as possible. Wash walls and ceilings once a month.

♦ **Work Tables:** Clean and sanitize tops after each use. Empty, clean and sanitize drawers and shelves weekly.
♦ **Hoods and Filters:** Empty grease traps when necessary. Clean inside and outside daily after closing. Clean filters weekly.
♦ **Broilers:** Empty drip pan and wipe down when necessary. Clean grid tray, inside, outside and top, after each use.
♦ **Utensils:** Wash, rinse and sanitize after each use.
♦ **Non-Food-Contact Surfaces:** Clear as often as necessary to keep equipment free of accumulation of dust, dirt, food particles and other debris.

Source: Applied Foodservice Sanitation, Education Foundation of the National Restaurant Association, (New York: John Wiley & Sons, Inc. 1985)

Monitoring the Program

A cleaning program that is flexible enough allows for changes in personnel and equipment. A manager should regularly review the program and consider the following questions:

1. Are maintenance workers among the highest-paid hourly personnel and recognized for their important contributions?
2. Is the program evaluated regularly? Is it reviewed when changes in staff, facility and menu occur? Does each facility follow a schedule based on its individual use and volume?
3. Do I have the proper tools for the staff to do each task correctly and quickly?
4. Is the staff given enough time to clean during hours of operation and after closing?
5. Do I have enough personnel for cleaning?
6. Is the program implemented properly, or are shortcuts taken?
7. Are cleaning workers properly trained?

Source: Applied Foodservice Sanitation, Education Foundation of the National Restaurant Association (New York: John Wiley & Sons, Inc., 1985)

Inspection Requirements

The Chicago Department of Health lists the following items as critical to check when conducting an inspection.

- **Food:** Sound condition, no spoilage.
- **Food Protection:** Potentially hazardous food meets temperature requirements during storage, prep, display, service, transportation. Facilities maintain product temperature. Unwrapped and potentially hazardous food not re-served.
- **Personnel:** Hands washed and clean; good hygienic practices followed. Restrict employees with infections.

- **Food Equipment, Utensils:** Sanitized at correct temperature and time with the proper detergent concentration. Equipment and utensils properly sanitized.
- **Water:** Safe source with hot and cold under pressure.
- **Toilet, Hand-Washing Facilities:** Proper number of toilets that are convenient and accessible and properly designed and installed.
- **Insect, Rodent, Animal Control:** No sign of insects or rodents. Outer openings protected. No birds, turtles or other animals in facility. ♦

THE CLEAN RESTAURANT

Employee Hygiene

by Jeff Weinstein

When was the last time your hands touched your mouth, face, arms or hair? Probably within the last minute. By doing so, you continually contaminate your hands with bacteria. In a foodservice setting, that creates the greatest danger to customers: Poor personal hygiene causes more than 90% of the sanitation problems in the foodservice industry, according to the Culinary Institute of America (CIA). Government statistics show improper hand washing alone accounts for more than 25% of all foodborne illnesses. Despite the statistics, a majority of foodservice employees still are careless about their grooming habits. Therefore, operators must explain the need for sanitary habits, state clearly what is expected of employees, and provide both necessary training and convenient facilities. Finally, they must supervise and lead by example.

This article explains what personal hygiene is, how to foster good grooming and hygiene on the job, and what the manager's role is in helping employees maintain safe and proper habits.

Watch Your Hands

The sanitation program at the Washington Regional Medical Center in Fayetteville, Ark., requires foodservice workers to touch a finger to a laboratory culture plate. Employees who think their hands are clean are astounded by what grows on those plates. "It makes a huge impression," says Nancy Bowen, R.D., the center's director of nutrition services. Managers in any foodservice operation must make a huge impression on their employees about frequent and thorough hand washing, the most important aspect of personal hygiene. Dirty hands are prime culprits in trans-

mitting contaminants to food products. Hands should be scrubbed whenever contaminated, after touching food or body parts such as the mouth, and always before performing the next job function. Keep in mind that the way hands are washed at home is not adequate for a foodservice setting. Lower-level pathogens, contacted by touching dirty clothes or surfaces, smoking, blowing the nose, sneezing, handling raw food, or touching the mouth, eyes, hair or face, are found all over the hands. These pathogens require a reasonable, one-time 30-second washing. High-level pathogens are found in feces, vomit, blood or other body fluids. They get onto the fingertips and under fingernails after using the toilet, picking at pimples or lesions on the skin, or caring for another person. These are dangerous organisms, and it is necessary to clean the hands more thoroughly, using a nail brush. When washing hands, pay special attention to trouble spots on the hands where dirt tends to hide. Work up a good lather to scrub the fingernails, cuticle beds, creases at the knuckles, the backs of finger joints and deep creases in the palms. Other sources of bacteria are exposed cuts or abrasions. Wounds should be antiseptically bandaged and changed several times a day.

Smoking and gum chewing should be avoided during the course of the workday. Both habits involve actions that are discouraged in a foodservice setting—putting hands around the mouth and nose. In addition, smoking and gum chewing tend to create a lot of saliva and often contaminate hands. While employees cannot be prohibited from smoking in designated areas, management must reinforce that hand washing is necessary before returning to the work area.

Since employees are encouraged to wash their hands several times during their shift, make it convenient for them to do so. Hand-washing sinks should be installed near all food-preparation areas. Also, make sure someone is responsible for refilling soap and towel dispensers. To avoid cross-contamination, do not wash hands in a sink where food is prepared.

In order to make the hand-washing experience as pleasant as possible, supply a soft and comfortable soap that is easy on the hands. Avoid harsh soaps that dry out the skin. Also consider providing hand lotion in the lounge or locker area.

As an adjunct to hand washing, many operators are installing hand-sanitizing systems. There are two types: The first is a spray system. Employees put their hands inside a box, where they are sprayed with a liquid sanitizing solution. The other uses a cream or gel, applied from a squeeze bottle or a wall-mounted machine, that sanitizes hands and keeps them from drying and chapping.

Sanitizers, however, are a supplement to and not a replacement for hand washing, warns Bob Harrington, assistant director of technical services for the National Restaurant Association.

Since hands can never be totally free of bacteria, the rule of thumb is to touch food as little as possible. Use tools or utensils to serve food whenever possible. For example, use a scooper for serving tuna or tongs for serving pastry.

Fashion vs. Safety

Employees' desire to make fashion statements on the job also causes a hygiene problem. In most cases, a foodservice environment is not the appropriate place to dress up with fancy clothes, big hairdos, nail polish and dangling earrings.

What follows is a list of fashion dos and don'ts in a foodservice setting, according to the NRA's Harrington.

Jewelry: It has no purpose, especially in the back of the house. Jewelry, especially rings, catches dirt, makes it harder to clean hands and can get in the way when cooking, serving or washing. Jewelry

also can be hazardous to customers because it could fall into food and become a physical contaminant. It is not as big a risk for servers because the degree of exposure is less. Servers may wear some jewelry, depending on the level and type of service in the dining room.

Hair: Long hair is not a problem, but what's done with it while on the job might be. Since people lose about 50 hairs a day, it must be restrained in such a way that it will not fly loose and deposit loose hairs. Restraints also discourage unconscious grooming with fingers. Hair nets should be worn in all food-prep areas.

Fingernails and polish: Long nails are not a problem; artificial nails are because they can pop loose and contaminate food. Nail polish is a low-risk item, but because it can chip and crack, it should be discouraged in food-prep areas. In the dining room, it is the manager's responsibility to weigh the cosmetic value against the risk. Nails and cuticles should be smooth and neatly trimmed.

Makeup, cologne, perfume: In a food-prep area, use of all three should be minimal. In the dining room, standards should be left up to management. Avoid habitual adjustment or reapplication of makeup or cologne to avoid the hands from coming in contact with the face or mouth.

Uniforms: Any back-of-the-house garments should be light in color to reveal stains. They should be cleaned every day. Work clothes should not be worn to work. They should be stored in a locker at work or carried to work in a garment bag.

Care should be taken to balance uniform policies, however. Too-strict uniform policies might hurt employee morale and erode their sense of dignity on the job.

At Good Samaritan Hospital & Medical Center, Portland, Ore., foodservice managers found the staff occasionally was deviating from the standard all-white uniform by dressing it up with jewelry or patterned stockings. The problem now is under control because management upgraded uniforms with a more fashionable look. Employees now wear white shirts with a thin gray pinstripe and burgundy slacks or skirts. The catering staff accessorizes the outfit with ties and vests.

"Employees are no longer as likely to test our standards by wearing jewelry and excessive make-up," says Barbara Clements, R.D., director of food and nutrition services. "When we do have a problem, I try to reason with the employee without putting them down. I tell them I know they feel good about their appearance but if they stop to think, it is not befitting of their position and not appreciated by those they serve.

"I know they feel good about their appearance, but I tell them to change for business reasons and to go wild when they are off on their own," adds Clements. "For the most part, that approach is very effective."

Despite standards for hygiene, employees will always test the limits of requirements. The key to good sanitation practices is leadership, not systems, policies or controls. Managers must set examples and serve as role models. If managers are seen constantly washing their hands and placing emphasis on its importance, hourlies will comply. Lead by example and support that with ongoing training.

Gloves Are Not a Panacea

Wearing gloves can go far toward improving sanitation. However, gloves should not give workers a false sense of security about cleanliness. Keep the following suggestions in mind:

Even if workers use gloves for safe food handling, employees still must wash their hands. If hands are not clean, they can contaminate the gloves.

Recognize gloves as a second skin. Anything gloves touch that would require hand washing requires changing gloves. For example, if workers are preparing different types of food, they should wash their hands and change gloves after working with each food item. If they fail to do so, the gloves become a vehicle for cross-contamination.

Gloves should not be worn when working around any open flame or other heat sources such as a flat-top griddle. They can melt or catch fire.

Also warn workers to be careful when handling knives while wearing gloves; they can prevent a solid grip.

The ARA Example

ARA Services, Philadelphia, has a reputation for having one of the best employee-hygiene training programs. Among the reasons:

All of its programs, both text and video, are customized. For example, ARA received permission from the Department of Agriculture to customize its "Food Safety Is No Mystery" video.

ARA brings in college faculty to teach sanitation training programs to unit managers.

Training is based on the Educational Foundation's Applied Foodservice Sanitation program. Managers must score 85% on the sanitation and food-safety standards test; nationally, NRA certification requires a 75% passing grade.

To train hourly employees, ARA believes the most successful programs are both informative and fun. The "Food Safety Is No Mystery" video is serious. Yet, in comic book-fashion, it traces how a police chief fell victim to food poisoning.

Unit managers reinforce training with regular ten-minute workshops. In addition, posters at all stations list proper sanitation and hygiene procedures.

A Reminder About AIDS

The HIV virus has not gone away. Operators who have not had an experience with an HIV employee eventually will, says Bob Harrington of the NRA. He recommends treating an AIDS-afflicted worker the same as any other employee with a serious, long-term disease. He recommends the following steps:

◆ Remember that the virus cannot be contracted through casual contact such as handshaking. There has yet to be a documented case proving that AIDS can be transmitted through food.

◆ Training is the best way to address staff questions and concerns about employees with AIDS. They will want to know exactly what the disease is and how it is contracted.

♦ Reinforce that if everyone exercises good sanitation practices, there is no risk of spreading the disease.

Handy Tips. Proper hand-washing procedures call for using water as hot as the hands can comfortably stand. Moisten hands and soap thoroughly, using a brush for nails. Wash 20 to 30 seconds, using friction. Include the wrist, forearm, up to the elbow and other areas that might come into contact with food. Rinse thoroughly under running water. Dry hands, using single-service towels or hot-air dryer.

Avoid Risks. People are the biggest culprits in passing along disease. Train personnel in clean personal habits and safe food practices. Rule of thumb: Avoid contact with the face and mouth. For example, avoid smoking, chewing gum and reapplying makeup.

Handle with Care. Limit hand contact with tableware that comes in contact with food or the customer's mouth. Handle glasses or cups by the base or handles—don't touch the rims. Pick up and carry utensils by their handles. Don't touch the rims of bowls, dishes and plates. ♦

Food Safety

by Jeff Weinstein

A line cook uses an unwashed knife to chop vegetables. A chef fails to make sure a roast cooks to 160F. A buser bumps into a pan of raw chicken, causing the juice to drip into a tray of broiled seafood. These are just a few examples of how the bacteria that cause foodborne illnesses can be transmitted.

If an outbreak takes place in your operation, the total cost of legal fees, settlements and lost business can be staggering. For example, the staff at D.B. Kaplan's delicatessen in Chicago had no way of knowing it purchased turkey crawling with bacteria one day in 1985, but the subsequent outbreak of food poisoning proved costly to the Levy Restaurants operation. Company President Bill Post estimates that business dropped off by as much as 85%, costing the restaurant $500,000 in sales. Legal bills added up to $75,000, while settlements with the public cost about $50,000. In addition, it took nearly two years to regain consumer confidence after a storm of negative publicity, Post says.

D.B. Kaplan's more than recovered its losses from a settlement with the supplier. But if the outbreak had been caused by an internal oversight in food-safety procedures, the company would have been forced to absorb the cost. That potential loss proves that food service operators must teach and constantly reinforce the principles of basic food safety. This article focuses on procedures and practical tips for safe food handling, from receiving and storing to preparation, service and cleanup.

Start at the Back Door

All food received at the back door must immediately be inspected for quality. If any product is in unacceptable condition, send the case back with the deliverer. If bad commodities happen to slip past inspection, destroy them immediately upon discovery so they cannot mix with safe foodstuffs.

The Old Spaghetti Factory, Portland, Ore., requires its crew to open every container of produce to inspect for spoilage and insect infestation, according to company spokesman John Dew. When employees accept dairy or other refrigerated items, they dip a thermometer into product to make sure the items are cold enough. "Refrigerated items should be held at 39F or less, so they should be delivered at the same temperature," insists Dew.

All frozen products, except ice cream, must be 0F upon delivery. Ice cream can be delivered and stored at 6F to 10F. Reject any item that shows signs of having been thawed or refrozen.

Since fresh eggs have been linked to outbreaks of foodborne illness, operators must make sure they are delivered refrigerated and immediately moved to cold storage upon reception. Eggs must be clean and whole, received with shells intact and no more than two weeks old.

Marriott has required its operations to use liquid pasteurized eggs for two years now. With the exception of single-service orders such as fried eggs, the company uses liquid pasteurized eggs for all recipes such as Caesar salad dressing and hollandaise sauce. "We don't want to take a chance of someone holding shell eggs out at room temperature or letting one contaminated egg slip into a large batch and have it incubate," says Don Grim, Marriott's executive director of quality assurance and food safety.

The Educational Foundation of the National Restaurant Association suggests these guidelines for receiving center-of-the-plate items:

Fresh meat should be firm and elastic to touch. Beef and lamb should be cherry red in color, while pork should be pink. Temperature should be 45F or below. Unacceptable meat will have discolored blotches or spots, a sour smell, and slimy, sticky or dry texture.

Fresh poultry also should be firm and elastic to touch with no discoloration. It should be packed in crushed ice; temperature should be 45F or below. Beware of discoloration around the neck and darkened wing tips.

Fresh fish should not have a fishy odor. It should be bright red with moist gills. Eyes should be clear and bulging. The flesh and belly should be firm and elastic to touch. It should be packed in self-draining ice at 45F or below. Do not accept fish with gray-green or dry gills with soft, yielding flesh.

Fresh shellfish should be shipped alive in the shell with no strong odor. A lobster shell should be hard and heavy. Clam and oyster shells should be closed. Again, temperature should be below 45F. A strong odor is a clue to unacceptability. If the shell is partly open, it means the animal is dead.

Simple Storage Rules

Store cooked food separate from raw food to prevent contamination, and keep food requiring refrigeration out of the danger zone, 45F to 140F.

When cooling in preparation for storage, use a method, such as water circulation external to a food container, that will not exceed four hours. At Haussner's restaurant in Baltimore, the staff uses large sinks (7-x-3-x-2-foot) in the cool-down process. Placing pots of soup or sauce in an ice bath with cold running water accelerates cooling. The process usually takes two hours to cool the food to 40F. The item in the pot must be stirred approximately every 20 minutes. To make sure stirring is not overlooked, The Old Spaghetti Factory kitchens keep a chart on the wall next to the cooling station. The staff must log every stir.

Ready-to-eat food should be stored above raw food, never below, because raw food juices could drip onto prepared food and contaminate it. As an added precaution, The Old Spaghetti Factory stores nothing below thawing chicken in a cooler.

Going one step further, the chain segregates different products so chicken juice cannot splash into cooling meat or fish. At Haussner's, color-coded trays make it easy for employees to make sure that the same product is stored on one rack.

Food-Prep Procedures

During preparation of food, it is most important to prevent cross-contamination. The rule is simple: Keep hot food hot and cold food cold. Avoid manual contact with food, and work with amounts that can be prepared in an hour or less. Batch cooking, preparing only as much food as is required at the last possible moment, helps assure minimal time in the temperature danger zone.

Other points to remember:

◆ Keep raw, cooked or ready-to-eat products in separate areas.
◆ Never use the same utensils for raw and cooked products.
◆ Never place a cooked product on a food-contact surface where a raw product has been without first washing, rinsing and sanitizing that area.

To make sure bacteria does not carry from one food or food-contact surface to another, Old Spaghetti Factory kitchen personnel wipe down any horizontal surface with bleach water, then with clear water, and confine the preparation of a product to that clean area. Once a prep cycle is completed, they wipe down the area again. In addition, they sanitize all cutting boards and knives.

At the Melrose Diner in Philadelphia, standardized procedures play a big part in quality control, according to President Richard Kubach. For instance, when cooks make chicken salad, they cut up and blanch the celery for 10 seconds to kill bacteria, then shock the celery in ice water to keep it crunchy. (All fresh produce should be scrubbed to remove visible dirt.)

Even though the Melrose Diner serves more than 3,000 people a day, menu items such as chicken salad are prepared in small, one-pound portions to reduce exposure to warmer temperatures. "Our philosophy dictates that we'd rather run out of something for ten minutes than have a large quantity held at growing temperatures throughout the day," says Kubach.

Marriott uses a similar procedure. When cooks make a salad such as tuna, they are required to put the tuna and all condiments in the refrigerator a day before the salad is made. That way, cooks can be sure the temperature of the product is below 40F.

Marriott takes an aggressive safety approach when it come to the preparation of shellfish as well. The company is working with suppliers who have the capacity to run certified shellfish through a 48-hour purification process. The fish are put through a filtered and sterilized water system to purge any remaining bacteria.

To make sure steam-table food is held at the correct temperature, Old Spaghetti Factory managers carry thermometers to test items such as spaghetti sauce. The kitchen manager checks the temperature of the steam tables to start; front-of-the-house managers then cross-check it at least every 30 minutes. Cooks are required to bring products up to 165F before placing reheated food on the serving line. They also stir hot food regularly to make sure all parts of it remain hot.

The Educational Foundation of the NRA recommends always using a metal-stemmed, numerically scaled thermometer to determine temperature of potentially hazardous food. Check temperature in more than one location, and make sure to check the product's center or thickest part.

Additional suggestions from the NRA for reusing prepared food include:

♦ Never save highly perishable food such as pudding or creamed casserole for use the next day.
♦ Label food with its preparation date and time.
♦ Do not mix reused food with fresh food portions.
♦ Never use hot food holding equipment for reheating, or cold holding equipment for cooling.

Guidelines for cleaning and sanitizing serving utensils, equipment and facilities complete the list of safety precautions.

Kitchenware and food-contact surfaces should be sanitized after each use. Hyatt Hotels uses ammonia-based cleaner for items such as knives and cutting boards. Also, the kitchen steward disassembles and cleans meat grinders, mixers and blenders after each use. At the Melrose Diner, management goes as far as to refrigerate all utensils at the end of the day to avoid a potential buildup of bacteria.

Food-contact surfaces of grills and griddles and other cooking surfaces must be cleaned at least once a day. Also, keep non-food-contact surfaces free of dust, dirt and food scraps.

Another danger zone is the garbage, which attracts flies and vermin. Haussner's restaurant avoids that problem by putting garbage in a separate refrigerated room. "It keeps out the flies," says General Manager Steve George. "Our trash is never put outside. It goes out only when the garbage man appears at the back door."

Enforce and Reinforce

All the food-safety textbooks and video training programs in the world are useless if managers do not enforce policies and reinforce good habits.

Several foodservice companies use internal auditors to make critical inspections of food-safety procedures. At Marriott, auditors make unannounced inspections two to four times a year at each operation. If a unit fails the test, the general manager is required to report to Vice Chairman Richard E. Marriott within 48 hours with plans for corrective action. Many Marriott divisions tie inspection performance to the management bonus program.

At Kansas State University, internal inspectors make monthly checks, looking for the same violations that might be on the health inspector's list. Each department is rated, and the winner receives an afternoon party.

The best reinforcement is hands-on, verbal reinforcement, according to George of Haussner's. "We don't believe in signs around here," he says. "We are very attentive to our employees' needs and physically help them through the processes that contribute to a safe and clean environment."

Whatever method is chosen, realize that the NRA reports that 89% of consumers are concerned about proper food handling in restaurants. The benefits of a well-conceived safety plan and the costs you save by preventing foodborne illnesses should persuade all operators to implement and enforce a food-safety program.

Wave of the Future

Hazard Analysis and Critical Control Points Systems, known as HACCP, is becoming the common method of producing high-quality, defect-free products. It enables an establishment to evaluate its operation, locate possible points of contamination and take preventive measures to protect against foodborne illness. HACCP stresses the process rather than the facilities. To implement the system, an operator must be able to set priorities concerning the hazards that exist according to severity and risk. For instance, time/temperature controls are more important than clean ceilings. Such controls must then be set up at each step of food preparation. An operator sets the system in motion by examining the menu and recipes, and by designing standardized procedures ensuring that all employees are trained in the HACCP system. Regulatory agencies across the country now conduct HACCP-based inspections. Inspectors observe the way an operator receives, stores, prepares and serves food. For more information, contact the Educational Foundation of the National Restaurant Association, 250 S. Wacker Dr., Suite 1400, Chicago, Ill. 60606-5834. Call (312) 715-1010.

Reference Guide

♦ Educational Foundation of the National Restaurant Association, 250 S. Wacker Dr., Suite 1400, Chicago, Ill. 60606-5834. Call (312) 715-1010 for information about SERV-SAFE food-safety training program and Applied Foodservice Sanitation coursebook.

♦ Educational Institute of the American Hotel & Motel Association, 1201 New York Avenue NW, Washington, D.C. 20005-3917. Call (202) 289-3193 for information on training material about sanitation management.

♦ National Sanitation Foundation, P.O. Box 1468, Ann Arbor, Mich. 48106. Call (313) 769-8010 for information about material on foodservice sanitation standards.

♦ Food Protection Certification Program of the Educational Testing Service, Princeton, N.J. 08541-6515. Call (609) 921-9000 for a listing of certified individuals by state.

♦ Charles Felix Associates, P.O. Box 1581, Leesburg, Va. 22075. Call (703) 777-7448 for information about posters, cartoon quizzes and handbooks teaching correct sanitation procedures. Spanish-language materials available. ♦

THE ACCESSIBLE RESTAURANT

Public Accommodation

by Jeff Weinstein

The sign on the door at 4,000 company-owned Pizza Huts is dated January 26, 1992, the date the Americans with Disabilities Act (ADA) public accommodation rules took effect.

"To our customers and the public: Pizza Hut is committed to implementing the Americans with Disabilities Act and pledges to take all reasonable steps to accommodate our customers and our employees." The telephone number for Pizza Hut's ADA hotline is posted at the bottom of the sign.

One week before the rules took effect, Pizza Hut gathered its regional managers for a conference to explain the company's commitment to removing barriers and changing service practices that could keep disabled customers from enjoying the full range of services. Initial modifications at existing units were to take place within 90 to 120 days of the January 26 date. Attitude and service training of crew members began immediately.

Pizza Hut has taken the steps necessary to comply with ADA, one of the most comprehensive pieces of legislation in U.S. history.

ADA requires operators to show they are making a good-faith effort to accommodate disabled persons by making changes that are "readily achievable" and do not pose "undue burden" to the business. Operators must evaluate their own facilities, making sure disabled customers can enter the facility, and then have access to goods and services.

Then, operators must put in writing the changes they plan to make and begin to make those changes. Every action should be documented.

Business owners who ignore ADA regulations risk legal action from disability-rights groups as well as the U.S. Attorney General. Recalcitrant operators could be ordered to pay attorneys' fees, remove barriers, provide aids and services, and modify policies. In egregious cases, the U.S. Attorney General can sue for civil penalties of up to $100,000.

Courts will rule on what is considered "readily achievable" or an "undue burden" on a case-by-case basis. Judges will take into account such factors as the cost of the changes, the amount the facility has already spent on barrier removal and overall financial resources.

Tax credits and deductions are available to help defer the cost of complying with ADA. Businesses can be granted a tax deduction of up to $15,000 a year for any ADA-related alteration made to existing facilities. Small businesses (with less than $1 million in gross receipts or fewer than 30 full-time workers) are eligible for direct tax credit of up to $10,250.

The rest of this article discusses various requirements and alternative means to providing access to foodservice establishments. While the letter of the law might seem overwhelming and confusing, in many cases, ADA boils down to inexpensive, common-sense measures.

For example, rearranging a few tables to provide aisle access for someone in a wheelchair is considered "readily achievable." But if the rearranging results in significant loss of serving or selling space, it could be considered an "undue burden."

If providing access is not easy to accomplish, ADA requires operators to consider alternatives. If an operator can't build a ramp up a long flight of stairs leading to the front door, for example, an alternative such as entry through another door or takeout food delivered curbside must be considered. In short, good faith can go a long way.

"Be open to suggestions and sensitive to potential problems," says Ginger Lane, who has been in a wheelchair for eight years. "If your intention is to serve disabled customers in the best way possible, they will have no reason to complain."

Getting in the Door

All the good intentions and sensitivity training in the world will not help a restaurateur one bit if a disabled customer can't get in the front door. Operators looking for a place to start to comply with ADA should look outside to the parking lot. For every 20 spaces in the lot, one should be set aside for the disabled. The space must be eight feet wide with a five-foot access aisle.

If you don't have a parking lot, don't worry; ADA does not require operators to provide parking if it doesn't exist. If the lot is small, the best alternative is to provide valet service for disabled customers. "Good service can get around the need for accessible service," says John Salmen, president of Universal Designer & Consultant Inc., Silver Springs, Md.

The next step is the ramp between the parking lot and the front door. If the slope to the front door isn't too steep, ramps usually are not expensive to build. "You're generally looking at replacing a 5-feet-wide, 20-feet-long section of sidewalk to install a ramp," says Tom Smith, national director of design and construction for Arby's, Miami Beach, Fla. "Depending on the part of the country, you're looking at a cost between $400 and $500."

In instances where a ramp to the front door isn't "readily achievable," consider installing a doorbell so restaurant personnel can be alerted to the presence of a disabled patron. Staff members can then send guests to a front or side door.

If access is achievable only through a kitchen door, make the experience a special event. Consider giving customers a tour of the kitchen and introduce them to the chef or manager. Also,

keep the back-door entrance as attractive as possible by placing items such as garbage cans at a distance from the door.

Temporary ramps are an option, but should be replaced with permanent ramps as soon as possible. Ramps can be purchased at medical supply houses and through publications for people with disabilities, for example, Paraplegia News, Spinal Network, Mainstream and Accent on Living.

A last-resort option is to carry a disabled person, wheelchair and all, up the front steps. However, if the staff isn't well-trained in this practice, most disability-access experts frown upon this idea. The guest and staff members could be injured, which could lead to a lawsuit.

For guests who can use the stairs, but are elderly or arthritic, make sure sturdy handrails are in place. Keep lighting strong enough for sight-impaired guests to see steps and doorways.

The next potential obstacle is the door itself. If the door is heavy, install a doorbell with a sign to ring for assistance. If a French door exists, one side should offer 32 inches of clearance when opened at 90 degrees. But that is not often the case, according to Salmen. In addition, it is difficult for a disabled person to open both doors. Alternatives: Install a doorbell or automatic door opener; keep a doorman on duty; change the door so one side is wider; or replace the entire doorway.

If a doorway vestibule fails to offer approximately 7 feet for a wheelchair to rest comfortably between two doors, the best alternative is to remove one of the doors. Also, consider changing the door swings so both swing out of the vestibule. The expensive solution is to reconstruct the vestibule.

Door handles also can present a challenge to disabled customers. Many restaurant companies are replacing all doorknobs, inside and outside the unit, with levers. This step is generally considered "readily achievable."

When a threshold in the doorway exceeds the maximum 1/2-inch, either replace the threshold or taper it with a small concrete slope.

Also, make sure employees who answer the telephone are trained to answer questions about access. They should know specifics, for instance, if the entrance is limited to a side door or via a temporary ramp.

Operators who provide curb service as an alternative should mention that fact in their Yellow Pages advertisements, or post a sign in the front of the unit. If a customer has called for take-out, make sure a staff member is on the lookout to bring the order to the automobile. Since people with disabilities are twice as likely never to have visited a restaurant, setting up curb or delivery service could increase business.

If all else fails, operators should keep a reference list of similar restaurants that are nearby and accessible. For example, Pizza Hut operations that are not yet accessible keep a list of Pizza Huts in the area that have ramps.

Getting to the Table

Providing 36 inches of clearance in restaurant aisles and 5% accessible tables set aside should not be difficult.

At Chicago's upscale L'Escargot restaurant, owner Alan Tutzer says creating an accessible dining room is as important as an outside ramp. "Guests in wheelchairs should feel comfortable at several tables and not be subject to poorer status in a corner," says Tutzer. He adds that fine-dining operations hit hard by the recession probably have the room to take out a few tables.

Proving an "undue burden" because of a loss of tables will be difficult in court, as well. "If seats are always full, an operator will have a hard time proving "undue burden," says Harvey Jacoby, president of Interplan Practice Ltd., an architectural firm based in Orlando, Fla. "If seats are not full, there should be no problem maneuvering tables to accommodate disabled customers."

Salmen recommends locating accessible tables near routes that lead from the entrance to the restroom, since that is the next step in providing accessibility. If that means seating disabled customers near the front door, so be it.

"I don't mind it if I'm seated near the front door, because I don't have to travel as far or worry about bumping into other customers," says Lane.

"First, the host should ask if the front seat is OK. Most people will not object, because the host is showing sensitivity. A lot has to do with intent. If a restaurateur is trying to serve a disabled patron in the best way possible, they have no reason to complain."

ADA also requires operators to provide services in the most integrated setting. Always placing disabled customers at the first table or in a corner near the kitchen could be considered discriminatory, especially if different amenities such as window views and piano bars are available in unique areas. At the Montgomery Inn in Cincinnati, a portable ramp is stored in the kitchen for disabled guests who prefer a window table that is located three steps down from the main dining area.

Seating and Service Requirements

According to Salmen, many restaurant tables have trouble meeting the 27-inch height required by ADA. Remedies, however, should be "readily achievable." First, raise the table with inexpensive leg extensions such as larger feet or blocks. If blocks are used, make sure the adjustment is made before the disabled customers reach the table to avoid subjecting them to embarrassment.

For tables that don't offer comfortable depth for a wheelchair customers, options include fold-out corners and oversize table overlays.

When Lane has trouble being seated, if the restaurant isn't too busy, she will ask that two tables be put together or to be seated at a four-top to provide extra room.

At the Montgomery Inn, hosts and managers are taught to position wheelchair customers at tables so they do not jut out into the aisle and get jostled by other patrons.

If the operation has a mix of pedestal and parsons tables, give disabled and elderly customers a choice. Older people or people with crutches or walkers often have trouble getting up from a seated position and prefer to lean on the table. Parsons tables are better at withstanding the weight, but pedestal tables allow more room for a wheelchair to maneuver.

NRA GUIDELINES

The National Restaurant Association offers guidelines for serving people with hearing, visual and mobility impairments.

Hearing impairments

♦ This is often a subtle condition. Staff should look for clues such as failure to respond to a verbal request.
♦ To get the person's attention, tap him or her on the arm or use a hand motion. Don't shout.
♦ To accommodate lip readers, face them directly and speak slowly and distinctly.
♦ Offer a pad of paper and pen so that the person can communicate with the server.
♦ Seat people who use sign language in a well-lit area. Try not to seat people with hearing impairments in a noisy area.

Visual impairments

♦ Greet guests in a normal tone of voice. Identify yourself and ask whether they want assistance to a table. If assistance is requested, offer your arm and warn the person of any level changes, steps or congested areas.
♦ If you don't have Braille menus, or if the person doesn't read Braille, offer to read the menu, including prices, to the person.
♦ Seat visually impaired customers in well-lit areas or provide penlights for better viewing of the menu.
♦ Instruct servers to announce their arrival and departure from the table. Frequent checks on the table are appropriate when the guest can't see where the server is to attract attention.
♦ When delivering an order, ask the guest if he or she wants to know the location of the food on the plate. Explain the locations using clock-face directions.

Mobility impairments

♦ Ask people in wheelchairs whether they want to be pushed before doing so.
♦ Don't seat them in a remote place, and make sure they have the option of a nonsmoking section.
♦ Ask guests with poor muscle control whether they would like their food cut up before it is served, and give them a flexible straw for their beverage.

Self-Service Solutions

At self-service areas such as buffets, salad bars, condiment tables and cafeteria lines, all items should be within reach of someone in a wheelchair. Arrange these items so they are no higher than 36 inches off the ground. Tray slides should be mounted at 30 inches. Once again, alternative means of providing service in these areas can improve access for disabled guests.

First, offer table service. If a salad bar or buffet is up a flight of stairs, the server can tell the customer what the choices are, ask for preferences and deliver the dish to the table. Servers also can offer to accompany the guest to the food bar and assist in preparing a plate.

In a cafeteria or fast-food setting, a crew member can help disabled customers through the line and escort them to their tables. At condiment counters, offer employee assistance or create a space to put down the tray so the dispensers can be operated without much inconvenience. Another option is to place condiments, including napkins, at the table.

Getting to the Restrooms

Of all its patron-accessibility guidelines, ADA's restroom requirements are the toughest and most expensive to meet. Entrance doors must have 32 inches of clearance. Stalls should be 5 feet by 5

ADA AT A GLANCE

The Americans with Disabilities Act prohibits public accommodations from discriminating against an individual with a disability in the full and equal enjoyment of goods and services. The National Restaurant Association states:

♦ You may not set eligibility criteria or special requirements.
♦ You must provide services in the most integrated setting.
♦ Existing facilities must remove barriers wherever "readily achievable."
♦ New construction and alterations to facilities must meet the higher standard of being "readily accessible."
♦ You must make reasonable modifications unless doing so would fundamentally alter the nature of services provided.
♦ You must offer aids and services to provide equal access, unless it creates an "undue burden."
♦ You are not required to provide services to disabled individuals that pose a threat to the health and safety of others.

FRONT-DOOR ACCESS

♦ At least 5% of parking lot spaces must be accessible with an 8-foot parking space and a 5-foot aisle.
♦ Ramps leading to the front door should be no steeper than 1/12 in slope.
♦ Thresholds at doorways should not exceed 1/2 inch in height.
♦ Entry doors should provide 32 inches of clearance when the door is open at 90 degrees.
♦ All fire exits must be accessible.

AISLE ACCESS

♦ Paths through dining areas, and at least one leading to the restrooms, should be at least 36 inches wide.
♦ Wherever booth or fixed seating is provided, at least 5% of the fixed tables, but not less than one, should be wheelchair-accessible.

TABLE ACCESS, SELF-SERVICE

♦ For wheelchair seating at tables or counters, leg space should be at least 27 inches high, 30 inches wide and 19 inches deep.
♦ Self-service areas, including utensil racks, salad bars, beverage dispensers and condiment areas, should be within reach of someone sitting in a wheelchair and no higher than 36 inches from the floor.
♦ Tray slides should run continuously from the tray stack to the cashier.
♦ The tray slide should be mounted at 30 inches.

RESTROOM ACCESS

♦ Doorways should have a minimum clear opening of 32 inches with the door open at 90 degrees.
♦ Rear grab bar should be 36 inches long.
♦ Accessible toilet should be 17 to 19 inches high.
♦ The furthest edge of the toilet-paper dispenser should be 36 inches from the rear wall.
♦ Lavatories should provide 29 inches from the finished floor to the bottom of the apron. The height to the rim of the counter of the should be 34 inches.
♦ Hot-water pipes and drain pipes under the lavatory should be insulated or configured to avoid contact.

feet so different approaches are possible. Newer restrooms already comply with these standards. Older restaurants, however, might need adjustments in this area.

In many cases, older restrooms offer little or no room to add space or remodel. Vestibules often are not arranged to accommodate the necessary space to open two doors. The space lacks maneuvering room, and stalls often are too small.

" 'Readily achievable' is defined as easy to accomplish and carry out without much difficulty or expense," says Jacoby of Interplan. "So the law should not require you to knock out a wall or cut into the kitchen to achieve the proper restroom size."

But the law does require operators to make their best effort, and many alternatives exist. If there is a vestibule, try to remove one of the doors. If maneuvering room inside the restroom is limited, replace large waste cans with smaller ones.

The best alternative, but not necessarily the easiest, is providing a separate unisex restroom on the main floor of the building, especially when individual restrooms are either up or down a flight of stairs. Changing both bathrooms into private unisex bathrooms could be a bit more realistic. One big stall in each room usually provides the necessary maneuvering space. Before taking this route, check with your building and sanitation codes because unisex restrooms are not acceptable in all municipalities. Also, consider whether your customers would be comfortable with a unisex restroom.

If two stalls are present, move the stall divider to make an accessible stall bigger.

In addition to adjusting stalls, install grab bars and adjust the height and location of the toilet-paper dispenser. Replace knob hardware with levers to make doors and faucets easier to operate. Either lower existing mirrors or put in a full-length mirror on a wall or the back of the door. Also, offer separate hand towels, or lower the cloth towel dispenser or adjust the dispenser to provide a longer loop that is easier to reach.

At the entrance, make sure the path of travel isn't blocked by displays, highchairs or cigarette machines. Also, avoid cute signs on the door, such as a hen and rooster, so mentally disabled guests won't be confused.

If making restrooms accessible is deemed an "undue burden" on the operation, the last resort is to make arrangements for your guests to use a nearby business's restroom.

When customers call to ask about accessibility, make sure the host or hostess explains restroom accessibility, for instance, that the facilities are down 15 steps or that they are equipped with lever handles and faucets.

Attitude Is Everything

Training staff to be sensitive to special guest needs can make or break a restaurant in the mind of a disabled person. A staff's poor attitude as opposed to less-than-perfect accommodations often leads to complaints. And an all-around good attitude might earn the restaurant a regular customer.

Most important, servers and other staff members should be honest if they are confronted with an unfamiliar situation. They should ask disabled customers how they would like to be helped. Both staff and management should be flexible and creative in addressing customer needs, as well as polite and nonconfrontational.

Generally speaking, staffs are not well-trained in handling disabled customers, according to Lane. She believes the best training comes from individuals with disabilities.

"Employees should say, 'Let me know how I can help you.' The guest will let them know they want help or that they are just fine on their own," says Lane. "Don't provide undue attention that someone might not want. A lot of disabled people like to act independently and don't want to be treated as though they can't do anything themselves."

And for those who just aren't comfortable working with the disabled community, Lane advises to give it time. "The more exposure people have to others with disabilities, the greater the comfort level."

Resources

♦ Architectural and Transportation Barrier Compliance Board. For technical information on ADA minimum accessibility standards. (800) 872-2253.

♦ U.S. Department of Justice. For information on accessibility requirements, barrier removal, auxiliary aids and services. (202) 514-0301.

♦ Internal Revenue Service. Contact your local office for information about disabled access tax credits and tax deductions for removal of architectural barriers. Or call (800) 829-3676 for a copy of Service Publication 907, "Tax Information for Handicapped and Disabled Individuals."

♦ National Restaurant Association. For technical assistance and information about operators' responsibilities under the ADA. (202) 331-5900. ♦

THE ACCESSIBLE RESTAURANT

Employee Accommodation

by Beth Lorenzini

For years, Harris Bank, Chicago, has followed the spirit of the Americans with Disabilities Act. The bank's foodservice department, a Canteen account, has traditionally offered employment opportunities to people such as Norbert Witulski, who is legally blind and has a hearing impairment.

Harris Bank has made a few adjustments to help Witulski do his job in the dishroom. First, it made it possible for him learn the job on site with his job coach, Len Scott, from the Chicago Lighthouse for the Blind, the agency that originally placed Witulski at Harris. In addition, Witulski's timecard is at the top of the card holder. A blue stripe across the top makes it easy for him to find. And in the employee locker room, Witulski's locker has a key lock rather than a combination lock.

While Harris Bank voluntarily made accommodations for Witulski, it is in the midst of reviewing its policy to be sure that it is in total compliance with ADA. And other well-meaning operators, like Harris, must follow the letter of the law as well.

Title I, which protects qualified people with disabilities from employment discrimination, became effective for all employers with 25 or more employees (including state and local government employers) on July 26, 1992. All employers with 15 or more employees had to comply by July 26, 1993. Employers with 15 or fewer employees are exempt.

ADA requires that operators make "readily achievable" accommodations to the known physical or mental limitations of otherwise qualified people. These accommodations must be made so that these people can perform the essential functions of a job, unless doing so would result in an "undue hardship" on the employer or if individuals pose a direct threat to the health and safety of themselves or others.

An accommodation poses an undue hardship if it is unduly costly, extensive, substantial or disruptive or would fundamentally alter the nature or operation of the business. Among the factors to be considered are the cost, the size of the business, financial resources and the nature and structure of the operation.

These factors have been called somewhat vague and relative; what might seem unduly costly to the operator might not seem so to the court. "Right now, it's hard to say what qualifies as an undue hardship," says A. Philip Nelan, director of Handicapped Employment Programs for the National Restaurant Association. Better parameters doubtless will emerge as cases are settled on an individual basis.

On the other hand, "readily achievable" accommodations usually are not very expensive. According to 1989 estimates by the Department of Labor and the Government Accounting Office, half of all workers with disabilities can be employed with accommodations that cost less than $50. Another 20% require accommodations that cost from $50 to $500, and another 20%, from $500 to $1,000.

In fact, foodservice operators should consider ADA an opportunity, not a burden, urges Steve Zivolich, founder of Irvine, Calif.-based Integrated Resources Institute, a not-for-profit consulting firm dedicated to including people with disabilities into all aspects of the community. "Complying with the employment portion of ADA generally is not that difficult," says Zivolich. "And it will lead some operators to find fantastic employees who happen to be disabled."

Job Descriptions

Under ADA, employers are not allowed to ask applicants whether they are disabled or about the nature or severity of a disability. They may only inquire as to whether or not an applicant can perform the essential functions of the job. For this reason, the written job description will become one of the most important factors considered by the Equal Employment Opportunity Commission (EEOC) and the courts when they decide whether an operator has violated ADA.

Changing those descriptions also will be the one of the most difficult task operators undertake. Operators need to be more detailed than ever before in writing down exactly what each position entails. At Schlotzsky's in San Antonio, for example, the description for the baker's job has been changed in part from "Baker mixes sourdough in mixer, pours dough into bus tubs and carries bus tubs to proofer . . ." to "Baker stands at work table 31.5 inches in height and mixes sourdough in mixer which is operated by handle located 50 in. above ground. Carries bus tub weighing xxx lbs."

"Basically, our bakers need to stand and move around to perform the essential functions of the job," says John White, director of training. "So I have to be sure to put in things like equipment heights and actual movement requirements."

Norb Weller of Weller Consulting, North Potomac, Md., provides an excellent how-to on writing job descriptions. Highlights include:

Job identification: A good job description starts with the job title, department, job title of supervisor, date the job description was prepared, preparer's name and approver's name.

Job summary: The description should provide the general purpose of the job. For a Kitchen Helper, for example, "maintains kitchen work areas, restaurant equipment and utensils in clean, orderly condition" would be appropriate. For a Table Server, "serves food and drinks to guests in dining room."

Essential functions: The description should list clear and precise statements of the responsibilities, job duties and major tasks as well as the percentage of time spent on each. For example, a Kitchen Helper "washes worktables, walls, refrig-

erator and floor, 20%; sorts and removes trash and garbage to dumpster, 20%; steam-cleans garbage cans, 5%;" etc.

Accountability: The major results and key outcomes expected of the employee should be listed. "Kitchen work area will be safe and clean so cooks and helpers will be able to work more efficiently" is an example. Accountability also can require that employees in certain positions meet specific dollar goals in revenue or cost containment.

Qualification standards: These are the personal and professional qualifications required, including skill, experience, education, physical and mental demands, safety, and other requirements. Some qualification examples include: "Lifts and carries sacks and cases of up to 70 pounds up to 20 times per eight-hour shift; places items on high shelves and in walk-in freezer. Frequent bending and stooping. Hazards include but are not limited to cuts from broken glass and metal cans, burns, slipping, tripping. Works frequently in hot and damp environment. No experience required."

Again, operators need to look carefully at the specific tasks essential to the job and put them in writing. To find out exactly what's involved in a job, talk to or observe employees currently working in various job positions, or have employees fill out questionnaires concerning their duties. Ask employees to review job descriptions after they've been drafted. And it might be a good idea to have an attorney review descriptions as well, since how they're written will serve as evidence should a discrimination charge arise.

Application Alterations

Job applications also need review, especially if operations have been using standard forms that were drafted years ago. According to EEOC, questions to avoid that pertain to disabilities include:

♦ List of diseases or major illnesses.
♦ Hospitalization history.
♦ History of mental-health treatment.

- Days absent from work in previous year because of illness.
- Disabilities or impairments.
- Prescription drugs being taken.
- Past treatment for drug addiction or alcoholism.
- Workers' compensation history.
- Height and weight, unless essential to the safe performance of the job.

In the view of the EEOC, which will enforce ADA regulations, not all of the above questions are in violation of antidiscrimination laws, but most serve no legitimate business purpose and should be left off applications. If any of the questions do in fact serve a legitimate business purpose, such as in the case of court-ordered affirmative action plans, then the questions might be exceptions to the avoidance rule; an attorney can advise. Also, although some of the information listed above might be needed for tax purposes, the EEOC recommends waiting until after a person is hired to collect the information.

On the other hand, questions that can be asked include:

- Job history and reason for leaving previous job.
- Education level, if job-related.
- Schools attended.
- Any name change employer should know to verify information about job history.
- Whether applicant is authorized to work in the United States.
- Whether applicant can perform specific job functions or would need a specific accommodation if hired (attach a job description).
- Whether applicant can meet attendance requirements (list hours and leave policies).
- Felony and misdemeanor convictions.

At the University of Washington, Seattle, for example, one application asks, "describe your ability to prepare a cycle menu" and "describe your ability to read and analyze a financial statement." All of the questions are specific and job-related. Applicants with disabilities that prohibit them from reading or writing can answer such questions orally, says Steve Hall, administrator of university foodservices.

Before Hiring

It is important to review interview policies and procedures and make specific preparations before you arrange an interview with an applicant who is disabled. The Job Accommodation Network (JAN), Morgantown, W.Va., offers these suggestions to prepare.

- Make sure that the facility and the interview area are accessible to individuals with disabilities.
- If the interview is exploratory, focus questions on skills, knowledge and abilities. If the interview is for a position, know the specific requirements of the job and have that job description in hand.
- If interviewees are expected to complete any paperwork such as an application, INS form or security pass, ask them beforehand if they will need any assistance in filling out the forms.
- At the time of the interview, proceed in the same manner that you would with any employee. Talk to the interviewee, not an interpreter if one is present. Don't lean on wheelchairs, but do sit at the level of the person in the wheelchair so that neither party needs to crane their neck.
- Shake whatever is offered, right or left hand, prosthesis, hook or elbow. Sit where lighting is good for applicants who are hearing impaired to accommodate lip-readers.
- Operators should be flexible in the way they communicate. For example, if a sign-language interpreter is not present with an individual who is hearing impaired, ask that individual how to communicate (pen and paper, lip-reading or computer terminal, for example).

Medical Examinations Dos and Don'ts

Not only are operators prohibited from asking about disabilities, but they also may not require applicants to take a medical examination before making a job offer. But an examination can be required after an offer is made if all employees working in that job category are required to take one. The information from the examination must be kept confidential and maintained in a separate medical file.

Under these post-hire requirements, employers can make employment contingent upon successful completion of a medical examination. If the exam turns up a disability, employers have two recourses. They can ask the individual what kinds of accommodations can be made to enable that person to perform the job (a shorter shift for a person with a heart condition, for example). Or the operator can refuse to hire the individual, but must be able to prove that the reason for exclusion is truly job-related and necessary for the conduct of the business. For example, if an employee is offered a food-handling job and his or her exam shows presence of Hepatitis A, the operator is prohibited from hiring that person in that position.

Operators also must be able to show that there was no "readily achievable" accommodation that would have made it possible for the individual to perform the essential job function.

Operators need not worry about being cited for discrimination against illegal drug users. Anyone who is using drugs illegally is not protected by ADA and may be denied a job or fired on the basis of such use. Also, under ADA, a drug test is not considered a medical examination. Therefore, ADA does not prevent employers from testing applicants and employees for current illegal drug use, even prior to the offer of employment.

While ADA excludes illegal drug users, it protects individuals who have completed or are currently in a rehabilitation program and are no longer illegally using drugs. ADA also protects individuals with AIDS and those who are HIV positive.

"Readily Achievable" Accommodations

Under ADA, what is considered "readily achievable" accommodation is going to run the gamut from replacing a combination lock with a key lock on lockers of employees who are visually impaired

to buying or modifying equipment. According to the EEOC, the principal test in determining whether an accommodation is reasonable will be its effectiveness. Does it enable a person with a disability to perform the essential functions of the job?

Such accommodations include altering work schedules to allow an employee with a disability time to get to work on special transportation. Reducing the number of hours in a shift, translating training manuals into Braille, improving lighting in the kitchen and installing handrails by steps are other examples. Lounges, lunchrooms and training areas on and off premises all must be accessible to employees with disabilities. If they're not, operators must provide those employees with accommodations equal to those enjoyed by nondisabled employees.

The best source for accommodation advice is the employee with the disability. Job coaches, too, will provide all kinds of tips and creative ideas to accommodate employees.

Employers are not obligated to implement or purchase the "best" accommodation, or necessarily the accommodation the individual with a disability would prefer. The accommodation simply needs to be effective. State departments of rehabilitation services often have or can acquire special devices to help employees function in their jobs. Included are such technical assistance devices as adapters that create large type on computer screens, voice-activated computer systems, Braille translators and printers, and special wheelchairs that hold people in an upright position. Often, these devices are tax-funded and cost operators nothing. If not, operators can get tax breaks on purchases.

Individuals with disabilities are not required to accept accommodations but will lose their "qualified individual" status if their refusal results in their inability to perform the job. And remember, not all employees with disabilities even need accommodation. At Romano's Macaroni Grill in Dallas, for example, employees who are severely mentally retarded are in charge of rolling flatware in napkins. The positions work beautifully both for these employees, who might have had difficulty finding employment, and for the restaurant, because a basic need is being filled efficiently. But no special accommodations are needed for these individuals to perform their jobs.

Training Tips

The methods operators use to train employees with disabilities are as unique as each foodservice operation.

More helpful than comprehensive lists of what to do for every possible case, however, are guidelines for finding training assistance, and plenty of resources exist. Across the country, thousands of agencies and organizations stand ready and willing to provide job coaches for on-site training as well as technical and human resources consulting. In most cases, such services are provided free of charge.

Begin by networking with fellow foodservice operators, says Zivolich of Integrated Resources. "If you know of another foodservice operation that has a good program, find out where they found help," he says. "Often, they'll recommend agencies and will give you the low-down on how well certain organizations work in specific situations."

Local school districts are another good source. Not-for-profit, supported-employment agencies are listed under Social Services in the Yellow Pages. And every state has a department of vocational rehabilitation services, which not only has programs of its own, but will know of local organizations that can help.

When employing individuals with disabilities, operators should expect to heighten their safety awareness, says Rob Nielsen, general manager of Brandenburg's in Madison, Conn. Brandenburg's, a training restaurant, is owned by SARAH, an agency that offers programs and services for people with "varying abilities."

"We take a lot of things for granted in a restaurant that we can't when someone has a mental or physical disability," says Nielsen. "You need to be aware of steps, bumps in the floor, lighting, sharp edges. You get very creative in the solutions you find." For example, one of his staff found an old crank-handle apple peeler at an antique fair and bought it for the restaurant. "We make a lot of strudel, but have employees who can't handle a sharp knife or a small peeler, so the crank-handle peeler is perfect," says Nielsen.

Incentives

Vocational rehabilitation programs will qualify employers of persons with disabilities to receive the Targeted Jobs Tax Credit (TJTC), a tax benefit of 40% on the trainee's first-year salary up to $6,000, or $2,400 per employee.

The National Association of Retarded Citizens (ARC) provides job-training salary differentials to employers of individuals who are mentally retarded. ARC reimburses 50% of the minimum wage for the first 160 hours of employment, 25% of the second 160 hours. Trainees must work 35 hours a week. Contact the NRA for more information.

Local vocational rehabilitation agencies can offer operators leads on other tax credits as well, including credits for the purchase of any special equipment to accommodate an employee with a disability.

ADA at a Glance

The Americans with Disabilities Act prohibits discrimination against a qualified person with a disability, who, with or without reasonable accommodation, can perform the essential functions of a job. Discrimination applies to hiring, firing, pay, promotions and other terms and conditions of employment. The National Restaurant Association states:

♦ You must reasonably accommodate the disabilities of qualified applicants or employees unless doing so would result in an undue hardship.

♦ You may not use employment tests to screen out people with disabilities unless you can show that the test is job-related and consistent with business necessity.

♦ You have the right to reject applicants or fire employees who pose a significant risk to the health or safety of other individuals in the workplace.

Writing a Job Description

♦ Try to begin each sentence with an action verb such as serves, wipes, mixes, cleans, cooks. Avoid such phrases as "responsible for" or "handles."

♦ Use simple, unambiguous language. "Slices cold meats and cheeses by hand or machine" is clearer than "uses sandwich preparation techniques and equipment."

♦ Describe duties in logical sequence and be specific about physical demands. For example, state that the job requires lifting 40-pound sacks 150 feet ten times per eight-hour shift.
Source: Norb Weller, consultant with Weller Consulting, North Potomac, Md., writing for the NRA.

Reasonable Accommodation

Work-environment changes that are "readily achievable" (easy to accomplish and carry out without much difficulty or expense) might include:

♦ Restructuring jobs.
♦ Modifying schedules.
♦ Allowing part-time positions.
♦ Modifying equipment.
♦ Adjusting exams, training materials and policies.
♦ Providing qualified readers or interpreters.

"Undue hardship," on the other hand, requires significant difficulty or expense, taking into account such factors as cost and a facility's and company's resources.

Hiring a Disabled Employee

♦ Compile accurate written job descriptions before advertising or interviewing. Carefully list the essential functions of each job.

♦ Review job-application forms. Limit questions to those that concern the applicant's ability to do the job.

♦ Eliminate questions on disabilities, past health problems, use of prescription drugs, hospitalization history and workers' compensation claims.

♦ Review the way you conduct interviews. Make sure questions focus on the applicant's ability to do a specific job. Offer an accessible location for interviews.

Employee Attitudes

Employees with disabilities are hired because they can do the job. Your staff should know this. They also should know:

♦ The best way to find out if an employee with a disability needs assistance is simply to ask that person.

♦ Employees should relax. People with disabilities aren't offended by statements such as "See you later" or "I've got to run" when those comments seem to directly relate to specific disabilities.

♦ Employees might feel that they are responsible for the safety of a co-worker who is disabled and fear they are not up to it. Dispel the fear through education.

Resources

♦ National Restaurant Association. For technical assistance about operators' responsibility under ADA. (202) 331-5900.

♦ Equal Employment Opportunity Commission. For information about ADA requirements affecting employment. (202) 663-4900.

♦ Job Accommodation Network. For free, practical advice for employers on steps to take to accommodate workers with disabilities. (800) 526-7234; in W.Va., (800) 526-4698.

♦ National Easter Seal Society. For excellent assistance on integrating people with disabilities into the community and work force. (312) 726-6200. ♦

THE SECURE RESTAURANT

Employee and Customer Safety

by Jeff Weinstein

As David and Cindy Jarvis watched their restaurant, Melange, go up in smoke on April 4, 1991, they couldn't help but think that they might have prevented the fire.

Not that the fire was due to their carelessness. Two weeks before the blaze, roofers hired by the landlord of the mall in which Melange leased space had a small fire in their tar wagon. The roofers, who didn't have fire extinguishers, used the restaurant's fire equipment to stop the blaze.

The day of the disastrous fire, Jarvis noticed more smoke than usual coming from the roofing project. Next thing he knew, the roofers were running back and forth with buckets of water, trying to extinguish a fire smoldering between the ceiling and the roof. Jarvis sent his sous chef to the roof with fire extinguishers and called the fire department, but it was too late.

"After the small fire, I was surprised there was no follow-up by the landlord to make sure that the roofers were better equipped to handle fires," Jarvis recalls. "If I had been nosier, I would have made sure the roofers had the right equipment and were properly insured."

No one was hurt that day in Wilmette, Ill., and Melange has since reopened at another site. But the Jarvis' insurance came up $200,000 short of covering the losses.

The Jarvis' story is a dramatic example of the safety issues restaurateurs face. It underlines the point that up-to-date safety programs are crucial to minimize liability and the number of job-related accidents and injuries.

This article on how to avoid workplace accidents and injuries is the first in a three-part series on restaurant safety and security. The second focuses on internal security measures that deter employee theft; the third on external security will show how to prevent robberies and vandalism.

Everyday Accidents

While devastating fires are rare, every day operators must deal with accidents: cuts, burns and falls that add up to big losses.

Godfather's Pizza, for example, paid $680,000 in workers' compensation claims in 1987. After that disastrous year, the Omaha, Neb.-based chain got serious about safety. As a result of operational and physical plant changes, last year the company paid only $168,000 in claims.

Two years since starting a strict safety program, Whataburger, Corpus Christi, Texas, has reduced the number of accidents by 15% and workers' compensation claims by $500,000, according to Mike McLellan, vice president of finance.

Built-In Safety

The best time to address the safety concerns of employees and customers is when the unit is being built.

The most often requested safety feature built into a new unit is nonskid flooring that is easy to maintain.

Bill Aumiller of Aumiller Youngquist P.C., Mount Prospect, Ill., says quarry tile with a non-slip grit or raised tread in traffic patterns is once again popular in kitchens. "Years ago, monocoat flooring was a very popular alternative to quarry tile," says Aumiller. "Operators could vary the amount of grit put into the floor so that it always had a rough texture and stayed slip-resistant. But many people have found that those floors don't hold up as well."

For operators who still prefer a poured floor, make sure the right amount of stone aggregate is used because too much or too little will hold grease and make the surface slippery, according to

---

PAINFUL STATISTICS

- In 1990, the foodservice industry reported 357,200 on-the-job accidents.
- On average, 35 work days are lost when a foodservice industry employee suffers a serious injury.
- Workers' compensation payments can cost a foodservice operator up to 16% of payroll.
- The most common foodservice industry injuries are sprains and strains (30%), cuts (20%), and burns (13%).
- Foodservice job injuries are most frequently caused by slips and falls on floors and walkways, mishandling of knives and machine slicers, inadequate knowledge of working with open flames, steamers and fryers, and overexertion from lifting and moving heavy objects.
- Approximately 90% of job-related accidents are the result of human error.
- Nearly 44% of all workers hurt on the job have been with their current employer for less than one year.

Source: Educational Foundation of the National Restaurant Association

---

designer Mark Knauer of Knauer Inc., Highland Park, Ill.

Creating enough kitchen space is another key to back-of-the-house safety. Knauer says there should be a minimum of 36 inches and a maximum of 48 inches walking space in traffic aisles or between work stations.

Knauer warns that traffic aisles that back up to work stations where food is being moved back and forth should be avoided. Traffic patterns perpendicular to work stations are the safest.

Other design features that improve safety include built-in space for trash cans; task lighting built into the bottom of shelves so cooks get a better view of their work; enough locker-room space for employees so they don't clog aisles with their personal belongings; and premix valves on faucets that keep employees from burning their hands in scalding water.

Doors leading in and out of the kitchen are another danger point. New York designer Susan Orsini recommends a buffer zone on each side of the doors where an abrasive carpet or mat removes grease from the bottom of employee's shoes.

In the front of the house, regular aisle maintenance and an aisle width of 42 inches help reduce the number of trips and falls by employees and customers.

For floors, carpeting is always the safest but often too expensive. Knauer recommends selecting a material with a nonskid or matte surface that has some abrasion. If the floor is tile or marble, a silicon sand finish will help prevent slips.

Because restaurateurs are concerned about atmosphere in booths, they tend to neglect lighting in the aisles. Knauer recommends using a recessed light fixture with a coiled baffle. It takes all the light between the source and surface and makes it disappear, yet highlights the surface itself.

With the enactment of the Americans with Disabilities Act, designers are avoiding multilevel surfaces in the dining room. But if stairways are built, make sure they are well lit, have sturdy railings and never have a run of fewer than three steps. "One or two steps are a trip hazard. Three becomes stairs," Knauer says.

Finally, to provide safe exit, especially in case of a fire, make sure there are two exits at extreme opposite ends of a typical restaurant with 150 to 200 seats. Also maintain the aisles and don't block off the exit by cramming in too many tables. All emergency exits should have panic hardware (crash bars) and thumb turns instead of key locks.

Accident Prevention

With workers' compensation premiums doubling over the last six years and the cost of a claim tripling over the past 10 years, operators finally started to seriously address safety in the late 1980s. What follows are examples of excellent programs that have led to a reduction in the number of falls, cuts, burns and repetitive-motion injuries.

Slips and falls: Cleaning floors properly is an integral part of preventing accidents. Bakers Square, Matteson, Ill., switched from a normal industrial soap to a stronger chemical that cuts through grease and emulsion. Since 1987, the company has reduced its accident frequency rate by more than 30%.

Restaura, Phoenix, found that employees were not applying floor treatments correctly. "If employees don't use clean water, it doesn't matter if you have the best floor-cleaning product," says David Davenport, risk manager. "We emphasize the correct procedure, regardless of the cleaner." In the past year alone, the company has saved 10% on workers' compensation costs by cutting down the number of slips and falls.

At Godfather's Pizza, Director of Safety and Risk Management John Garland found the key to slip-free floors is in the equipment. Instead of using mops that just push the grease around, according to Garland, Godfather's switched to deck brushes and power washers for efficiency. Between 1987 and 1990, the company saved $520,000 on insurance costs, he says.

Proper footware also prevents kitchen wipe-outs. Restaura has started a pilot program with shoe manufacturers that send mobile shoe stores to its contract-feeding sites. Employees are required to wear proper footwear and Restaura picks up half the price.

A number of companies continue to experiment with floor surfaces at trouble areas in the restaurants. Lettuce Entertain You Enterprises, Chicago, is testing a process in which floors are coated with a very strong acid chemical that etches microscopic pockmarks into quarry tile. It provides a more abrasive surface and grease soaks into the newly created pores, which are cleaned out every night.

Restaura is using more rubber mats in high slip areas. "We are getting away from abrasive floor strips because they wear out faster and the edges start peeling up and create trip hazards," says Davenport.

By installing mats at ice machines and next to

COST OF WORKPLACE INJURIES

- Back strain: 31%/$23,916
- Other sprains/strains: 19%/$13,611
- Fracture: 11%/$23,138
- Concussion/bruises: 11%/$12,055
- Laceration/puncture: 10%/$9,722
- Dislocation/crushing: 3%/$47,249
- Hernia: 3%/$24,499
- Burn: 3%/$12,833
- Infection/inflammation: 2%/$13,805
- Amputation: 1%/$40,249
- Occupational disease: 1%/$31,305
- Cumulative injury: 1%/$29,166

Source: National Council on Compensation Insurance

dish tanks, Godfather's has cut the number of slips and falls by 35%.

Cuts: The best way to prevent cuts is to reinforce the importance of wearing nylon-mesh gloves when working with knives and other sharp equipment. Godfather's has reduced cuts by 75% since it started requiring employees to wear safety gloves.

Restaura is going a step further by testing a new fabric treatment for gloves. According to Davenport, he can ladle 400F grease onto the new gloves and it runs right off. They cost twice as much as average models, but reportedly last four times longer.

Sharp corners are big cut threats in kitchens, as well. To fight that problem, Whataburger is installing equipment with rounded corners at new units.

Burns: Once again, gloves play a major role in the prevention of burns. Whataburger employees wear heat-resistant gloves that reach the elbow. "Previously, our employees were getting burned because gloves were too short," says McLellan.

Whataburger also is buying grease-retrieval equipment, which reduces the contact employees make with hot items such as the oil that is drained from fryers. The pump system sucks the

EMERGENCY PROCEDURES

If an emergency situation presents itself at Village Inn restaurants, employees immediately consult a red safety manual. It explains how to assemble a crisis management team and initial steps to take control of the situation.

The Denver-based chain's program is exemplary. Overall, the company has reduced accidents by 15% and saved $500,000 in workers' compensation claims. But few restaurant companies go beyond training their managers in CPR and how to shut off the gas and electricity.

Glen Garey, legal counsel for the Texas Restaurant Association, has devised a checklist of what to do when a customer or employee has an accident.

- Make the injured person as comfortable as possible.
- Arrange for prompt first aid or medical care.
- Ask the injured person how the accident happened.
- Ask for names and addresses of all witnesses.
- Have all employees present fill out a witness report at once.
- If no employees saw the accident, have two or more of them inspect the scene and then fill out a report.
- Inspect, verify conditions of premises for any structural defects.
- Note the condition of the area: Is it clean and dry? Well-lit? Are any fallen objects lying near the injured person? If so, were they dropped by the injured person, another customer or an employee?
- Do not enter into a dispute with the injured person over the cause.
- Do not reprimand any employee at the scene.
- Do not offer to pay all medical expenses.
- Do not admit responsibility.
- Do not mention insurance.
- Do not discuss the accident with strangers, now or later.
- Do not permit photographs to be taken by anyone other than your company representatives.

grease into a canister mounted on wheels. The canister is then rolled outside, where the shortening is pumped into a grease trap.

Repetitive-motion injuries and back strain: Because of the constant lifting they do, foodservice employees are prone to carpal tunnel syndrome, characterized by chronic pain and numbness of the hand, wrist and arm caused by repetitive motion. Operators are just starting to learn about the ailment and are adapting systems to prevent it.

Since Godfather's pizza makers must constantly press down and flatten dough, they use wrist guards to keep their wrists in a neutral position and therefore avoid the syndrome.

Bakers Square has redesigned its pass-through window and counter to allow servers to make more natural arm movements. The counters are lower and shorter so servers can get closer to plates when pulling them from the window.

According to William Tamulis, the chain's manager of safety and loss prevention, Bakers Square is looking at eliminating bus-tub areas in the middle of the dining rooms. A full bus tub weighs about 34 pounds and can take its toll on a buser's back.

As an alternative, the chain is having servers and busers make more frequent trips to tables and take dirty dishes on a small tray directly to the dishroom. Back-injury claims have reduced to the point of nonexistence in units where this system is in place, according to Tamulis.

To control back-injury claims, Restaura and Godfather's require employees to wear plastic weight belts when lifting heavy objects. As a result, both companies have witnessed a decrease in the number and severity of lifting injuries. Godfather's also trains employees to let suppliers deliver heavy loads directly to storage areas.

Motivational Tools

No matter how detailed the safety program, it is useless unless employees are motivated to follow it.

Several companies have developed incentive programs that encourage employees to work safely.

Bakers Square: For every quarter a restaurant remains accident-claim free, all employees receive a reward such as a $20 gift certificate to a local merchant. That reward doubles to $40, $80, and so on, for each consecutive quarter the unit stays accident-free.

The Loss Sensitive Allocation program uses a unit's safety performance to determine its workers' compensation payments. All units used to pay an equal amount into the workers' compensation pool. Today they are charged an average cost per claim. Accident-free restaurants don't sustain any charges, enabling managers to take that savings right down to the bottom line and improve their bonuses.

Village Inn: The company's Credibility of Image program includes one announced and one unannounced safety inspection at every unit once per quarter. The comprehensive quality assurance program asks 496 questions about sanitation, cleanliness and safety. While unit managers aren't expected to get a perfect score, the outcome determines a significant amount of their bonus, according to J.B. Bettinger, director of human resources.

A safety lottery is held each quarter in each region for hourly employees who haven't had an accident requiring medical attention. They can receive additional entries if the unit as a whole has fewer than 15 accidents a quarter. Winners of the regional lotteries each get a $200 gift certificate to

a department store and a pair of safety shoes. All entries go into a year-end drawing for a $500 gift certificate.

Restaura: The contract feeder is piloting a safety bingo game at 70 locations in Missouri, New York and Michigan. Hourly employees receive a bingo card. Each day the unit is accident-free, a number is drawn. Each employee who makes a bingo receives $10. If there is an accident that requires medical care, everyone turns in their card and two days pass before the game starts up again. The program was created by the loss-prevention division of Western Media Associates Inc., Danville, Calif.

A Safe Attitude

All the safety experts quoted in this story say that incorporating safety training into employee orientation programs and operations training is crucial to the success of any safety program. It helps raise awareness from the get-go.

Many of these companies also have safety committees that have daily ten-minute meetings to remind the staff about safety issues and to look around the unit for potential problems.

"Intensity is the key," says McLellan of Whataburger. "Operators must stay on top of the safety issue every day and make this a top-of-mind issue along with sales."

Inspection Checklist

Here's what to check to prepare for either fire department or Occupational Safety and Health Administration (OSHA) inspections:

- Gas hoses and quick-disconnect systems in good condition.
- Fire-protection system in "on" position, serviced and tagged within past six months.
- Adequate portable fire extinguishers, accessible and serviced annually.
- Sprinkler valves open, marked and accessible.
- Sprinkler heads operable, unobstructed, 24-inch clearance, and free of paint and corrosion.
- No storage adjacent to heaters, motors, electrical panels, etc.

- Hood and vent cleaned by service quarterly.
- All hood filters in place (no gaps between side-by-side hoods) and cleaned daily.
- OSHA posters properly displayed.
- Accident records and reports kept for five years.
- Hazard communication training current; hazardous bottles labeled.

Source: Bakers Square Restaurants

Walk, Don't Run

To prevent slips and falls:

- Never run—walk as fast as is safe.
- Wear properly fitting shoes with skid-resistant soles and leather uppers.
- Clean up dropped food, liquids and grease immediately.
- Keep aisles and walkways free of carts, boxes, trash cans, mop buckets and other obstructions.
- Close oven doors immediately after inserting or removing food.
- Select a ladder that fits your size and is sturdy enough for the job.
- Carpets, rugs and runners should fit smoothly and tightly to the floor. Rug and runner edges should be unfrayed, securely bound and beveled with rubber or plastic to avoid catching shoes.
- Stairs, ramps and raised areas should never be obstructed or used for storage.

Source: Educational Foundation of the National Restaurant Association

Rules for Preventing Back Injuries

Since sprains and strains account for 30% of foodservice injuries, it is important to follow proper lifting procedures.

- First establish solid footing. Check the condition of the floor to make sure it is dry and clean. Stand close to the load, feet spread shoulder width. Place one foot slightly in front of the other to establish a focal point for the weight of the load.
- To maintain alignment and balance, stand with your head in line over your legs and feet, facing the load. Then bend at the knees to reach the load.
- Grip the load with your whole hand, not just fingers, and pull the load close while it is still on the ground. Tighten your stomach muscles to help concentration and further align the back. Arch the lower back in by pulling your shoulders back and sticking your chest out.
- Lift slowly, keeping the load close to the body with the legs taking the weight of the load.
- To set the load down, bend at the knees and go down smoothly, reversing the steps from the lift. Set down the corner of the load and slide your hands out from under it before settling the load.

Cut Down on Cuts

To prevent cuts:

- Keep knives sharp. Dull knives slip.
- Cut three feet away from your body and don't hack.
- When chopping, curl your fingers under while holding the food item being cut.
- Wear cut-resistant gloves when using knives, handling or discarding cans, or opening boxes.
- Let falling knives fall. Never attempt to catch them.
- Wash one knife at a time with blade pointed away. Never leave knives soaking under water because they cannot be seen well.
- When carrying a knife, point the blade down and the cutting edge slightly away.
- When passing a knife, put it down first.
- If you break a glass item, use a broom and dustpan or a damp paper towel to pick up the pieces. Never use your bare hands.

Source: Educational Foundation of the National Restaurant Association

Don't Get Burned

To prevent burns:

♦ Set patterns so traffic is one-way wherever possible.
♦ Maintain adequate traffic and working space around heating and cooking equipment.
♦ Keep doorways and aisles clear of obstacles.
♦ Forbid horseplay around heat sources.
♦ Have chefs wear long-sleeved, padded or double-breasted coats.
♦ Buy hand protectors such as oven mitts and potholders that are grease-, liquid- and heat-resistant.
♦ Avoid crowding the range top.

♦ Avoid setting pot handles over burners.
♦ Adjust burner flames to cover only the bottom of the pan.
♦ Ask for help when moving any heavy, hot items.

Source: Educational Foundation of the National Restaurant Association

To help operators improve safety and reduce costs incurred from injuries, the Educational Foundation of the National Restaurant Association has released the SERVSAFE Employee and Customer Safety training program. For information, call (800) 765-2122. ♦

THE SECURE RESTAURANT

Internal Security

by Beth Lorenzini

Bob Chinn grosses $14 million a year at his Wheeling, Ill., restaurant. And he makes sure he knows where all of it goes. One of his veteran bartenders discovered this the hard way. After Chinn found out that the bartender had been in a liquor-storage area at 2 a.m., the bartender was fired.

How did Chinn know about the bartender's early-morning escapades? Linda McMillen, office manager, demonstrated the sophisticated security measure as she put her key in the door of the general managers' office. It didn't open. The door, like many throughout the restaurant, is equipped with a Marlok computerized lock system. "I guess I'm denied access right now," she said. "But listen." From within the office, the sounds of a computer printer could be heard. "The computer is printing that I tried this door at this time on this date and was denied access."

In addition to computerized locks, Bob Chinn's has closed-circuit surveillance cameras on such areas as the loading dock, a wait station and personal-property room, a secured money-counting room, front-door entry only for staff, and alarm systems on doors. Owner Bob Chinn also has two trusted employees, his nephew and grandson, check in deliveries. Such precautions against theft are mandatory in an operation that employs more than 200 and grosses up to $370,000 in a single week.

"Operators can reduce internal theft by 60% simply by letting employees know that management is watching," says Fred Del Marva, chairman and CEO of Food & Beverage Investigations, loss management investigators in Novato, Calif.

More than that, owners and managers could take expensive marketing plans that are designed to increase sales by 25% and toss them out the window if they would just make a minimal effort to control theft, says Francis D'Addario, director of loss prevention for Hardee's Food Systems, Rocky Mount, N.C.

With so much money at stake, why are so many operators reluctant to face the issue? "Theft control is a hassle," says Del Marva. "Who likes playing cop?" Also, many operators hate to admit they're being taken. The majority of employees caught stealing have worked for the operation an average of five to seven years.

Signals of Theft

Spotting theft isn't necessarily difficult; it just takes diligence, says James Meyer, president of Professional Information and Testing Services, Toledo, Ohio.

A variance of more than half a percent in food cost should be considered odd enough to check out, says Meyer.

An unusual food-cost variance can mean cash is going out the front door or food is going out the back. To detect cash-register theft, Meyer suggests following up on certain clues.

Tally systems to track under-rings. If a customer orders a burger, fries and a soft drink, the employee rings up a soft drink alone. The extra money goes into the register, but the employee uses slash marks on a scrap of paper, toothpicks stuck in an orange, pennies in the dime slot or dollars under the register to keep track of how much extra money they can take when they cash out the drawer.

The best way to prevent under-rings is to audit the drawer mid-shift unannounced. Have a new cash drawer ready to replace the drawer being audited.

Hardee's is experimenting with an audio-visual camera system at drive-thru stations. The employees are trained to welcome customers, repeat orders, state the price and give customers receipts. Managers can watch and listen to see that the price stated is the price displayed on the register. The chain has seen a reduction of theft, speedier service and an improvement in hospitality in the 14 units equipped with the system, which can cost from $3,000 to $6,000, according to D'Addario.

Follow your no-sales. If a customer asks for change, it gives the employee an opportunity to open the drawer and keep it open for the next few sales, so that transactions can be made without ringing them up.

Meyer says ten or fewer no-sales a shift are probably all right, depending on the operation. If there isn't a reason for a no-sale, even 10 is too many. More than that is a problem. Managers should check the register tapes after every shift. Low customer counts and low sales compared to other registers, especially in a fast-food operation, are good signs that the employee was working out of an open drawer. In a full-service operation, at the bar, for example, long lapses between sales (a good register system dates and times each transaction) is a sign to watch.

Void voids. Voiding sales is one of the most common forms of theft. An employee makes a sale, voids out the transaction or a portion and pockets the money. In a full-service operation, no employee should be allowed to void a sale unless a manager keys in to the register to allow the function.

Many times, managers get lazy and lend their key or simply leave it in the register. Not only does this give all employees access, but ambitious crooks can take an imprint of the key, watch for and memorize manager passwords (if the system requires one), and have a key made to void whenever the opportunity arises. Lending and leaving the key should be strictly prohibited on pain of firing.

In a fast-food operation, the need for speed often dictates that cashiers need to be able to void without manager input. To prevent theft, many quick-service cash-register systems buzz each time a void is done. Teach managers to respond to the buzzers to find out why the void occurred.

Document all cash-drawer activity. Watch for distorted or incomplete paperwork when cashing out drawers. Do random inventory double-checks (count the beer bottles left in the bar cooler, for example) and require that employees write their reports in pen and correct in red.

On reports, include a line that reads "To the best of my knowledge, this report is true and accurate," and make employees sign at the bottom. Because they have signed their name to the reports, they have involved themselves legally.

Back-of-the-House Theft

One hospital foodservice director had no choice but to play cop when he arrived on the job at a 350-bed hospital.

"The foodservice department never took inventory. If invoices said $30,000 worth of food was bought in March, then that's what they submitted as food cost. It was unbelievable," he says.

Employees also never bothered to lock the storage areas even though locks were on the doors. The final straw came when one employee was asked why there were 11 cases of bacon when six or seven would suffice. "I don't want to run out," he replied. "And I always count on two cases walking."

The director immediately ordered monthly inventories, a grueling four-day process. Computerization eight months later turned inventory into a one-day affair because all price changes already were entered into the system.

Other policy changes ensued. Inventory was cut in half with products delivered under the just-in-time method. The director estimates that these new security policies save the department $50,000 to $100,000 annually.

The security measures enforced by the food-service director are right on the money, according

EXPENSIVE STATISTICS

- The foodservice industry loses approximately $20 billion a year to theft and cash mishandling.
- One out of every three employees will steal if given the opportunity. This includes theft of cash, merchandise and time.
- Approximately 5% to 8% of gross sales is lost to internal theft.
- 75% of all missing inventory is from theft.
- 73% of job applications are falsified.
- The majority of employees caught stealing have worked for an operation for an average of five to seven years.

Source: Fred Del Marva, chairman and CEO, Food & Beverage Investigations, Novato, Calif.

to Del Marva. He offers these tips to reduce back-of-the-house theft:

- Conduct frequent inventories. Once a month is a must, once a week is better, and daily for expensive items is best.
- Distribute receiving responsibilities. The person who checks in deliveries should not be the same person who conducts inventory or orders food.
- Pare stock. The less inventory on hand, the less there is to count and to steal.
- Refuse off-peak-hour deliveries. Make sure that a trusted employee and manager oversee the delivery and check items off the invoices line by line. They should never sign an invoice that includes items on back order, but should instead insist the driver cross off that item on the invoice. In other words, never pay for items before they're delivered.
- Use insider accounting. Hire accountants familiar with restaurant accounting needs such as food cost, food usage and quality control.
- Designate an employee entry/exit. Have a manager stand at the door at quitting time. Other doors should be equipped with alarms. This way, employees can't go through the

doors with merchandise without triggering the alarm, and the doors don't violate fire and emergency exit codes.

- Discourage duffel bags. Let employees know you reserve the right to search bags and other totes.
- Oversee trash disposal. At Bob Chinn's, garbage dumpsters are locked in a free-standing garage so that they can't be reached after hours. Buy clear garbage bags. Designate one person to take trash out and have a manager accompany the employee. Buy a trash compactor; it necessitates fewer trips to the dumpster and discourages employees from putting good food in the trash because the food will be crushed.

Get Outside Help

Many chains use pre-employment tests to filter out high-risk employees. Companies such as London House, Park Ridge, Ill., offer more than 200 different employee tests, including those that rate integrity and honesty. (See "Hiring for Security" for more information on employee testing.)

Besides pre-employment testing, operators can filter out high-risk employees in the hiring process. Credit reports and criminal and driving records can reveal high debt and alcohol and drug use, all of which provide motives for stealing. Reference checks also help.

Objectivity is one of the best defenses against theft. Methods of theft can be so clever that they are difficult for operators to spot, especially if a trusted employee is doing the stealing.

Hiring a private investigator might be one of the most worthwhile investments an operator can make. Several agencies specialize in foodservice theft (see "Resources"). Fees vary depending on the job, but many start at $250 a day plus expenses. A few days, and sometimes only one day, might be all it takes for a professional to spot your problem employee. Investigators can:

- Send in professional spotters to watch cash-register transactions.
- Suggest and evaluate security systems.

- Audit accounting systems.
- Provide undercover employees.
- Provide pre-employment screening.
- Help put security policies in writing and teach operators how to follow through on apprehensions.

If you don't want to deal with the problem yourself, bringing in an objective professional might be the answer.

Establish a Policy

One of the worst mistakes operators make is failing to establish a policy both spoken and written that lets employees know that theft is not tolerated. Unless a policy is in place, employees charged with theft can claim ignorance.

For new employees, clarify policies regarding:

- Eating and drinking on the job.
- Cash-register procedures for voids, no-sales and shift-end reports.
- Giving food and drinks to friends.
- Inventory, delivery and invoice procedures.
- Garbage disposal—designate who is to do it, when and accompanied by whom.
- Employee entry and exit.
- Personal property, what employees can and cannot bring on premises.

For minor offenses, set up a warning system: If employees fail to follow policy after three warnings, fire them. Following through on your word shows you mean business. Failing to follow through invites others to ignore policies.

Hiring for Security

Pre-employment tests that rate integrity and honesty can filter out high-risk employees, but they must be applied correctly for legal, accurate assessment. (Integrity tests are not allowed in Massachusetts.)

Beware of companies that have a "one test fits all" policy. Tests should fit a very specific business need, be it honesty, customer service, safety,

drug avoidance or turnover. Tests cost between $8 and $16, depending on the test and the number purchased.

Before opting for pre-employment tests, check the company, says Jack Jones, vice president of research and development at London House. It should be able to provide:

- Research to back up its tests.
- Validation studies to show the tests work.
- Certification that its tests meet professional standards of scientific associations.
- Full credentials for licensed staff.
- And a statement that the test is fair to all.

Security Hardware

Operator awareness combined with security hardware can sharply reduce employee theft.

- **Computerized POS systems:** Should generate paper trails that state transaction date, time and server; should have a large display so that prices are visible; should not allow unauthorized voids; and should allow frequent, hassle-free code changes.
- **Closed-circuit television cameras:** Placed on registers, at loading docks, on garbage dumpsters, in personal-property rooms and at access doors, these make would-be thieves think twice. Hooked up to a VCR, tapes are valuable evidence in prosecution. Some operators even use dummy cameras.
- **Computerized locks:** Tell operators when someone had or was denied access to secured areas. When a personnel change occurs and on a regular basis, locks can be recoded.
- **Door alarms:** Alarms let everyone out in an emergency, but don't allow employees out without bringing attention to the act.

Resources

- Food & Beverage Investigations, 175 San Marin Dr., Ste. 111, Novato, Calif. 94945; (415) 892-1027, Fred Del Marva.

- Professional Information and Testing Services, 3609 West Alexis Rd., Ste. 112, Toledo, Ohio, 43623; (419) 475-6701, James Meyer.
- London House, 1550 Northwest Highway, Park Ridge, Ill. 60068; (708) 298-7311.

- Stanton Corp., 6100 Fairview Rd., Charlotte, N.C., 28210; (704) 552-1119. ◆

External Security

by Jeff Weinstein

As a member of the closing crew at Lee's Famous Recipe Chicken, Tulsa, Okla., went to lock the front door at 10 P.M. on August 17, 1992, he was greeted by an unexpected sight—a former employee and three other men.

Led by the former employee, the four forced their way through the door, took the restaurant keys, locked the front door and turned off the lights that would normally be off at closing time, according to franchisee and unit manager Roy Whitworth, who recounted the story for *R&I*. After making sure panic buttons had not been pushed, the former employee herded the four-member crew to the walk-in refrigerator at gunpoint.

Using a key he recognized from his days on the job, the ex-employee activated the time-delay safe and started the 15-minute countdown to take the day's receipts.

While waiting for the safe to open, the robbers told the four employees to kneel, then shot each in the back of the head. Three died at the scene. The fourth died later at a local hospital.

Witnesses identified the robbers, one of whom turned himself in. A second was captured in Tulsa, while two others were apprehended in Michigan. All four were charged with four counts of first-degree murder and one count of robbery.

Since the robbery, Whitworth has installed security surveillance cameras and hired an armed security company to pick up receipts. But no one can say whether the upgrades would have made a difference on August 17.

"I thought about security upgrades previously, but it was a matter of cost," says Whitworth. "In our business, you try to take as much to the bottom line as possible and don't do everything you want to do."

Many operators might have to stretch to afford the latest in security hardware and software. But tragedies such as the one that occurred at Lee's should have restaurateurs asking themselves if they can afford not to make the investment.

A Secure Appearance

Thieves can case a restaurant and quickly recognize weaknesses in security, a lackadaisical attitude displayed by the staff, for instance.

"Your restaurant must look secure," says Fred Del Marva, a private investigator who specializes in hospitality industry security. "If it doesn't, thieves will mark it as an easy target."

Starting on the outside, proper lighting is an important safeguard. Drug dealers as well as thieves favor dark parking lots. Even if no robbery occurs, drug deals that go bad can end in violence, including gunfire.

Del Marva says he has nine cases pending in which guests were beaten in the parking lot. He says too many owners believe such crimes are not their fault because they didn't happen in the unit. But federal law dictates that as long as operators benefit financially from their parking lots, they are responsible for such occurrences.

Some consultants say sufficient illumination in the parking lot starts at two-foot candle power. Others prefer a case-by-case approach. Earl Lundquist, loss prevention manager for KFC, Louisville, says the chain does not conduct formal lighting surveys on site. Instead, KFC's safety experts use common sense to decide when more light is needed. "In higher-crime areas, we try to keep drug dealing away from our unit by lighting the lots as though an NFL night game was going on," Lundquist says.

SHOCKING STATISTICS

- The FBI reports 687,732 robberies in 1991. Robbers grabbed $562 million in cash and property.
- The FBI reports 80,448 robberies in commercial sites in 1991, up from 65,600 in 1987.
- Excluding banks, gas stations and convenience stores, the FBI reports 11.7% of all robberies in 1991 occurred at commercial sites.
- The FBI reports approximately $1,456 was stolen per incident at commercial sites in 1991.
- The FBI reports the use of firearms by robbers increased by 22% in the first six months of 1991.
- Robberies are most frequent from 9 p.m. until 3 a.m. Most occur between 1 a.m. and 1:59 a.m., according to the National Institute of Justice.
- The average robbery takes 90 seconds, with one robbery in the United States every minute; 30% of all robberies at commercial sites occur during closing procedures, according to McGunn Safe Company, Chicago.

Francis D'Addario, director of loss prevention for Hardee's Food Systems, Rocky Mount, N.C., recommends installing timers for outside lighting.

"Too many operators are on energy-saving schemes that call for turning off all parking-lot lights when the closing crew is leaving," says D'Addario. "Robbers waiting two blocks away can get on the lot in no time, intercept the crew leaving the building, take them back inside and do the robbery."

Set on a timer, the pole sign and reader board can switch off at closing time so customers know the restaurant is no longer open. Parking-lot lights can be timed to shut off 15 minutes after the crew leaves, allowing them to depart from a fully lit lot.

Video cameras as parking-lot security measures also are gaining in popularity, especially in high-crime areas. They should be positioned in lots so they are obvious to a robber, but high enough so they are out of reach. Depending on the climate, operators might consider placing cameras in weather-proof housing.

For full-service operations, valet service adds a degree of outdoor security. If a few of the valets are not busy, instruct them to patrol the lot instead of standing idle.

An unarmed guard also can serve as a good defense for the parking lot. Because of the expense, however, guards most often are employed by restaurants that have a problem with noncustomers who park their cars in the lot for extended periods.

Sound the Alarm

Alarms are an absolute necessity for a secure restaurant.

D'Addario recommends installing motion detectors over main-entrance doors, and behind and on top of the building. The presence of someone lurking around the building will set off the lights, and call police attention to the area.

David Craig, director of security for Long John Silver's, advises placing contact alarms on all exterior doors for burglary protection. These systems need to be replaced every six or seven years.

To further discourage robbers, alarms should be accompanied by a clearly visible sign stating the presence of the alarm.

TV to the Rescue

Not long ago, thieves wouldn't risk armed robbery for $20. But cheap drugs, such as crack and sniffable heroin, make $20 an adequate heist for robbers in need of a fix.

"Many people committing robberies today are in it for the quick hit, so they can buy drugs," says Lundquist. "They are willing to go out and do three robberies a day at $20 a hit and keep coming back. And they will come back to the same place until they get caught."

To combat theft during operating hours, the most popular technical deterrent today is closed-circuit television systems focused on cash registers, loading docks and parking lots.

Long John Silver's recently purchased 100 CCTV systems for chronic high-crime units. Since the chain installed cameras, videocassette recorders and monitors at the first units selected, the problem has almost completely disappeared, according to Craig.

The Long John Silver's system cost $2,350 per unit, which pays for itself in 12 to 18 months, Craig says.

For operators who can't afford a $2,350 system, Del Marva advises going to a warehouse club to buy a monitor and camera for as low as $250. "While it is not connected to a VCR for a recording, someone in the office can monitor the screen for potential trouble," he explains.

Safe Safes

Because thieves target the safe first, a sturdy, hard-to-open model is an important deterrent. Time-delay safes are quickly replacing combination safes, because thieves have to wait as much as 15 minutes for it to open once the key is inserted.

At KFC units, the area surrounding the time-delay safe is covered by motion detectors. In addition, seismic sensors are placed inside the safes. If any vibration is felt, a loud alarm goes off. "It drives robbers away before they can get to large amounts of money or property," says Lundquist.

Even more sophisticated is the electronic safe, which can include a time delay. It provides an audit trail so operators know who has been in the safe, at what time and how long it was open.

Eventually, money must be taken out of the safe and transferred to the bank. Rather than have an employee place what is often in excess of $1,000 in a deposit bag and personally deliver it to the bank, the restaurant can hire an armed security company to handle the transaction for $250 to $500 a month.

Cutting-Edge Security

Because of the growing incidence of violent robberies, operators want to give employees as many security options as possible.

A popular device for restaurants located in tough neighborhoods is the bandit barrier. Double-hung windows of bulletproof glass lock to the counter in front of cash registers, separating the customer from the server. Customers pay and are served through a turnstile.

Instead of installing bandit barriers, many fast-food operations lock the front door after dark and serve only through the drive-thru window.

A more advanced tool is the mobile alarm, which can be hooked to an employee's clothing. If the employee wearing the alarm is forced into a cooler, he can still get to the panic button on his person.

Long John Silver's is considering putting locks on the inside of coolers so employees can lock themselves in, denying access to the robber. The employee will still be able to send an alarm because all coolers and freezers have panic buttons mounted 18 inches off the ground.

Some robberies occur when an employee takes out the trash. Because headsets are already in use at drive-thru windows, Long John Silver's decided to take advantage of the technology by requiring employees to wear them while emptying the trash. If there is a problem en route, the employee can communicate with crew members inside the unit.

Policies and Procedures

Experts in this field say too many operators take only minimal precautions, thinking they will never be victims. After all, it always happens to the other guy. Right?

"The fact is, we are the other guy, and we let our guard down," says Joe Szvetitz, loss prevention manager, Circle K, Phoenix. "Foodservice and convenience-store operators need to raise their level of awareness, must have involvement and commitment at all levels, and constantly reinforce policies and procedures."

Local police departments usually offer free security consultations. Security consultants charge about $200 an hour. If an expert advises taking measures that are too expensive to handle all at once, begin by correcting the most serious deficiencies immediately. Perform the rest in steady, planned increments.

Here are some steps operators can take to upgrade security policies.

♦ Schedule at least three crew members to close. This is a new requirement at Long John Silver's, and it requires the closing crew to leave the restaurant together. "Robbers like to see as few people as possible," says Craig. "The more clerks, the more interference during a holdup."

♦ Pull excess money from registers. $1,000 is too much to keep in a drawer, according to security experts. Adopt a policy to drain off excess cash into a floor safe, time-delay safe or vault every time the drawer exceeds $200.

♦ Vary cash-handling and money-transfer routines. Robbers look for consistency. So don't let the same employee clear out the register near the front door at 11 p.m. every night. Count cash in a secured room or manager's office after all customers have left, all outside doors have been locked and the building has been checked for "hide-ins."

♦ If there is no armed service, vary the time of deposit by at least an hour. Disguise the deposit in something other than a bank bag. Vary the route and the vehicle driven to the bank. Assign two people to make the trip.

♦ Place cash registers in the most visible areas. The ideal location is in front of the windows facing the street. Keep areas above and around registers well-lit.

♦ Don't fill windows with promotional material. Obstructed windows conceal holdups from the outside.

♦ Maintain stringent door policies. Don't admit anyone through the back door after dark. Prohibit anyone from entering through the front or back door after closing. Do not let employees take out trash after dark. Make sure doors are locked during cash-counting procedures. Equip rear and side service doors with peepholes.

♦ Regulate entry to storage rooms. Once there is no need to enter storage areas, they should be locked and the keys hidden.

♦ Make temporary policy changes when necessary. KFC units in high-crime areas were hit when suppliers made deliveries before store hours. Those units temporarily decided to stop deliveries and outside activities before store hours.

Be Prepared

If employees are prepared for robberies, they will be better conditioned to deal with one when it happens.

Constant training, including role playing and reinforcement of policies and procedures, has helped Hardee's reduce crime by 30% to 40%.

Hardee's also sends out a loss-prevention newsletter, The Stop Watch, which stresses re-view of security policies and procedures.

Perhaps the most important aspect of training is how to react to a situation.

Experts list several rules of thumb:

♦ Don't delay or fight back. People who resist robbers are 49 times more likely to be killed than those who cooperate.

♦ Remain calm and obey all reasonable commands. Keep movements slow and deliberate with hands in plain sight.

♦ Never lie. The threat of violence skyrockets if a robber thinks an employee is lying.

♦ Give robbers what you can. Tell them about any equipment, such as time-delay safes, to avoid surprises.

♦ Try to get the robbery over as soon and as easily as possible to avoid injuries. Don't chase or follow.

♦ Lock up the business and call the police immediately after the event.

♦ Ask witnesses to talk to police and write down details about the robbery as soon as possible.

Security experts stress over and over the need for employees to follow security procedures because, yes, it can happen to you, too.

"Never in a million years did I think it would happen here," says Whitworth, franchisee and manager of the Tulsa Lee's. "My advice to everyone is not to get complacent and comfortable with the way you do things, because I learned it can happen to anyone, anywhere."

The Cost of Security

How much of an investment do leading security devices require? Loss-prevention experts offer these estimates.

♦ **Closed-circuit television (CCTV):** A single-color chip camera mounted on a panning motor with a black and white monitor and time-lapse videocassette recorder in a locked security cabinet: $5,500. Three black and white solid-state chip cameras, monitors, event recorder with time/date generator and audio: $2,500.

♦ **Time-delay safe:** Fully programmable with identifying key lock, audit trail, seismic sensor and deadlock for overnight: $2,200.

♦ **Bandit barriers:** Individual, bullet-proof panels that can be locked into place at night, with speaker system: $14,000. Fixed barrier without speaker system: $6,000.

♦ **Perimeter alarm system:** Contact alarms for doors, glass-break detectors, passive infrared motion detectors, proximity alarm for safe, panic buttons: $1,300 to $1,800. Monthly monitoring fee extra $16 to $45 a month.

Stop Inside Jobs

Robberies often are triggered by security leaks from current employees working with thieves or by ex-employees who learn the security system, quit and return to rob the unit.

The best solution to this problem is to hire trustworthy employees. Signals that an employee isn't trustworthy often appear on employment applications or tests:

SIX TIPS TO PREVENT DELIVERY CRIME

Growth in the delivery market has produced a new mark for criminals: the restaurant delivery person.

Round Table Pizza, San Francisco, posts in its restaurants a list of safety tips for delivery drivers.

1. Enter and exit the restaurant through the front entrance after dark.

2. Drop excess cash after every delivery run in a secured drop-box located in the delivery area.

3. Carry only a minimum bank, no more than $20 or $30. This bank might include two $5 bills, 10 $1 bills and a few dollars in change. Order takers should tell delivery customers that drivers will not accept bills larger than $20 for payment of food.

4. If available, carry a two-way radio. It allows the driver to contact the restaurant or police in the event of a threatening situation.

5. Always lock vehicles and leave headlights and emergency lights on, and use a flashlight when making a delivery. After exiting the car, scan areas around the house, especially in darkened areas to the sides of the home.

6. Use extra caution in case of darkened homes or areas. If the situation seems threatening, do not make the delivery. Call the restaurant and have them phone the customer again, requesting they leave the front light on.

♦ Gaps in job history.
♦ References not professionally related.
♦ References' addresses don't appear in telephone directory.
♦ Applicant skips portion asking if convicted of crime.
♦ Social Security prefix, which identifies state of issuance, doesn't match state where applicant was born.

♦ Applicant fails written integrity test that identifies undesirable applicants.

Is It Worth the Risk?

Before opening a restaurant, look into the neighborhood's crime rate. Talk to local police and do an area crime survey to determine whether it pays to open and how much security equipment will be needed.

Taco Bell uses a crime index prepared by CAPINDEX, King of Prussia, Pa., to predict the crime activity in any area. For $250, the CAPRisk Crime Vulnerability Assessment provides a three-page report or a color-coded map identifying the risk of crime in a three-mile radius of the proposed site. For $350, you get the report and the map.

The index produces crime projections for homicide, rape, robbery, aggravated assault, burglary, larceny and auto theft.

The reports also can be used as litigation support to counter allegations of failure to provide proper security.

For information, call (215) 354-9100.

Safety in Numbers

To learn more about foodservice security, consider joining a professional association. The American Society for Industrial Security has a foodservice committee. Call (703) 522-5800 for information. The National Foodservice Security Council is made up of loss-prevention professionals from most major restaurant chains. For information, contact Earl Lundquist, KFC, at (708) 449-7888. ♦

MEETING THE ENVIRONMENTAL CHALLENGE

What the Chains Are Doing

by Brian Quinton and Jeff Weinstein

When giant McDonald's gave up the foam clamshell for paper sandwich wrappers, it seemed the foodservice industry was on its way to a Green Revolution.

McDonald's switch was supposed to herald a new ecological consciousness in the foodservice industry. Customers would sort their refuse. The polystyrene-recycling industry would wither for lack of product. "Green marketing" would sweep the industry, as ads pushed chains' earth-friendliness. And forward-thinking companies would build ecological concern into their corporate structures, signaling that environmental responsibility was as important as the fiscal kind to business in the '90s.

So, How Goes the Revolution?

Much more slowly than expected. An *R&I* survey of the top 50 chains in the foodservice industry found that only a few have departments of any size devoted solely to overseeing their environmental affairs; among them, McDonald's, Kentucky Fried Chicken, Domino's, Dunkin' Donuts and Walt Disney dedicate one specific department or manager to supervising their total ecological impact. Most of the rest give responsibility for all things ecological to operations or to purchasing, or spread it out among several departments.

The survey results show that environmental initiatives drop off among the second 25 companies. The major exception here is the lodging chains, most of which piggyback foodservice ecology onto their custodial waste programs.

Among foodservice companies, McDonald's, Oak Brook, Ill., has positioned itself at the head of the green brigade with its well-publicized

packaging changes and the McRecycle initiative, which commits $100 million to the purchase of products from second-use materials.

McDonald's is also the only company to collaborate with an outside agency on an ecological study. That joint project with the Environmental Defense Fund resulted in 42 current or planned moves to test source reduction, recycling, reuse and innovative waste disposal.

But Marriott Corp., Washington, while not publicizing its efforts as well as McDonald's, is as environmentally active as the burger giant, responding "yes" to 23 of the 27 initiatives on *R&I*'s survey. For instance, to reduce food waste, its Management Services division is purchasing more precut and cleaned produce. Many accounts also are going back to cloth cleaning rags because they can be laundered and reused.

Walt Disney World, Orlando, Fla., produces 35% of the energy it consumes by burning nonrecyclable trash. The company, which already recycles in the back of the house, is currently researching ways to get visitors to recycle the waste of 80 million meals and snacks consumed annually in its theme parks.

Another active company is Orlando, Fla.-based Red Lobster. The General Mills-owned chain has eliminated all paper products from the dining room and has contracted with a glass recycler in the Southern California market. Among other creative projects, every unit is reusing the ink cartridges for computer printers.

As the survey shows, most of the others are implementing, or at least testing, some form of solid-waste solution—usually recycling, reduction and reuse programs.

Recycling: Most of these efforts begin with recycling, which holds out the prospect of reduced waste-carting costs and landfill tipping fees by thinning a store's waste stream. The most widely mentioned recycled item is corrugated cardboard. Atlanta-based Arby's stores, for instance, recycle 150 pounds of corrugated cardboard a week. Some chains, such as Domino's, arrange to have their suppliers back-haul cardboard to their plants in areas where trash haulers are reluctant to pick up cardboard for recycling.

The Ann Arbor, Mich.-based pizza giant also recycles its takeout boxes. The octagonal box, reconfigured from a square to save 10% on materials, is a hot item with customers. Many operators offer a bounce-back coupon that pays customers 25 cents for each pizza box they recycle. Domino's Environmental Coordinator Larry Hull says 20% to 30% of franchisees' customers participate in the program.

Red Lobster recycles fryer oil in almost every unit. Grease is poured into a lockable 55-gallon square bin behind the restaurant. A tanker truck from a recycling company comes by regularly to siphon out the grease and clean the bin. The grease is recycled to produce, among other things, dog food and makeup.

Reduction: Red Lobster also has rolled out one of the industry's largest waste-reduction programs. The chain expects to reduce front-of-the-house trash by 4.7 million pounds per year sys-temwide by switching from paper place mats and napkins to linen ones. (The cost of leasing and laundering linens is six times that of using paper.)

As part of ARA Services' "Earth Sense" campaign, 28,000 refillable mugs have been sold to clients. At one hospital account with 500 employees, this action has eliminated 1,500 disposable cups a day. This action saves the hospital $10,000 a year, ARA says. The mugs range in price from $35.25 per case of 22-ounce mugs to $106 for a case of 12-ounce mugs. Philadelphia-based ARA uses the money generated for a variety of environmental programs.

Reuse: Subway is working with a meat supplier whose cartons can be transformed into carryout trays. Customers are encouraged to bring the tray back for further reuse. A box is good for four or five uses before losing its integrity, executives for the Milford, Conn.-based chain say.

International Dairy Queen, Bloomington, Minn., sends the packaging for delicate waffle cones back to the manufacturer for reuse around later shipments of cones.

Composting: In composting, organic wastes are broken down naturally and processed into soil enhancers. It is expected to become an important resource-recovery technique, capable of transforming up to approximately 80% of foodservice trash into soil enhancers, according to Glenn

---

WHEN OPERATORS TALK ABOUT WASTE

Many of the top chains cite suppliers as the No. 1 source of their best waste-reduction ideas. A survey by the International Foodservice Manufacturers Association identified operators' top solid-waste concerns:

◆ The need to eliminate excessive packaging
◆ Rising disposal costs
◆ Negative consumer perceptions
◆ Need for recycled content in packages and shipping containers
◆ Impending legislative restrictions on packaging
◆ Limits on trash storage space
◆ The mechanics of setting up recycling or reuse programs
◆ In-house waste separation
◆ Finding out what is recyclable
◆ The desire to make all disposables biodegradable

White, a senior packaging engineer in KFC's research department. But the industry is still in its very early stages, and only a handful of major chains are testing composting programs.

This summer, Louisville, Ky.-based KFC conducted a three-week composting test in eight Massachusetts units, hauling presorted trash to a composting site in Maine. A KFC supplier underwrote the test, which turned store garbage to usable compost in 45 days. "We found that 80% of our waste stream is compostable," says White. "That should be the case in most fast-food restaurants."

A complete composting infrastructure is still five years away, according to White, making cost calculations rather theoretical now. But he believes landfill closures and climbing tipping fees will make composting competitive. "Besides, this is a long-term thing," he says. "We're proving that we can make it work operationally, so that when the composters get their ducks in a row, we're ready for them."

These are all admirable efforts, and, taken together, they show that the 50 industry sales leaders are pursuing a range of options for becoming better planetary citizens. But the chart of these efforts still shows a disturbing amount of blank space, and a surprising number of big companies testing three programs instead of 13 or 30. Why aren't more companies trying to recycle in the front of the house? Or looking for ways to reduce the number of individually wrapped items? Why is only 0.002% of foodservice polystyrene now being recycled? Why haven't more chains dropped chlorine-bleached paper? In other words, what's holding up the green revolution?

Technological Confusion

Years of conflicting expert opinion and lobbying by interested parties make it harder than ever to answer some solid-waste questions, which tends to freeze some companies into inaction. The paper vs. polystyrene foam debate hinges on which part of the product's life cycle is studied. Paper takes up less landfill space and is biodegradable in

theory—when exposed to sunlight and the elements; but foam makes less trash by weight, and its manufacture consumes less energy and creates fewer harmful byproducts. Paper can be recycled. So can foam—but under current Food and Drug Administration guidelines, not into packaging that comes in direct contact with food.

This confusion is one reason most companies do not advertise the ecological steps they're taking. The feeling is, just do it, whatever it is, and let the customers who care know that you're doing it. But don't shout it from the rooftops, or you might wake up one day to find a panel of experts holding a press conference about your impact on the nation's rivers and old-growth forests.

Domino's exemplifies the low-profile approach to ecology. "We've seen what happened to other companies that started waving banners," says Hull. "It turns out more negative than positive. People start turning a magnifying glass on them and saying, 'What about this, this and this?' We just do these things, get them under our belt, so that when the glass is turned on us someday, we'll look pretty good."

Markets for Recycling

A more important obstacle to greener dining, say many of the chains surveyed, is the incompleteness of the current solid-waste infrastructure. The right market conditions for recycling currently do not exist in many parts of the country, making it tough for national chains to implement cost-efficient national policies on reprocessing their solid waste.

Once again, polystyrene foam stands out. The food-related polystyrene-recycling industry is in a very early stage of development. Even among the growing ranks who say it can be recycled, foodservice polystyrene has a reputation for being tough to recycle because so few processing facilities currently exist: Only 13 reprocessors now handle polystyrene that has been in contact with food, far fewer than the number recycling and remaking other plastics. Add to this scarcity the cost of teaching customers to sort the recyclables, or of having employees do so in the back, and these figures can put a big dent in any operator's projected cartage savings.

Success has its problems, too. The high 30% to 50% recycling rate for corrugated cardboard is undercutting the price of that commodity, discouraging further recycling. "When we started testing recycling, cardboard was $40 a ton," says Michael Murphy, director of consumer affairs for Randolph, Mass.-based Dunkin' Donuts. "Now it's $20 and falling. It's down to $5 a bale in this area. That's almost more than it costs to bale it." He now is considering getting the franchisee-run distribution centers to dedicate some trucks to hauling cardboard rather than paying someone else.

Even a Dunkin' Donuts test that got consumers to recycle 70% of front-of-the-house waste was discontinued because it did not offset the special handling and hauling costs. "Our franchisees want a cost-neutral program," Murphy says. "We had hoped we could lop enough off the weekly waste pickup to bring costs down to that level." But the income from the sale of recyclable material just did not offset the special handling and hauling costs.

Economic Considerations

"Cost neutral" is the key term for ecology in a sluggish economy. Most chains report they are not really determined to pay less for recycling; they just don't want to pay more. As Arby's Will Fisher, vice president of technical services, says, "We're not putting stuff out at the curb in order to get a check at the end of the week. But if a hauler comes once a month and charges too much, the store managers will balk."

Those balky managers also make companies think twice about the availability of recycled product, further impairing the steady growth of the recycling industry. White says KFC's "single greatest concern" about going to a recycled-paper chicken bucket is the fear of a shortage of recycled paper. "It would be sad to have to switch back six months later," he says. "We want to be sure that when we change, it's a long-term decision."

Unfortunately, the unformed state of the post-consumer infrastructure means that participants might indeed come out in the loss column—until precisely such big companies begin getting involved. Their publicized commitment to and active participation in solving the solid-waste problem could do a lot to foster the growth of the infant solid-waste-handling industry.

No one's saying that ecology has dropped off the consumer's radar screen. But chains in the *R&I* survey say environmentalism is mellowing into just one more criterion for many customers, right along with price/value, convenience and nutrition.

Every year since 1986, the research firm Yankelovich Clancy Shulman, New York, has reported that the group who says it is "concerned about the environment" has grown larger, to 29% of Americans in 1990. However, in 1991 the proportion dropped back to 24%. Meanwhile, an August 1991 *Wall Street Journal* poll said 8 in 10 American voters call themselves "environmentalists," but only 5 in 10 translated that belief into action by buying a green product during the previous six months.

Easier Said than Done

Chains point to this dichotomy to explain the lack of consumer-targeted recycling programs. Chains that have tried to get customers to sort their in-house trash report discouraging results. Los Angeles-based Carl's Jr. tested voluntary paper and plastic recycling in its dining rooms, but discontinued the project in the face of irregular cooperation. Fisher says Arby's test of polystyrene-foam recycling got 80% customer participation in some stores, but only 40% in others. "It was too unpredictable," he says. "Surveys showed 80% of our customers felt good about what we were doing. But between what people say and what they do, it was eye-opening."

Still, some companies, notably McDonald's and Burger King, say they will keep testing consumer recycling despite less-than-total compliance, and in the face of the old argument that half of fast-food waste goes out the drive-thru window.

Rules and Regs

In a sense, what they say about politics holds true for ecology, too: It's all local. Laws and regulations differ, as do market conditions; and franchisees often must be persuaded, not presumed interested. But experts inside and outside of foodservice think broad statewide waste laws will emerge from the present localized confusion, forcing both the markets and the franchising rules to change.

Preparing for these coming effects demands a highly centralized effort now. For one thing, many companies are in relative darkness about the size and nature of their own waste stream, and it takes a highly organized, unified effort to analyze a company's trash output. McDonald's found that 80% of its waste came from behind the counter; that might not be true of another chain.

Spread the Word

Once the waste problem is described, companies must find out what individual stores are doing now to solve it and then spread that expertise among other operations. Unit managers and franchisees aren't solid-waste experts, nor should they have to be. They should be able to draw on corporate headquarters as a clearinghouse for data and practical suggestions. For example, ARA put its accounts into an environmental database and linked managers to a consultant hotline with advice on waste haulers and recyclers around the country.

Instead, as noted earlier, most companies spread ecological responsibilities out among several departments or hand them to executives with other duties, such as purchasing and operations. All too often, those other tasks demand active management, daily decisions and round-the-clock monitoring. Put next to these more urgent, less abstract concerns, environmental issues can fade into invisibility. They demand special scrutiny, a long view though a wide-angle lens.

Ecological Ombudsmen

Without a designated ecology ombudsman, you "risk losing your focus on environmental initiatives," says Domino's Hull. "The environment is always in the background, and you know you ought to be paying more attention to it. But if it's not screaming at you, you naturally turn to the things that are, whether it's government regulation or minority employment or minors in the workplace. You tend to pick up the pot that's boiling over."

Environmental solutions don't always balance out on the profit-and-loss statement. When managers have to decide which of two competing projects is worth their scarce resources, says KFC's White, they often choose the one with the most clear-cut return on investment, and ecology is never clear-cut. "It's so difficult to quantify ecological values, to put your hands around something real," he says. "Many people are just more comfortable going straight to the bottom line."

"A lot of these changes involve a whole range of functions within the company," adds KFC spokesman Dick Detweiler. "Dedicated people, whose sole job is to be advocates for a more ecologically sound company, can be engines for driving the cause." ♦

MEETING THE ENVIRONMENTAL CHALLENGE

Independent Innovations

by Jeff Weinstein

Is recycling, reusing and reducing waste a chore? Not according to John Zehnder, food and beverage director at Zehnder's of Frankenmuth, Frankenmuth, Mich. "Once you see how great the return on investment is, recycling starts to become a game to see where else money can be saved," he says.

At his 1,300-seat restaurant, it's a game that the whole staff plays. Thanks to the wait staff's brainstorming, for instance, the restaurant recycles soft-drink cans and parks the refund money in an employee-support fund. The cooks found ways to reduce supplier packaging, and the maintenance staff devised a system to recycle cooler/freezer compressor water.

And the savings are substantial. Between recycling compressor water and corrugated cardboard alone, Zehnder saves $12,000 a year. Although the cardboard compacting machine cost $8,000, it saves between $250 and $750 a week in carting fees, and paid for itself in eight months. Since he bought the compactor three years ago, it has saved the restaurant more than $20,000.

"A lot of people hesitate to get involved with recycling because of the initial start-up costs," says Zehnder. "But I tell people that the payback is there. Find two or three items within your organization that will return the largest amount of money."

Results of *R&I*'s latest survey among owners of the nation's 50 highest-grossing independent restaurants show they have a spirited environmental conscience, despite a lack of labor and resources in many cases. And like Zehnder's, their motive is not strictly humanitarian. "We have to recycle to keep costs down," says David Oster, facilities director at the Manor, West Orange,

N.J. "The skyrocketing cost of hauling waste to the landfill made us do it." Since starting a recycling program in 1989, Oster has saved the Manor approximately $72,000 a year in carting costs.

Here are the ten most popular waste-reduction practices, based on responses to *R&I*'s independents waste survey.

♦ 84% use bulk-pack liquids.
♦ 79% reuse utensils, wares and permanent cups.
♦ 79% use less water.
♦ 73% use less electricity.
♦ 73% use trash compactors.
♦ 66% recycle fryer oil.
♦ 61% recycle corrugated cardboard.
♦ 59% use bulk condiment containers.
♦ 55% recycle glass.
♦ 52% have reduced supplier packaging.

The most vigilant operators can cut their carting costs by as much as half in urban areas, according to Pete Berghoff, vice president of the Berghoff restaurant, Chicago.

Survey results found The Berghoff t be among the leaders in the independent-restaurant environmental movement. Berghoff's latest brainstorm calls for buying a pulper and water press to reduce the amount of solid material that runs down the drain. He expects to save "big money" because the restaurant is billed on parts per million of solids in the waste stream. In addition, he won't have to spend as much money routing clogged sewer lines.

Berghoff already has reduced the restaurant's garbage load by recycling all waste meat, bones, fat and other stock byproducts. Even on a slow week, the rendering company that picks up the

RECYCLING RESOURCE GUIDE

Resources for operators who want to start a waste-reduction program:

State or city restaurant associations: Better than the national association because they are more aware of what recycling programs are available in your community.

Local recycling project: Often a volunteer group or program set up by a city. Call City Hall or the chamber of commerce for contacts. Often the best sources for information on what companies are buying recyclable materials and where to go to buy the necessary equipment.

Local waste-management company: Often have person in charge of recycling who can lead you to outlets for glass, cardboard, plastic, etc.

Raw-material trade associations: Polystyrene Packaging Council, Washington, (202) 822-6424; Glass Packaging Institute, Washington, (202) 887-4850; National Solid Wastes Management Association, Washington, (202) 659-4613; Solid Waste Composting Council, Washington, (800) 457-4474; Council for Solid Waste Solutions (800) 243-5790.

garbage collects 1,600 pounds and gives Berghoff a nominal payment. The waste is used for make-up bases and soap.

Before the Manor restaurant started its solid-waste management program, waste haulers emptied the compactor twice a week. When the $400 pull and tipping charge was added, the cost of removing garbage was $93,000 a year. Today, haulers empty the compactor every five weeks for an annual cost of just more than $20,000.

One of the more innovative recycling efforts at the Manor involves a machine called "The Cannibal," which pulverizes clam, mussel and oyster shells. The remains, along with additives, are used as a soil conditioner for the restaurant's grounds or sent to owner Harry Knowles' other restaurant, the Highlawn Pavilion in West Orange, to line the parking lot.

The Manor also separates its glass and has it picked up for free by a glass company. An average load is 15 tons. If a waste hauler picked up the glass, it would cost approximately $109 a ton.

Since the Manor receives approximately 150 boxes of oysters per month, it returns the empty boxes to the supplier for reuse. The same is done with milk and ice-cream containers, and aluminum-coated frozen ice packs that arrive with the fresh lobsters. In an average month, this amounts to about 200 pieces, weighing 800 pounds.

The restaurant also obtained a permit from the state to use its 40-yard van as a waste-removal truck. It is used to transfer nonrecyclable dry waste (waxed cardboard, wood boxes, crates and nonrecyclable plastics) to the new "waste to energy" incinerator in Essex County, N.J., to be used as fuel to create electricity.

All equipment purchased to handle the program should have a payback within three years, according to Oster.

A few of these top independents make recycling and waste reduction look easy, but they are the exceptions to the rule. Even finding the resource material to help develop a program can be a struggle.

When Zehnder started his program, the state environmental agency delivered a cardboard box for recycling envelopes and left ten minutes later. Unsatisfied with the agency's help, he made the necessary contacts by becoming a charter member of the Frankenmuth, Mich., environmental awareness organization. "Members of groups such as this can tell you who buys what recyclable products, who sells the equipment and who is willing to lend a hand."

While most businesses tend to shy away, Zehnder recommends getting in touch with the radical environmental groups in the area. "They are my most important resource for whatever I need," he says.

At the Manor, Oster contacted the recycling expert at the Essex (N.J.) County Waste Management Company, who led him to the outlets that could help get rid of plastic, tin, aluminum and more.

As more plastic, glass and paper is recycled, the lower the price for the recycled material becomes. In addition, the market for these materials is sluggish because industry hasn't created enough uses for recycled material. Furthermore, the market for recyclable materials varies from city to city.

"If we could get glass pickup, we'd sort it," says David Laxer, president of Bern's Steak House in Tampa, Fla. "But there is no market here. We used to separate glass and have a private company pick it up but it became unprofitable for the recycler and they stopped. Now all our bottles go into the dumpster, which is a waste."

Another example is Scoma's Restaurant, San Francisco, where a truck used to come by and pay to pick up fryer oil. Today, Scoma's has to pay to have it removed.

However, the market for recycled material is not as bearish in other regions of the country. Zehnder's, for instance, plans to start glass- and plastic-separation programs because two new companies in the area are starting recycling operations.

Another challenge operators face is training employees to recycle. Because of the industry's high turnover rate and employees' long-standing bad habits, constant training and supervision can become burdensome.

The Manor set up an in-house environmental training program and, at regular staff meetings, constantly reinforces its commitment to any resistant employees. Oster says it took about six to eight months before the program sunk in with hourly workers.

The Manor uses a color-coded system for separation of waste. All waste items are mounted on a multicolored pegboard adjacent to the trash-compactor door. The compactor has a red door, and only the waste that has been sent through a red pulper machine, and other items mounted on the red section, are placed in the compactor. All other color-coded items on display are placed in the corresponding receptacle by color for proper disposal.

Coaxing suppliers to reduce the amount of product packaging they use is a crucial step toward running an environmentally friendly restaurant. To date, operators are meeting with limited success as suppliers continue to search for alternatives that still will present their products in an attractive fashion.

"Suppliers have to take into consideration the appearance of their products, so they have a way to go before they can offer an abundance of products with reduced packaging," says Oster. "But if more restaurant operators would raise their voice about this issue, something could be accomplished sooner."

Zehnder also believes in the strength-in-numbers route. As president of his local American Culinary Federation chapter, he is asking members to tell him about products that arrive in excess packaging. He is keeping a list, and if one product keeps showing up, the group will submit a letter to the supplier, explaining the organization's concerns.

While some of the smaller independent operators don't have the resources to develop a solid-waste management program, this group of high-volume operators generally has the means to make a contribution that will protect the environment.

Restaurants such as the Manor, The Berghoff and Zehnder's are taking leadership roles, while others see recycling programs more as a burden and someone else's problem.

In the end, recycling, reuse and reduction of waste becomes a dollars-and-cents issue. Operators really can't afford not to get involved. "When I talk about recycling, I prefer to refer to it as 'waste management,'" says Zehnder. "A restaurateur wouldn't throw a prime rib in the trash can, but they throw away metal, glass and all these other recyclable objects that in the long run cost them dollars."

Independent Innovations

What follows are some of the more original waste-reduction and recycling practices in place at the nation's independent restaurants:

♦ Old Ebbitt Grill, Washington, plans to cut out all beer bottles in the house by going to a $125,000 all-draft beer system.

♦ Tavern on the Green, New York, cuts up unusable dining-room linens, dyes them green and uses them as cleaning rags in the kitchen.

♦ Bern's Steak House, Tampa, Fla., saves electricity and water by recapturing water runoff from ice machines and pumping that already chilled water back into the machine.

♦ Philadelphia's Sansom Street Oyster House owner David Mink has formed a committee to work with the Pennsylvania Environmental Council to develop a standardized set of criteria for the restaurant community. Restaurants would be evaluated and rated on the soundness of their environmental practices, and findings would be made available to the public.

♦ Catch 35, Chicago, recycles the wire hangers delivered with the clean kitchen laundry.

♦ Sufficient Grounds, Berkeley, Calif., donates its coffee grounds for fertilizer.

♦ Smith & Wollensky, New York, donates leftover food to local City Harvest and Meals on Wheels programs.

♦ Legal Sea Food, Boston, sells its seafood scraps to fish farms for feed. ♦

MEETING THE ENVIRONMENTAL CHALLENGE

Ideas from the Institutions

by Beth Lorenzini

Talk about concerned consumers: When Associated Students of University of California, Los Angeles (ASUCLA), tried to decide whether to convert to mostly polystyrene disposables on campus, students revolted. "They were adamant about us using paper only," recalls Rob Clarke, division manager.

ASUCLA decided to let students help make the decision. It set up a public forum at which students, faculty and environmental experts could debate the issue. Part of the forum included a demonstration of "biodegradable paper" vs. polystyrene. After hearing and seeing some evidence—including seeing uncoated paper "melt" under the weight of hot gravy—students agreed with the disposables plan.

ASUCLA's battle shows just what hurdles colleges as well as hospitals, schools and other noncommercial operators must overcome to get recycling, reduction and reuse programs in place. Despite the hurdles, however, institutions are beating commercial operations in cutting down on solid waste. When compared with the first waste survey of the top 50 *R&I* 400 companies, it's clear that institutions are leading the Green Revolution.

In fact, vocal customers are one of the reasons institutions are steps ahead of their commercial peers in reusing, reducing and recycling. It's easier to get "semicaptive" audiences into the reduction and recycling mode than a clientele that changes daily.

The depth of institutions' dealings with the waste issue is as impressive as the breadth. More than 70% of those who responded to the *R&I* questionnaire have in place at least 10 of the 29 projects listed on the survey. More than 60%

recycle cardboard, aluminum and glass; 50% recycle fryer oil; and more than 50% use permanentware coffee mugs to reduce paper- and foam-cup usage.

The most successful programs have a few things in common:

♦ Most programs start out small, first by reducing waste and then by recycling the items they generate in volume that can make revenue or save landfill fees such as cardboard, office paper, aluminum and glass.

♦ There is a designated coordinator and/or strong communication among custodial, business services, graphics, media, foodservice and human resources departments.

♦ Operators with successful programs talked to other operators in their areas and to city officials and trash haulers to find out what was happening in terms of reduction, reuse and recycling.

♦ Operators with good programs realize that environmental programs cost money up front. They practice the "spend now to save later" strategy.

♦ Good environmental programs have easy-to-read, easy-to-implement guidebooks, literature, signs and policies. Reducing, reusing and recycling is made easy for the customer.

Strategies in Reuse

More than half of the institutions surveyed have mug programs. Customers purchase a mug and receive a discount on beverages when they use it. Every time someone refills a mug, one less disposable goes to the dump. One tip from the Associated Students of the University of California-

Los Angeles, which offers hot/cold plastic and ceramic mugs: Charge the lowest price possible for the mug. Take only a minimal profit, because savings from disposables will more than cover the cost.

The mug program extends to vending at Stamford, Conn.-based Service America. Vending machines throughout the company's accounts can be fitted with $200 mug-sensor kits. Customers simply put their permanent mug in the beverage dispenser. The sensor acknowledges the mug, cancels the paper cup and fills the permanent mug.

Many of the institutions surveyed have purchased or plan to purchase pulpers and balers. At Pennsylvania State University, University Park, foodservices is working with the college of agriculture to mix foodservice pulp waste with manure for fertilizing local farms.

Los Angeles Unified School District, which saved $177,000 in landfill fees by recycling polystyrene in 1991, will now recycle 80 million milk and juice cartons annually as well. Warren Lund, director of foodservice, believes his district is one of only two in the country to take advantage of this latest technology. The machinery for the milk-carton process, which separates the polystyrene coating from the carton paper, was donated by a paper company.

Two institutions launched excellent environmental programs with help from M.B.A. students. National Medical Enterprises (NME), Santa Monica, Calif., and ASUCLA both had the help of students who researched and developed environmental programs as their master's theses. "If an operation doesn't have a program going, I would recommend calling the local college to see if there are M.B.A. students looking for projects," says Clarke.

At NME, Trudi McComb, director of food and nutrition services, worked with administration to get funding for the project. She appointed Stacy Gurrola project specialist. Gurrola, an NME employee and M.B.A. student, spent almost a year researching waste and waste legislation, analyzing costs, surveying customers and

units, and finding out what kind of reduction and recycling options were available. With the information, she set up a formal three-phase recycling plan for all of NME.

ASUCLA says it saved $100,000 outright in 1975 when it switched from permanent stainless utensils to heavy-gauge plastic. At that time, about a dozen trash bins were fitted with mini receptacles for utensils so they could be washed and reused. But it took the efforts of M.B.A. student April Smith to get ASUCLA in environmental gear in 1989.

"She told us that we should fit every trash bin with a utensil receptacle, that we should improve the signage on it and that we should watch to make sure employees weren't trashing the utensils rather than sending them to be washed," says Clarke. ASUCLA also began washing its plastic coffee cups in the Kerckhoff coffeehouse. "We did what April asked and watched our utensil and mug purchases go down by $24,000 in the '89 to '90 year and 50% more in the following year." Smith also was a key player in ASUCLA's new recycling policy.

"If you are making any environmental decisions, it's mandatory that you get your entire facility involved in the decision-making process," says Clarke. "It's vital to have a policy and it's vital that your 'community' agrees on it.

"Recycling program how-tos can come from the manufacturers as well. Los Angeles Unified's recycling program began with the help of Amoco Corp. Because one of the nation's four National Polystyrene Recycling Co. (NPRC) plants is located in southern California, recycling was a viable option. Amoco also is working with Chicago schools to get a similar program up and running. Chicago, too, has an NPRC facility.

But distance from a plant shouldn't be an excuse not to consider a program. "We have lots of polystyrene programs going in areas that don't have NPRC facilities nearby," says Colleen Holmes, Midwest/Southwest Region Director for Amoco. She says many cities have local solid waste entrepreneurs who will devote half their truck space to compacted polystyrene. These people also are willing to haul it to recyclers at great distances because in many cases, the money they receive for the polystyrene covers the trip, with a profit.

Many institutional giants have found innovative and effective ways to get the word out about how to reduce, reuse and recycle. Some of the most sophisticated material comes from contract companies.

For example, ARA's extensive Earth Sense environmental program, an easy-to-understand, 55-page guidebook, gives operators workable tips to become environmentally friendly. For example, the guide suggests purchasing food in bulk to cut down on supplier packaging. Asking suppliers to take back and refill plastic tubs, buckets and pails is another suggestion. The guidebook answers environmental questions, suggests who to contact to recycle, who to get involved in programs and how to analyze a unit's waste flow and cost out recycling. The guidebook is available free to ARA's accounts.

ARA's and other contract companies' environmental programs are simple, include small steps and are well-presented.

"So many people get overwhelmed by what dealing with the waste issue entails," says Gurrola. "The trick is to start out small and work your way up to more—bit by bit." ◆

INDEX